Anthrohistory ❧

Anthrohistory ❧ Unsettling Knowledge, Questioning Discipline

Edward Murphy, David William Cohen, Chandra D. Bhimull, Fernando Coronil, Monica Eileen Patterson, and Julie Skurski, editors

THE UNIVERSITY OF MICHIGAN PRESS   ANN ARBOR

Copyright © by the University of Michigan 2011
All rights reserved
Published in the United States of America by
The University of Michigan Press
Manufactured in the United States of America
Printed on acid-free paper

2014 2013 2012 2011   4 3 2 1

No part of this publication may be reproduced,
stored in a retrieval system, or transmitted in any form
or by any means, electronic, mechanical, or otherwise,
without the written permission of the publisher.

A CIP catalog record for this book is available from the British Library.

Library of Congress Cataloging-in-Publication Data

Anthrohistory : unsettling knowledge, questioning discipline / Edward
   Murphy . . . [et al.], editors.
      p.   cm.
   Includes bibliographical references and index.
   ISBN 978-0-472-07135-7 (cloth : alk. paper) — ISBN 978-0-472-05135-9 (pbk. : alk. paper)
   1. Ethnohistory.   I. Murphy, Edward.
GN345.2.A57   2011
909'.04—dc22   2010040247

Finally, at this stage in interdisciplinary relations, one hopes to see progress toward a superior stage which would be "transdisciplinary," that would not be satisfied with achieving interactions or reciprocities between research fields but rather would situate these connections within a system without disciplinary borders.

JEAN PIAGET (1974, 170)

Contents

List of Figures ix

Openings

1. A Prefatory Piece, *Chandra D. Bhimull, Edward Murphy, and Monica Eileen Patterson* 3

2. The Pursuits of Anthrohistory: Formation against Formation, *David William Cohen* 11

Part 1 Encountering Boundaries

3. Notes on the Difficulty of Studying *el Pueblo*, *Paul K. Eiss* 37

4. Step into Anthrohistory, *David Pedersen* 48

5. Genealogies of Mediation: "Culture Broker" and Imperial Governmentality, *E. Natalie Rothman* 67

6. Childhood, Memory, and Gap: Reflections from an Anthrohistorian on Georges Perec's *W or the Memory of Childhood*, *Monica Eileen Patterson* 81

7. Working in the In-between: Archives, Ethnography, and Research in Gaza, *Ilana Feldman* 97

8. The Past and Present of the Future Perfect in Anthropology and History, *Deirdre de la Cruz* 110

Part 2 Unsettling Knowledge

9. Past Warfare: Ethics, Knowledge, and the Yanomami Controversy, *Julie Skurski* 121

10. Disaster Preparedness, *Shannon Lee Dawdy* — 140

11. Reclaiming Tradition, *Zareena A. Grewal* — 156

12. Impressions: An Interval — 171

13. The Miracle of History: Temporality and Uncertainty in Southern Arabia, *Mandana E. Limbert* — 181

14. The Politics of Burial in Post-Apartheid South Africa, *Kerry Ward* — 191

15. Losing the Phenomenon: Time and Indeterminacy in the Practice of Anthrohistory, *Oana Mateescu* — 208

Part 3 ❧ Questioning Discipline

16. Anthrohistory and Phantom Limb Syndrome: Transdisciplinarity in a Disciplinary World, *Thomas C. Wolfe* — 225

17. On the Subject of Governance, *Anupama Rao and Steven Pierce* — 240

18. Between Disciplines, After Modernity, *S. C. Humphreys* — 252

19. The Politics of Naming: Ethical Dilemmas and Disciplinary Divides in Anthropology and History, *Dorothy L. Hodgson* — 257

20. On the Importance of Having a Method, or What Does Archival Work on Soviet Atheism Have to Do with Ethnography of Post-Soviet Religion? *Sonja Luehrmann* — 273

21. Wanderings beyond Codification and Desire, *Setrag Manoukian* — 286

Openings ❧

22. Pieces for Anthrohistory: A Puzzle to Be Assembled Together, *Fernando Coronil* — 301

Bibliography — 317
Contributors — 343
Index — 347

Figures

FIG. 3.1.	Dead deer in the Yucatán	38
FIG. 4.1.	Prehistoric glacial movement and lake shapes	51
FIG. 6.1.	Casper David Friedrich, *Der Wanderer über dem Neblmeer* (Wanderer above the Sea of Fog, 1818)	80
FIG. 7.1.	Gaza records removed to Israel	103
FIG. 10.1.	Holt Cemetery, New Orleans	150
FIG. 10.2.	1849 map of New Orleans, depicting flooding in 1831	154
FIG. 12.1.	Conference poster "Trans/Formations of the Disciplines," February 2004. René Magritte, *Le Parc du Vautour* (1926)	172
FIG. 12.2.	Katsashuki Hokusai (1760–1849), *The Great Wave at Kanagawa* (from a Series of Thirty-six Views of Mount Fuji, ca. 1829–32)	173
FIG. 12.3.	José Guadalupe Posada, *Don Quijote* (ca. 1895–1913)	174
FIG. 12.4.	Tshimbumba Kanda Matulu, *Lumumba in Buluo Prison* (1974)	175
FIG. 12.5.	Paul Klee, *Angelus Novus* (1920)	176
FIG. 12.6.	Sarah Wyman, *Blanket* (2008)	177
FIG. 12.7.	Philippe Petit between the Twin Towers (1974)	178
FIG. 12.8.	Deborah Howard, *Labyrinth* (1999)	179
FIG. 12.9.	M. C. Escher, *Drawing Hands* (1948)	180
FIG. 14.1.	9/11	207
FIG. 20.1.	Architect's drawing of the Cinema MIR (1961)	279
FIG. 20.2.	Evangelizing concert of Pentecostal church	279
FIG. 21.1.	Fursat with other poets in Shiraz, Iran (1903)	288

Openings

1 ❦ Chandra D. Bhimull, Edward Murphy, and Monica Eileen Patterson

A Prefatory Piece

In the 1950s, anthropologists, who had long been accustomed to bracketing history, began to imagine an anthropology that would be, if anything, historical. Historians subsequently came to imagine new forms of history that would succeed only with the incorporation of insights and approaches from anthropology. Over the decades that followed, the exchanges of prominent anthropologists and historians would contribute important energy and direction to the fields of social history, cultural history, ethnohistory, microhistory, and historical anthropology.

In many instances, these exchanges formed part of intellectual movements that sought to rework and even radically change the ground on which academic work would stand. Beginning in the late 1970s, scholars influenced by the emergent currents of poststructuralism, postmodernism, and postcolonialism attempted to inhabit new spaces that would transcend inherited assumptions and practices constrained by unexamined power relations and provincial perspectives. Many of the interdisciplinary connections between anthropology and history nourished and fed off these currents. Historical anthropologists and anthropological historians were now taking part in a multidisciplinary dialogue that often spurred great debate within disciplines and led to the formation of a number of new interdisciplinary institutions, publications, and forums. This development helped university leaders promote fresh investments in *the interdisciplinary* as a viable means of reform and renovation in higher education. As interdisciplinary connections spread, they could take inspiration from a lesson that anthropologists and historians working together had often learned: that interdisciplinarity can make possible the creation of critically important, transformative intellectual projects.

Yet in spite of this, as scholars working between anthropology and history had also sometimes discovered, interdisciplinary projects bear the burden of legacies and contexts shaped in part by their disciplinary roots. They can frequently fail to find common dialogue and understanding. Practitioners of one discipline may borrow from another, but they do not necessarily engage deeply with the other's debates and complexities. Likewise, in seeking to reassert control over their disciplinary boundaries, both intellectual and institutional gatekeepers may end up excluding the perspectives of outside scholars. It is no wonder, then, that interdisciplinary projects are often short-lived and superficial. But even with these potential pitfalls, such projects nevertheless have the potential to open opportunities for critical reflection on the boundaries and possibilities of disciplinary formations. Crucially, they can help scholars who seek to create forms of knowledge that appropriately engage with their objects of study, rather than rotely following academic practices and expectations.

This volume presents work by scholars who embrace this impulse to produce engaged and reflexive scholarship at the crossroads of anthropology and history. As such, the volume is not a compilation of work by historical anthropologists and anthropological historians. We have neither sought to privilege one disciplinary perspective over the other nor have we attempted to confect a perfect equilibrium between anthropology and history. The collection instead features intellectuals whose work seeks to produce knowledge between and beyond the two disciplines. In doing so, the contributors have attempted to develop perspectives that not only transcend and unsettle the conventions and relationships that shape academic disciplinary fields, but also the broader fields of power that constrain intellectual production.

As a collection, the essays presented here attempt to practice anthrohistory, a transdisciplinary project that moves beyond a partial integration of the disciplines. The volume's contributors seek to bring anthropology and history together in order to build on the possibilities and insights of each while also resisting their constraints and limitations. In developing this critical space, *Anthrohistory* searches for ways to produce ethically responsible knowledge in a world riven by violence and dominative forms of power.

The authors who appear in this volume work in numerous academic settings, archives, and field sites around the world. Yet at some point in the past twenty years, each has had an intellectual connection to the Doctoral Program in Anthropology and History at the University of Michigan (subsequently referred to as "the Anthrohistory Program"). This program first formed in the late 1980s amidst the burst of enthusiasm for the interdisciplinary and reflexive work that began to gain traction in the 1970s and 1980s. It has persisted even as other interdisciplinary projects forged at the same moment have disappeared. In certain respects, the Anthrohistory

Program has been a unique, ongoing experiment in interdisciplinarity, surviving despite changing dynamics in campus institutions and broader intellectual trends. Throughout, it has sought to be an expansive location of critical reflection that is relevant and resonant with scholarly work taking place across the globe.

While engaging its two academic departments and disciplines, the Anthrohistory Program has developed in an independent and interstitial space full of varied trajectories and openings. This volume is the culmination of a long-standing effort to take stock of this space. In 2004, scholars at the University of Michigan marked the fifteenth anniversary of the program by hosting a conference called "Trans/Formations of the Disciplines: Evaluating the Project of Anthropology and History" (see fig. 12.1). The conference was an effort to contextualize and assess the range of scholarship coming out of the Anthrohistory Program. To what extent, for example, had it succeeded in transcending the disciplinary constraints of anthropology and history? What were the broader transformations in both the academy and the world that had shaped how anthrohistorians could practice their crafts? How had this particular interdisciplinary configuration affected the experiences and scholarship of students and faculty who had taken part in it?

This was about cohabitation: about beginning to live not in "the archive" or "the field," but in the world—a world in which it was no longer clear to me where "field" ended and "archive" began, or what it meant to compartmentalize life in that way.

&. PAUL EISS, THIS VOLUME

For participants, the answers to these questions, particularly the last one, were multiple. Although the Anthrohistory Program has always been small and at times it has tenuously clung to its institutional setting, it has nevertheless produced dozens of PhDs. These students have not only combined anthropology and history in often surprising and unforeseen ways, but they have also forged connections with scholars working in a number of other intellectual frameworks. Students (and their faculty advisers) have formed seemingly organic connections with scholars working in such areas as semiotics, archeology, subaltern studies, race, geography, museum studies, the environment, gender, the history of science, urban planning, and area studies, to name only some.

Despite their diverse and multidisciplinary experiences, however, participants in the conference also had a partially shared repertoire to draw on, facilitating the creation of an intense and at times unsettling dialogue.

If research experiences for anthrohistorians are of great temporal and spatial breadth, they also form the basis for a deep intellectual and political engagement with specific circumstances and peoples, a process that inevitably transforms the researcher. While anthrohistorians have a set of authors that they loosely share, they also each engage with the perspectives of their own particular interlocutors. And as they search for openness and possibility in their intellectual pursuits, anthrohistorians also maintain a hard-edged commitment to producing responsible forms of knowledge.

The shared orientations that have been critical to the individual and collective work of scholars involved in anthrohistory were evident in the papers presented at the Trans/Formations conference. These orientations point to the varied ways in which anthrohistorians have grappled with a host of methodological, epistemological, ethical, and political questions that have challenged academics from across the humanities and social sciences for decades. They include imaginative thinking about the uses and valences of time and space in the interpretation of culture and history; serious attention to the worlds of people rendered outcast, subordinate, or marginal; inspired regard for connecting the material to the cultural; studied concern for the possibilities and limits of archives and sources; critical reflection on the privileged position of scholar, observer, teacher, and expert; and an unreticent experimentalism in the representation of life worlds found, understood, and reconstructed. Underscoring how shifting contexts and inequitable social formations shape scholarly work, the conference drew attention to critical questions of power and ethics in the production and uses of knowledge.

Most of the essays here bear threads back to the 2004 conference, but three—David William Cohen's, Fernando Coronil's, and the present preface—developed after the conference as the editors and many of the participants met on several occasions to consider further the possibilities and limitations of anthrohistorical work. We have located these three pieces as "Openings," as they each suggest directions that can guide readers through not only the particularities of *Anthrohistory* but also the more general ways that working through it can aid in developing politically engaged and ethically responsible scholarship.

The papers presented at the Trans/Formations conference primarily followed standard academic form, as conference participants produced essays designed for academic journals and, inevitably, personal professional advancement. The conference thus demonstrated how a number of academics trained in an anthrohistorical milieu had come to practice and produce their own forms of scholarship. While the essays comprising this volume are a follow-up to the conference, they respond to a different impulse, reflected in the fact that they are shorter and more evocative, exploratory, and explicitly reflexive.

The form of the essays is deliberate. There is, as Hayden White (1986) has insisted, a content to the form, and ours suggests central concerns and perspectives that emphasize the kind of anthrohistorical work we seek to produce. In the first instance, the experimental style is meant to free our contributors from the often taken-for-granted assumptions and practices of academic writing. This permits them to expand creatively on the possibilities of anthrohistorical work as they each attempt to engage critically with their own academic projects. In this way, each contributor provides both an opening for new approaches and a critical reflection on aspects of the state of anthrohistory and the currents of thought within which anthrohistorians engage. If "Openings" bookend the volume, they also take shape in each article, breaking down the conventional and often hierarchical dichotomy between editorial overview and contributing article.

The design and organization of the book's layout seek to foreground orientations and possibilities embodied in transdisciplinary, anthrohistorical work. The volume's sectional headings point to these orientations, and their interconnected thematics underscore the considerable overlap between the issues and concerns presented throughout the book. As the first part's title indicates, anthrohistorians are constantly "Encountering Boundaries." They must grapple with not only the boundaries of the disciplines, but also the multiple borders and frontiers that mark and shape social life as well. The heading also invokes the double sense of the word *encounter*, in terms of both experiencing boundaries and seeking to counter or transcend them. Our authors show that these boundaries often exist in surprising locations, as in the ways that imperial categories in sixteenth-century Venice resonate with current assumptions about subjectivity and difference, or in how understandings of the future affect forms of analysis and narrative in anthropology and history.

As a part of our engagement and experimentation with anthrohistory, visual fragments throughout the book perforate and suture the text. Photographs, drawings, and quotations explore, connect, and extend the papers and their themes. As fragments, they are shards and particles of revelatory residue that fracture, rupture, shatter, disintegrate, and crack. They are mischievous interruptions weaving in and out of the papers. They unsettle fixity. They open.

Similarly, "Unsettling Knowledge" suggests that knowledge needs to be problematized and taken away from its comfortable or convenient status. At the same time, the pieces in this section also address knowledge that is itself unsettling; knowledge that disturbs, troubles, and perdures, as in the debris of Hurricane Katrina, the demeaning of the Yanomami in South America, or the presence of the dead in South Africa. In "Questioning Discipline" our authors not only unsettle the conventions, norms, and assumptions of disciplinary boundaries, but they also probe the strengths of disciplinary power as they attempt to build a discipline better equipped to pose critical questions. Such building and unsettling can happen while evaluating the dynamics of a North American history department, considering the dilemmas of governance in former English colonial contexts, or probing the value of adopting analytical approaches that are historicist or phenomenological in nature.

Building and unsettling require support. Attempting to recognize all who helped make this volume possible is a seemingly impossible task. Such recognition might begin with an absurdly long list that would demonstrate the multiple schools of thought and the varied thinkers who have sustained the analytical engagements of *Anthrohistory*. The list would include a number of social thinkers who have inspired critical work across disciplinary boundaries and broader sociopolitical domains. It would acknowledge scholars who, at different moments and with different levels of intensity, forged connections between anthropology and history. It would recognize the fact that the engagements of anthropologists and historians were thickly involved with all the significant "turns" of the past thirty years in the humanities and social sciences: literary, cultural, linguistic, and historical.

Each essay, address, article, and book carries the full history of its formation. In other words, what the various texts are, in the most concrete sense, includes all that went into their creation and also all that continues to condition their existence. Most acknowledgment sections in articles and books allude to only a portion of this content.

ॐ DAVID PEDERSEN, THIS VOLUME

Such a list would underscore the varied and yet often interconnected intellectual fields within which the anthrohistorians in this volume tread. It would recognize the fundamental and expansive role of the past in shaping the institutional cultures and academic projects of the present. It would emphasize, as any good microhistory must, how the view of the small and the particular opens up vistas that are extensive and vast. Such acknowledgments would be simultaneously celebratory and cautious, appreciative and yet unsatisfied. They would indicate that the scholars involved in the project of anthropology and history have produced their own scholarship, but not under conditions of their own choosing.

Ultimately, such a list would be contrary to the conventional practices of compiling acknowledgments in academic work. It would, moreover, be inadequate and incomplete. We tried to create one, yet with continuing consideration it never ceased to demand new entries. We struggled to identify our shared influences as we battled over which individuals to include. There was no clear or singular genealogy from which to construct an essential list of interlocutors for the project of anthrohistory. While the debts that anthrohistorians owe do point to a shared academic orbit, they also suggest an inchoate and expansive dialogue, one that can encompass connections across many temporal, spatial, and epistemological boundaries. How might one, for example, acknowledge an intellectual movement that may have traveled from Franz Boas, Carlo Ginzburg, and Carolyn Kay Steedman to Walter Benjamin, Joan Scott, and Dipesh Chakrabarty?

In the end, we can only nod to these broad and diverse connections, limiting ourselves here to a more conventional, if no less deserved recognition of specific individuals and institutional bodies. Since the Anthrohistory Program is small and has minimal overhead, the sustained participation of faculty and students has been essential to the work that has made this book possible. The people involved in the program and in this volume have grown accustomed to intermittent and at times frenzied planning sessions, marathon meetings, long e-mail exchanges, and the writing of numerous grant proposals and reports. If much labor power has been spent negotiating these often bureaucratic pathways, it has nevertheless led to extensive funding, a testament to the University of Michigan's commitment to interdisciplinary work.

On behalf of all six editors, we would like to thank the International Institute, the Institute for the Humanities, and Latin American and Caribbean Studies, each of which provided essential support for the 2004 conference. The Department of History, the Department of Anthropology, and the Office of the Vice President for Research also helped to fund the conference, in addition to numerous other events hosted by the Anthrohistory Program. For four years, the Rackham School of Graduate Studies, through the Rackham Interdisciplinary Workshop, has backed anthrohistorical work in all of its activities, including reading groups, planning sessions, parties, the 2004 conference, and the 2007 roundtable. The Office of the Provost supported a forum hosted by the Anthrohistory Program that explored the controversy over scientific research among the Yanomami. Since 2004, the Office of the Dean, College of Literature, Science, and the Arts, has funded a monthly Friday colloquium series.

Numerous individuals have contributed to making possible the spaces of intellectual collaboration that resulted in this publication. For pivotal leadership in the development and sustenance of the Anthrohistory Program, we thank Nicholas Dirks, Sally Humphreys, E. Valentine Daniel, Ann Laura Stoler, Kali Israel, Fernando Coronil, David William Cohen, and Paul C. Johnson. Participants at the 2004 conference who do not appear in this volume include Kathleen Canning, Liviu Chelcea, John Collins, Andrew Conroe, Isabel Cordova, E. Valentine Daniel, Laurent Dubois, Geoff Eley, Juliet Erazo, Heloise Finch, Lessie Jo Frazier, Jenny Gaynor, Anjan Ghosh, Simon Gikandi, Ema Grama, Sergio Huarcaya, Nancy Hunt, Kate Jellema, Dong Ju Kim, Ken MacLean, Bruce Mannheim, Genese Sodikoff, Eric Stein, and Ann Laura Stoler. Josh Coene participated in the 2007 roundtable workshop but does not appear in the volume. Federico Helfgott and Stephen Sparks expertly produced a detailed record of the conversations that took place there.

Many of these individuals have contributed to other events sponsored by the Anthrohistory Program, in addition to the following: Danna Agmon, Daniel Birchok, Charles Bright, Sueann Caulfield, Sharad Chari, Robert Chidester, Fred Cooper, Joshua Cole, Nicholas Dirks, Christopher Estrada, Gillian Feeley-Harnik, Krisztina Fehéváry, Karen Hébert, Gabrielle Hecht, Matthew Hull, Webb Keane, Stuart Kirsch, Alaina Lemon, Purvi Mehta, Erik Mueggler, Janam Mukherjee, Grace Okrah, Julia Paley, Tasha Rijke-Epstein, Sonya O. Rose, Estaben Rozo, Neil Safier, Damon Salesa, Rebecca J. Scott, Carla Sinopoli, Ian Stewart, George Steinmetz, Thomas Truatmann, Katherine Verdery, Christian Williams, Andrea Wright, Yiching Wu, and Norman Yoffee. For assistance in putting the volume together, we are grateful to Cristián Doña-Reveco, Sergio Huarcaya, and Deborah J. Merzbach. We give special thanks to Diana Denney who, with extreme patience and extensive knowledge of the University of Michigan's resources and procedures, has made possible every anthrohistorical event and gathering of the past nine years. More so, Diana has translated her own sense of the importance of the hidden spaces of academic work and life into exceptional and timely support for the Anthrohistory Program and for its students.

2 ❧ David William Cohen

The Pursuits of Anthrohistory: Formation against Formation

We begin with two scholarly disciplines—anthropology and history—and with the boundary that has distinguished them. In the context of the university, this boundary is a distinction marked in the everyday by a distance down a hallway, or across a campus, the defining words on office doors, in lobbies, and etched so permanently into the exterior wall or cornice of a building. It is a distinction understood in farther travels to different professional meetings and conferences, and to the closer journeys of self- and mutual identification. It is a distinction marked practically in the name on the check to whom the dues are paid, in the journals most likely scanned for the latest in findings, arguments, and books reviewed, and, poetically, in the types of stories that constitute the important folklore of professional practice. More deeply, it is a distinction reflected in modes of professional training, in the ways questions are asked and research planned and evaluated. Equally, the distinction is marked in the relative significance attached to words like *documents, archives,* and *the field,* and in the respective obligations, ethical and otherwise, that the professional owes her subjects. The distinction is substantial enough that few are encouraged to cross the boundary in any more than the most cursory or perfunctory way. And the distinction is sufficiently constrictive that conversations on one side of the boundary often run out of energy and pertinence before they reach the other side, *despite* the many and frequent calls of leaders of the two disciplines to take the other seriously . . . and *beyond* the substantial incentives that higher education across the globe has given over the past several decades to the construction of "the interdisciplinary."

The Disciplines

With some early and tentative developments in the 1950s and 1960s, interdisciplinarity, multidisciplinarity, and transdisciplinarity have come to occupy a prominent position in the conversations, plans, and actual approaches taken in universities, interested foundations, and government agencies. Interdisciplinarity became—and remains—a central piece of major reform efforts in higher education in North America. Well placed or not, a confidence in the values of such development has extended more broadly to the reform and restructuring of higher education in Europe, South Africa, and beyond.

These experiments in the physical sciences, natural sciences, social sciences, humanities, arts, and the professions have drawn variously, and at various times, on senses of crisis in specific disciplines and also from anxieties regarding the openness of higher education to calls for innovation and change. Some universities and research centers bring different units together simply to salvage the weaker or poorer partners, producing new departmental conjugations without transgressing or transcending disciplinarity. Such experimentation has also grown out of a sense of the possibilities (or, as some would claim, necessities) for turning new alignments of expertise and teaching into fresh and effective engagement with critical issues in the world, some new and some old, from global climate change to the structure of DNA, from child soldiers to genocide, from pandemics to the conservation of flora and fauna. Consequently, over the past half century, the boundaries of disciplines have been transfigured from the vital materials of professional distinction, esteem, and identity into architectural components of higher education, conveying what seemed greater value not just in Clifford Geertz's "blurring" (1983) but, also transcendence.

The early interchanges of anthropologists and historians served as signs of the possibilities of such blurring, yet they could also appear to be little more than a kind of smuggling, with scholars reaching into the other discipline to borrow or appropriate what seemed a useable approach or idea (Cohen 2009). Here, the achievement was not in the blurring of a boundary between the two disciplines but rather in the simultaneous animation of distinctive materials or elements or methods drawn from the two disciplines. Indeed, in the 1980s and 1990s, the disciplines of anthropology and history became especially *hot*, attractive, to scholars in other fields and professions and also to university administrators. While encouraging of reading outside one's own discipline, these exercises in smuggling could in fact be quite limited and shallow as certain ideas—symbol, ritual, archive, memory, structure, process, thick description, narrative, meaning, subjectivity—were extensively milked. But the multiplication of such "transgressions"—and the fact that they carried the signatures of influential scholars in both disciplines—would suggest that the disciplines were themselves in transformation even if there were few scholars who would pronounce the need for, or actually take the steps to construct, new interdepartmental and interdisciplinary formations such as have appeared at the University of Michigan, or earlier at Emory, Santa Cruz, Johns Hopkins, and Chicago, or later at Erfurt.

In time, these borrowings across the disciplines—whether mining new areas of research or revisiting old questions, or engaging critically the unexamined linkages between power and knowledge—have had broad import. The trade in ideas and approaches among anthropologists and historians has led to sophisticated work on persistently difficult and influential questions of race, class, time, work, faith, culture, gender, ethnicity, nation, and empire. They have brought fresh perspectives to the study of the meanings of nation and citizenship. They have opened important conversations regarding capital and capitalism; established strong grounds of critique of concepts of modernity, civilization, and globalization; and supported the critical examination of convenient models such as core and periphery, and family and state. They have initiated new inquiry into questions of scale of analysis; the force of position and location in the perspectives of actors, subjects, authors, and audiences; the relative import of different types of sources; the situatedness of reading, translation, interpretation, analysis, and representation; and the social and political ground of objectivity and truth.

> *A reader may ask: What is the writer's relationship with the place and the people he writes about?*
> — BERGER 1979, 5

These openings across the disciplinary boundary between anthropology and history have emboldened some to experiment with practices of representation and narration. They have the feel of an intellectual movement, of something in motion, of a *project* of reshaping the practices of producing and reproducing knowledge. These openings have even led scholars to recognize the most testing of issues, requiring them to engage with questions of uncertainty and indeterminacy that would have once been virtually unthinkable in historical and anthropological inquiry. Contributors to this volume have stepped boldly into these issues. For example, in her contribution for this collection, Oana Mateescu examines the unsettled accounts in Romania relating to an ambiguous figure in a 1950 "uprising"—known as *chermeza*, also bearing the meaning of a revel. Mateescu's goal is not to solve the puzzle of Victor Lupa but rather to act—in the mode of an anthrohistorian—to explore "just how ambiguity and indeterminacy are produced and made into resources constitutive of a history." She reveals how "indeterminacy is the practical achievement of people."

Monica Patterson, in her essay, also takes on an exemplary challenge: getting at the powerful instabilities in the uses of the concept of childhood and also at the problematic assumptions inherent in the project of gaining access to the memory of childhood. Patterson's piece calls up a close reading of Georges Perec's *W or the Memory of Childhood* (1988) to reflect on the idea of the anthrohistorian working with indeterminate categories and fragments of texts, images, and memories, as well as silences, in attempting to reconstruct memory and experience. At the center of this is the "gap," not just as an epistemological challenge of finding the tools to fill in a hole in the inventory of knowledge of society, culture, and history, but also a knot of ethical and philosophical questions regarding the work of silence, uncertainty, absence, ignorance, disappearance, and suffering. The quest for knowledge is not only unsteady but also—in all its absences—full of weight.

In his contribution to this volume, Paul Eiss reflects on the unsteady state of the quest for knowledge located not only "in the field" but also between the lines and images contained in a field journal and later reflections on the challenge of coming to know *el pueblo*. The thing most manifest, most obvious, most resembling a given, reintroduces itself as the unexpected challenge along the path to knowledge.

In a somewhat quixotic parallel to the point that Eiss makes, however institutionalized and durable the framework of *anthrohistory* may turn out to be, however self-evident and fixed its procedures and expectations may become, its essence is likely to be more revealed in what is unsettled as opposed to what one could take as given or fixed. For the readers of Eiss's contribution, a bloodied dead deer on a path, seemingly too heavy to carry, evokes the sense of a project that can perhaps never be completed. In this sense, the mutual engagement of anthropology and history is more *a project* than an achievement, a burden to be carried, yet a burden that— in the gathering of a sense of the weight—may be productive.

In his piece for this volume, Tom Wolfe foregrounds the ways in which, in practice, the engagement of anthropology and history may also be about erasure, a "phantom limb," in which the anthrohistorian may find herself working, teaching, and writing in the lived spaces of one discipline while carrying forward the little used or lost "limb" of the other. The "phantom limb" of the other discipline is disabling and perhaps also—

with respect to the gaze of anthropology on history—enabling, for it may permit one to grasp the powers, languages, and cultures that constitute *discipline* in its departmental and disciplinary procedures.

As discipline's self-regard is constituted within professional practice, so discipline's work is deeply engaged in the intersections—and the thickly gendered and racialized intersections—of professions, classes, nations, and empires. Rena Lederman (2004, 8) has pushed this further, asserting that "attention to the ethical ordering of disciplines may trace out the complex interweaving of intellectual and moral justifications for our ways of meeting responsibilities to research subjects, and for our expectations about trust and truth-telling within specialist communities. Such attention may help also in the remaking and broadening of those communities." In her essay for this volume, Dorothy Hodgson underlines the very different expectations and effects of ethical concerns in the two disciplines. As Hodgson suggests, anthrohistory serves as a space within which the critique of discipline, and of *the* disciplines, finds a possibility if not also a necessity. For Hodgson this is not simply a question of contradictory expectations but more about the consequences of the far more complex interplay of different ranges of ethical concerns relating to intervention, representation, participation, and dialogue, not to mention of the protocols for protection of human subjects, rights issues in publication, and appropriate venues of publication.

Another challenge of getting at discipline is in recognizing that at one level, or in one orientation, a discipline appears to be one thing, while in a different orientation, the same discipline appears so diverse as to defy generalization. A commonplace experience of anthropologists and historians in conversation with one another is that a sense of one's own discipline may seem so unsettled while the other's view of it seems so confident in singular ascriptions (Ohnuki-Tierney 1991, 2). The question of discipline is sharply marked in such conversations; a familiar trope in such conversations is a focus on *method*, a term implying limits without specification, and specification without limits.

In a different context, and with different intent, Sonja Luehrmann, in her essay for this volume, offers a most suggestive discussion of "method" as it transited substantially different contexts of Soviet and post-Soviet practice, from the Soviet methodology of promoting scientific communism to the methodology of those promoting and proselytizing religion in these post-Soviet times. The recognition of transcendent method, of continuity in the practices of the methodicians, reveals underlying protocols for conveying ideas and practices, with a juxtaposition of sorts between *method* as connoting a universalist idea on the one hand and the particular dispersals of content, of approaches, in the practices that are recognized as method on the other.

Paradoxically, the search for universals, whether in practice, theory, or knowledge, may actually produce diversity and division. Six decades ago, important humanistic and social science scholarship was organized and also fragmented, within disciplines: anthropology, art history, classical studies, economics, history, literary studies, government and political science, psychology, and sociology. Today, the same could be said, but with a difference: extraordinary constellations of centers, departments, institutes, and programs have become almost necessary fixtures within higher education across the globe: from African American studies programs to humanities centers, from science and technology programs to East Asian institutes, from Jewish studies centers to performance studies programs. If these interstitial developments, these interdisciplinary centers, institutes, and programs together represent a statement, it is that somehow "the disciplines" of the humanities and social sciences are, or have been, *insufficiently* powerful vehicles for the production and reproduction of knowledge. The saturating effects of a highly valued *interdisciplinarity* may have brought into existence more entities within higher education that function as commensurate with disciplines. Each of these new entities commands some level of associational identity or loyalty, multiplying such possible associations without necessarily delivering to the individual scholar or teacher the advantages of being both a part of and an other to a disciplinary home. Significantly, the consensus in support of interdisciplinarity, with its thematic proliferation, with its openings to restructuring of higher education, has proceeded without re-

> *We maintain that sociocultural anthropology contains more than a series of discrete conceptual items that can be consumed at will by historians, that it is more than a type of textual or discursive analysis that converges with other like efforts from other disciplines, and that it is more than a "genre." Therefore, historical anthropology cannot be a small-scale variation of history, a useful repository of useful concepts, or just a technique. Rather, it approaches the past with a coherence that is derived from its own histories, the persistence of (and rebellions against) its own traditions, and the long-term conflicts (some old, some new) among its component parts.*
> ❧ SILVERMAN AND GULLIVER 1992, 52

quiring or producing a serious engagement with, and critique of, discipline, as exemplified in Wolfe's piece here.

Still, deep engagement with one discipline may encourage, even construct, reflexivity with respect to the other. This reflexivity may include, as Lederman has argued, experiencing distinctions among disciplines as not just "socially real" but also as "ethical affronts" (2004, 8). This may not be easy stuff for the "interdisciplinarian." We see in Wolfe's chapter that, as the anthrohistorian works with colleagues in the history department, the coproduction of academic work may induce an everyday sense of *discomfort* through the harboring of critical ethnographies of practice neither shareable nor reciprocated. Optimistically, Wolfe sees these circumstances as stirring insight that could actually be instrumental in the reform of the university.

> *Much of the difficulty of interdisciplinarity has to do with the fact that attention, recognition, and authority are channelled by disciplinary institutions.*
> ❧ SPERBER 2003

In a different vein, Sally Humphreys suggests in her piece for this volume that a profound and largely unrecognized challenge of being "bidisciplinary" is to be capable of a double reflexivity: "being able to stand outside as well as inside two disciplines." By contrast, the typical mandate of interdisciplinarity is more modest: to find a productive reflexivity within the practice of one's discipline through engagement with another. While interdisciplinarity—in this modest form—is a piece of a broader critique and reform of higher education, David Pedersen argues in his essay here that anthrohistory's project brings attention to the burden, the weight, of discipline while considering the values of other ways of producing knowledge. In this aspect of anthrohistory, the challenge is to get at the meanings, powers, logics, and work of "discipline" abstracted from the discipline's conventional moorings in the literatures, conventions, and identities of professional practice. As Pedersen notes, beneath the boilerplate histories of a discipline one can see the materialities of local and global situatedness along one axis as well as the professional and scholarly and political along another. He locates the particular terms of the 1987–89 formation of the Anthrohistory Program at the University of Michigan in the context of a *specific* set of time and space conjunctures and conditions in which social science programs were then imbricated.

Perhaps the question remains open as to whether interdisciplinarity gone viral has been at the expense not only of the disciplines but also of the very promise of interdisciplinarity. At the same time, the mutual engagements of anthropology and history have produced spaces of critical engagement with the disciplines and even with the very idea of discipline, while also generating new and significant scholarship drawing on interests, orientations, and strengths associated with each of the disciplines. As exemplified in the work represented in this volume, anthrohistory has both seized the possibilities and encountered the challenges and limits of the call to interdisciplinarity, giving impetus to transgressive practice in the constitution of general and useable knowledge.

Critique

Anthrohistory's "transdisciplinary" ethic opens out of earlier goals of bridging disciplinary distinctions but encompasses other routes to knowledge beyond "the academy." At the core of this ethic is *critique,* not simply confected to distance old scholarship but also to unveil and conjugate the threads of hierarchy and domination that run almost silently between programs of knowledge production and programs of power. It is also a *critique* of the projects of bringing anthropology and history within the same frame, in support of the values of continuous *self-critique,* drawing attention to the force of "location" in one's own scholarship as Pedersen foregrounds in his piece; questioning the associations of means and ends in research as Eiss does in his essay; and giving attention to the possibilities of constituting and reproducing ethically responsible knowledge (as Hodgson discusses in her piece).

And it is a *critique* that is also playful and experimental, never quite satisfied with the reasons for given protocols of scholarship, expertise, and audience; desirous of being open to new possibilities for remaking the grounds of expertise, of qualifying authority, of sharing learning; and aware that the productions of knowledge develop at many sites and moments. Anthrohistorians, as represented by those whose work is included in this collection, are simultaneously studying in the disciplines; working among cohorts and faculty dedicated to the reproduction of best practices, theory, and priorities of the disciplines; and studying apart from each and both disciplines' programs of reproduction. Put another way, the engagements of students and faculty within the framework of anthrohistory bear the promise of not only pressing a double-disciplinary and doubly reflexive training but also cultivating critical, alternative, and unsettling perspectives on knowledge and expertise.

From one angle the doubly reflexive ambit of an anthrohistory—as projected in this volume—may seem strange and inchoate if not impossible, at least a pedagogical stretch. Yet such formation toward the unsettling of given perspectives and programs of knowledge and expertise—*formation against formation*—unfolds within this collection, and in the broader body of work that this collection represents, as anthrohistorians inevitably bring into conversation diverse fields of research, different periods of time, and varied scales of observation, with shared recognition of other productions of knowledge, other ways and interests in knowing. In these cross-field conversations, the question of *scale* is one that emerges early and reasserts itself often, as anthrohistorians work through debates over the relative merits or powers of approaches characterized as *microhistoire* or macrohistorical, or as they grapple with contending analytical frames of global and local, or as they engage key words in the literatures of the disciplines such as *field, informant, community, process, system,* and *structure.* For example, with respect to the *scope* of observation or analysis, the engagements of anthropologists and historians carry the question beyond one of aesthetic, technical, or practical choice. Certainly *scale* invites attention to variables of size and depth of units of analysis, bringing into focus how shifting temporal and spatial scales can bring important light to the productions of institutions, routines, subjects, markets, and commodities. Yet, difficult ethical and political contingencies travel with such seemingly direct choices of the dimensions of the research (which are most often made in the early stages or even pre-stages of research). In the foreground of conversations, of training, is the quixotic or double realization that little can be understood without engagement with the "big structures, large processes, huge comparisons"— to cite the late Charles Tilly's exquisite phrase (1984)—and that little can be understood without a close understanding of how people experience

> *Imagine, suddenly, the substantial material world (tomatoes, rain, birds, stones, melons, fish, eels, termites, mothers, dogs, mildew, salt water) in revolt against the endless stream of images which tell lies about them and in which they are imprisoned! Imagine them, as a reaction, claiming their freedom from all grammatical, digital, and pictorial manipulation, imagine an uprising of the represented!*
> ❧ BERGER 2001, 202

and render into understanding the big forces with which their lives may be engaged. And, similarly, the great changes must be studied over the longue durée *and* in the immediate moment.

In part, these variations in fields of scholarship develop as students and faculty channel through uncommon congeries of literature in seminars and courses. And they are discovered when one ventures beyond the academy and beyond the conventional sources and methods considered authoritative in the two disciplines. Training in "the disciplines" is complicated and enriched as students take up courses that draw them into architecture, dance, law, literature, music, performance, urban planning, and visual arts. These are not only "outside" studies—"cognates"—but also the means to a broadened interdisciplinary practice and to a thickened engagement with the naturalized routines, paradigms, certainties—the *framings*—of each of the disciplines of anthropology and history. *Framing* suggests choices that we make, as if we, as scholars, are free to choose. Less obvious, but obviously more significant, is that framing underlines the conditioning structures in which scholars pursue their work, in which the choices that one may seem to have the authority to make are already shaped if not determined. The engagements of anthropologists and historians self-critically raise the question of the logic and power of the frame of study, bringing attention to the assumptions, categories, and narrative structures employed to produce scholarly texts *and* to the ways in which the shapes and boundaries of relationships, organizations, and social performance are produced and conditioned. Moreover, such attentions to scale and framing—as choices with assumptions and implications—lead into a further range of reflection and critique on *the stakes* of choices made in the frames, scales, sites, and methods of research.

> *The struggle for life is the matter. We can find its germinations and ruins in fields, those expanding spaces where social activity continuously unfolds, and archives, as the ever-more-varied containers of its readable traces and signs.*
>
> ❧ CORONIL, THIS VOLUME

In her contribution to this volume, Julie Skurski examines the explosive 2000–2001 Yanomami controversy at the University of Michigan—and necessarily beyond—in terms of the differing research agendas, professional alliances, institutional bases, and definitions of ethics revealed among contending parties. The controversy opened with the publication in late 2001 of Patrick Tierney's *Darkness in El Dorado: How Scientists and Journalists Devastated the Amazon*. The University of Michigan was roiled by charges in the book against former faculty and then by actions of university leaders and faculty to dismiss the book. Students and faculty associated with Michigan's Anthrohistory Program organized a series of three colloquiums to open a space for discussion of Tierney's charges and of the scholar's and institutions' responsibilities in the supervision of research and in handling critical reviews of that research. Here, the conditions of field and archive were revealed to be closely and deeply connected to the ostensibly distant institutional anchorages of scholarship. As Skurski shows, the colloquiums moved beyond denunciation to foreground the positive values of layered ethnographies and histories. Exquisitely exemplifying a transdisciplinary anthrohistory, the colloquiums foregrounded the inherent linkages among the subjects and objects of research, linkages that are often obscured by the boundaries, practices, and norms of disciplines and professions. Skurski argues that the colloquiums opened for discussion the simultaneous proximity and distance constituted in the relations of metropolitan institutions of higher education with the subjects of research. On the one side, the colloquiums exposed some of the effects of hierarchy in the organization of scholarly and scientific research; on the other, the colloquiums raised once again the question Robert S. Lynd memorably asked, "knowledge for what?" (1939).

The World

As a relatively young, active, and flexible scholarly project in an era of extraordinary change, anthrohistory encounters most directly the question of whether university-based programs of training and research can comprehend and account for a world in change and the related shifts in knowledge: from the recognition of the tensions of multiple perspectives to the interpretative conflicts among different institutionalized frames of knowledge; from the deeper understandings of the workings of silence to the recognition of ritualized modes of representation, interpretation, and commemoration; and from the strong authority of expert knowledge, metanarratives, and general theory to the mediations and instabilities introduced into global knowledge production from other sites and sources of knowledge, theory, and interpretation. As scholars have engaged the world beyond the disciplines, beyond the academy, and beyond North America—that is, as they have moved *outside* the more accessible if not also privileged ranges of discovery and knowing—they also find themselves inevitably turning *inside* in questioning the relative authorities of established practices of interpretation and representation amid the powers and poetics of other narratives, other theory, other programs of knowledge. Ilana Feldman, in this collection, suggests that war, violence, neglect, and despair call for difficult work of addressing specifically the "in-between" spaces of experience, creating an "in-between ethnography."

In a moving essay published in 1998, Arundhati Roy explored the abyss revealed in May of that year in the moment of India's nuclear tests and the beginning of a nuclear arms race in South Asia. Roy related how, in this moment of horror, she attempted to explain to a friend from New York that "the only dream worth having . . . is to dream that you will live while you're alive and die only when you're dead." On a paper napkin, she drafted for her friend an ethic of living, her protest for life, a protest that seems so lonely, so marginal, and so impossible in the face of the drafting of weapons of mass extermination to the cause of *nation*.

In similar ways, young scholars have found their ways to anthrohistory at the University of Michigan and elsewhere through their struggles to engage the unspeakable, and to disclose and remediate disparity. Shannon Dawdy, in a contribution to this volume, found herself in post-Katrina New Orleans experiencing "anthropology and history—not as objects, nor precisely as professional activities, but as ways of living in the world." As Dawdy suggests, echoing Feldman, hierarchy in the world, the embedded hierarchies of knowledge, and "the unspeakable violence and the vulgar disparity of life" require a set of different arts, practices, and orientations than those that seem to have been so well supported, so thoroughly privileged, so capable of infinite elaboration and reproduction as have been those inhabiting well-defined disciplines.

Inevitably, the intersections of anthropology and history call up the challenges of identifying and problematizing hierarchy in the constructions of power and knowledge. In his essay, Fernando Coronil reflects that "non-dominative knowledge excavates deep within and beyond given fields and archives." Feldman echoes this critical concern for the objectification of "field" and "archive" that are recognized

To love. To be loved. To never forget your own insignificance. To never get used to the unspeakable violence and the vulgar disparity of life around you. To seek joy in the saddest of places. To pursue beauty to its lair. To never simplify what is complicated or complicate what is simple. To respect strength, never power. Above all, to watch. To try and understand. To never look away. And never, never, to forget.
❧ ROY 1998, 1

not only as archetypes marking prime objects, or means, in the one discipline and another, but additionally as the veritable sites where the ancestors lay hold of our contemporaries and ourselves, shaping the limits and possibilities of what we can or will do with the knowledge that we find, or are bequeathed.

Such weight from the past hangs heavily in Kerry Ward's contribution to this volume, as she narrates the struggles in South Africa over the territories of the dead among a considerable range of interested actors. The dead in a sense not only lay claim to their spaces but condition the terms of negotiation of landscapes, properties, zoning, and development as well as cemeteries and monuments. Likewise with the Yanomami debates, the subjects of research ultimately condition the terms of their representation.

Here, the powers and limits of "master narratives" may be grasped even while revealing the difficulties of constituting alternative practices of knowing, representing, and engaging the world amidst ambivalence and uncertainty. More so, scholarship itself, as in explanations and alibis mooted in the defense of the Yanomami research, may be implicated in the workings of hegemony. Less delicately, conversations on these questions of hierarchy and resistance at the intersections of anthropology and history over the past few decades echo, sustain, and may in some instances elaborate the 1968 critiques of university-based knowledge of non-European societies. As Skurski reminds us with the Yanomami controversy, university-based knowledge of non-Western societies is *part of* the armature of Western domination and privilege rather than *about* the continuing domination, neocolonialism, impoverishment, and underdevelopment.

> *The encounter between anthropology and history unfolds as a highly theorized enterprise that constantly questions and reshapes its domain.*
> — MATEESCU, THIS VOLUME

Practice

When anthropologists and historians seek productive engagements with one another, and with one another's discipline of formation, they draw into the foreground the question of how scholars may produce ethically responsible knowledge in the contexts of hierarchies of power in the productions of scholarship, amidst the commodification of knowledge and the misapplication—even the violence—of expertise. As the Anthrohistory Program's colloquiums on the Yanomami controversy highlighted, a release from the authority of the respective disciplines reveals the situated and privileged protocols and values of national, professional, and disciplinary practice, unsettling the more conventional and accessible grounds upon which to formulate and conduct scholarship. Recognition of the powers of alternative accounts destabilizes dominant frames of reference, locating knowledge as imbricated in collective myths and fictions, national and otherwise. Coming to know is a project of coming to understand oneself, one's own formation, the foundational strengths and privileges of given concepts and expectations, of even coming not to know . . . heavy work indeed. Humphreys suggests, "if the idea of a 'cultural turn' still has any energy, it is in the invitation to think critically about disciplines as cultures."

In her piece on "culture brokers" and imperial governmentality on the verges of Ottoman and European worlds, Natalie Rothman reflects on the heavy work involved in the constitution of cultural boundaries that "are made to seem natural, immutable, and all-encompassing." Rothman's intermediation—organizing authority and constructing representations and outcomes—is an exercise in and of expertise and power. On the one side, such examples as Rothman uncovers on the verges of Ottoman and European worlds would seem to portend the possibility of transcending difference between disciplines—for example, anthropology and history—as well as cultures and regions. Yet intermediation speaks to another range of stakes involved in the mastering of difference, suggesting the political effects of programs of translation and representation, whether we are referring to borderlands of empires or to transnational and globalizing processes or to claims of interdisciplinary and transdisciplinary programs in the academy. Once understood, Rothman's remarkable intermediaries appear to have the capacity of intellectuals to shape, subsidize, silence, and overdetermine categories as well as to reproduce and circulate knowledge.

The multiple nodes of knowledge production have given considerable force to debates across the academy regarding the uses and abuses of research, the roles of states in the constitution of knowledge and silences, the fates of particular kinds and claims of experts, and the relative powers—and the suppression or dismissal—of other ways of knowing. Noisy debates regarding the content and purposes of "Western civilization" and "core curriculum" courses, and struggles over the content as well as the idea of "the canon," have marked the territory of these conflicts over the proprietorship and reproduction of knowledge. This is evidenced in virtually every field of research from health, development, and poverty to fertility and reproduction, mental health, work, environment, resource extraction, citizenship, and human rights. These conflicts have contributed energy *to* and drawn energy *from* core analyses of the work of gender, race, nation, and class in the production and circulation of knowledge in the academy and wider society. In these openings to new veins of critique and scholarship on poverty, inequality, war, exploitation, and empire, on struggles for rights and remediation, anthropologists and historians have been active and important players. Sometimes they share common concerns across the disciplinary boundary while not necessarily sharing a common grammar of critique transcending discipline. An anthrohistorical perspective will not find reassurance within the explicit and implicit protocols of one, or any, discipline. It is a perspective, or an approach, that finds its bearings through its critical approach to the received certainties in the disciplines, whatever the topic, site, or period.

It is important that, through their own practice, the contributors to this volume have not only exemplified this thickened and more complicated engagement of scholarship with the world model of interdisciplinary exchange but have constructed a space that both "bridges" the disciplines (engaging the protocols, languages, and claims of each) and "works between" the disciplines, organizing a productive space simultaneously *between and outside* the two disciplines. In developing the collection for this volume, we have come to speak of this "space" as *anthrohistory*. One would suggest that this "space" has fostered *its own* republics of practice, "rules" or procedures, discursive fixtures, and goals, while significantly open to the sometimes intoxicating but often productive influences of underdevelopment theory, subaltern studies, race and gender theory, performance studies, media studies, and radical political activism secreted not only from other parts of the world but also from outside the academy itself.

Another test for those seeking to engage the approaches and literatures of anthropology and history is to get at affect, or *sense*, especially at the meaning of experience for another. In her essay, Zareena Grewal seeks to recuperate the concept of "tradition," not only looking for a stronger theorization of tradition to counter the dismissive effects of generations of critical deconstructive scholarship in the frame of "the invention of tradition" but also to counter the subtle and powerful ways in which "treating tradition as a shallow term, particularly in the case of Islam," situates scholars as "complicit in a new harmful, violent, and imperial project." This is not only a hermeneutical or an ethical challenge; it is also a challenge to work through the privileged nexus of ascription versus self-realization toward understanding the politics of description, representation, internalization, and authenticity.

As one "senses" the ways in which commodities, markets, and states are fetishized, one also may come to see how sense and affect bear the imprint of broader forces and processes, as in intersubjective and collective "structures of feeling" (Williams 1973). Indeed, it may seem that the most internal and intimate effects claiming the scholar's attention are already beyond the competences of our most familiar research tools. Luehrmann, in her essay on method, notes that a comparison of Soviet and post-Soviet "methodicians" is not just an opportunity to deconstruct contemporary practice or "to establish chains of historical causality" but also to understand the pride with which a member of a collective farm reported to authorities her considered use of propaganda posters and with which a study leader recounted having combed the Bible for appropriate verses. Here is an opportunity for the anthrohistorian to use juxtaposition to grasp the terms, protocols, and meanings of practice that go deeper than or beyond specific ethnographic observation and historical accounting.

As Coronil notes, "of this world but not at home in it, anthrohistory resists being disciplined in existing institutions or contained by definitions." Like Feldman, contemplating the "in-between spaces" of experience and research in Gaza, Dawdy locates her post-Katrina position between the Federal Emergency Management Agency (FEMA), which hired her to perform surveys of the disaster on historical sites in New Orleans, and the victims of the flood and government neglect. For Dawdy, a first-order task was to constitute "a perspective that balances somewhere between necessary patience and useful outrage." And she notes how differently she was experiencing the catastrophe from the ways that "Katrina" was experienced by its direct subjects.

Epistemes

One of the challenges of attending to the labyrinthian intersections of anthropology and history, of anthropologists and historians, of anthrohistory is to gain a competent and usable understanding of the unfolding of the bridging of the two disciplines (Axel 2002; Cohn 1987; Dirks 1996; Dube 2007; Roseberry 1989; Silverman and Gulliver 1992; Tanner 2004; Willford and Tagliacozzo 2009). There have been many calls, programmatic and intellectual, for anthropologists and historians to move onto common ground, to take account of the possibilities of a sharing or exchange of ways of working, to overcome the boundedness of discipline. While there have been a few attempts to diagram the history of these relationships, there remain many ways to tell this story of anthropology and history. One inclination is to view these engagements as following a path from an originary moment, or moments, toward the unfolding of a new paradigm or discipline. An emergent journal such as *Historische Anthropologie* founded in 1993 or the Doctoral Program in Anthropology and History founded in 1987 to 1989 are signals of professionalization a-fresh, signs of the unfolding of a new discipline out of its parents, these specific developments located in some mid-term between an original conceptualization of a possibility and a future achievement. One appealing line of interpretation locates "the margins" as the nurturing context of anthropology and history's juncture (Axel 2002), while another would see the juncture called up by the recognition that "Europe" must engage and understand the rest of the world, the "other" (O'Brien and Roseberry 1991). A less "natural" story would identify diverse constitutive threads, each traceable to influential lines of work from Boas-ian anthropology in North America to the *Annales* school in France, from pioneering work in *microhistoire* to Marxist analyses of third world underdevelopment, from the efforts of British social anthropology to escape functionalism to the struggles for history in new nations, from new lines of work in symbolic and linguistic anthropology to the influence of histories claiming "indigenous" authority, from the calls to comprehend the experience of victims traumatized by the horrors of slavery and violence to the sometimes vexed and paradoxical efforts to give "voice" to those counted as the silenced (Sider and Smith 1997; Trouillot 1995). Other narratives could track the changes within each of the disciplines, pointing to areas of scholarly work where the boundaries between work in one discipline and work in the other have been traversed, for example, with respect to issues of agency and hegemony (Willford and Tagliacozzo 2009). Still others could draw on shifts in generations of scholarship broader than the particular disciplines.

There is also an inclination to formulate these engagements in terms of what one discipline has taken to be the more prominent distinctions of the other, such as the characteristic sites of research, field or archive; closed versus enlarged scales; varying conjugations of time and temporality; incommensurate equations of the symbolic and material; different values of concepts of culture and structure; and varying practices of narration. These have been well-exercised tools of distinction arguably more useful than real ... overwhelming what might have been significant commonalities. One of the convenient fictions that has shaped the way the story of anthropology and history has been told is that the discipline of history could claim a heightened sense of the significance of time in an era in which anthropologists reckoned that their own discipline lacked a capacity to explain change or transformation. Such a distinction is so nominal and ill-informed as to be useless except as a way of evading more studied examination of what anthropologists and historians do with time. Within the actual engagements of anthropologists and historians, as they are exemplified by contributions to this volume, *time* connotes, first of all, contingency and force in the engagements among subjects, scholars, and audiences as each confronts, or presents, different temporal conditions in which inquiry and representation may be organized, different temporal codes, different valences associated with tense, even in the different temporalities in which respective changes within the disciplines of anthropology and history may be discerned, even in the different temporicities through which change is experienced and represented.

Temporalities and temporicities are subtly and powerfully produced in situations of duress, stress, domination, resistance, and violence. In her contribution, Limbert shows that temporalities are not redolent with certainty, whether for observer or historical actor, but rather they are "mysteries," conjured of uncertainties, manifesting the interplay of multiple and different trajectories, from the timeline of oil revenues to the contemplation of theocratic revival. Feldman situates this question in terms of the multiple and layered frames of time that condition memory and reflection for retired civil servants in Gaza. On the one side, the layered administrations of Gaza have produced a layered stratigraphy of archival material and contexts of governmental service and experience. On the other, in her conversations with retired civil servants, "no single time ... provides the correct interpretative frame for them. These conversations take place ... in-between time."

The exquisite incapacity of practitioners of anthrohistory to summon a credible unified history of their own practice reveals the effects of deeply contingent deployments of time in observation, description, analysis, and explanation. In her essay, Deirdre de la Cruz examines the ways in which—at an almost unconscious level—the future perfect, *anticipation,* conditions research and educes theory at the intersection of anthropology and history. "Here the horizon of a fine work only ever recedes, and the literal closure of a story is an open invitation to read anew. Here the future perfect is goading in nature, holding out the promise of what will have been learned for what I am in the process of discovering." Her essay calls for a more conscious, more open recognition of a "reciprocal engagement with the future," that while all writing—anthropological and historical—is inevitably about the future, the challenge is in writing "from a place of obligation—without calculation of return." The settled protocols of scholarship, nested in conventions of language and practice, do not lead so much to settled knowledge but rather into the realms of the uncertain, the indeterminate.

In her essay on the project of anthrohistory, Mateescu shows how "the practical historians of *chermeza*" work with and also produce indeterminacy. In doing so, they "lose the phenomena" through an anticipation of the stories, and the values and contingencies of the stories, that may be produced. By extension, Mateescu offers the possibility of looking at the project of anthrohistory as more than a work in progress, indeed as a "form of anticipation, prospectively orienting the attention of its practitioners to a world where past and presents are still being made."

While there is no straight line of work or positions extending from the first programmatic statements and the first exemplars of an anthropology formally informed by history and a history formally informed by anthropology—and, following de la Cruz and Mateescu, all such writing is arguably full of a supposition, of a will, to produce a future—it is important that there are different ways to tell the story of the engagement of the disciplines of anthropology and history. In his essay, Setrag Manoukian marks the distinction between two prime framings, one which he terms "states of affairs" and the other "blocs of sensations." In the former, the regime of study involves the acts of contextualization—the ways in which events, experience, or institutions are produced, with anthrohistorians keenly attentive to the "com-participatory work of researchers and others" in confecting social reality and crediting their analytical work to getting at "'the construction of' whatever one is researching." On the other hand, Manoukian's concept of "blocs of sensations" connotes the "expressive possibilities and limits of the material we think through, and the effects of thoughts and affects they project." The implications of Manoukian's distinction is to look at the disciplines in different ways, turned in a manner of speaking 180 degrees, from how we have been most disposed to look at them. Here, the potential of engagements with affect, in the context of the sense of possibility of theory's mastery of "states of affairs," would seem to call up a different frame of scholarship.

Following Manoukian, we view this engagement of disciplines as comprising sometimes unsettled, multiple, and alternately independent and interrelated developments, signaled by both the "expressive possibilities of the material" we study and the open-ended inventories of literature to which we attend. Constituted both within and apart from the disciplines, drawing upon them and establishing critical distance from them, anthrohistory is inevitably marked by and continues to engage a broad range of intellectual and political movements and institutions, including the Frankfurt school, surrealism, subaltern studies, native or indigenous claims commissions, the *Annales* school, peasant studies, orientalism and its critique, history workshop projects in several arenas, underdevelopment theory, radical anthropology, oral history, the new American history, comparative slave studies, feminism, the Birmingham school, world system theory, historical archaeology, deconstructionism, the new African history, the new social history, postmodernism, women's studies, cultural and ethnic studies, black studies, postcolonial studies, human rights activism, microhistory, environmental studies, Atlantic studies, Alltagsgeschichte, along with independent and globalized indigenous peoples' movements.

Notably, anthrohistorians have been attentive to and involved in the literary, cultural, linguistic, and historical "turns" in the humanities and social sciences. In his chapter, Pedersen reviews the ways in which "the turns" are narrativized by four scholars he locates as natives of the "Great Lakes Basin World" and the ways in which their situatedness in that world is joined with the project of the Anthrohistory Program at Michigan. The four narratives provide a coherent and persuasive account of the constitution of an interdisciplinary program at the University of Michigan but, as Pedersen notes from his research into university records of the 1980s, they evade or understate the degree to which the context of foundation was thickly joined to the university leadership's attempt to rebound from disgraceful acts of racism on campus—at the University of Michigan and elsewhere during the Reagan years. The foundational account of Michigan's Anthrohistory Program remains unsettled, as does that of historical anthropology and anthropological history more broadly.

Recognizing the multiple threads of work and influence, the contributors and editors of this volume take this sense of the unsettled account of anthropology and history as productive, providing openings to experimentation as well as pivots for critical reflection on the practices of scholarship. It is intriguing to consider the will to render the histories of this project of anthrohistory into a deterministic genealogy. Such accountings tend to be conjured in the difficult gaps between generally apprehended trajectories on the one side (historicization) and the local evidence and immediate experience on the other (contextualization) that themselves rehearse the essential characters that each discipline's practitioners recognize in the other's. Still, echoing Patterson, there is also the additional "gap" in which anthrohistory unfolds its projects and programs; this is between a sense of possibility and breakthrough to new vectors of knowledge production and circulation—see Coronil's play with Marx: "The poetry of the present holds the prose of the future"—and a sense, shared at virtually every meeting of students and faculty associated with the University of Michigan's Doctoral Program in Anthropology and History, that this program is always on the verge of disappearing.

It must also be noted that such a will to authorize this project of anthrohistory via historicization may have effects on the shapes of work that claims to have or is seen as having bridged the disciplines. In their contribution, Anupama Rao and Steven Pierce move the attention of scholars from the extensively rehearsed questions of governmentality and rights viewed in the contexts of the postcolonial and globalization toward a deeper historical interrogation of "the human" and the "the role of (colonial) violence in constituting ideologies of the partial humanity of colonial subjects." Humphreys echoes this view seeing the intersections of the disciplines making it possible to return "to the eighteenth-century conception of anthropology as the theory of what it is to be human," including, as she draws on Rebel (2005), "the capacity to be mystified, to repress obvious elements of experience, to learn what not to know." In conversation with Manoukian's suggestion to rethink the given, or privileged, stories of the intersecting ambits of anthropology and history—and Mateescu's suggestions on the possibilities of recognizing how indeterminacy in the production of knowledge is produced—bring to the fore the questions of what it has meant and what it will yet mean, and not mean, to be "human" in this world.

Anthropologists and historians may have found some important common ground in the attempts to bring into words or narratives the story of this encounter between disciplines. They have come together recognizing the possible values of a historical anthropology or an anthropological history; or of a discipline of anthropology more deeply marked by the approaches and contingencies of historical investigation and historical explanation and a discipline of history "thickly" marked by anthropological approaches and theory regarding the work and power of symbols, languages, and structure. Yet, the "stuff" of this possibility may lie beyond the obvious frames of biography of disciplines or the programmatic calls for enriched disciplinary practice, or the potentially influential calls to bring disciplines (or the practitioners of disciplines) into spaces of common work. A sense of the essential "contract" of Anthrohistory (here, one is tempted to invoke the term in a privileged and formal address) clearly lies beyond the declaration of need, good, or opportunity.

To be blunt, as the hard questions of the powers and ethics of knowledge confront the privileged confidence of the academy and its core disciplines, this project implies more paradigmatic virtuosity than paradigmatic unity. The collection of remarkable work presented here reveals important dimensions of a project with the promise of further growth and the promise to challenge power and privilege in the productions of knowledge; yet within the project is located a dis-ease with the actual possibilities of remaking the power-knowledge relationship, at least as it reproduces itself in the academy in the metropolitan regions. Here, the uncertainties and ambiguities of pursuing a "formation against formation" press forward toward different ways of knowing, addressing, and engaging the world.

This essay began with the juxtaposition of practices and directions in scholarship sustained in their distinction by secure boundaries of strongly supported and well-rehearsed disciplines. It closes with a more complicated and also opportune sense of difference, a difference quite *other* than the motifs of crossing or blurring strong boundaries. If the relationships of anthropologists and historians began—as this essay began—in a context of separate hallways and different cultures, where breaking across difference suggested the possibility of a new synthesis, the mapping of anthrohistory resembles, in Coronil's expression, "a labyrinth whose exits become entrances into an expanding labyrinth, its arrivals are points of departure and its answers pose new questions."

In his last writings in 1985, Italo Calvino reflected that across his working lifetime he had sought "to remove weight, sometimes from people, sometimes from heavenly bodies, sometimes from cities; above all I have tried to remove weight from the structure of stories and from language" (1988, 3). He offered for "the new millennium" a goal of lightness. Lightness is offered up as a "value rather than a defect." Lightness carries fresh and transformative possibilities in the business of finding, knowing, and understanding (Cohen 2009). In the idea of weight, there is an echo of

Eiss's bloody deer on a path, too heavy for *him* to carry any further. In weight, there are the constrictions, inhering in the inertia of disciplines, of given structures, institutions, programs of expertise, ways of seeing and knowing. For Calvino, lightness—through multiple and powerful vectors that are connective yet weightless—can relieve the burdens of an overbuilt world.

For anthrohistory—not quite of two disciplines, not quite bridging them, not quite between them, and not quite aspiring to any of these postures—lightness is also a value, a tool, a strength, catching the light of several vectors. Indeed, anthrohistory's *formation*—formation here conveying several meanings: modes of learning, groundedness, cadres, processes, and open temporality—organizes itself along multiple vectors: the promise of experimentation in the constitution of new standpoints and fresh logics, including the exploration of the pluriversal, the multiple languages of justice and equality, and other frames of knowledge standing outside the built structures that have actively privileged the "universal" values descending from the Enlightenment; a growing attention to and understanding of the powers and poetics of uncertainty and indeterminacy; the continuing development of alternative radical politics, embodying a strong sense of responsibility to the subjects and audiences of anthropological and historical investigation; and a renewed sense of the particular responsibilities that bind our fates with those of our subjects.

> *Whenever humanity seems condemned to heaviness, I think I should fly like Perseus into a different space. I don't mean escaping into dreams or into the irrational. I mean that I have to change my approach, look at the world from a different perspective, with a different logic and with fresh methods of cogitation and verification. The images of lightness that I seek should not fade away like dreams dissolved by the realities of present and future . . .*
> ❧ CALVINO 1988, 7

Part 1 ❦ Encountering Boundaries

3 ❧ Paul K. Eiss

Notes on the Difficulty of Studying *el Pueblo*

> He writes about it without having felt it yet.
> —SETRAG MANOUKIAN

Well here I am, standing alone on a trail in the middle of the woods, somewhere in Tetiz's woodlands, but very far from Tetiz. . . . I am guarding a deer, just killed by my hunting buddies. Here's the blood: [*stain on the page*] I thought I was guarding it from other people—who the hell would be out here anyway—but I have just realized who the real enemy is, who just stopped by to pay a visit: a big, black vulture. A few badly thrown rocks keep the things away—now at least I can make myself useful for a change.

So it's October 1995, and I'm in Yucatán sitting on the ground by a deer carcass, alone. After a day of pushing through the brush in hundred-degree heat, I am covered with dirt and twigs, and small ticks that I picked up along the way. I am trying to remember the initial symptoms of heat exhaustion, and comparing those to the dizziness and nausea I feel. But I am not too tired to feel embarrassed about what has happened. After tagging along with a hunting party, uselessly, all day, I and another man had been given two deer to carry back to camp—in traditional Yucatecan fashion, which involves trussing the deer and then hoisting it onto your back. A rope runs from the carcass over your forehead. I am no expert in this. The first couple of times I try to get the animal on my shoulders, it flops around, throwing me off balance. I fall over, twice. Finally, I succeed in hoisting it up, and hobble forward, with the brutal cord cutting into my forehead and hands. I make it about one hundred feet, before the deer shifts again, snapping my neck back and I fall, one last time, atop the carcass. While I struggle to get up, my companion continues on his way. "I'll send help," he says. Then I sit beside the carcass and begin writing in my notebook, pausing to stain the page with the deer's blood.

Let me put this differently: "Imagine yourself suddenly set down surrounded by all your gear, alone ~~on a tropical beach~~ [in the woods] close to a native village, while the ~~launch or dinghy~~ [hunting party] which has brought you ~~sails~~ [walks] out of sight" (Malinowski 1922, 4). Did I already expect that it would be like this—that I might experience, or write, something like this? As a student in Michigan's Doctoral Program in Anthropology and History in the 1990s, I was exposed to an abundance of scholarship bearing on the historical and epistemological critique of anthropology's founding figures and their methods—including the heroic mode of ethnographic writing and self-presentation. Nor did "history" emerge unscathed. Like other students of my generation, I had been schooled in a variety of styles of analysis—discursive, materialist, semiotic, constructionist—which easily lent themselves to the critique of the pretensions of historicist narratives, archives, and of the historian's own heroic romance, set in the archives. In their conjunction, this training made for a critical stance toward both "field" and "archive" as arena of practice, experience, and knowledge—a vaccine, it would seem, against the conceits of earlier times.

FIG. 3.1. Dead deer in the Yucatán. Photo by Paul Eiss.

Yet on arrival in Yucatán, I found myself seduced by the romance of archive and field, and the heroic roles they seemed to offer to ethnographer and historian. Both seemed to offer themselves as places of encounter with *el pueblo*—a word that translates in English into a political abstraction ("the people"). In Spanish, however, the term is richer, and more grounded, as it is used to refer to small or rural settlements (towns or villages), and to the communities that inhabit those places (typically involving "face-to-face" relationships and shared communal possessions or qualities), as well as to "the people" as an abstract entity. In my work in the state archives, and in the dilapidated offices of the Secretariat of Land Reform, I dedicated myself to searching out documents relating to rural indigenous *pueblos*, and especially their conflicts and struggles with landowners and state officials before, during, and after the Mexican Revolution (1910 forward). I imagined, as I diligently amassed photocopies of thousands of pages of material, one day carrying these documents with me to the communities named in them, in hopes of triggering discussions and recovering a "secret history" of indigenous mobilizations. I imagined countering an official, statist historiography that presented indigenous workers and pueblo residents as essentially passive, backward, and racially inferior objects of benevolent uplift by agents of the state, with a history of continued indigenous struggle against ethnic, class, and political exploitation, during and after the Revolution, as much as before. The guiding principle of my archival work was thus a general sentiment of solidarity with *el pueblo*, against its exploiters, and a belief in the emancipatory possibilities attendant on the recovery of historical consciousness of the varied *luchas*, or "struggles," of *el pueblo*. This was the basis for my enchantment by what some call the archival fetish, but also, perhaps, by the prospect of remaking myself as a certain kind of historian, cast in a romantic and heroic mold, a historian of *el pueblo*.

As for "the field," over the course of time and according to expectation, I had found "my" ethnographic community—a pueblo called Tetiz—where I had begun living, studying Maya, had made contacts and some friends, and had started taking part in many aspects of daily life in the *pueblo*, from work, to fiestas, to religious processions. Long before I had an inkling of what might become the focus of my work, I was motivated by the classic ethnographic imperatives—to participate and to observe, and to write. I sought in so many ways to be "of *el pueblo*": through ways and expressions in speech that were *mayero* (i.e., Maya in nature or inflection); by refusing spoons and forks handed to me (alone) at meals, to eat with my hands; by participating in largely communal activities of *el pueblo*, like religious processions and fiestas; by spurning the use of hired bicycle taxis; to walk miles in the hot sun when I visited nearby haciendas; in occasional bouts of public drinking. I yearned to be given a nickname—that was how most people I knew in Tetiz were identified locally, by Mayan or Spanish words for "cow," "armadillo," "corn," "dragon," or even "monkey thief," rather than by their given names—and I even tried to drop hints about names that I thought would be both appropriate and cool. In the field, as in the archive, I was guided, I think, by an assumption that my vague but well-meaning sentiments of solidarity with *el pueblo*—"the people," in the abstract, but also *this* place, and *this* community—were the credential that might provide me a means of access and recognition in a place where I had no roots, and where my attachment to the forms of communal life were shallow and tenuous at best. Throughout, I remained faithful to Malinowski's injunction to observe, as well as participate, taking time each evening to chronicle my efforts at being in, and of, *el pueblo,* in field notes. Beyond capturing information in writing, I thus evoked, and imagined, the prospect of authoring a future "public" ethnographic text, whose spectral authority somehow might be conjured, through the evening ritual of writing field notes.

It is in this spirit that, in October 1995, I head off to the woods near Tetiz as part of a communal hunting group (illegal due to violation of both laws protecting animals and laws forbidding foreigners to carry firearms). I aim to prove myself in what I take to be the archetypical way not only of being "of *el pueblo*" (with connotations of working class, and indigenous or mestizo identities, or affinities) but just as importantly, of stereotypical ways of being male in *el pueblo.* But as I sit, exhausted, by the deer, these romantic aspirations are pushed to the breaking point, as the weight of *el pueblo,* becomes, quite literally, unbearable.

> Nothing can rescue me from this crisis of manhood. *I can't carry really heavy shit with my head,* not this deer, and not the huge loads of wood that men carry. Not for 10 kilometers. Not for 5 kilometers. Not for 100 meters. I feel like a failure. I would not be able to be a man in this culture, for the simple fact of not being able to strap shit heavy objects to my head and carry them for great distances.

The deer twists on my back, dragging me to the ground, it bends and breaks these stereotypes, this romance. It exposes the futility of my attempts to know *el pueblo,* by becoming part of it or through mimesis, provoking me into objectifying it as an alien entity that I might know, but to which I might never belong ("this culture"). The only salvation, it appears to me, is to turn to writing itself, to author field notes in the very moment of the debacle. Or rather, to author fragments of a diary—ethnography's third genre, though a dark-side one, whose writing is equally expected, as a testimony to the "reality" of ethnographic experience and the making of the author as ethnographer. As I pen words, throwing the occasional rock at the gathering vultures, I return to the charged image of my painful walk with the deer. But now it is my own personal calvary—not an ignominious fall but rather a redemptive drama that might save me, and "my" discipline.

As I walked along, I kept saying, like a mantra, as the deer slid back and forth on my back, its blood seeping through my shirt, my back and neck in agony: "Fuck anthropology! Fuck anthropology!" That gave me an extra burst of strength and I made it another 50 feet before collapsing, a third and final time, on top of the carcass. And then I started writing this. Broken in practice, but not in theory. Deer one, anthropologists zero. But then again, I continue to write, and the deer is *bien muerto*.

There is a momentary comfort in this—the use of writing to render alien the setting to which a moment before I intensely, if naively, desired to "belong." Even more so, in the act of projecting an internal conflict into the domain of nature, posing the situation as a contest pitting me against a poor dead animal, whose blood I use—as both a stain of otherness and a mark of authority—both to notarize the "reality" of my ethnographic testimony and to refocus my anger, away from my companions, away from myself. It was as if I had written: "'Exterminate the ~~brutes~~ [deer]!'"— echoing Malinowski's diaries (1989, 69), and their Conradian pre-text, evoking a violence that might set things to rights in the end. It is surely true that field notes and ethnographic writing are, as Geertz argued (1988), crafted in an attempt to create the effect of the author's "being there" and to derive authority from that presence. Yet as I sit in the woods, to author these fragments of a diary is not so much to "be there" as they are to *not* be here, or to be elsewhere. They are about removing myself from unendurable surroundings, to a space of dialogue with an imagined audience—the future version of myself who will be the reader of these blood-stained pages.

Such psychodramas play in the archive as well. Another flashback: it is October 1995, or thereabouts (the keeping of "archive diaries" not being, unfortunately, a reflex of historical discipline). I am sitting at an old metal desk

> *Be wise, Ariadne, you have small ears, you have my ears: let a wise word slip into them: Must one first not hate oneself, if one is to love oneself? I am your labyrinth . . .*
>
> ❧ FRIEDRICH NIETZSCHE 1984 AS CITED IN DELEUZE 1997, 99

perusing old petitions for land in the dusty, hot, and decaying offices of the Secretariat of Agrarian Reform. As on other days, I pretend not to overhear indigenous rural dwellers that come, literally hats in hand, to an official seated at the next desk, to request the attentions of agrarian officials. I have come prepared for the typical physical challenges of this place, which seem symbolic of the abandonment of agrarian reform, amid the sweeping neoliberal reforms instituted by President Carlos Salinas and continued thereafter. Thus, I am ready to jump to another desk if rainwater pours through the leaky roof, or to wrap my mouth and nostrils with a bandanna when documents are covered by mouse droppings and dust from a fallen wall nearby. But I am not prepared for this: severe abdominal pains and churning, telltale signs of the imminent, explosive onset of an intestinal infection. I have never dared to enter the bathroom in this place before, but its state—filthy, without water in the commode—is a deterrent no more. With relief, I become more aware of my surroundings, noticing a pile of old papers atop the commode: land reform documents and correspondence from the archives—perhaps akin to the documents being received or drafted by officials in the room outside. Someone must have forgotten them here! But then my eyes stray to a pail on the floor—the wastepaper receptacle. It is filled with other such documents, now crumpled and covered in excrement, as they are meant for use as toilet paper. What is a historian of *el pueblo* to do?

It does not occur to me, initially, as I suffer and write in field and archive, to reflect on what lessons such situations might offer, regarding the difficulty of studying *el pueblo*—specifically, regarding the tension between, on one hand, a mimetic expectation that one claims access to an understanding of *el pueblo* by being, or appearing to be, part of it, and on the other, the fact that in the very act of knowing and objectifying *el pueblo*—making use of it, in effect—one locates oneself outside its boundaries. Yet over the course of time, episodes like this, particularly those characterized by bodily discomfort or disorienting sensory overload, will pave the way for some insights, by fits and starts.

In the archives, and outside of them, such situations led to a growing awareness of the contradictions of my own assumptions regarding *el pueblo* and of those inherent, perhaps, in the very idea of *el pueblo* itself. Both the documents I read and the interactions I overheard in the agrarian reform archives were framed by generic references to and presentations of *el pueblo* that clearly ratified long-standing practices of class and ethnic rule and subordination. Years of plowing through documents produced and collected by government officials led me to question the task that I had assumed to be my own, that of searching out and collecting documents for a history, from below, of an elemental entity called *el pueblo,* that is, "the people," in opposition to that from above, of the state and its agents. Instead of that opposition between state and *pueblo,* I came to see the construction of each to be deeply implicated in the construction of the other.

For me, *el pueblo,* to paraphrase Abrams's (1988) classic discussion of the nonexistence of "*the* state," began to seem like a mask—an artifice, a fictitious entity ("*el*" *pueblo*) sutured out of the conflicted realities of community, place, and politics. It was an ideological fiction, whose construction shadowed that of the state—or rather the *idea* of the state—as the mystical corpus that was at once the state's field of action, its condition of possibility, and a legitimating smokescreen for structural relations of subordination. I began to see that "mask" peering out of varied kinds of documents that I found in my archival research on western Yucatán. Creole nationalists wore it, in the early nineteenth century, as they busied themselves dismantling indigenous republics and stripping away communal lands and political autonomy, in the name of *el pueblo.* So did late nineteenth-century landowners and government officials, who oversaw the conversion of the region to commercial hacienda agriculture based on indigenous indebted servitude. They masked themselves as well, notably in public events in which they boosted and promoted the modernization of *el pueblo,* even as they invented, celebrated, and performed *pueblo* traditions, ranging from religious processions to "traditional" dances and fiestas. Above all, that mask was donned by government officials and political organizers, from revolutionary and post-revolutionary Mexico to the present. They claimed to constitute the state as a legitimate government of *el pueblo,* which would put indigenous and working-class interests first, even as they set in place a corporatist political system and forms of interaction (as I had witnessed in the Land Reform offices) that replicated the old forms of exploitation and racial and class domination in a new guise. In every case, *el pueblo,* or perhaps better, the *idea* of *el pueblo,* emerged as a reified counterpart to what Abrams called the idea of the state, a mythical unitary social object for that mythical unitary political subject.

But masks do not merely serve to dissimulate or conceal. When donned in a ritual context, they may allow for possession by spirits. So it was that even as it emerged as a privileged political object, *el pueblo* was appropriated as a political subject, emerging as a protagonist of oppositional and emancipatory political appropriations, in which the linkages between place, community, and political agency were reconfigured—even if also reified—in radical ways. In my archival work, as in my fieldwork, I started noting the appearance of that "mask" in many times and places. As they donned that mask, indigenous communalists in the early nineteenth century took possession of the political language of liberalism, authoring petitions aimed at defending communal lands from encroachment, in which they translated and broadened indigenous conceptions of community, into demands and rights of *el pueblo*. The mask was worn by communalist insurgents from the late nineteenth century forward, who took to the woods as the haciendas expanded, eventually leading a decades-long campaign of guerrilla actions against haciendas, police, and federal army, also in name of *el pueblo*. I recognized that mask in the documents of the revolutionary and post-revolutionary periods, as working and indigenous populations—and even a few revolutionary political organizers—made claims in the name of the Revolution, in ways that challenged government officials' more conservative understandings of *el pueblo* and its interest. Finally, in my fieldwork, I saw that mask donned by striking workers, residents of Tetiz and outside labor organizers, as they contested exploitative labor conditions and the conditions associated with "neoliberalism" more generally. In such moments, *el pueblo* seemed to emerge, even if ephemerally, not as an object of control by and source of legitimacy for "the state" but rather as a political subject. It is one that continually escapes control, and indeed projects a utopian horizon of possible actions, relations, and alliances that call into question the legitimating fictions of the state, leaving signs of its passage like traces of blood on pages written by others.

Yet, as my continuing experiences in "the field" constantly brought home to me, to consider *el pueblo* solely as mask, construction, or political rhetoric, is to ignore its power and depth as a kind of second nature (thus, as Coronil has argued in a critique of Abrams's account of the state's "masking" practices, entailing "not concealing a preexisting reality but trans/forming it" [1997, 114–15]). In this sense, as a lived or inhabited entity, *el pueblo* seemed to me to expand far beyond, above, and below the domain of the political, structuring and framing the most varied domains of life. I came to appreciate this first in the context of religious practices—the performance of rituals surrounding the Virgin of Tetiz—*la Vírgen del pueblo*—notably via regular processions marking out and sacralizing the spatial compass of Tetiz and neighboring settlements. *El pueblo* constituted the most powerful and ubiquitous framework of social or collective memory—that is, as the collective point of reference through which people gave accounts of the past—and it occupied the deepest register of poetry and written history authored by area residents. It seemed to be embedded in an extensive set of implicit understandings about personal behavior and character ("He/she is *del pueblo*," people would often say—a statement that might convey any number of things, depending on the context). It even seemed that *el pueblo* had become embedded in the land itself—as if by inhabiting, working, or even traversing the roads, houses, and woods, one unavoidably encountered a consciousness of *el pueblo* inscribed in the landscape. To live in Tetiz was to be confronted, always, by *el pueblo* as both the mask above the face and as the face beneath the mask, at once the most abstract of concepts and the most concrete.

Recently, in the context of writing a book on this topic, I have been confronting the difficulty of studying *el pueblo*, in ways that are driven by theoretical concerns and the burdens of writing itself. I have been trying to move from a fragmented and compartmentalized understanding (*either* place, *or* community, *or* political entity—as "the people") to one that takes place, community, and politics as coproduced, and deeply and mutually imbricated; and I am trying to move away from posing *el pueblo* as a "mask" (à la Abrams) or as an "empty signifier" (à la Ernesto Laclau), toward a view of *el pueblo* as a concrete abstraction that is filled, and deeply inflected, by the history of struggles that have produced it as a concept and as a "reality." In a task that occupies me still, I am trying to put my archival and fieldwork to use in a study that explores how *el pueblo* came to have its hold, and continues to have a hold, on life in places like Tetiz, in large part through an *allegoresis* of possession that structures *el pueblo*'s manifestations. But that is now. A decade ago, when I was immersed in fieldwork, and archival work, the difficulty of studying *el pueblo* was different—more existential than theoretical. It was more than a task, as Abrams prescribes for the study of the state idea, of "demystification." This was about cohabitation: about beginning to live not in "the archive" or "the field," but in the world—a world in which it was no longer clear to me where "field" ended and "archive" began, or what it meant to compartmentalize life in that way. This was thus, for me, about learning, or beginning to learn, about how to "bear" *el pueblo*. My way of bearing it, in writing, was no less a part of this place, and no less of a masquerade fitted from without. The deer's blood, in other words, was not the deer's alone; it also stood, allegorically, for that of others, and perhaps for the act of writing itself.

But in October 1995 awareness of this is still very much in the future. I sit by the deer in the woods, caring only about using pen and paper to find momentary and deluded solace, in a moment of severe discomfort. That delusion disappeared about an hour later, when two short old men appeared, one of whom picked up the deer like it was a bag of feathers, strapped it to his head, and trotted off toward camp. I followed, distracting myself from the embarrassment of my fall by snapping a few photos. Soon, we had reached the camp where the rest of the men were resting, pouring scalding hot water on themselves to dislodge dirt and ticks from the hunt.

Already, when I entered the woods with my shotgun-toting companions, I had been subjected to unrelenting teasing—which my limited Maya allowed me to understand, vaguely, as joking threats of a *Deliverance*-esque nature. Now, by the time of my ignominious return to camp, the story of my "dance" with the deer carcass already had begun to spread. I went with it, reenacting my writhing fall several times, to general mirth. Along with a few other similarly pathetic stories, it began to circulate widely in Tetiz and would be recounted to me, and to others in my presence, for years to come. It wasn't that they disrespected me or considered me a subject of ridicule. Rather, I, an initially inexplicable and somewhat threatening presence (at first some hid their children when I visited, out of fear that I intended to steal their organs), had been exposed, once divested of my own privilege, as only too human, and clownish at that. Over time, they came to accept my oddities—my penchant for sitting around writing notes, snapping photos, and asking naive questions—and they seemed to be somewhat entertained by having me participate in processions, fiestas, the occasional hunting trip, and the rest. I even was given a nickname, much to my chagrin—*El Gringo* (that is, people who initially called me by name, with time and acquaintance began to address me that way: "Hi *Gringo,* how are things?"). I became reconciled to this after hearing one man introduce me to another who did not know me, adding, "but this *Gringo* is not like the others." He then proceeded to tell tales of my hunting prowess that both of us knew were patent falsehoods. Not through my failed efforts at mimicry but rather through cohabitation, I had been "possessed," as a mask-wearing *gringo del pueblo,* and that was enough.

But all of this is yet to happen, as I sit in the woods waiting for rescue, penning what seem to me to be clever words, and sealing them with a

Does one read a text as if it were lying on the couch?

❧ DE CERTEAU 1986 (1982), 52

deer's blood. Reading those notes now, I recognize that there is something that can be rescued in them—perhaps the beginnings of insight into the difficulties of bearing *el pueblo,* and into the contradictions of being at once within, and without, its bounds. But however revealing, those words strike me now as among the worst I have ever written. They are marred by the deepest of deceptions: that the blood on the page is not our own.

4 ❧ David Pedersen

Step into Anthrohistory

> Though pretensions to systematic knowledge may
> appear more and more far-fetched, the idea of totality
> does not necessarily need to be abandoned. On the contrary,
> the existence of a deeply rooted relationship that explains
> superficial phenomena is confirmed the very moment
> it is stated that direct knowledge of such a connection
> is not possible. Though reality may seem to be opaque,
> there are privileged zones—signs, clues—which allow
> us to penetrate it.
> —CARLO GINZBURG (1986)

This chapter is about sustaining a critical stance toward the production of professional academic knowledge. It explores how the Doctoral Program in Anthropology and History (the Anthrohistory Program) at the University of Michigan, since its inception, has taken up and embodied this vital space. This posture, where the taken-for-granted forms, categories, practices, and social relations that make up university life and comprise its varied knowledge-products may be held up for scrutiny, remains surprisingly hard to hold. The Anthrohistory Program came into being only through a remarkable confluence of events, trends, and contingencies not all immediately detectable from any single vantage point. The critical position of the program has been made possible—indeed, necessary—because of the bulk and durability of what counts as mainstream, conventional, and discipline-specific academic knowledge production. Figuratively, Anthrohistory has been like the evanescent foam on the tip of a wave that emerges at and from the interaction of strong uninterrupted winds, large open bodies of water (with tides, in the case of oceans), and their varied seabeds.

The comparison with wave tips is not just metaphorical. Although the earth's largest water bodies and atmosphere have been well studied, wave bubbles as the boundary zone of water and air remain one of the most intriguing and challenging objects of research. Surprisingly little is known about wave bubbles' properties and causes of formation (Deane and

Stokes 2002). Similarly, while the disciplines of anthropology and history each carry well-worn presuppositions about what the world must be like, how it can be known better—and often at least an implicit answer to the questions of "why" and "to what end" for both of these—there has been less examination of these questions at the two disciplines' intersection. Discussions have tended to highlight important differences between anthropology and history and focus on how best to combine research techniques (archival, ethnographic) for specific topics.

This chapter seeks a fresh ontological, epistemological, and ethicopolitical stepping-off point, arrived at by dealing directly at the crossroads of the two disciplines. For lack of a better term, I call the resultant theoretical bargain *anthrohistory*. To "step into" this incipient space entails some basic and perhaps unconventional assumptions about how to relate part and whole while keeping both in motion—the figurative relationship between waves and water, and, following the opening epigraph by Carlo Ginzburg, getting to the real by way of its clues or signs.

The chapter illustrates the anthrohistory modality by exploring how the Anthrohistory Program itself formed, in wavelike fashion, out of a larger though still very much open whole, which I label the "Great Lakes World." To wrangle this conceptually, especially the enigmatic notion of "open whole," the chapter begins with a brief examination of work by scholars who have specific connections to the Anthrohistory Program. The initial objective is to make sense of these published texts through both their content and what

The initial problem is one of perspective. . . . It is clear, of course, as this journey in time is taken, that something more than ordinary arithmetic and something more, evidently, than ordinary history, is in question.

❧ RAYMOND WILLIAMS 1973, 9, 10

appears to be their most immediate cause. This endeavor sets the ground for developing the modality of anthrohistory, illustrated through continued analysis of the program's formation in relation to these texts. Working through text to context, sign to fuller real object, uncovers the assemblage of tendencies, events, and chance that yielded the program and lie dissimulated within its knowledge products, especially the initial works considered. In the process of this detectivelike endeavor, I wish to show that the openness and capacity to move about and connect associated with anthrohistory is, in fact, a feature of its own historical and institutional formation as the Doctoral Program in Anthropology and History at the University of Michigan. The chapter concludes with the suggestion that to sustain the project of anthrohistory, and by extension the program, requires something like "surfing" amidst and against the strong currents that push for the re-production of professional disciplinary-specific knowledge and the kinds of boundaries, separations, and continuities that this presupposes.

The Great Lakes World

Following on the hydrous theme for a moment, about ten thousand years ago, a glacier more than a half mile thick receded across the middle part of North America, leaving behind three major depressions in the land and several minor ones all together filled with some five thousand cubic miles of fresh water. Currently more than forty million residents of Canada and the United States—and countless other life forms—thrive in this water-dominated world, known by its ecologists as the Great Lakes Basin (Annin 2006). Though most people accept this account prima facie, to actually perceive the Basin's formation at this scale would require a vantage point about a thousand miles above the Earth's surface, the upper limit of what is known as a "low earth orbit." This is the realm in which most human space flights have occurred and where all man-made artificial satellites of the earth revolve. This view would have to be held steady for several thousand years in order to immediately perceive the actual formation of the Great Lakes World.

Shifting to a more grounded perspective with a much smaller spatiotemporal extension and a more narrowly human or social focus, in 2002, in the lower half of the Basin (not far from Lake Ontario and Lake Huron), a group of about fifteen students and faculty associated with the Anthrohistory Program gathered to discuss a precirculated paper written by Webb Keane, a professor in the Department of Anthropology at the University of Michigan.[1] The essay was titled "Self-Interpretation, Agency, and the Objects of Anthropology" and offered a challenging and provocative genealogy of the discipline of anthropology, moving briskly through the twentieth century to identify two central tendencies. Keane argued that despite varied concentrations of effort and schools of thought, the discipline, at least as concentrated in the United States, has tended to privilege geographical and historical particularity, specificity, and detail. At the same time it has struggled to develop more general theoretical claims applicable across particular contexts. Amidst this tension, according to

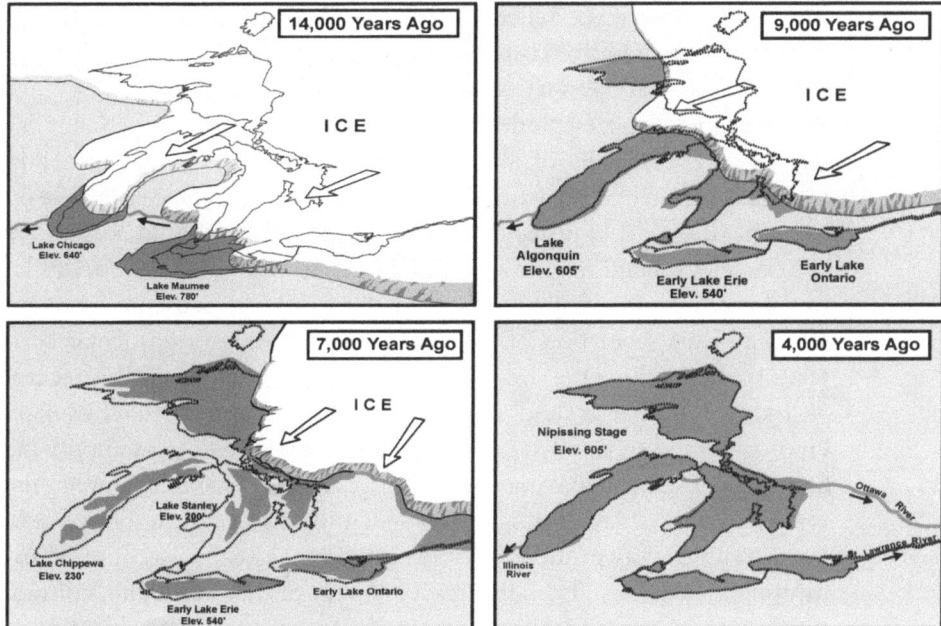

FIG. 4.1. Prehistoric glacial movement and lake shapes. Copyright U.S. Army Corps of Engineers and the Great Lakes Commission (2000 [1999]).

Keane, the object of anthropological knowledge has tended to be a concern with human agency, social action, self-understanding, and their limits. Keane (2002, 85) concluded with a call for keeping the tension alive both around human agency and its limits and also the unique intersubjective quality of ethnographic inquiry along with the requirement that "our analyses must take us away from them and demand some portable objectifications."

Keane also reflected on the particularity of his account, offering one sense of the context of its formation. "I guess in some ways the paper is about coming to terms with my relationship with Marshall Sahlins and David Schneider," Keane remarked. Like others in the room, he had pursued graduate studies in the Great Lakes Basin, completing his degree on the shores of Lake Michigan at the University of Chicago's Department of Anthropology where Sahlins and Schneider had held professorships.

Several months after this event and within a couple miles of it, Geoff Eley, a professor in the Department of History at the University of Michigan, delivered what was billed as the "Sylvia L. Thrupp Collegiate Professorship in Comparative History Inaugural Lecture." The title of his talk was "On Your Marx: From Cultural History to the History of Society." Like Keane's paper, the presentation was mildly autobiographical in that it described several decades of intellectual ferment in the field of history in which Eley had directly participated. It concluded with some reflection on what the discipline of history had become and what it should be. Eley recounted the general move away from larger-scale accounts of social history to new kinds of smaller-scale analyses, which focused on human selves and the formation of intersubjective meaning in particular contexts. He highlighted the signal work of Carolyn Steedman in this regard, well-known for her groundbreaking book *Landscape for a Good Woman*. "In many respects, Carolyn Steedman (born 1947) seems to exemplify the arguments I've been making about changes in the discipline between the 1960s and now" (Eley 2005, 172). Eley's identification of the importance of human subjectivity in the field of history echoed Keane's account of anthropology. But Eley also called for a recovery of that which the "cultural turn" was much in opposition to—some kind of capacity for identifying more general tendencies, structures, and mechanisms as they might operate at particular (often large) geographical and historical scales. Encouraged by the response to his Sylvia Thrupp address, Eley expanded his argument into book form, appearing that year as *A Crooked Line: From Cultural History to the History of Society.*

Around this time, William Sewell, Jr., a professor at the University of Chicago who had been a member of both the Departments of History and Sociology at the University of Michigan during the 1980s, began to assemble his reflections on the discipline of history and his own role in ushering it through the "cultural and interpretive turn." In early 2005 he presented this at Michigan in conjunction with nascent efforts to found what has become called the Eisenberg Institute of Historical Studies at the University of Michigan. Later in the year, it appeared as the second chapter of his book *Logics of History: Social Theory and Social Transformation*.[2] Like Eley, Sewell recounted the gains and the losses of the cultural turn and made a similar call for recovering the capacity to study larger-scale social processes, especially through quantitative analysis.

Coinciding with this, George Steinmetz, a professor of sociology and German studies at Michigan, published an edited collection that contained revised versions of Eley's Thrupp address, Keane's essay, and

Sewell's book's second chapter, titled "The Political Unconscious of Social and Cultural History, or, Confessions of a Former Quantitative Historian." Steinmetz's book was called *The Politics of Method in the Human Sciences: Positivism and Its Epistemological Others*. The essays by Keane, Eley, and Sewell contributed important overviews of the disciplines of anthropology and history and, besides addressing the cultural/interpretive turn, commented specifically on the role of positivism in shaping their respective disciplines. In this respect, Steinmetz's collection of the Keane, Eley, and Sewell essays in his volume represented a particular coagulation of Basin work.

Parallel Developments in the Basin

There is another microcosm of debate and discussion about the two disciplines that has occurred in the Basin, overlapping partially with the Keane, Eley, Sewell, Steinmetz assemblage. This one involves a constellation of scholars broadly concerned with the study of colonial and imperial systems of rule and exploitation. Often glossed as "colonial studies" and in some cases as "postcolonial studies," this work was such a presence in the Anthrohistory Program for a period of time that some observers remarked that the program had become near synonymous with that project.

Among many goals, the past two decades of work on colonial studies has sought to distinguish itself from exactly the earlier generation of large-scale work that people like Eley and Sewell had recently gestured toward. Anthrohistory Program–affiliated faculty such as Fred Cooper, Fernando Coronil, Val Daniel, Nick Dirks, Nancy Hunt, Ann Stoler, and many others each sought in different ways to alter or at least free up the assumed scale of inquiry, the level of focus, and the geohistorical perspective of analysis. By adding finer-grained studies alongside larger-scale ones, this work helped to show more clearly the mutual though also asymmetrical formation of colony and metropole and the multiplex forms of domination, exploitation, and control within colonial and imperial systems. Related to this, the new work also sought to point up the way that such systems constantly were "in motion." Scholars directly took up the challenge of how to adequately study, make sense of, and write about all manner of social dynamism and interaction, rather than only seek after systemic continuity and processes of self-reproduction.

In one representative way, Ann Stoler, a Basin dweller who taught at both the University of Wisconsin and the University of Michigan, describes this goal of capturing such change in her book about Dutch colonialism and its archival recording, *Along the Archival Grain:* "[The book] seeks to identify the pliable coordinates of what constituted colonial common sense in a changing imperial order in which social reform, questions of rights and representation, and liberal impulses and more explicit racisms played an increasing role" (2009, 3). Stoler emphasizes that this kind of inquiry involves identifying "the *mutating* assignments of essence and its predicates in specific time and place." As an example she points out that colonial racial distinctions "were protean, not fixed, and subject to reformulation again and again" (2009, 4). Yet Stoler avoids a formalistic distinction between change and stasis. Her book at the same time seeks after and is organized around what she describes as the near permanently inscribed "watermarks" that can be discerned in colonial history. In this book and across much of Stoler's previous work, these often entail lasting (both historically and geographically) hierarchical distinctions around race, sexuality, gender, class, age, and family form. Borrowing her turn of a phrase, Stoler's relational approach captures together both the vigorously palimpsest and hidden indelibility of colonialism.

At the risk of slighting the subtlety and significance of this work by Keane, Eley, Sewell, and Stoler, my rudimentary summary is meant to point out some themes that they all share. First, all of them congealed out of the Great Lakes World, written by major participants and protagonists in recent scholarly turns. More specifically, each author has had some connection to the University of Michigan and involvement with the Anthrohistory Program. In this regard, all of the works assess several decades of research in order to offer a form of situated commentary. Keane explicitly discusses anthropology, Eley and Sewell comment on history, and Stoler writes on colonial studies. In most basic form, all of the essays reflect on the challenges and importance of shifting across larger-scale generalities and smaller-scale particularities. Keane, Eley, and Sewell discuss this explicitly in terms of disciplines. Although Stoler frames it as an issue for "colonial studies," the relevant disciplines are history and anthropology and, to a lesser extent, literary studies. At this level of analysis it is clear that the essays overlap in terms of place, time, and thematic concerns (though with different conclusions). What is the significance of this, if any?

Explaining a Phenomenon

One way to approach this question is to assume that since all the authors take up roughly the same issue in the same place, there likely is some sort of common or shared cause that has brought this about. A first-order explanation would simply be that recent turns in scholarship have generated this moment of reflection. One also could separate causes that are more internal or external relative to the object of study. Thus, regardless of the topic, it is possible that multidecade perspectives like these tend to be produced at particular moments in people's professional careers. A variant of this way of explaining knowledge production is suggested by Arjun Appadurai (2000, 13), once a Basin dweller at the University of Chicago as both student and professor: "For most researchers, the trick is how to choose theories, define frameworks, ask questions, and design methods that are most likely to produce research with a plausible shelf-life." Appadurai specifies that the challenge is how to navigate between too big a set of questions that would not be funded and too narrow a theme that, even if funded, would (to continue the water theme) "sink without a bubble in the ocean of professional citations." Finally, perhaps the most obvious correlation is between the authors and the place: "It's a Michigan thing."

Regardless of why these works appeared and their significance, there is a shared logic to the line of questioning and explanation that I have followed so far. It is the premise that because all the authors take up the same issue (micro/macro; change/stability) in roughly the same time and place, there probably is a shared cause. In slightly different language, it is the assumption that every cause of a given quality has a related effect of a given quality. In simplified terms, it means roughly "if x, then y." A more sophisticated definition labels this epistemological and methodological habit "regularity determinism" and stipulates that it is the assumption that "for every event y there is an event x or set of events $x_1 \ldots x_n$ such that x or $x_1 \ldots x_n$ and y are regularly conjoined under some set of descriptions" (Bhaskar 1975, 69). This basic relationship may be expanded also so that y includes unperceived or conceptual events, such as a structure or some sort of force or mechanism like Appadurai's "shelf-life" seeking. Similarly, the relationship may be softened in the form of "whenever x, then likely (probabilistically) y." In whatever form, however, regularity determinism rests on a more basic presupposition: the spatial and temporal domain of analysis necessarily must be finite and closed. Otherwise any conjunction of events could not be called constant or regular. As an example to help grasp this point, it is this logic and the realization that it is an unexamined habit that yields the significance of the popular story about Zhou Enlai, the first premier of the People's Republic of China, who was asked sometime in the 1950s to name the major consequences of the French Revolution. According to legend, he replied, "It's far too early to tell."

Open Holism

Another way of approaching the apparent phenomenon of the four interrelated accounts would be to begin from a logic of spatiotemporal openness, rather than one that emphasizes constant conjunctions within closed systems. As a first step this would entail the assumption that each essay, address, article, and book carries the full history of its formation. In other words, what the various texts *are,* in the most concrete sense, includes all that went into their creation and also all that continues to condition their existence. Most acknowledgment sections in articles and books allude to a portion of this content. Yet the people and places accorded gratitude by Keane, Eley, Sewell, and Stoler are as much causes as effects. For example, Keane acknowledges that his essay is a reflection of his relationship with Sahlins and Schneider. Besides the efforts of the parents of these two famous anthropologists, what else could have gone into Sahlins's and Schneider's capacity to have an influence on the work of one of their former students? And what shaped that? Remarkably, Keane's essay has all of this hidden inside. To inquire after this content is to presuppose an open whole of relations. In this way, the larger whole of which the essay is a part can be found by beginning with and moving through the part itself, treating it as a sign, clue, or symptom of something more. Part and whole, cause and effect are not formally separate and discrete in this modality.

To reach toward including more of what constitutes the various articles and books requires moving about, varying the locus, focus, and spatiotemporal scope of analysis. In the course of developing a more complex multidimensional account of this scholarship, the qualities of their many determinants come into view. Some are more contingent, like the comments of the anonymous reviewer of Keane's essay. Other determinants may be more general: all of the essays are written in English and are about largely English-language debates.

In a more open-ended fashion, the question then becomes, what likely had to occur for the appearance of the work? The immediate challenge of beginning this way is that the answer could be infinite. Short of arriving at the end of such a list, however, it is nevertheless possible to pursue a few currents that go beyond Appadurai's shelf-life seeking as a simple causal mechanism. Beginning with the essays concretely and moving backward and outward, provisionally filling in more of the conditions of their formation and existence, constantly reasking the question, "what possibly or likely has or had to occur?" at every juncture yields some important distinctions and complexity. Larger trends, minute interaction, and moments of pure chance appear together, all reciprocally constituting each other.

Returning to the specific texts and beginning such inquiry, it becomes clear that there is a slight variation in emphasis around the way that Keane, Eley, Sewell, and Stoler refer to the conditions out of which their academic scholarship has formed and the ways that it should or must respond. Keane concludes his essay in a subtle manner, pointing out that anthropological knowledge—all that goes into its making, from fieldwork to publication—is never outside of the social and historical conditions of its formation. In practice, though, his article goes only so far as to say its purpose is to characterize and define the discipline of anthropology and that its origins largely rest on relations between the author and his teachers. Eley, Sewell, and Stoler share the general perspective of relating knowledge to its conditions of formation and use, but they are slightly different from Keane. All three regard their work as being directed at specific historical conditions. They are cautious about using terms like *capitalism, imperialism, colonialism,* and *racism* as near-universal placeholders. But, nevertheless, they do use these terms explicitly to specify the conditions to which their scholarship responds and what they seek to examine. In addition, Eley, Sewell, and Stoler all explicitly acknowledge the signal importance of *interdisciplinarity* in this project, especially at the University of Michigan, in the past and for the future. Keane alludes to this in his conclusion, acknowledging the importance of the "historical turn" in anthropology in sharpening sensitivity toward "power effects." But I believe Eley, Sewell, and Stoler make a slightly stronger claim. But rather than compare, however, I wish to just note this quality of emphasis found in Eley, Sewell, and Stoler by considering excerpts from their acknowledgments.

Eley
Pride of place goes to the University of Michigan, both to my colleagues and graduate students in the Department of History and to the wider in-

terdisciplinary culture fostered so uniquely by this university, whose crucible in many respects was the Program in Comparative Study of Social Transformations (CSST) formed in 1987.

Sewell
The origins of this book go back to the late 1980s, when I was serving as the first director of the Center for the Study of Social Transformations (CSST) at the University of Michigan. CSST was a university-funded experiment in interdisciplinarity, a collection of historians, anthropologists, and sociologists—as brilliant as they were argumentative—who met regularly to thrash out questions of theory and method. Our discussions were intense and absorbing; they spilled over into lunches, parties, and countless ad hoc seminars in the corridors. The discussions certainly vindicated the founding group's assumptions that scholars in these three disciplines had plenty of interests in common and much to learn from each other. They also made clear that disciplinary divides were very real; disagreements between those hailing from different fields were often sharp and sometimes heated.

Stoler
I thank first of all those who became such dear friends as we collectively built the Doctoral Program in Anthropology and History at the University of Michigan. . . . The years in which this book took form coincided with the heady rush of another intellectual venture of which I was privileged to be a part: the program in Comparative Studies in Societal Transformation, a dynamic constellation of faculty from the departments of Sociology, Anthropology, History, Comparative Literature, and Political Science who reveled in reaching beyond their prescribed disciplines to engage one another's work and the different understandings of social critique and history that each brought to it.

Despite their notable differences, all three passages mention the acronym CSST with a quality of praise. This is a clue that slightly disaggregates the Basin, even the context of the University of Michigan.

Interdisciplinarity and Change

Regardless of the exact words that the letters stand for, CSST indeed formed at the University of Michigan, literally out of a reading group organized at first by faculty members from anthropology, history, and sociology. Members of the reading group, including Sewell and Eley especially, proposed that it be expanded to become an interdisciplinary venue for regular discussion and debate among faculty and invited guests. In 1986 Sewell with appointments in both history and sociology, together with Terrence McDonald in history, Sherry Ortner of anthropology, and Jeff Paige in sociology, wrote a successful proposal and received funds from the newly created Presidential Initiatives Fund at the University of Michigan. This fund had been started by University of Michigan president Shapiro with the help of a grant of $5,000 from the W. K. Kellogg Foundation, across the state in Battle Creek. The university contributed a matching amount.

The Kellogg grant was awarded as part of the foundation's Education and Youth Programming and specifically earmarked to "encourage education and scholastic excellence by helping the University of Michigan to bolster interdisciplinary scholarly activities."[3] The foundation had been established in 1930 by Will Keith Kellogg, the inventor of the toasted corn flake. The Kellogg grant, passed through the the University of Michigan Presidential Initiatives Fund, allowed CSST to embark on a three-year project organized on the premise that the disciplines of history, sociology, and anthropology, especially as represented at the University of Michigan, all were converging on a single shared question, each bringing specific theoretical, methodological, and rhetorical approaches: "How do groups of actors constituted and constrained by social and cultural structures act so as to transform the very structures that constituted them?"[4] According to the proposal, the new program would include thirty faculty members from the three disciplines and be centered on a yearlong seminar series for members. It also would include lectures and seminars by invited speakers, team-taught graduate courses, and research support for selected graduate students. In the proposal, the authors listed five explicit goals to be achieved during the three-year period of support.

> (1) develop a core of faculty capable of moving freely across the disciplinary boundaries that now divide scholarship in history, anthropology, and sociology, with a consequent increase in the power and sophistication of our research; (2) establish a unique interdisciplinary graduate program that will make the University of Michigan the prime choice of graduate students interested in comparative historical social science; (3) establish in the larger academic community, by means of scholarly visits, conferences, and publications, the well-founded impression that Michigan is at the epicenter of a major reconfiguration of historical social science; (4) launch a variety of new individual and collective research projects by both faculty

and graduate students; (5) secure outside funding to continue the project beyond the initial three years.[5]

A review of the program after one year, written by Eley and discussed in one of the faculty seminars, expressed optimism, but not without careful note of important issues that limited discussion:

> First, some sociologists had the most difficulty with "discourse." . . . Secondly, anthropologists still seemed to be asserting an excessively proprietary relationship to the discussion of culture, and responded somewhat allergically to discussion that sought to deal with culture in a different way. . . . Last . . . if sociologists seemed the most disconcerted by the extra-disciplinary discussion, and the anthropologists the most comfortable within their given disciplinary problematic, then the historians were the ones that seemed to be without coherent disciplinary stance to call their own.[6]

Despite the divisions, if judged by its self-stated goals, CSST was nearly a complete success during its first three years. Although it did not form an explicit CSST graduate program, a group of affiliated scholars were able to bring together faculty in anthropology and history to form the Doctoral Program in Anthropology and History. Indeed, the interdisciplinary climate stimulated by CSST and supported by the university created the possibility for the Anthrohistory Progam. There was an important stumble, however, that like another clue, redraws the boundaries of analysis.

As part of its goals, leaders of CSST drafted a second proposal to seek outside funding from a U.S. government source, the National Endowment for the Humanities (NEH). According to Eley, the proposal was well-received and moved successfully through the review process, only to be directly vetoed by NEH chairperson Lynn Cheney.[7] Her appointment as chair was a feature of the Reagan administration's efforts to substantially reduce the resources of the agency. In 1980, when Reagan came into office, the Heritage Foundation, a DC-based conservative policy organization, released its "Mandate for Change," which championed a long list of conservative political projects to be undertaken by the new administration. This "Mandate" criticized the NEH for supporting poor quality scholarship and work that did not properly qualify as "humanities" (Nash, Crabtree, and Dunn 1997).

The expansion of conservative political control during the Reagan presidencies of 1980 through 1988 included also the growth of conservative student organizations on U.S. campuses. A climate of reactionary conservatism spread, including strong arguments about the primacy of Anglo-European descent, Christianity, heteronormativity, and the English language in dominant definitions of U.S. national identity and character. On campuses this fostered debate, but it also coincided with an upsurge in violent confrontations, marked especially by white assaults on black students. In the late 1980s, brief exchanges grew into major conflicts at Columbia University, University of Massachusetts, the Citadel in South Carolina, Wellesley College, Hamilton College, University of Virginia, Howard University, and the University of Texas at Austin (where two students wearing Ronald Reagan Halloween masks and dressed in sheets beat up a black student in his dorm room). Frank Matthews, publisher of the magazine *Black Issues in Higher Education*, commented on the context of this violence, saying that white students appeared to be "reading the message" from the Reagan administration: "It's all right to be a racist" (Kantrowitz and Turque 1987, 30; see also Vallela 1986, 3).

The University of Michigan figured as well in the campus clashes. In late February 1987, operations at the student-run radio station, WJJX, were suspended after a student host invited callers to share their best racist jokes on air. Students also had slipped notes calling for "open hunting season" on blacks under the door during a meeting of black women students in a dormitory common room (Wilkerson 1990, A12).[8] In this context, university students formed the United Coalition against Racism (UCAR) and organized several public assemblies and protests. Students also founded "Black Action Movement (BAM) III," echoing the history of two earlier BAM formations, BAM I in 1970 and BAM II in 1975, both of which were instrumental in bringing about change on the campus. Both organizations challenged the university administration to respond to a list of proposals to improve racial/ethnic relations on the campus. After almost a week of confrontation, Rev. Jesse Jackson, head of the Rainbow Coalition/PUSH, made a well-publicized visit to the campus and met with students and administrators. According to the *University Record* (1987, 1):

> After 24 hours of intense negotiations, President Harold T. Shapiro, the Rev. Jesse Jackson, University Administrators and representatives of two student anti-racism groups late Monday afternoon announced a plan of action to remedy racial inequalities at U-M. The six-point plan is designed to achieve representation of blacks throughout the University, "proportionate to their numbers in the population," and to hold each area of the University accountable for meeting affirmative action timetables and goals

within individual units. It also provides for the creation of a new vice provost position with responsibilities for minority affairs, including recruitment and retention of students and faculty.

Further contributing to the national attention focused on Michigan and the quality of shock felt by many faculty and students on the campus over how grave the conflict had become, University of Michigan regent Sarah G. Power committed suicide two days later by jumping from the eighth floor of the 212-foot Burton Tower.[9]

The Mandate

Among the significant outcomes of the protests and negotiations was an acknowledgment by the next University of Michigan president, James J. Duderstadt (who succeeded Shapiro in 1988), that the University of Michigan had failed to properly address racial diversity and conflict on the campus, leading up to the student protest (Sporn 1999, 124). The singular project that resulted was what became known (probably without intending to echo the title of the Heritage Foundation report earlier in the decade) as the Michigan Mandate. This Mandate was an ambitious three-part plan to transform the university into a more "international," "technologically advanced," and "diverse" institution. As part of achieving these objectives, the Mandate called for expanded efforts to recruit and develop minority students and faculty. One aspect of this entailed allowing multiple appointments across departments and between departments and new interdepartmental programs established on the campus. Several of these hires specifically, as well as the climate of interdepartmental collaboration directly funded and encouraged by the Mandate, formed the financial and institutional backdrop, the conditions of possibility for the new work associated with CSST and the newly formed Anthrohistory Program.

Judged by Duderstadt's many public addresses and published retrospective accounts, the Michigan Mandate was in line with a broad strand of multiculturalism that had appeared in corporate contexts throughout the United States over roughly the same time period (Dolgon 1999). In this register, it was a gesture toward the importance of "diversity," though according to a fairly narrow culturalist definition relatively divorced from their larger historical, social, and political-economic context.[10] In addition, despite being closely identified with the singular voice and vision of Duderstadt (and also criticized for its appearance as an elitist top-down initiative), the Mandate was a remarkably collective document. At a first level, it reflected significant discussion and debate among a group of "authors" working closely with Duderstadt.[11] According to one member of what Duderstadt called his "team":

> The Mandate was an open work-in-progress for two years. We presented it to *everyone* and incorporated their feedback. It wouldn't have been legitimate to do otherwise. We met with Black organizations in DC, including anti-apartheid (in South Africa) campaign members. We met with organizations in Michigan, in Detroit. . . . We went to the churches—we worked very closely with Charles Adams. We talked with different alumni groups, women's groups, black faculty groups and academic organizations . . . It was a huge effort.[12]

Nevertheless, Duderstadt and his close advisers did not publicize these meetings and worked hard to foster the image of single authorship.[13] They were acutely image-conscious, regularly checking how well their arguments and empirical data corresponded and also how particular kinds of language would be publicly regarded.[14]

With more effort it might be possible to further anchor the collective authors and show their visions and ideas to be as much a reflection of their broader social position in the region as their personal invention. Some of this context would include the university in relation to dominant activities across the region, especially the U.S. auto industry concentrated in southeast Michigan and extending across the Great Lakes World. As scholars have well documented, this area has been marked in recent decades by the loss of relatively high-wage, manufacturing jobs as firms have shifted aspects of industrial production to regions of Latin America and Asia (Bluestone and Harrison 1982). Much of daily life in the United States instead has became increasingly organized around the production of both high- and low-wage services, the latter yielded especially by a new migrant workforce from Asia and Latin America.

Viewed in this larger context, the University of Michigan Mandate calling for the university to become a diverse, international, and technologically advanced university is as much a reflection as an instrument in this aggregate transformation, often glossed as part of the process of "globalization." Moving outward and backward, it becomes possible to appreciate that "globalization" is the current moment of a much longer process that began when an otherwise backward European hinterland was able by the sixteenth century to colonize the hemisphere of the Americas, exploiting and extracting unprecedented resources and wealth (Dussel 1993, 1998).

Among the indigenous resources harnessed in the context of European New World colonialism was the tall grass known as maize or corn (the former of which was popularly adopted as the term for "yellow" in reference to the University of Michigan school colors: "Maize 'n' Blue"). Biologists have shown that maize's evolutionary development is inseparably tied to its human use, especially the relative ease with which it can be cross-bred. Were it not for human manipulation of the grass over the past five thousand years, corn itself would not have evolved as it has. This is the same period in which the fully formed Great Lakes have existed. Understood together at this scale of analysis, the development of the corn flake in Battle Creek and the later funding of interdisciplinary work at the University of Michigan paid for with corn money are just fleeting moments in a larger combined socionatural process.

Implications: Surfing

This concluding gesture to the co- and unfinished development of corn and the Great Lakes World is delivered to reemphasize anthrohistory's stance toward "open holism." Things like books, articles, authors, grants, university programs, campus affairs—even crops and water bodies—rest on and embody at any moment an unclosed ensemble of determining relations. To inquire into this rests on the capacity to shift about scales, foci, and perspective, remaining sensitive to multiple trends, events, and open possibilities all at once. The racist attacks on the University of Michigan campus were the hard and inchoate edge of broadly conservative forms of U.S. nationalism and ethnocentrism that emerged in the face of worldwide patterns of integration and reorganization. Student protests were part of struggles since the 1960s (BAM I, II, III) that similarly stretched the University of Michigan conflict into a broader critique of racism and forms of social oppression and domination in other contexts. The 1987 confrontations helped to yield the Michigan Mandate, which in turn fostered the conditions within which an adept group of interdisciplinary scholars were able to use those resources to build a shared project of inquiry into: "How do groups of actors constituted and constrained by social and cultural structures act so as to transform the very structures that constituted them?"[15] The ability to pursue this question across disciplines at the University of Michigan has rested on the historical conditions of its asking. To produce knowledge that can record, actively choose, and, in fact, play an explicit role in a broad and unfolding transformation of cultural and social structures is not always coterminous with shelf-life seeking or substantiating a specific discipline. Nor is it the necessary outcome of efforts to diversify a university.

The challenge with the anthrohistory modality, as the corn gesture also illustrates, is that whenever a temporal, spatial, or conceptual domain is drawn—wherever inquiry necessarily starts and stops—this involves an active choice. As an action it is infused not just with logical dimensions, as I have tried to illuminate by contrasting "regularity determinism" with "open holism." It also carries aesthetic, ethical, and political ones. The totality of determinant relations is potentially infinite, and one could use the resources of all past, existing, and yet-to-be-invented academic disciplines—and more—to trace out what has gone into the formation of the essays, chapters, and books introduced at the beginning. Out of choice, my account lingered longest on evidence gleaned from the past two decades, mostly in the vicinity of the University of Michigan. The manner of my explanatory investigation was inherent in the terms and the boundaries that I chose. The effect, I hope, was to show the relationship between the interdisciplinary question that CSST organizers posed in their initial proposal, its practical answering over the past two decades, and the geohistorical conditions of its asking. This was the purposeful small-*t* truth achieved.

It suffices for a short time to follow the trace, the repeated course of words, in order to perceive, in a sort of vision, the labyrinthine constitution of being.
  ❧ GEORGES BATAILLE 1988 (1954), 83–84

The challenge is that our set of available choices, in terms of categories, spatiotemporal frames, levels of emphasis, and perspective is not completely ours to newly make. Some of the essays discussed here begin and end with stories of disciplines, what they have had and what they need. Their potential, like that of the intersection of anthropology and history more generally, however, is of opening up and refashioning the boundaries and terms of inquiry according to purposes other than shelf-life or citations in a discipline.

NOTES

1. For the past 335 years, many people have marked the geographic coordinates of the house where the discussion occurred as about 83° 45′ 01.29″ to the west of a

building called the Royal Observatory, located in the city of Greenwich, England. The house, built in 1927, also lies about 42° 17' 15.09" north of the equator and sits 245 meters above sea level.

2. See my commentary on the book (2009) in *Social Science History,* along with the analyses in the same issue by Riley and Steinmetz, together with Sewell's response.

3. From the record of the grant publically available on the foundation website, http://www.wkkf.org/Default.aspx?tabid=97&CID=1&CatID=1&ItemID=730&NID=95&LanguageID=0

4. William H. Sewell Jr., Terrence J. McDonald, Sherry M. Ortner, Jefferey M. Paige, "Program in Comparative Study of Social Transformation," CRSO #344/CSST #1, May 1987, 7.

5. Sewell et al. 1986, 3.

6. Geoff Eley, "Taking Stock: The First Year of CSST," CSST Working paper #21, CRSO Working Paper #384, February 1989, 4.

7. In response, the University of Michigan's president's office agreed to fund CSST for a second three-year period.

8. The flyers had used the slur "porch monkeys" to refer to African Americans.

9. "Sarah G. Power, 52, Dies in 8-Story Fall; Michigan U. Regent," *New York Times,* March 26, 1987, D27.

10. Great Lakes Basin anthropologist Terrence Turner (1993) of the University of Chicago has labeled this strand "difference multiculturalism," distinguishing it from a more critical variant.

11. In e-mail correspondence, Duderstadt told me that these authors were Mark Chesler (social work), Joe White (business), Chuck Vest (engineering), and Charles Moody (education). Early drafts also appear to have been circulated to Shirley Clarkson, Robin Jacoby, Connie Cook, Ejner Jensen, and Susan Lipschutz of the University of Michigan.

12. Confidential interview. Charles Adams, a University of Michigan graduate and African American, is the widely recognized pastor at Hartford Memorial Baptist Church in Detroit.

13. Duderstadt Papers, Bentley Historical Library, Box 22. In one instance, Marylynn Knepp, at the time working in the Office of the Provost as a policy adviser to the dean, asked Shirley Clarkson, a Duderstadt adviser, to identify the larger working group that was working to formulate the Mandate.

14. On August 17, 1988, a version of the Mandate was exchanged in draft form between Shirley Clarkson, a close Duderstadt assistant, and Vic Schlitzer, a member of Gehrung Associates in Keane, New Hampshire, a firm that specialized in consulting on public relations issues for universities. Duderstadt Papers, Bentley Historical Library, Box 22.

15. William H. Sewell Jr., Terrence J. McDonald, Sherry M. Ortner, Jefferey M. Paige, "Program in Comparative Study of Social Transformation," CRSO #344/CSST #1, May 1987, 7.

5 ✤ E. Natalie Rothman

Genealogies of Mediation: "Culture Broker" and Imperial Governmentality

In a famous formulation, Mary Louise Pratt defined contact zones as "social spaces where disparate cultures meet, clash, and grapple with each other, often in highly asymmetrical relations of domination and subordination."[1] Yet as Pratt herself shows so meticulously, the ongoing history of cultural mediation does not unfold through anonymous "clashes" between discrete, well-bounded, and fixed entities but through the practices of actors, embedded in particular institutionalized projects and genres of interaction. This raises the question of the analytical insights to be gained by focusing attention not on an abstract "culture clash" (an untenable concept, despite its unfortunate recent resurgence) but on specific processes of mediation, their agents, institutional sites, and genres. It further points to the stakes involved in considering the myriad ways in which historically shifting settings—imperial for the most part—have shaped such processes of mediation and our analytical accounts of them.

The following essay addresses this cluster of questions by turning to an archival case from an early moment of imperial governmentality, sixteenth-century Venice. I suggest that those whom both the early modern imperial state and modern social scientists understood as brokers par excellence between distinct "kinds" were in fact active participants in the definition and redefinition of these kinds and their prototypical centers. Through a case study of the inquisitorial trial of a commercial broker accused of assisting a runaway Ottoman slave I also examine how the marketplace, an essentialized locus of mediation often conceptualized as an anonymous, impersonal space for exchanges between discrete individuals, might be understood rather as enmeshed in a wide range of institutionalized forms of sociability and practices of boundary making.

In early August 1573, word reached the Venetian Holy Office[2] of a teenaged slave named Zorzi (Venetian for George), who had run away from the house of his patrician master. According to the initial deposition, Zorzi, formerly a Muslim, had been baptized and had received communion and other holy sacraments. But now, having gone into hiding in the attic of a house "where several Turks live," he had allegedly returned to Islam ("tornato a far Turco") "having shaved his head and dressed as a Turk in order to go secretly to Turkey." Five days after Zorzi's escape, his master, Marcantonio Falier, visited Zorzi's place of hiding. He was met by an uncooperative landlord, a Greek commercial broker named Francesco di Demetri Litino, better known by his nickname, Frangia, and his wife, Giulia. The couple claimed complete ignorance of Zorzi's whereabouts, but Falier persisted in demanding that his slave be returned. That evening Frangia sent Zorzi to spend the night at a friend's house nearby, and the following morning Zorzi was unceremoniously returned to his master.[3]

Despite this "happy ending" from Falier's point of view, and the apparent restoration of Venetian social order, the Holy Office did not drop the case. Rather, it arrested Frangia and opened a lengthy investigation, in the course of which the inquisitors interrogated not only Zorzi, but also Frangia, Giulia, their eighteen-year-old son, and the family's neighbors and friends. Their depositions reveal the deep tensions between how inquisitors and witnesses drew moral, religious, and social boundaries between Venetians and Turks, Christians and Muslims, masters and slaves, merchants and brokers. They also underscore the important role of diffuse networks of trans-imperial subjects, including merchants, slaves, interpreters, and brokers, in the process of mediating these categories, that is, in articulating and shifting their prototypical centers within specific genres and institutions.[4]

Frangia's inquisitorial trial is exceptional among the archival traces left by early modern Venetian commercial brokers. The overwhelming majority of documents conserved in the archives of the Venetian brokers' guild concern legal attempts to regulate the activities of commercial brokers in the market. Indeed, the Venetian state entrusted brokers with the important task of mediating between foreign and local merchants. Venetian law envisioned brokers—ideally, if not in practice—as the impartial, vigilant agents of the state, who noted down their transactions in a special notebook, collected taxes and duties from foreign merchants, and protected their interests vis-à-vis less than scrupulous trading partners.

Unlike the archives of the brokers' guild, the record left by Frangia's inquisitorial trial underscores the extent to which the marketplace and the home were—and are—intermeshed, and the importance of domestic arrangements and personal ties in forging and cementing alliances between commercial brokers and their clients. Indeed, the various testimonies reveal a complex set of interests, hierarchies of authority, and modes of interaction between locals, localized foreigners (like Frangia himself), and Ottoman sojourners. Such interactions clearly violated patrician notions of a perfected social order premised on Christian morality and civic unity in the face of religious and political Others. Moreover, rather than bring into contact the supposedly preexisting categories of "Venetian" and "Turks," Frangia and his household members played an active role in shaping these categories.

Early modern commercial brokers operated at the interface between local governments and foreign subjects, between the mercantile and artisanal sectors of urban societies, between state institutions and the market, and between rich and poor. Brokers' intermediary and transformative role is particularly significant given the predominance of trans-imperial subjects among the ranks of this profession. In early modern Venice, Christian converts, Jewish, Armenian, and Greek-Orthodox Ottoman and Safavid subjects, redeemed slaves, war refugees, retired soldiers, and other émigrés from Venice's Eastern Mediterranean and Adriatic colonies all vied for appointment as brokers. Brokerage seems to have been an appealing occupation for colonial subjects too, whose property was lost or threatened by Venetian-Ottoman warfare, and who moved to the metropole in increasing numbers in the wake of the Ottoman conquest of Venetian Cyprus in 1571. In petitioning the government for employment or sinecure in the metropole, dispossessed colonists hoped to restore their wealth, if not their status.

The unique position of trans-imperial subjects in the Venetian commercial sphere is well attested in the unfolding testimonies in Frangia's trial in the summer of 1573. The various testimonies—including those by Frangia, Giulia, Zorzi, their Ottoman tenant-merchants, and these merchants' slaves—underscore how deeply embedded trans-imperial subjects were in extensive social networks in Venice and beyond. As important, they suggest the transgressive nature of the witnesses' domestic arrangements, at least from the point of view of Frangia's patrician interrogators.[5] Such arrangements belie a simple parsing of their milieu into "Venetian" and "Turk," and bring into the limelight the important role of localized émigrés, such as Frangia and Giulia, in facilitating a range of interactions across linguistic, religious, and juridical boundaries.

Indeed, some of the transgressive consequences of the domestic arrangements between Frangia's family and its Ottoman sojourners were exposed by the escaped slave himself. Zorzi claimed that he had planned to go back to the Ottoman Empire in the hope of finding his Christian Bulgarian parents, whom he had not seen since his kidnapping as a young boy. He had been encouraged to escape from his Venetian master, he said, by several friends of similar circumstances. All of them had purportedly managed to escape Venice on board a ship heading for Izmir just a few days earlier. They were all aided not only by Ottoman merchants and their slaves, but also by Frangia's family.[6]

From the beginning of the proceedings, then, Zorzi presented himself as reluctant to abide by the rules governing Venetian domestic slavery. Rather than endorse his new identity as a baptized slave, he asserted his wish to return to his *ur* identity—not that of an Ottoman Muslim convert, but that of a kidnapped Christian boy. To that end, he related how he had recruited an extended network of accomplices, crossing spatial, social, and religious boundaries. His professed desire to reunite with his parents was, moreover, a powerful indictment against his current servile state, challenging the legality of his very enslavement.[7] In order to befriend Frangia's Ottoman tenants and secure their assistance in his escape, Zorzi implied he was even willing to "reactivate" his Muslim past and resume Muslim bodily practices such as having his head shaved and wearing a white turban.[8] It is impossible of course to determine what exactly transpired between Zorzi and his Ottoman hosts in Frangia's house, but we can assume that Zorzi was convincing enough in invoking his Muslim background for the merchants to collaborate in his ultimately unsuccessful attempt to return to the Ottoman Empire.

If Zorzi's testimony pokes holes in patrician representations of a perfected Venetian social and religious order, other witnesses similarly undermine notions of a stable domestic order. Throughout the trial, Frangia sought to present himself as the master of an orderly household, and to claim authority over his wife, children, and tenants. But two revelations seriously compromised his claims to authority: that the keys to his house were actually kept by his Ottoman tenants, and that as a broker-landlord he was utterly dependent on the translation skills of his tenants' slaves, for he himself did not speak a word of Turkish.[9] Not only did these slaves possess vital communicative skills, but their friendship with a diverse group of young slaves, servants, and apprentices across the city gave them broad social access, belying their supposed isolation. Furthermore, these slaves apparently exerted enough authority to conduct Zorzi's ceremonial headshaving. This act transgressed not only religious but social hierarchies as well. It mirrored and reversed Zorzi's baptism by his patrician master only eighteen months earlier, an important ritual enactment of ownership and presumed spiritual transformation.[10]

Thus, in order to act as a broker, Frangia depended on a much larger network of intermediaries. The testimonies of his wife, his son, and his neighbor reveal the extent of this network. The position of Frangia's wife, Giulia, emerges as particularly ambiguous, as she only partially adhered to the religious and moral boundaries sanctioned by Venetian officialdom. Although supposedly subordinate to her husband's commands, she was the one who during the visit of Zorzi's master Falier deftly negotiated with the irate patrician and knowingly lied to him about his slave's whereabouts. Well before that, as becomes clear from her testimony, she was in daily contact with her Ottoman tenants about eating arrangements and may have tacitly collaborated with them not only in hiding Zorzi in her house but other runaway slaves as well.[11]

The inquisitorial record further allows us to explore some Venetian officials' implicit concerns regarding brokers' person and profession. From the start, Frangia's dual social position, as both a Venetian civil servant and a "Greek," could raise suspicion of political as well as religious subversion.[12] As if being Greek were not enough, Frangia rented rooms to Muslim Ottoman merchants. This was in clear violation of the law, which forbade anyone to lodge foreigners except for licensed hoteliers; brokers were specifically warned against the common practice.[13] This was a repeated point of contention, as brokers were ideally placed to offer newly arrived foreign merchants lodgings and other services. Brokers frequently claimed ignorance of this law and insisted that they were simply doing merchants a favor by welcoming them into their homes.

The ban on brokers' lodging of foreign clients was part of an effort to monitor foreigners' presence in the city and to secure revenue from the tax collected through licensed hoteliers. But it also was linked, and increasingly so, to religious concerns regarding Muslim Ottoman merchants' freedom of residence. Indeed, Frangia himself vaguely alluded to "scandals" that the lodging of Muslim merchants in Christian households had caused. The occasion for these assertions was his petitioning—only a year after the trial discussed here—for an exclusive privilege to operate a *fondaco* (an exchange-house, from the Arabic *funduq*) for "Turks." The Senate granted his request to establish a "special hotel, like the ones of many other Nations, and people in this city, and also like the ones the Turks in their countries of the Levant have provided for the Christian Nation," on August 16, 1575.[14]

Frangia's shrewd emphasis on the need to prevent scandals struck a sensitive chord. Already during the trial, beyond an obvious concern over Zorzi's planned escape and ostensible apostasy, inquisitors questioned the moral well-being of Frangia's family itself and located it precisely in the crossing of social and spatial boundaries. Throughout the interrogations, inquisitors repeatedly asked Frangia, Giulia, and their son about the nature of their interactions with their Ottoman Muslim tenants. Inquisitors wanted to know who cooked the tenants' food, what kind of food it was (in particular, whether tenants ate meat on Friday, a clear sign of religious transgression), and whether the family and the tenants had ever eaten together. Giulia was particularly careful in her replies, assuring her interrogators that no contact through food (let alone through the sociability presupposed and reinforced by commensality) had taken place between her family and her tenants. Concern over food restrictions and their violations typified the Holy Office's attempts to expose and uproot heresy, and Giulia was clearly conscious of the link between the violation of Catholic food restrictions and ostensible heresy.[15] Her detailed answer about what her tenant had given her to cook for dinner on Friday evening when Zorzi was discovered in the attic suggests she was well aware of what her interrogators were after.

> He eats meat every day, and we don't eat meat, neither on Wednesday nor on Friday for any reason, and it is true that he gave one of my little girls, who is four years old, a pumpkin roll, and I told her not to eat anything with grease or meat, so the cat ate it in the pantry.[16]

Giulia thus emphasized that she deemed the food that her tenant had given her little daughter worthy only of the cat, and in the pantry, out of sight. On the other hand, the fact that her tenant offered food to the girl at all may well suggest that affective ties between these specific tenants and landlords went beyond polite greeting on the staircase.

This case study therefore illustrates the specific role of trans-imperial subjects in articulating differing conceptions of religious boundaries, orthodoxies, and their transgression within and across early modern Mediterranean empires. In this case, as in others, intermediaries did not actually forge a bridge between distinct kinds. What Frangia performed was not the bringing together of clear-cut, mutually unintelligible, and well-bound sociocultural groups. Rather, his task—endorsed by Venetian officials—was to police and contain, to establish boundaries and maintain them as best he could. At the same time, Frangia himself defied the official boundary between "Venetians" and "foreigners" on many levels: juridical, linguistic, religious, and affective. His mediation was vital for the smooth operation of the Venetian economy, which at that period increasingly depended on Ottoman trade for its survival. But his practices of mediation could not be "normalized" without undermining Venice's constitutive political myths of purity. The boundaries formed and transformed through Frangia's and Giulia's actions therefore did not always overlap with the contours of moral community as Venetian elites understood them. Like other understudied trans-imperial groups and institutions, Frangia, Giulia, and their tenants/clients partook in circuits of exchange that sometimes eluded Venetian officialdom, but into which the state repeatedly attempted to insert itself, through regulating mechanisms such as broker licensing, taxation, and supervision by an officially designated interpreter. These circuits, nonetheless, remained for the most part impervious to official interventions. The uniqueness of Frangia's court record, therefore, is not so much in the practices and networks it reveals but in their ample textual elaboration.

From turn-of-the-twentieth-century European administrators in Southeast Asia on the lookout for collaborators to help pacify the colonies, to 1930s Chicago school sociologists seeking to understand the plight of the bicultural "marginal man" in U.S. immigrant neighborhoods, to 1950s anthropologists hopeful about the propensity of village teachers in Latin America and Africa to mediate "local" and "national" cultures in the (post)colony, to 1970s economists and urban planners captivated by the phenomenon of "middleman minorities" operating successful small businesses in the otherwise collapsing American inner city, social scientists have sought to explain what seemed like the special predisposition of certain ethnic minorities to act as cultural intermediaries. Despite important methodological and epistemological differences, scholars identified the groups in question as "culture brokers" because they either partook in interregional networks of exchange or could be understood to be of "mixed blood."

In a somewhat different vein, much recent work in both history and anthropology has highlighted how cultural intermediaries operating in imperial contact zones could articulate, negotiate, consolidate, contest, and transform power structures.[17] While breaking much new ground, this body of work has dealt only in passing with the epistemological assumptions and imperial legacies underwriting its basic analytical vocabulary, namely, *culture* and *mediation,* and has left implicit the model of commodity exchange between enterprising individuals in a marketplace on which it is often premised.[18] This billiard ball view of cultures as "internally homogenous and externally distinctive and bounded objects" was memorably critiqued by Eric Wolf.[19] It was in part at least the legacy of an imperial optic that understood taxonomies of colonial alterities as signs of "global difference."[20] The relationship between a billiard ball view of bounded cultures and an imperial optic is best exemplified by the influential theory of "plural society." According to British colonial administrator-turned-anthropologist John Sydenham Furnivall, a plural society comprises

> two or more elements or social orders which live side by side, yet without mingling, in one political unit ... rulers and the ruled are of different races ... Native, Chinese, and Europeans have distinct economic functions, and live apart as separate social orders.[21]

The concept of "plural society" thus was premised on an image of colonial societies as neat, pyramidal structures, where powerful ethnic and class divisions coalesce. Furnivall of course was interested in identifying potential agents to use in colonial administration, not in addressing the question of cultural mediation per se. Yet by positing ethnicity as the chief cleavage in society and by suggesting that certain ethnic groups may facilitate colonial governmentality through their actions as go-betweens, Furnivall articulated a theory of mediation of sorts, premised, not surprisingly, on a transactionalist model of exchange.

The legacy of the "plural society" paradigm is evident in some of the most influential theories of cultural mediation developed by sociologists, economists, and anthropologists throughout the first half of the twentieth century, from Chicago school sociologist Robert E. Park's "marginal man" theory,[22] via the economic theories of "marginal trading peoples" and "middleman minority,"[23] to anthropological work on cultural intermediaries in the 1950s and 1960s.[24] In one way or another, these various traditions tended to conflate cultural mediation with the capacity to serve the interests of an established political order, and generalized from Furnivall's policy-driven emphasis on ethnic minorities as potential collaborators to an ontological propensity of such minorities to function as cultural intermediaries.[25]

Significantly, in both Furnivall's "plural society" and some of its later theoretical elaborations, the market provides the meeting place par excellence for the different ethnic groups, while little attention is paid to cultural mediation in other domains.[26] Yet, as Frangia's case above suggests, brokers rarely operate in an anonymous commercial sphere external to their actions and composed of discrete individuals pertaining to discrete social categories. Rather, brokers actively participate in constituting the commercial sphere and its concomitant legitimate subjectivities through myriad practices, constrained and enabled by the matrix of power of a particular contact zone. This conclusion counters much of the extant scholarship on early modern commercial brokers, which has tended to describe them as disinterested agents of the supposedly universal logic of capitalism, and their activities as having taken place in an anonymous marketplace. Although I cannot elaborate on this point here, cases such as Frangia's suggest a far more haphazard and tangled development of commercial practice, where brokers and other trans-imperial subjects played an essential role.[27] Indeed, as I have argued, the mediation that early modern brokers engaged in was rarely limited to commercial transactions. On the contrary, it was multilayered, fraught with other social obligations that encompassed various actors (brokers, their kin, friends, patrons, and clients) and which occurred through a host of institutions, including, prominently, domestic ones.

Beyond tangible commodities, brokers transacted affect and ways of categorizing the social world: notions of trust, profit, morality, honor, and risk are all essential to the shaping and reshaping of economic action. When Frangia and Giulia welcomed Muslim Ottoman tenants into their home and entrusted them with the house keys, when they allowed their toddler to roam about on the staircase leading to the tenants' quarter, when they tacitly accepted runaway slaves hiding in their attic, and when they lied to their patrician interlocutors both in their home and at court, they redrew important boundaries in ways that clearly transgressed Venetian elite notions of what was moral, honorable, and legal. Later, when Frangia petitioned the government to allow him to operate a *fondaco* for Muslim merchants, he sought to capitalize on precisely those increasingly threatened boundaries of the Venetian moral community. His petition (and, much

> We must . . . read the great canonical texts, and perhaps also the entire archive of modern European and premodern and European and American culture, with an effort to draw out, extend, give emphasis and voice to what is silent or marginally present or ideologically represented.
>
> ❧ EDWARD SAID 1993, 66

later, his alleged maltreatment of tenants as the *fondaco*'s manager) set in motion a host of other processes and intermediaries, which in turn led to an ever more consolidated spatial and conceptual segregation between Venetian and Ottoman subjects, between Christians and Muslims, and between different categories of Ottoman subjects operating in Venice. These reconstituted boundaries were in part the result of his actions, rather than their precondition.

My brief exploration of the nexus between commercial practice and affective ties in early modern Venice has identified brokers' households as an important domain where patrician notions of foreignness were contested and transformed. Venetian officialdom (and many modern scholars) understood commercial brokers as disinterested agents of the state, operating in an anonymous marketplace composed of discrete, individual actors. Against such an understanding, Frangia's trial record suggests how brokers and their clients often acted in concert, forging intimate ties across religious, linguistic, and political boundaries. According to early twentieth-century conceptions of cultural mediation, such a case could seem to exemplify how "marginal men" functioned on the margins of the religious and political boundaries assumed by elite officials. However, such a conclusion would be premature. Frangia's case underscores how unstable these boundaries are and why their durability should not be assumed a priori. Here, mediation occurs not in a marketplace of free exchange but within a host of interlinked, institutionalized domains where gendered, ethnicized, and classed subjects act upon one another. Perhaps even more important, none of the categories transacted by Frangia, Giulia, Zorzi, and their numerous patrician interlocutors, be it "Christian," "Turk," "local," or "foreigner," necessarily remained fixed throughout the process of articulation. Exploring how specific trans-imperial subjects operated within particular institutional domains offers a better understanding of the reconstitution of boundaries in one early modern contact zone. Such an approach should also generate further insights into how historically shifting cultural boundaries were and are made to seem natural, immutable, and all-encompassing.

NOTES

1. Pratt 1992, 4.
2. Established in 1547, the Venetian Holy Office was a highly autonomous chapter of the Roman Inquisition, administered by clerics who for the most part

came from Venice's patrician ruling class. For a bibliography on this well-studied institution, see Ruggiero 2001, n3.

3. From the opening statement in Archivio di Stato di Venezia, Santo Uffizio, Processi, b. 35, fasc. 12 (henceforth: SU 35), fol. 1r (Aug. 15, 1573). All subsequent archival references are to materials in the Venetian State Archives, unless otherwise stated. For a different perspective on this case, see Burke 2006.

4. Briefly, I define trans-imperial subjects as actors who straddled and thus mediated religious, linguistic, and political boundaries across imperial domains, in this case, the Venetian and Ottoman states. For a fuller discussion of this concept, see Rothman forthcoming.

5. Like Zorzi's master, the inquisitors sitting on the case were themselves, for the most part, Venetian patricians.

6. SU 35, Zorzi's testimony, fols. 1v–4r (Aug. 15, 1573).

7. In theory, if not in practice, Venetians were not supposed to trade in—and certainly not to possess—Christian slaves. If slave owners overlooked this moral dictum as a matter of course when it came to recent converts to Christianity, they found it harder to ignore when a slave could prove he or she had been born to Christian parents. Not surprisingly, in their inquisitorial depositions, slaves in Venetian households commonly claimed to have been kidnapped from Christian parents at a tender age. See Rothman forthcoming, chapter 3.

8. Early modern Venetians widely regarded head shaving and the sporting of "Turkish" clothes as signs of conversion to Islam. Significantly, Ottomans similarly held change in dress to be a sign of a convert's new religious affiliation. See Minkov 2004. For the relationship between outward appearance and presumed inner spiritual transformation in early modern Venice, see also Head 1990; Wilson 2003.

9. SU 35, Frangia's testimony, fols. 6r–6v (Aug. 20, 1573).

10. On religious conversion as a practice of subject making by the early modern Venetian state, see Rothman 2006.

11. SU 35, Frangia's testimony, fol. 5r (Aug. 20, 1573).

12. On the triadic relations between Greeks, Latins, and Muslims in the early modern Mediterranean, and specifically on Venetian anxieties regarding Greek-Ottoman collaboration, see Greene 2000. The profession of Venetian commercial brokerage became increasingly "ethnicized" and suspect in the wake of the loss of Cyprus (1571) as the government granted many refugees from the lost colony license to exercise the trade.

13. Arti, b. 517, fasc. 1, fol. 2v (June 26, 1497). See also Urban Padoan 1990, 18; Manno 1995, 127; Costantini 1996.

14. Cinque Savii, Seconda serie, b. 187, fasc. 1, unfoliated (1574). While Frangia, his son, and eventually his grandson all served as custodians of this institution, it only became mandatory for Ottoman Muslim merchants to lodge there in 1621. The numerous struggles against government efforts to force all Ottoman and Safavid merchants to move into the *Fondaco dei Turchi* in the course of the seventeenth century are discussed in Rothman forthcoming, chapter 6. On *fondachi* in the Mediterranean more generally, see Constable 2003.

15. On the Venetian Holy Office's interest in food consumption as index of religious (un)orthodoxy in the age of confessionalization, see Head 1990.

16. SU 35, Giulia's testimony, fol. 13r (Aug. 22, 1573). Abstention from meat on Wednesday and Friday would not have marked Giulia and her family as Catholic as opposed to Greek Orthodox, but simply, in this case, as neither Lutheran nor Muslim, the two major concerns of the Venetian Holy Office at the time.

17. The literature here is vast. For some suggestive examples, see White 1991; Austen and Derrick 1999; Robinson 2000; Richter 2001; Cohen 2003; Alam and Subrahmanyam 2005; Metcalf 2005; Jasanoff 2005.

18. For a critique of "academic discussions of ethnic identity framed in individualist terms, which seem to suggest that maximizing, goal-oriented 'actors' switch or cross boundaries in pursuit of their ends, approaching questions of identity in consumer terms, as a matter of optimal selection," see Li 2000, 150.

19. Wolf 1982, 6; Wolf 1994; see also Barth 1969 for an earlier emphasis on boundary maintenance and boundary crossing as interrelated aspects of the constitution of ethnic categories.

20. Connell 1997.

21. Furnivall 1944, 446. Furnivall (1878–1960) was educated in Cambridge and joined the India Civil Service in 1901. He arrived in Burma in 1902, where he worked until 1925. Following his retirement to Britain he became Lecturer in Burmese Language, History and Law at Cambridge University. In 1940 he published a Burmese-English dictionary, and in 1942 he wrote *Reconstruction in Burma* for the Burmese government.

22. Park 1928; Stonequist 1961 [1937]. The concept has a much longer history, of course, and is heavily indebted to Simmel's famous ideal type of "the Stranger" (1950) as "someone who crosses boundaries and therefore defines and defies boundaries, or builds bridges over them." See Cassidy 2000, 15. On Simmel's contributions to interwar American sociology, see Coser 1965; Alexander 2004.

23. Becker 1940; Becker 1956, 225–37; Blalock 1967, 1982; Bonacich 1973.

24. See, inter alia, Fallers 1955; Geertz 1960. At least in the case of anthropology, however, the theoretical shift to consider social systems as inherently composite, open-ended, and multilayered prompted scholars already in the 1960s to look at the longer trajectories of the specific societies they study and situate them within the global power structures of colonialism and capitalism (Wolf 1956; Press 1969). Indeed, many anthropological accounts of cultural mediation have gradually incorporated historicity itself, as understood and enacted by members of the societies studied, into their analysis of the objectification of "culture." A very partial list includes Taussig 1986; Cohen 1994; Trouillot 1995; Stoler and Strassler 2000; Boym 2001.

25. See the call to historicize and deessentialize the concept of "minority" in Asad 2000.

26. The emphasis on the marketplace may explain at least in part why much of the literature on "cultural brokers" employs capitalist vocabularies, either in overemphasizing brokers' economic role (particularly in middleman minority theory) or in envisioning culture itself as a commodity to be transacted (partic-

ularly in early anthropological literature). I cannot address here the conceptual implications of this emphasis on the "marketplace" but should note in passing its structural resemblance to the notion of "comprador bourgeoisie" in Marxist theory.

27. For a critical assessment of how the historiography of commercial brokerage has been subjected to the teleological paradigm of "the rise of capitalism" see Reyerson 2002, 1–8.

FIG. 6.1. Casper David Friedrich, *Der Wanderer über dem Neblmeer,* "Wanderer above the Sea of Fog" (1818).

6 &ed; *Monica Eileen Patterson*

Childhood, Memory, and Gap: Reflections from an Anthrohistorian on Georges Perec's *W or the Memory of Childhood*

> My childhood belongs to those things which I know I don't know much about. It is behind me; yet it is the ground on which I grew, and it once belonged to me, however obstinately I assert that it no longer does . . .[1]

> That mindless mist where shadows swirl, how could I pierce it?[2]

> Childhood is neither longing nor terror, neither a paradise lost nor the Golden Fleece, but maybe it is a horizon, a point of departure, a set of co-ordinates from which the axes of my life may draw their meaning.[3]

In his autobiographical novel/memoir *W or the Memory of Childhood*, Holocaust orphan Georges Perec attempts to penetrate the mist of muddled memories of his traumatic childhood using various strategies he perceives to be neutral and objective. In alternating genres, Perec gathers fragments, gaps, and uncertainties in an attempt to write about a childhood he can't remember. I happened quite unexpectedly upon this remarkable work, yet it so thoroughly captures, questions, and represents my own encounters with South African adults remembering childhoods fringed by or grounded in trauma.[4] Perec sparked an important theoretical intervention in my work on memory at a crucial time for me as I was confronting the holes in my own research and attempting to determine what I had learned. This was a discovery that was modeled by some of my own heroes of anthrohistory who have also found theory in unlikely places. In many ways Perec's book is an organized, schematic attempt to access his early life using the tools and approaches of anthropologists and historians. Ultimately, it is only within the *gaps* between verifiable truths and misrememberings that Perec finds meaning in and access to past experiences. It is in sentiment—in all of its patchiness and supposed evidentiary weakness—that a sense of Perec's childhood may be found. Residing in the ephemera of "gap," sentiment is what renders his childhood visible and meaningful.

Perec was working as a scientific archivist in Paris when he first attempted to write fiction around the age of twenty. Some twelve years later in 1967, he joined a collective called OuLiPo, short for "**Ou**vroir de **litté**ra-ture **po**tentielle," which roughly translates to "workshop of potential literature." The collective included mainly French-speaking writers, scholars, and mathematicians,[5] who sought to "assist the renewal of literature by inventing, refining, and refurbishing *formal devices,* which can be thought of equally well as tools, or constraints, or constrictive forms" (Bellos 1986, 10). Utilizing structures drawn from the realms of mathematics, logic, and chess as constraints, Perec and his fellow writers were "astonished by the way that through this apparently conscious process, the unconscious appears more likely" (10).

Noted for his creative energy and intense love of wordplay, Perec proved to be quite prolific before his premature death in 1982, just four days before his forty-sixth birthday. He produced more than twenty works including a 300-page novel written without the letter *e* (1969, 1994), a 1,247 word palindrome, an oral history project about Ellis Island (1995 [1980]), dozens of crossword puzzles, and a survey of the 124 dreams he recalled having between May 1968 and August 1972 (1973). In an interview in 1981 he said it was his ambition to have used all the words in the dictionary by the end of his life. He further declared, "I would like to say everything in every way possible" (1993).[6] Perec was an observer and recorder of "everydayness" and saw his work drawing most prominently from the fields of sociology, autobiography, the "ludic," and narrative (Bellos 1986, 12).

W or the Memory of Childhood was reportedly Perec's most challenging work, taking thirteen years to complete.[7] The first of his intertwining narratives spins a lurid fictional tale of W, an island society ruled by "boundless terror" in which conscripted athletes are forced to compete against one another in increasingly sadistic events designed to maximize their suffering and humiliation. Based on a set of drawings that he had produced around age thirteen, the parallels with Nazi ideology and the horrific conditions of the concentration camps are clear. Spliced throughout this gradually unfolding narrative are autobiographical fragments from Perec's childhood in France around the time of the German occupation.

Perec marshals his evidence and presents it to his readers, including an attempt made fifteen years earlier to capture and record everything that he knew about his parents. Believing that by discovering and disclosing the inaccuracies of his account he could discern a deeper truth about his early years, Perec forces his readers to witness the whittling away of his narrative through an exhaustively critical exegesis. The six pages of original text are subsumed by eight pages of interruption in the form of footnotes consisting of documentation, clarification, speculation, interrogation, refutation, reevaluation, reflection, revelation, qualification, confession, emotional expression, interpretation, denunciation, and correction. The critical interventions Perec makes into his own text are often totalizing in scope: "There's no basis for any of this," he claims, in reference to one of his long-held beliefs, and "I do not know the source of this memory, which nothing has ever confirmed" (1988, 13, 37). Perec admits to his own inventions, calling himself out by exposing evidence and contradictory accounts that destroy the credibility of his original text.

Like an anthrohistorian, Perec seeks to assemble and read a range of fragments in his quest for a more intimate engagement with his past: stories, old journal entries from his youth, newspaper articles, photographs, fantasies, scars. Perec invokes the disciplines' foundational methodologies early on: "For years I sought out traces of my history, looking up maps and directories and piles of archives. I found nothing, and it sometimes seemed as though I had dreamt, that there had been only an unforgettable nightmare" (1988, 3); and "in what I am about to relate . . . I wish to adopt the cold, impassive tone of the ethnologist: I visited this sunken world and this is what I saw there" (4). The tangible traces of his parents are painfully few: five photographs of his mother, only one of his father. He searches for patterns and strives to determine what is characteristic and what is exceptional, plumbing the details for more knowledge, broader understanding, and deeper feeling. The circumstances of his separation are profoundly traumatic on both the personal and collective level: born to Jewish immigrants from Poland, Perec first lost his father, who bled to death from wounds received fighting against the Germans, and shortly thereafter his mother, who was deported to Auschwitz and murdered.

While Perec's interruptions are abrupt, they are made in a language that is often unsure. His narrative is thus marked by an interesting juxtaposition: uncertainty sits alongside precision, feelings and imaginings are accompanied by a preoccupation with numbers, facts, figures, and dates. He does a lot of counting, as if numbers can fill the abyss of silence and uncertainty with something settled and fixed.⁸ He strips his narrative down to only verifiable facts, dissecting his memories with obsessive zeal. In the process, Perec's own knowledge and understanding of who he was and what he experienced are fragmented even further: any loose claim he may have once had on his childhood has slipped away. He relentlessly pursues exactitude, verification, ordered chronology, and underlying meaning, seeking to distill the "Truth" from multiple sources. The result, however, is not a clarification but an obfuscation—in fact an *annihilation* of any salvageable meaning or memory of substance. The objectivity he seeks leads him not closer to his truth but further from it, temporarily distracting both him and us from the devastating void of a childhood without parents.

Perec presents a wonderfully complicated exploration of the inner workings of memory. Acknowledging the overwriting that shapes and partially constitutes his memories, he confesses that one of his fondest was likely inspired by a Rembrandt painting, raising the question of what popular icons can do to memory.⁹ Upon close inspection he finds Hans Christian Andersen and Victor Hugo, the 1937 film *Bizarre Bizarre,* and illustrations from children's books trespassing in similar ways (1988, 39-40). His excavations of memory reveal a fusion of fiction and life, along with the sometimes arresting, sometimes sneaking power of images—whether from literature, art, history, imagination, or constructions of childhood—to overwrite one's access to pasts in complex ways.

Another of his most treasured memories is destroyed when Perec realizes that he has co-opted a classmate's experience of an accident as a personal remembrance of his own. Recalling a mutual friend, Philippe Gardes, the author and his acquaintance Louis Argoud-Puix discover that they all attended the same school and were, in fact, in the same class. Louis remembered Philippe, but not Perec, who then asked him about an accident that he was "supposed to have had." Louis remembered the accident in precise detail: it was "identical in every way" to Perec's memory of himself, only Louis was sure that it "had happened to the self-same Philippe" (1988, 80).

As stories circulate among people and within one's own personal narratives, the boundaries between reality, fantasy, self, and other(s) can be difficult to discern. Fantasy both obscures and fills gaps, and sometimes even creates them. Fantasy accommodates metanarratives, and the foundational narratives of our selves as they shape-shift. We all cling to our own personal mythologies to fill gaps—sometimes the gaps between who we are or have been, and who we would like to be. Dreams also feed memory. Perec shares one of his: "several versions of it exist, and overlaid upon one another, they make the memory itself more illusory. The simplest statement of it would be this: my father comes home from his work; he gives me a key. In one version, the key is made of gold. In another version, I swallow the key, everyone fusses, and the next day it turns up in my stool" (1988, 14). The symbolic possibilities are not lost on the author. Perec reminds us that memory, identity, and experience also inform and shape our tastes and desires: "The memories I have of my father are not many. At a particular time in my life, in fact at the time I referred to previously, the love I felt for my father became bound up with a passionate craze for tin soldiers" (28).

Among others, David William Cohen's Camella Teoli (1994) and Alessandro Portelli's Luigi Trastulli (1990) have demonstrated how "untrue" stories can elicit deeper understandings of the past. Similarly, Perec teaches us more about his childhood by exposing contradictions and contestations, such as those raised by his aunts and cousins, than a single, consistent account could ever provide. It is through engaging with these "misrememberings" that Perec provides a rare glimpse into his own interior world. Strikingly, several of these inconsistencies involve injury and illness, typically inflated or chronologically shifted onto the period of life after he lost his parents. In Perec's own (self-) analysis,[10] this is not coincidental but rather a symbolic symptom of his experiences: "The Red Cross evacuates the wounded. I was not wounded. But I had to be evacuated. So we had to pretend I was wounded. That was why my arm was in a sling. But my aunt is quite definite: I did not have my arm in a sling; there was no reason at all for me to have my arm in a sling. It was as a 'son of father deceased,' a 'war orphan,' that I was being evacuated by the Red Cross, entirely within regulations" (1988, 55).

While narratives of redemption, conscientization, and becoming tend to neatly order and frame, Perec suggests that there are not always straight lines between a former child self and the adult he grows into. Much lies beyond these frames, and cannot be captured by them or held within them. An unframing is required, and an acceptance and acknowledgment both of the many gaps in research and the fact that these have the potential to create more honest and inclusive scholarship. As Perec and so many other Holocaust writers have shown, there is an "ethics of emptiness" that allows for and works with—rather than against—spaces of gap, silence, and absence. In fact, neutrality and objectivity seem not only flat and void of substance, but inappropriate, inhumane, abhorrent.

Through an alternating double narrative of dissected memoir and dark fantasy, Perec's construction of "childhood" is revealed to be more of a sieve than a frame. By moving back and forth across the two main story lines, he exposes something that neither narrative can fully contain. There is something else that we as readers—and especially as anthrohistorians—must recognize in the space between.

> The adventure story is rather grandiose, or maybe dubious. For it begins to tell one tale, and then, all of a sudden, launches into another. In this break, in this split suspending the story on an unidentifiable expectation, can be found the point of departure for the whole of this book: the *points of suspension* on which the broken threads of childhood and the web of writing are caught. (1988, preface)

Part of the work of anthrohistory then may be seen as mapping these "points of suspension" and engaging with them: taking them up and wrestling with them for a while. It is within these spaces that the alchemy of memory, imagination, and sentiment can transmute and subsist—a crucial recognition if we are to produce textured histories of childhood that make the social worlds of children more accessible. The gaps of childhood are often preemptively filled with superficial and sanguine scripts that serve to reinscribe children's subordinate status as nonsubjects—"preadults," "empty vessels," "blank slates"—effectively avoiding meaningful engagement with their thoughts and experiences.

Much of our knowledge about our own childhoods is derived from others. If growing up severs us in certain ways from our childhoods (certainly in terms of shifting our subject-positioning into the dominant and hegemonic field of adulthood), what can take us back? What prompts reconnection, reformulation, reevaluation, and understanding of one's childhood? In *The Mysterious Flame of Queen Loana,* Umberto Eco (2005) makes a compelling case for the singular power of sensory triggers such as scents, images, sounds, and textures. Perec also explores the range of ways that we know about our childhoods: through firsthand memories, the stories relatives tell, photographs, archives; through dreaming, imagining, feeling, and sensing; and by plugging into the larger frameworks of history, film, novels, and popular culture.

Memories of childhood are especially episodic, and often articulated in the language of superlatives and firsts. What factors within our childhoods and ensuing lives contribute to the highly selective, unstable, and ongoing memory process that enables us to carry or keep on hand certain experiences that may then be brought forward, laid out, offered up? In Perec's account, memory is a hub of emptiness. Perec exposes the holes in his memory and narrative accounts until they overwhelm what he thinks he once knew or experienced. His analysis subsumes content and severs sentiment. In trying to fill in the gaps, Perec distills his early life story down to nothingness and obliterates his own memory. By filtering out the inconsistencies, the interpretations, the speculations, and the unverified, he pushes us further from any real understanding or sense of his past. It is through this annihilation of personal memory that we as readers confront the utter devastation of the Holocaust by witnessing a relentless pursuit of a truth so fleeting and fragile it is destroyed through the very means used to find, fix, and reinforce it.[11]

For Perec, sentiment activates, animates, and grounds the fragile sense of meaning in his early life. In the beginning of his narrative he writes, "I possess other pieces of information about my parents; I know they will not help me to say what I would like to say about them" (1988, 14). He shows that sentiment is not merely memory's dross but a fundamental part of its very constitution. Sentiment is one of the lenses through which children become visible. Perec is thus more available to us in the early part of the book, when he is still capable of registering emotion.[12]

Unfolding the most tragic events of his life, Perec describes his last contact with his mother with clinical sparseness: "One day she took me to the station. It was in 1942. It was the Gare de Lyon. She bought me a magazine which must have been an issue of *Charlie*. As the train moved out, I caught sight of her, I seem to remember, waving a white handkerchief from the platform. I was going to Villard-de-Lans, with the Red Cross."[13] We have here been given the basic facts of this separation but none of the feelings it may have invoked. Finally, achieving his desired but devastating degree of "neutrality and objectivity," he finishes her story: "I've been told that later on she tried to cross the Loire ... She was picked up in a raid, together with her sister, my aunt. She was interned at Drancy on 23 January 1943, then deported on 11 February following, destination Auschwitz. She saw the country of her birth again before she died. She died without understanding" (1988, 33).

As he excises the subjective and speculative from his memory, the more dispassionate he becomes. With the authority of neutral objectivity, his narrative is rendered flat and yet overly saturated with meaning: "We never managed to find any trace of my mother or of her sister. It may be that they were deported towards Auschwitz and then diverted to another camp; it is also possible that their entire trainload was gassed on arrival. My grandfathers were also both deported" (1988, 41). Perec's multiple ways of *not knowing* are much fuller and constitutive than the facts. As his story unfolds, there is less and less engagement with the finality of what is known because the medium for knowing has been extinguished: for him, it is only within the spaces of uncertainty that sentiment can be held. "From this point on, there are memories—fleeting, persistent, trivial, burdensome—but there is nothing that binds them together" (68).

We are constantly engaging with the past. When we gaze up at the night sky or peer through a telescope, some of the light that we see may be from stars that have been extinguished for billions of years. Accounting for this vision is not simply a matter of a time-space continuum, however. A certain mindfulness toward simultaneity is also required. Different time-moments constitute the skyscape, and the objects we are closest to do not necessarily appear most clearly. As Perec notes,

> I could generalize a little, that in almost everything I am producing there is, we could say, a story and the story of the story. A fiction and a fiction about the fiction and like, it's like mirrors, and it doesn't end with the fiction and the fiction about the fiction—there'll be speculation about the fiction of the fiction and so on. And there is, I could say there is several levels.... But I can't know exactly what the fiction is. It's like a mayonnaise, I should say. (1988, 26)

One must also consider the intensity and strength of certain bodies in relation to one another. Strong memories can trump more recent ones in their power and sway, and the clarity of their vision in both detail and impact. So too, the brightness of stars is ever and always relational. Without other celestial bodies to compare them to, we would have no way of determining either their place or size, nor their significance in the universe.

Employing innovative sources and unconventional methods, Georges Perec excavates a rich palimpsest of perspectives through a shifting range of temporal, emotional, and conceptual vantage points that speak through the gaps existing between them. The very inaccuracies and imaginings that overwrite most of Perec's memories of his murdered parents largely constitute his connection to them. The source of meaning in his childhood is only visible when viewed through the sedimented sentiment of the unsayable.

In Perec I have found a theorist of memory who inspired my idea of gap as a means of keeping something alive, engaged, and dynamic.[14] Of course, there can be no singular reading of gap, for gaps are attributable to many things. There are several types of gap that constitute, shape, and define the ways in which we produce and engage with our memories of our own childhoods. Each of these gaps overlaps with the others, compounding and destabilizing them further. Not every gap is imbued with equal significance.

When it comes to children, one of the most frequently invoked is a cognitive gap in which a child's worldview, analytical skills, life experience, maturity, and understanding are recognized as different from those of adults. The prominence of imagination in children's thinking creates a space between adult and child, and real and fantasy. Far too often, however, adults assume that children lack understanding rather than seeking out what their understandings are. Usually subordinate in their family and society, children's subalternity engenders many kinds of gap deriving from issues of power, voice, and choice. Metanarratives, including those of cultural texts, notions of nation, and the concept of "childhood" and "self," can serve to both situate and occlude past experiences as accessed through memory.

Could we not understand something quite significant by looking harder for the patterns in what is missing, and what *doesn't* appear, alongside that which does? What if we aimed to produce a photonegative image of history, inverting the traditional process of "historian as sleuth" to foreground gap? What would a biography look like that consisted of the stories *not* told, the events and people and experiences *not* remembered? If one could gather all of the holes and silences encountered, how would such an archive of absence be ordered? How would it be read?[15]

The problem is that much analysis is dominated by serious examination of only that which is believed to be known with certainty, thus ignoring or flattening out the rich dynamics that explorations of gap can reveal. Narratives of childhood memory are marked by a layered ambiguity of definition: blurred boundaries between self and others, real and imagined, firsthand and borrowed, and an alternative grasp of temporality. An act of translation to oneself is required to make sense of the child one once was. Stepping off from *W or the Memory of Childhood*, I would like to consider the costs and consequences of trying to overwrite the gaps of memory. I would like to pause and hold open a space for gap in my work: to acknowledge and (re)consider it as a dynamic and productive space for anthrohistorical scholarship, to learn from it, to take it on its own terms, and to try to understand what those are. For it is not enough to say that memory is a process, or to acknowledge the belatedness of testimony. We must also tend to the patterns in *how* these processes work, and what their shaping influences, logics, and constraints are.

Like the imagined rulers of the totalitarian state of W, the architects of apartheid engineered brutality into every facet of South African society: its laws, landscape, discourse, social practice, educational system(s), and economy. In apartheid society, black people were systematically denied their individuality and subjectivity through an exhaustive array of legal, social, and economic structures: laws reifying their racial and ethnic identities, consignment to supposed "homelands," jobs that clothed them in anonymous uniforms and assigned them new names, a substandard educational system designed to produce subservient automatons, and the myriad rules of "petty apartheid" in which the conditions, context, and character of interpersonal interactions were dictated and delimited.

One of the bitterest ironies to be found in what was finally declared a crime against humanity[16] was the fact that apartheid ideology inverted expectations of black children and adults. Treated in so many ways as adults when they were actually children, black South Africans caught within the apartheid system were often only regarded as children after reaching adulthood.[17] This was reflected in a wide range of ways: from the ubiquitous terms of address ("boy" or "girl") to the clothing African men had to wear in prison (including short pants, otherwise worn only by white children). There is also a perduring preoccupation among many whites with "teaching" black people and disciplining them, typically the kind of concerns that adults have with children. Infantilized and coded as children, black adults were often unable to act as the authorities, guardians, and protectors of their own children as a result of their emasculation by the state.[18]

What and how we know about children's lives during this critical period of recent South African history is limited. Thus my efforts to research childhood in the late apartheid period involved constant confrontation with what was not available, what had been forgotten, what had not been recorded or understood, and what was simply beyond an empiricist ken. Methodologically I engaged in an archaeological process of trying to bring under scrutiny the found remains of late apartheid South African childhood. The initial phase of this process consisted of determining the densities around which childhood congealed. Through everyday interactions, archival research, formal and informal interviews, participation in national holiday and public events, volunteer work at nongovernmental organizations, and regular visits to museums, monuments, and memorials, I identified several fruitful areas of inquiry, to touch down on specific nodes or sites of meaning-making around which particular constructions of childhood may be tracked (Patterson 2009).

But my attempts to unravel the meaning of these constructions did not yield any sense of singular settledness and, as I discovered, could not be done in isolation. It seemed at times that the closer I got to my subject, the concept of childhood, the more it eluded me. Like a mirage, "childhood" seemed to be visible only when I looked at it peripherally, in relation to something else. I eventually came to realize that it is impossible to settle on one definition of childhood. Based on my research on apartheid South Africa, my understanding of childhood is one that resists such stabilization. Mine is not a project that seeks to determine the suitable age of responsibility in South Africa, nor is it one that merely aims to demonstrate that childhood is socially constructed.

Rather, inspired by Perec, I attempt to use the idea of gap to see deeper into the constructions of childhood that circulated at the end of apartheid by considering them in relation to one another. For a gap is also an opening. Just as it is the spaces *between* letters that make words and meaning, I have found that the spaces between knowing and not knowing, between certainty and uncertainty, and between memory and forgetting define the task of studying children and childhood. Arguably, such gaps not only suggest the challenges of such studies but, in themselves, produce children and childhood as rich objects of political engagement and political imagination.

Semantically, socially, and intellectually, "childhood" is fundamentally constructed in its meanings and usages. As a concept, childhood has a great deal of force. It is an especially emotive category often claimed as universal. It relies upon familiar narrative structures and often manages to evade the contradictions among them. The political, cultural, and social work of childhood lies in these conventions. The discourse of childhood is embedded in deep sentiments (particularly nostalgia), ideas of innocence and purity, and (Eurocentric, classist) assumptions about children spending most of their time playing. But childhood is also a space of struggle, contested by those both within and outside of it. That it can be used so powerfully without much definition, contextualization, or problematization becomes part of its capacity to do so much work. In contrast to the romanticized notions of the universality of childhood that cast children as transcending the need for narrative, they demand and deserve the same kind of textured, contextualized, and complex readings that adults are accorded in anthropological and historical analysis.

Violence shatters. It creates holes in people, families, and landscapes. Within universalist and human rights-based frameworks and evaluations of violence, one's degree of "childness" typically translates into presumed degrees of victimhood and extends the surface area of what counts as violence.[19] But the pervasive presence of various forms and threats of violence in the everyday lives of young people amplifies the instability and uncertainty of childhood in ways that push ambiguity into any naturalization of children as victims, for children have been seen to have extraordinary agency and responsibility. In the apartheid system and the forms of resistance that sought to destroy it, violence and childhood were both structurally and practically linked.

While violence, or the memory of violence, vexes and complicates constructions of childhood in South Africa, the frequent exposure to and participation of children in it confounds our understandings and explanations, particularly in terms of how violence should be evaluated, forcing open new questions about how to understand culpability, power, and intentionality, for instance, when *children* use violence.[20] Likewise, the unsettled nature of evaluations of pain and violence leaves questions of agency and responsibility open to additional reflection, revision, and debate. In the context of apartheid, these two highly unsettled and unstable constructs—childhood and violence—are inextricably entwined. The pervasiveness of violence in the late apartheid period disrupts the efforts to settle constructions of childhood in South Africa, both now and then. Each nurtures the complexities and possibilities of the other.

I have often been asked to reveal my definition of childhood, as if there is a clear-cut answer that I am withholding. But for an anthrohistorian, the question is one that I believe yields more by remaining open than any attempts on my part to settle it could provide.[21] In excavating the found remains of childhood from the broken grounds in which their constructions are embedded, I have attempted to trace their contours and track their mobilization and manipulation to consider not only what constructions of childhood may tell us about children in this particular cultural context and historical milieu but what these understandings reveal about the society from which they come. Tending carefully to the gaps in this pocked and perforated landscape is made uniquely possible using an anthrohistorical approach like the one I have demonstrated here. In attempting to investigate what dominant notions of childhood do for communities, states, and the global politic, I seek out the complex and often opaque ways in which such understandings resonate, travel, and transmute by shifting my focus between local, national, and international settings that are dynamically linked and engaged.

In my research, "the points of suspension on which the broken threads of childhood . . . are caught" consisted of a set of fragments and artifacts I gathered, more notable for what was missing than what I found (Perec 1988, preface). These remains point to overwhelming loss: young lives broken and impaired by trauma, malnutrition, lack of opportunity, and the premature imposition of the burdens of adulthood. Living lives meant to be bound by never-ending negation, "nonwhites" were treated as nonentities—foreigners in their own land, lacking freedom of movement, stability, privacy, security, and unfettered opportunities for fulfillment. But children in this period also possessed incredible resilience, ingenuity, resourcefulness, and creativity, all of which found expression in a variety of forms. Unfortunately, many of these expressions have not received adequate attention or engagement by the custodians of history either within or outside of academe. Constructions of childhood are powerful and have a tendency to blot out the complex subjectivities and experiences of children as dynamic social actors.

The power of these constructions derives from their familiarity, emotional potency, and reflection of social values. The gaps between and within these constructions mask the complex and varied roles and experiences of young people and reinforce their subalternity socially, politically, and within South African historiography. These gaps have also enabled a nation to look away from the reprehensible realities of then and now, even while purporting to hold them up for acknowledgment and examination. The Truth and Reconciliation Commission was ultimately unable to resolve the fundamental contradiction of acknowledging and celebrating both the contribution of young people in the struggle and the horror of what those contributions so often entailed. How could such horror ever be resolved? As Martha Minow has argued, because of the inherent brutality and scope of mass violence, "there is no punishment that could express the proper scale of outrage," there is no market measure that can put a value on "living an ordinary life," and no apology that is adequate for the harms inflicted (1998, 104–21).

At one time in South Africa's recent history, the instability of childhood was the liberation movement's greatest resource. The vitality, hope, and impatience of young people forced one of the most authoritarian regimes ever known to eventually relinquish their ill-gained monopoly on state governance and power. But these contributions, which could not have been given (or taken) with a full understanding of the consequences involved, have had devastating consequences for many who made them. There remains a tremendous gap between the promises of freedom articulated in South Africa's new Constitution and the poverty and suffering that continue to plague the majority of people in the "free" South Africa. There is also a gap in the renderings of young people and their contribution to this ambiguous phase of freedom and the complexity of their lived experiences, their internal struggles, and their ongoing hardship and lack of opportunity in the new South Africa.

The costs of compromise in negotiating the terms of a democratic South Africa have been high. Continuities across apartheid and the post-apartheid era abound. Apartheid is all around. It is inscribed on the landscape, manifest in the distribution of wealth and resources, reflected in life expectancy and infant mortality rates, and it endures in the social conditioning that continues to poison the way many white people look at, talk to, and think of black people. As political exile Mbulelo Mzamane once exclaimed, "Show me the corpse of the dead apartheid!"[22] Contemporary divisions in the new nation are not only between white and black, however. So too they live on in acts and attitudes of xenophobia. Paradoxically, the most enduring achievement and greatest failure of the apartheid system was in dividing people based on fear, hatred, greed, and bigotry. Deep divisions among all kinds of people still remain.

The former youth who fought for freedom and who today are unemployed and undereducated are often referred to as "the lost generation." The pathologizing defeatism of this appellation not only obscures the varied roles of the young in the struggle, it also occludes the historical and continuing contestation of these very categories. It is important to remember the very real stakes involved in these constructions. They are palpable and devastating, particularly to those for whom the least has changed. The vast majority of the children and youth of the antiapartheid era continue to live in extreme poverty.[23] Inequality pervades every space and every aspect of South African society.

If childhood is, as Perec suggests, "a horizon, a point of departure, a set of co-ordinates from which the axes of . . . life may draw their meaning" (1988, 24), what happens when people live in a world in which the terrain is marked by terrible voids, absences, gaps, and contradictory representations that can't be reassembled in some coherent sense of identity or purpose? What if the destination of childhood turns out to be a dead end, where all universalisms fail? Given the abject inequality that continues to plague South Africa today, it is vitally important to wrest away the concept of childhood from simplistic victim-based or celebrationist accounts that gloss over unsettled and unresolved tensions, and to lay bare the gaping holes in this story of nation-building. Only then will it be possible to engage in a more honest and effective consideration of the interconnections between race, violence, and childhood—and, of course, class—in the apartheid structures of the past and in their pernicious (re)incarnations today.

> *A roar: truth itself has appeared in the blizzard of metaphors.*
> ❧ PAUL CELAN 1967, *ATEMWENDE*

NOTES

1. Perec, *W or the Memory of Childhood* (1988, 12).
2. Raymond Queneau, as quoted in Perec 1988.
3. Raymond Queneau, as quoted in Perec 1988.
4. I stress the *theoretical* contributions of such comparison. I do not intend to equate the Holocaust and apartheid, or to rank experiences of mass suffering.
5. Including Italo Calvino, François Le Lionnais, Oskar Pastior, Raymond Queneau, and Jacques Roubaud.
6. Perec's declaration brings to mind Jorge Luis Borges's "The Library of Babel" (1964, 51–58).
7. The narrative pieces of W were submitted in their earliest form in 1969 as a serial to the French journal *La Quinzaine litteraire*.
8. For example, noting the number of his own spelling mistakes in a single name.
9. "The subject, the softness, the lighting of the whole scene are, for me, reminiscent of a painting, maybe a Rembrandt or maybe an invented one . . ." (14)
10. It is worth noting that Perec was undergoing psychoanalysis when he completed this manuscript.
11. Perec's quest to uncover more about his and his parents' past resonates with that found in George Sebald's novel *Austerlitz* (1992).
12. Like Martin Amis's *Time's Arrow* (1992), another unconventional work about the Holocaust that experiments with temporal frame and structure, it may be argued that Perec's *W* only makes sense in reverse.
13. This journey was actually his rescue through the Kindertransport.
14. In *The Texture of Memory,* James Young speaks to this notion by arguing that memorializing something can limit and even deaden public engagement with it (1993).

15. Jennifer Cole's work *Forget Colonialism? Sacrifice and the Art of Memory in Madagascar* (2001) suggests such an approach.

16. See United Nations General Assembly Resolution 1761, passed on November 6, 1962, and United Nations International Convention on the Suppression and Punishment of the Crime of Apartheid, November 30, 1973.

17. Apartheid laws offered little or no protection for children, even in regard to their detention in jails. Common law stipulated that only children younger than seven would not be held responsible for their criminal conduct. Even babies were not immune from the effects of incarceration. The systematic use of torture in South African jails and police stations during apartheid was extensive. Children and youth were frequently placed in jail cells with criminal inmates who were encouraged by security forces and police offers to assault them. The proliferation of gangs in the prison world often held dangerous consequences for the young in particular. Many youth suffered assaults, theft, stabbings, and rape while held in criminal cells. In particular see the section "Special Hearing on Children and Youth, Prisons, and Human Rights Violations Hearings" in volume 4 of The Truth and Reconciliation Commission of South Africa's Final Report (1998).

18. In 1960, the Children's Act, No. 33 reinforced the legality of incarcerating children when it included a police cell in its definition of "a place of safety." Children could be held in the more numerous and readily available police cells or in adult penal facilities, and in both places there was little difference between the treatment of adults and children. Solitary confinement, meal deprivation, and corporal punishment were used against detained children and allowed by law in cases involving viciousness or cruelty. The emotional, physical, and mental harm suffered by children detained in prisons and police cells was profound.

19. Assumed to draw force from individuals' innermost core of humanity, both violence and childhood have transcendent political and cultural authority, and yet they are inherently unstable, and engaged with sensibilities and undersdtandings that are individualized, and culturally and historically specific.

20. I explore these questions in my dissertation (Patterson 2009).

21. In addition, myriad practitioners, researchers, marketers, and lawmakers have established entire subfields, industries, and legal codes based upon various definitional notions of what childhood is or should be.

22. "Reimagining South Africa and the Political Imagination of South Africans," conference organized by African History graduate students at the University of Michigan, Ann Arbor, January 13, 2001.

23. I have focused here primarily on the ways that the vectors of violence and childhood come together in the case of black children, but there is much more that could be written about childhood constructions and their connection to particular forms of violence affecting white children during this period. Although apartheid accounted for a tremendously disproportionate amount of suffering among black or so-called nonwhite people, the inhumanity at its core diminished everyone within what has been aptly referred to as a sick society.

7 ❧ *Ilana Feldman*

Working in the In-between: Archives, Ethnography, and Research in Gaza

The June 1967 war, in the course of which Israel occupied the West Bank and Gaza Strip (along with the Sinai and the Golan Heights), had an immediate, dramatic, and obvious effect on Palestinian lives. It also had an immediate and dramatic—though perhaps less obvious to the casual observer—effect on the archives of Palestinian history. Explaining the state of United Nations records from its work in Gaza, one UN official described how records being stored in Jerusalem got caught up in war.

> Everything was going quite smoothly until the fighting started on the 5th of June 1967. I witnessed the destruction of some of the UNEF [United Nations Emergency Force] records. This was due to the fact that Government House came under heavy mortar and artillery fire. We built a barricade at the main entrance of Government House and some of the boxes were used to reinforce it. The door was blasted open and set afire and the boxes burned. Thus we will never really know what is missing.[1]

This account of archival destruction is preserved within the remaining (and still extensive) archives of UNEF. I encountered this description at a considerable remove from the event, both temporally and geographically. UNEF records are now stored in the UN archives in New York, and I spent some very pleasant weeks in 2006 working through these materials. My experience with UN records echoed many other experiences I have had in the course of conducting research on and in Gaza over a number of years.

Each of the many wars that have punctuated Palestinian history has introduced new disruptions in the archival sources of that history. Such loss is regularly noted in the often still rich and detailed archives that remain. In the course of my research I have encountered numerous records of archival destruction—of British Mandate files, of Egyptian Administration records, of personal papers. Similarly, conversations with people about mundane aspects of their lives regularly circle back to dramatic moments of dispossession and displacement. Gaza—and Palestine more generally—is certainly not unique in having a history of violence and conflict that presses in on nearly every aspect of life, and therefore of research. My work has without doubt been impacted by the history and persistence of conflict in Palestine, but I have also sought to explore other facets of the Palestinian experience.

Indeed, even as my work has been directly impacted by the dramatic events in Palestinian history, these events have not been the primary subject of my research, which has rather been about the quotidian bureaucratic mechanisms through which Gaza was governed. My interest is in "life and government in the in-between" (Feldman 2008)—in the daily work of governing and the space for living that continues even in places marked by turmoil and conflict. What I did not know when I was in the field in 1998 and 1999 was that my work was made possible by this same kind of in-between moment. Considering the periods of the British Mandate (1917–48) and the Egyptian Administration (1948–67), I focused on low-level civil servants—Palestinian employees of "foreign" governments—to understand how bureaucratic authority was produced and challenged and how the dynamics of service provision helped shape the place and people of Gaza.

Even as my focus was on bureaucratic practice rather than exemplary events, one of the problems for government work in Gaza has always been that events continually impede and redirect this work. The ways that the history of successive and rapid regime change has helped shape the place, its people, and its government are evident almost anywhere one turns in Gaza. The makeup of the population itself—two-thirds refugee—is a direct result of the 1948 war over Palestine and the displacement of much of the Palestinian population. The very shape, size, and even name of the territory are a result of this same war. Walking around Gaza City, one sees buildings that have been in successive turns prisons, schools, and administrative offices. The laws that govern the place are an amalgam of amendments enacted by British, Egyptian, Israeli, and Palestinian bodies on an existing Ottoman framework. When I was doing fieldwork in Gaza, one of the difficult issues facing the Civil Service Commission of the new Palestinian National Authority was how to bring the different civil service regulations in the West Bank and Gaza—reflective of their different governmental histories—into agreement.

Conversations with retired civil servants revealed a persistent tension between the goal of regularity in their work and the often exceptional conditions under which that work was conducted. In the course of my research, I spent a lot of time at the Retired Civil Servants Association. The old men who gathered here, whether the association officers for whom work here had replaced work in a government office (there is mandatory retirement at age sixty, and there are plenty of people who still want to work when they leave government service) or the members who came by for coffee, conversation, and complaint, had a lot to say about Gaza's various governmental moments. Conversation often shifted rapidly among complaints about corruption in the Palestinian Authority, to recollections of Israeli occupation policy, to debates about the impact of the British Mandate.

The research I conducted during the uneasy quiet of the Oslo years was at one remove from the histories I encountered in archives and conversation. My work on Gaza in the years since has been at a different—and more discomforting—remove. In recent years, my work has necessarily been more "on" than "in" Gaza, as circumstances have made getting in quite difficult. In today's conditions the extended research I conducted in the late 1990s would be impossible to undertake. My work took me all around the Gaza Strip, from Gaza to the West Bank, and from the West Bank into the western, Israeli part of Jerusalem. Palestinians could not move the way I did, but the lull in overt conflict made my research trajectories possible. This period proved to be the waning days of the Oslo Accords (agreements signed in 1993 that led to the creation of the Palestinian National Authority [PNA] and the pullback of Israeli troops from Palestinian population centers). People talked a lot about the possibility of another uprising, but frustration—with what was perceived as Israeli intransigence and PNA corruption—had not yet been transformed into revolt.

The second *intifada* broke out in September 2000, not long after I completed my research. In addition to an enormous increase in violence (on all sides) this intifada resulted in dramatic new restrictions on Palestinian movement. Not only did the Green Line—the boundary between the Occupied Territories and Israel—become more impermeable, travel between Palestinian towns in the territories has been severely curtailed by checkpoints, bulldozed roads, and other militarily enforced restrictions. By the time I returned to Palestine for follow-up research, Gaza was essentially closed—foreigners working for NGOs or as journalists now need to be on an approved list to enter. As I have sought to continue to deepen my understanding of Gaza's history, I am acutely aware of how little firsthand knowledge I have of the tremendous difficulties of its present.

The past and present are regularly in tension in Palestine (and the future too often seems unavailable), and one necessarily feels this tension when working here. The imperative to report on the immediate can feel very strong. And, given the difficult, and increasingly desperate, conditions in which many people live, it is not entirely misplaced. Nonetheless, there are other imperatives that remain important as well, and one of the challenges facing scholars of the Palestinian condition is to keep those imperatives in mind. Scholars have a responsibility both to recall that things have been and can be other than they are now and to explore the connective threads in practices and policies that may appear radically new. The Palestinian experience poses challenges to both of these demands. Daily living under occupation requires that people constantly adjust to a new normal—to new roads they cannot drive on, new places they cannot go, new restrictions in almost every aspect of their lives. As someone who comes and goes, I am regularly stunned by the developments in my absence—a wall snaking across the landscape, a checkpoint where there used to be open road, an elaborate border crossing where there used to be a checkpoint—and am nearly equally amazed by how quickly (though certainly not happily) people have altered their daily rhythms to manage in these new conditions. While people need to adjust in order to live, researchers are obliged to account for the trajectories of politics and power that produce these new circumstances. They need also track the older techniques and mechanisms of control that are often utilized in new forms (whether from the British period or from the military government of Israel's Palestinian citizens).

In the brief space I have here, I want to explore the particular challenges of working on and in spaces in-between dramatic outbreaks of violence. I consider the tracks of such violence through archives and people's imaginaries as well as the particular challenges that emerge in working one's way through this complicated terrain. Conditions of research—the materials preserved or destroyed, the ease or difficulty of access, the silences and the revelations—speak as directly as do the fruits of this work to the politics and histories of the places scholars investigate. Research site and subject cannot be imagined as separate from research space and method. Making sense of their relation requires precisely a consideration of "the in-between": in-between event and habitual practice; in-between life as lived and life as recorded and recalled; in-between destruction and accumulation.

Archives and the Politics of History

My time in Gaza was not an experience of fieldwork under fire (Nordstrom and Robben 1995), but I was researching a place that has often experienced such conditions and whose archival and ethnographic record bears clear marks of such a history. Not being part of a nation-state, Gaza has no national archives. Being a frequent site of war and conflict, documents "belonging" to one state are often in the hands of another (Israel seized and holds both British and Egyptian records). In the wars that accompanied the many changes in rule over this place, many documents were lost or deliberately destroyed. Assembling an archive of Gaza's history required, therefore, pulling together the disparate records of different offices, individuals, and archives as well as engaging with several different states and their institutions (including Egypt, Israel, Great Britain, and the Palestinian Authority).

My work explores, and relies upon, many different types of files—personnel, police, administrative correspondence, *waqf* (Islamic endowment), municipal council, association, and report files—all of which have particular conditions of production and retention. Anyone who has spent any time chasing after archival materials will certainly be cognizant of the importance of serendipity to the success of this endeavor. My own experience is no different. Whether the boxes of records from the Gaza administration that appeared lost in *Dar Al-Watha'iq* (the Egyptian national archives) on one visit, only to reappear the next time I tried, or the Egyptian records held under uncertain classification in the Israeli archives to which I was granted access, gathering materials required a certain amount of luck and a great deal of stubbornness.

The dramatic conditions of Gaza's archive illuminate a more extreme instance of the power relations evident in all archival production. The violence that has accompanied the shifts in regime and status—taking place always through war and in chaos—has meant that the documents of its history have followed particularly troubled paths. While no system of archiving documents, however comprehensive in its regulations, is ever perfectly actualized, in the Gazan case many documents have been preserved without being archived. That is, they were kept, but not according to the procedures for preservation that had been defined for them. Or, in other cases, documents have been preserved that might not have qualified as archive-worthy at all within their systems of production. At the same time, many records that did have a place in the archives were lost or destroyed in the wars over Gaza and their aftermaths.

Even with this difficult history, records of Gaza's history do exist and were available to me. In many ways Gaza's uncertain political status sometimes made research easier. The departure of Israeli occupation forces from administrative functions, and their replacement by a still-in-formation Palestinian Authority, made those records that are held by government offices in Gaza relatively more available. In the absence of an overarching policy or procedure for determining access to government files, my ability to research files of different offices was dependent on the determination of the head of each bureau. Much of my early research time in Gaza was spent going from one ministry to another inquiring about whether they had any "old documents." I had greatest success in offices where the records were still in active use (personnel files in the pensions administration, land sale registries in the housing ministry)—where they remained "files," and had not been fully transformed into "archives." In these places I was frequently granted broad (though not entirely unrestricted) access.

One of the things I explored in my research was precisely the relation between files and archives, and the process through which government files are transformed into historical archives. As the considerable body of work on archives has clearly shown, their production always involves mechanisms of exclusion, even in conditions far less fraught than those in Palestine (Trouillot 1995; De Certeau 1988b; Stoler 2009). Archival conventions permit entry to only certain materials, according to criteria that may not reflect the active life of the files and that can reshape the import of documents. In order for files to become archives, they need to be extracted from their original working networks. As I argue in my work, it is precisely these kinds of networks that lend authority to government documents, and in this regard archiving has to be seen as an act of disempowerment of these files. To be sure, they are re-placed within another network of documents, and thus accrue new kinds of authority, but this authority is not the same as governing authority.

The archives of the British Mandate include many documents that describe the procedures of archival storage and culling—both in the calmer times and in the increasing chaos that preceded the end of British rule in Palestine. In these final days clerks worked overtime to try to copy significant records—such as land registries—to be able to both retain the files and to leave a copy for the "successor regime." To the last, Mandate

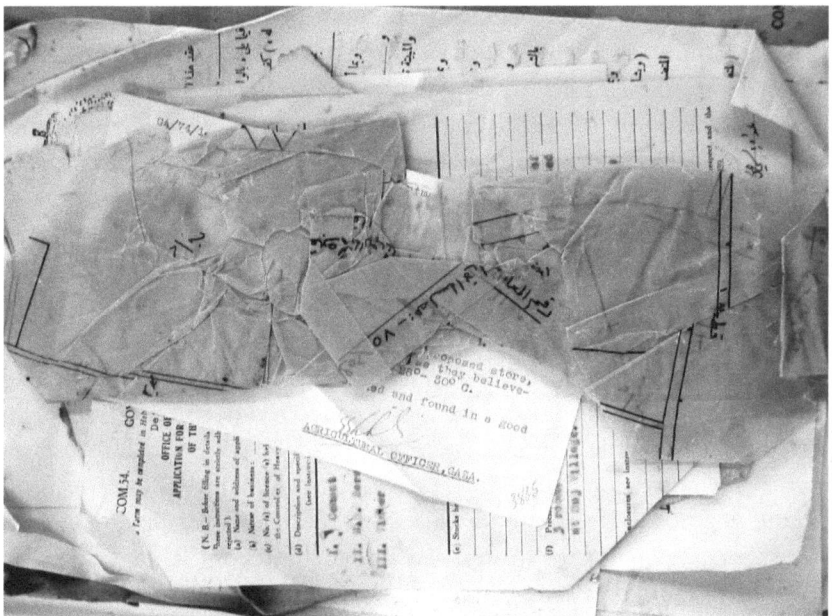

FIG. 7.1. Gaza records removed to Israel (1967). Photo by Ilana Feldman.

officials tried to manage an orderly procedure of archival production and transfer, but they were not wholly successful. The records of the Palestine government that are currently housed in the Israel State Archives were not, it seems, supposed to be left behind at the end of the Mandate. Apparently, the documents were prepared for shipping back to Britain, but in the chaos that accompanied the departure something went wrong and they never made it there. Most of the materials were lost, and those that were found were preserved in the archives of the new Israeli state (Alsberg 1991). Even if these records did not end where they were supposed to, they do look like regular archives. They are indexed according to meaningful criteria and are relatively straightforward to work with.

The records of the Egyptian Administration in Gaza are much less simple. Many of these files are also housed in the Israeli archives—taken when Israel occupied Gaza, first in 1956 and then in 1967. These records were seized in the middle of their active lives—they were fully "files," unlike the Mandate records, which were already on their way to being archives. Among these records there is, for instance, a town planning directorate registry book whose entries stop abruptly (and in the middle of the page) on October 31, 1956—just before Gaza was occupied by Israeli forces. Had they been able to follow a regular archival trajectory, many of these documents would no doubt have been culled from the records. That they were not makes this collection an extremely rich source for historical research, but this unusual path also means that they are not as readily accessible as other archival materials. The collection seems to have been kept in its entirety by the ISA. It has not, however, been catalogued, organized, or, as it turns out, formally declassified. When I began my research these records had an ambiguous status, and I was given access to a considerable portion of them (not materials deemed to be politically sensitive). When another researcher's interest in the Jordanian equivalent of the Egyptian papers raised concern, a decision was made to shut these files until such time as someone with both Arabic skills and security clearance could examine each document and make a decision about whether to declassify it. This seems unlikely to happen any time soon. Fortunately for my work, I was able to photocopy large portions of these files before they were closed, thus contributing to a further archival wrinkle in the life of these papers.

Even as Gaza's archival trajectories track the Palestinian experience in violence and conflict, the documents in these archives illuminate other aspects of this history. The files show the mundane work of government proceeding under difficult conditions, the efforts of ordinary civil servants to do their jobs and be recognized for their efforts, and the continued desire of Palestinians for features of life that would appear normal in many places—comfortable housing, adequate services, and the opportunity to live their lives as they pleased. The files show as well that not only did events impact governmental practice, this practice sometimes influenced events—providing mechanisms for managing political crises, shaping social relations, and defining the space of Gaza.

In-between Ethnography

It is not only archives that record the history of documentary loss and fragmentation. In my conversations with retired civil servants in Gaza we often talked about what was gone and what had been kept. People told me about destroying documents when Israel occupied the Gaza Strip, fearful of what might be done with the information they contained. People also told me—and showed me—how they had saved records of their lives prior to their dispossession in 1948. People showed me land deeds, identity documents, and an assortment of other papers that were not only mementos of their past lives but material evidence of their claims to land and home. Even when I talked with people about fairly mundane aspects of their civil service jobs, these records and rememberings of loss regularly entered the conversation.

Not every loss leaves such a clear trace, however, and not every memory is recounted. Working through this field is one of the inevitable challenges of ethnographic research about the past. Indeed, such research by definition occupies an in-between space. When you research the past you talk with people in the here-and-now about the there-and-then, and keeping the temporalities at play in any given conversation straight can be challenging. In the case of my research on bureaucratic practice, the critiques that people rendered of existing governing arrangements (the Palestinian Authority in this case) through their descriptions of past regimes are perhaps the most persistent example of this layered temporal concern. Working through such conversations involves coming to recognize that there is no single time that provides the correct interpretative frame for them. These conversations take place, as it were, in-between time.

Because of this complexity, I have thought a lot about how to describe my research conversations. The most self-evident label for conversations about the past—oral history—does not seem adequate in this case. For instance, we weren't talking only about the past (though one never is) but quite explicitly about people's current evaluations of what government could and should be—evaluations honed over a life's experience with multiple regimes. As much as I wanted to understand what people did in their jobs, what challenges they faced, what benefits derived, I also was trying to gain a better sense of what it meant to people to be a civil servant. I was interested, that is, in both memory and judgment—and these were clearly intertwined. Memory is always a process, not an inert fact (Stoler and Strassler 2000; Amin 1995; Swedenburg 1995).

If this is true of any ethnographic exploration of the past, as I think it is, in the case of my particular research in Palestine one has to confront the additional factor of being in the in-between of violent conflict. What is at stake here is not simply that I did my research during a lull in violence that made my work possible (though this is obviously a crucial issue) but that everyday bureaucratic practice creates such an in-between space even in the midst of violence. Though it is certainly possible for violence to overwhelm this work, and sometimes it does, more often bureaucracy persists in the face of extraordinary events (Feldman 2005). This other aspect of the in-between also helped make my research possible, but in a somewhat different way than the political quiet that let me travel everywhere I needed to go. It was in part due to the persistence of bureaucracy (which itself became a focus of my analysis; see Feldman 2008) that people were interested in engaging with me and my questions.

As I began my research in Gaza, I had not been entirely sure how my project would be received by people. I was not so much worried that people would be hesitant to speak with me; Palestinians are generally eager to tell their stories to anyone who will listen and who may be able to transmit those stories to a wider audience. It was in fact the Palestinian awareness of the importance of the circulation of knowledge about their suffering that made me wonder whether they would find my project—which did not focus on the national struggle or the Israeli occupation—irrelevant to their concerns. What I found was that the retirees with whom I spent much of my research time were by and large delighted that someone was interested in hearing about their work—work which generally meant a great deal to them—and were quite willing to share their insights with me. They thought their work had enduring importance—despite the many changes in regime and the ongoing absence of a Palestinian nation-state—and they were eager to share their thoughts on this importance. Understanding the civil service persona meant exploring the habits of both thought and action that shaped this position. As became abundantly clear to me in talking with people, these habits did not become irrelevant when civil servants retired from their jobs—nor, in fact, did habit formation cease. As I came to see it, my conversations with people were part of the continued, and continual, production of civil service habits (Feldman 2008).

However much bureaucratic practice occupies an in-between space, and however much conversations about the past equally occupy an in-between time, neither is *out* of place or time. One of the ways that both time and place became evident in my conversations with elderly Gazans was in the gaps, silences, and elisions that sometimes occurred. Sometimes people expressed concern about whether their words would be reported in the press (which I assured them they would not be), reflecting anxiety about the possible response by Palestinian Authority security services to public criticism of this government. The particular place and time of my research created distinct areas of concern.

Other arenas of reluctance were connected to complex social phenomena, phenomena that were also linked to the place of Gaza. I was interested in understanding more clearly the relationship between native Gazans and the refugees that make up two-thirds of Gaza's population. Although I heard and saw enough to make it clear that there was a degree of tension between these groups, many people were unwilling to say very much about this issue and many insisted that there were no problems. I think this reluctance stemmed from both the centrality of the refugee issue to Palestinian politics—and to the sense of the Palestinian national identity—and a desire not to call attention to social distinctions within the population. Of course, my understanding both that there were such distinctions and of the reasons why they might be downplayed itself developed through the accumulation of conversation and archival detail over the course of my research. In this particular case, the awareness I acquired around this issue and the many questions that remained led me to new research on the Palestinian experience with humanitarianism in the years since 1948, research that has helped me better understand these dynamics (Feldman 2007a, 2007b).

Conclusion

I want to conclude by reflecting further on the analytic value of the "in-between," as well as its tenuous and therefore challenging status. At a very practical level, it was the possibility of such a space that made my research possible—both my movement through the field and the accumulation of archival records that enabled me to explore the past. In my work I have always sought to participate in creating ways of understanding the Palestinian experience that are not wholly dominated by the "Palestinian-Israeli conflict." And, indeed, my research has highlighted a broader palette of Gazan experience. People worried about doing their jobs well, they worried about raising their families, and they certainly worried about how political conditions impacted their ability to do these things. At the same time, both ethnographic and archival research show how often and with what significant effect this in-between space is intruded upon by dramatic events and upheavals. These events need to be recognized not simply as intrusions into bureaucratic procedure or archival management, but as crucial to shaping and redirecting these spaces and life around them.

In January 2009 Gazans experienced another dramatic intrusion into their everyday lives. Already suffering enormously from an economic blockade of the territory Israel imposed in the wake first of the Hamas victory in Palestinian parliamentary elections in January 2006 and escalated after the kidnapping of an Israeli soldier in June of that same year, Gaza was devastated by three weeks of Israeli aerial bombings and ground attacks. In the aftermath of this assault—called Operation Cast Lead by the Israeli military—Gaza entered a new, peculiar, in-between. While destruction ceased, Israeli restrictions on the entry of goods into Gaza meant that little reconstruction was possible. It was not until July 2009 that the UN began a project to clear away the rubble from January's bombings.

In 2009 Gazans grappled with many of the same challenges I explored for an earlier historical period—how to house, feed, and care for a population whose lives have been upended by war. The recent in-between conditions mean that the overt violence of destruction has, for the moment, been replaced by a discourse of humanitarian concern and bureaucratic regulation of the boundaries of that concern (Feldman 2009). Israeli officials maintain that the government "helps fully on the humanitarian issue. Thereafter it is a redline" (*New York Times,* January 25, 2009). What constitutes humanitarian assistance is a matter of some dispute and is subject to both policy and bureaucratic decision making. The cement needed to rebuild is deemed to be beyond this line, but so too, for a moment, was pasta.[2] Decisions about resources across the spectrum of human needs become part of Israel's strategy in dealing with Gaza. Understanding both the dramatic and the mundane is vital for making sense of this situation and for comprehending the broader Palestinian experience in the twentieth and into the twenty-first century. The sometimes fleeting spaces in-between provide one means of entry into this understanding.

> *Transdisciplinarity goes beyond the dualism of opposing binary pairs: subject/object, subjectivity/objectivity, matter/consciousness, nature/divine, simplicity/complexity, reductionism/holism, diversity/unity which have marked the history of ideas for millennia.... Because transdisciplinarity is radical, in the sense that it goes to the roots of knowledge, and questions our way of thinking and our construction and organization of knowledge. It requires a discipline of self-inquiry that integrates the knower in the process of knowing.*
> ❧ MONTOURI 2008, xii, xvi

NOTES

1. UN S/0378/0034, File 1, "The Historical Background of the Records of the United Nations Emergency Force, 1956–1967," J. Belwood, Chief of Registry, UNTSO, April 22, 1968.

2. When Senator John Kerry visited Gaza in February 2009, he learned that Israel was prohibiting the entry of pasta into the Strip. As reported in *Ha'aretz* "he was told by United Nations aid officials that 'Israel does not define pasta as part of humanitarian aid—only rice shipments" (February 25, 2009). With Kerry's intercession, Israel changed its policy.

8 ❧ Deirdre de la Cruz

The Past and Present of the Future Perfect in Anthropology and History

Anthropology has taken a keen interest in futurity as of late. Ethnographies have cropped up within the last five years covering all manner of domains and phenomena to which some sense of the future is deemed constitutive: economies of speculation; philosophies and practices of hope; and of course, the time-to-come entailed by the religious messianic (which, in this emergent milieu of inquiry, has taken on an almost familiarly cozy quality). *American Ethnologist,* one of the most important journals of the discipline, dedicated an entire issue to discussing a single article by Jane Guyer, entitled "Prophesy and the near future: Thoughts of macroeconomic, evangelical, and punctuated time" (2007, 409–21). If this issue of *AE* is any indication of ascendant trends, this moment in ethnographic production seems to be one that is drawing some attention away from histories of the present to its futures.

Not that the future has been solely the province of anthropology, however, for historians too have sometimes been concerned with the futures envisioned by a given past.[1] It is the aim of this essay, however, to focus in on a particular modality that has been employed in past endeavors to merge the fields of anthropology and history: neither futures of the present nor futures of the past, but pasts that anticipated something of their own futures, and thus possibly our present.

Let me begin with a historical ethnography whose architectonic form as much as historical content reveals this temporal logic. Writing about the convergence of eighteenth-century manuscripts that document a newly formalized royal ritual (or more precisely, "ritual" as a new royal form), on one hand, and a colonial interest in the "traditional" culture that these texts would appear to authenticate, on the other, John Pemberton, in *On the Subject of "Java,"* argues:

> The "Java" of [Dutch] Javanology's disciplinary gaze had already been constructed in just the fashion that would render it naturally recognizable as

an object of cross-cultural, cross-lingual desire. That is, the subject of "Java" retraced here through palace manuscripts (of the late eighteenth century on), seems to have *anticipated*—to have predated and, perhaps, *looked forward to*—formal Javanological attention. Thus, although "Java" was very much a working construct of modern Javanological discourse (as Tsuchiya demonstrates), it nevertheless foreshadowed that work by supplying Javanologists a subject ideally fit for analysis, a subject *already* constituted discursively in Javanese. (1994, 104)²

Here *anticipation* is neither a strictly prophetic condition nor simply a vague orientation toward the future but performed as a prefiguration (or "foreshadow," in Pemberton's words) of a future moment, in this case, the future production of colonial, disciplinary knowledge. The analytical purchase for Pemberton in employing this anticipatory mode—especially relevant for the joint project of anthropology and history and one of its enduring occupations—is that of circumventing an easy dichotomy of colonial epistemologies from without and colonized retention of "culture" within, of constructivism versus essentialism, as well as that of discontinuity versus continuity. Less immediately evident, however, is the underlying logic that makes such a claim of anticipation possible: that of apprehending the significance of a past (text, event, etc.) via a retrospective reading of its future recalling, in other words, only from the perspective of the future perfect, or *what will have been.*

This is a temporality that some of us who work at the intersections of anthropology and history occupy, whether we give heed to it or not. And it is more common, I think, than Pemberton's somewhat unique materials and meticulously laid-out argument might suggest. This essay strives to draw attention, by way of example or citation, to this tense of the future perfect, or more broadly, to the state of *anticipation*, as it has frequented our sites of study, work, and materials. Part of this reflection shall be discussion or reference to the various theoretical and philosophical strains that I understand as being relevant or having inspired this mode of thinking about time in the joint fields of anthropology and history. The essay will then address what I see to be the implications of this often vexing conceptualization of time, in the spirit of thinking what is to come for our field, and

I know of one Greek labyrinth which is a single straight line. Along that line so many philosophers have lost themselves that a mere detective might well do so, too.
&. JORGE LUIS BORGES 1962a, 141

for the task that pursues—from the future—our research always, that is, writing.

Futures Closed: Technology and Exhibition

Perhaps nothing imbues in us a more acute sense of anticipation, and specifically, of what will have come to pass, than those artifacts produced by technologies of mechanical reproduction. Entailed in every act of representation and documentation—not accidentally known also as "capture"—produced by a photograph, a reel of film, or a sound recording is the future of a present that will have no longer been. Roland Barthes's (1981) famous meditation on the photograph of the downright beatific-looking Lewis Payne right before his execution—*he is dead and he is going to die*—starkly summarizes this confounding reality, one that inheres in every object recorded and reproduced by mechanical means. In the history of anthropology and ethnographic method, this paradox of posterity and vanishing has motivated, albeit at times to abominable consequence (see Rony 1996), the enthusiastic employment of such technologies, put to the service of archiving cultural practices deemed destined to extinction.

But the tense of the future perfect (sometimes called future anterior) particular to these technologies and the modes of perception that they transform is quite different from that which Pemberton, for example, describes in his analysis of Javanese texts. It is not that of a speculative self-fashioning that anticipates (without wholly predicting) its future historical significance, but the collapse of time altogether, a mode of thinking about time that in fact evacuates history, rather than shore up the productively disruptive power of prefiguration. True enough, when Barthes associates the photograph with *flatness* he is not merely speaking of the physical properties of the object itself, but of the experience of time that the photograph provokes, and with that, the instantaneous transformation of Death from that which is buoyed by a plenitude of reference (symbolic, transcendent, affective) to a "platitude" of hollowness.

> The horror is this: nothing to say about the death of one whom I love most, nothing to say about her photograph, which I contemplate without ever being able to get to the heart of it, to transform it. The only "thought" I can have is that at the end of this first death, my own death is inscribed; between the two, nothing more than waiting; I have no other resource than this *irony:* to speak of the "nothing to say." (Barthes 1981, 92–93)

This irony about which Barthes speaks (where all that exists to be said is that there is nothing to say) may call to mind the hyperreality of the self-referential sign that emblematized postmodernism. In the postmodern condition, its best-known interpreters tell us, what self-referentiality is to the sign the future perfect is to the temporal: "Not modernism at its end but at its nascent [yet constant] state" (Lyotard 1984); the "blockage ... crisis or paralysis" of historicity (Jameson 1991); time-space compression (Harvey 1990); and so forth, the past and future but introjections of a present that exists without any real historical consciousness.

In the collaborative project of anthropology and history, this critique of the ahistorical as generated by new technologies of seeing and depiction found some of its best material in the representational genre of the *exhibition*. From Egypt in Paris of the 1880s (Mitchell 1988), to the Philippines in St. Louis in 1904 (Kramer 2006), to again, "Beautiful Indonesia" of the late twentieth century (Pemberton 1994), the exhibition itself became an object upon which the imbricated methods of reading at once historically and ethnographically could productively turn its scrutiny. Though occurring within, in fact, different historical periods, and analyzed to different critical ends (in the works I've cited above, colonialism and discipline; imperialism and race; postcolonial regimes and their recuperation of "culture"), the *exhibit* exemplified for many contemporary scholars a common politics of "picturing" that, precisely for flattening out history and culture into an order of representability, provided a site of inquiry rich for examining the production of historical and cultural difference, and power.

Just because *flat* may be the ontology of reproductions and representations generated by modernity's technological regimes, however, does not mean, of course, that these regimes themselves are not historical. Most recently, students of anthropology and history have turned to explore exactly this tension between the profoundly historical shifts in what Friedrich Kittler has coined "discourse networks"[3] and the subjects and objects to which these shifts give rise, subjects and objects whose influence and domination in a given social and political context stem precisely from the assertion of their naturalness (see Mitchell 2009), in other words, from the disavowal of their own historicity. Here a logic of *anticipation* serves to document the subtle workings of *emergence*, drawing attention to the structures of feeling (Williams 1977) or visibility (Sakai 1997, 73) that prepare a society or community to be receptive to that which has not yet come fully into being or prominence. By attenuating the "new," furthermore, the logic of *anticipation* (or foreshadow, prefiguration, "opening a space for," "making available to be taken up"—there are indeed many ways to express this) may present a potent critique of the conception of modernity that presumes a radical break with that which preceded it, that asserts even the very distinction between continuity and discontinuity as abstractions that permeate consciousness (Lefebvre 1995). *Anticipation* challenges modernity's representational and totalizing claims—including those instantiated by technologies of depiction—by casting off the belief that the present is the best or only vantage point for the production of knowledge.

Futures Open: Writing and Reciprocity

Despite some scholars' recent turn to the future as a fruitful domain of inquiry, there has been little active reflection overall among anthropologists and historians on the future as a historical tense that deeply structures our own research, analysis, production, and pedagogy. I say *active* because we are certainly aware of the future at all times; it is perhaps the most palpable tense for us, as well as the most anxiety inducing, appearing as it often does as a field of deadlines, expectations, hurdles, and so on. But rarely, I think, do anthrohistorians or historical anthropologists situate our work in relation to the future as much as we do, practically by second nature, to the past. We examine the genealogies of our intellectual thought and study the historical trajectories of our disciplines. We choose our research topics in history, often, because we think they will illuminate our present circumstances. We turn reflexively to critically assess the production of the past and the timeliness of certain historical imaginaries. In short, we produce our work in reciprocal engagement with the past.

So what would it mean to write in reciprocal engagement with the future? I do not mean prognostication (indeed, the pursuit of some social sciences). Nor am I speaking of a drive for posterity (for certain, the disenchanted motivation of some). For these future-oriented modes and motivations of scholarly production are primarily invested in *governing* what is to come, rather than in allowing the radical indeterminacy—the foreignness—of the future to engage and affect the present. What I am suggesting here is that we enlist anew a theory whose ideas about reciprocity have been foundational to anthropology and of great use to thinking through various histories of exchange and economy, but have yet to be deployed in thinking about the temporal dynamics of anthrohistorical production: that of the *gift*.[4] We might sum up the contribution of the theory of the gift as follows: while all writing is writing for the future, to write as gift is to write from a place of obligation—without calculation of return. It is to write in ethical address to a desired future, knowing that what may be heard is little more than speculative noise.[5] It is to write with deep consideration for a future reader—for forging a social bond of sorts—but in submission to the fantasy of pure gift as that which does not seek acknowledgment of receipt. We all write because we fancy we have something to say, a story, ours or someone else's to tell. But writing as gift means to write precisely because something has yet to be said—always. This remainder is constitutive, perpetual, propulsive, for to write in the spirit of the gift is to write about becoming. This gerund we might think of as the future's gift to us, and writing is how we reciprocate. Ad infinitum.

This is not meant to be as cryptic as it may sound. In fact, we participate in this cycle of exchange all the time, most intensely at the other end of the circuit, as readers of literature. Here the horizon of a fine work only ever recedes, and the literal closure of a story is an open invitation to read anew. Here the future perfect is goading in nature, holding out the promise of what will have been learned for what I am in the process of discovering (for the first time, in this second, third, sixth, etc., reading).[6] Here too, finally, is one of the greatest sources of pedagogical enthusiasm and reward. Neither rational forecast nor prophesy, then, the anticipatory relationship our writing might have to the future would be one that is defined by an adherence to its poetic possibilities; to being consciously, perhaps even heretically, antidefinitive in scope.

The Future (Other than) Perfect

In the introduction to a marvelous historical ethnography by Amanda J. Weidman, several dimensions of anticipation and futurity I have briefly outlined here are instructively articulated. Weidman's work on the historical emergence of Karnatic music as emblematic of South Indian "classical" culture exemplarily addresses several sets of concerns and topics that have occupied scholars of anthropology and history for years: colonialism and empire, subjectivity and agency, nationalism, gender, and the politics of cultural production. At the same time, it is a study that signals where the history of anthropology and history, at its best, may lead us, for *Singing the Classical, Voicing the Modern* heeds and extends the interdisciplinary imperative by opening itself up to more than just these two fields, engaging musicological theory and media studies, among others. Weidman herself is a "classically" trained violinist, both in the Western and Karnatic traditions, and thus her involvement with music teachers and practitioners in Madras, under the dual commitment of developing her personal practice and gathering material for her scholarship, serves at once to validate her musical mastery of a genre and call into question the very basis of her specialization. She had not yet realized this at the beginning of her musical apprenticeship, however, as she willingly confesses at the start of the book.

> In the fall of 1994 I found myself in the dubious position of auditioning, unsuspectingly, before a music teacher who was determined not to take me as a student. As a student of South Indian classical music, I had sought out this particular teacher after hearing about the extraordinary qualities of her violin playing. I had announced my desire to study with her in a letter, which preceded my arrival in Madras by a few weeks. Since she was retired from her job as a staff artist at All India Radio, I assumed she would probably have time to spend with me, and I looked forward to apprenticing myself to her in the kind of disciple-guru relationship that is considered crucial to the education of any student of Indian classical music. I felt that once I had inserted myself into such a relationship, I would really have "arrived." (2006, 1)

Her expectations registered in a confident future conditional ("I would really have 'arrived'"), Weidman realizes over several years of her apprenticeship with this guru that she would never really get to where she had thought, that is, to a level of inheriting a specific cultural tradition. This is not to say that she did not "arrive" elsewhere, however, an "elsewhere" furthermore brought to her in a photograph.

> In the spring of 1998 a reporter for a Madras newspaper interviewed us [she and her guru] for a feature story. When he asked how long she had been teaching me, instead of answering the questions, she said, "This is not teaching. This is gurukulavasam" (a mode of teaching and learning in which the disciple lives with the guru for years while the guru imparts musical knowledge). We posed for a photo that was supposed to capture us in the act of gurukulavasam, sitting on a mat with our violins, each facing stiffly outward toward the camera.

I realize now that at that moment I *had* arrived, if not at what I had imagined the authentic role of the disciple to be, then at one of the central oppositions through which Indian classical music, at the beginning of the twenty-first century, has come to be defined. (3)

Here a politics of futurity is terrifically rendered in the flat surface of a photograph: the image appearing to deliver precisely that which Weidman had, at the beginning of her journey as apprentice, desired. But her critical eye refuses to accept the photo as a fulfillment of a future once sought out and foretold by her own expectations, seeing it instead as a startling slice of a history much greater than that of her musical biography, one that nevertheless deeply informs it.

Weidman's frank admission points to what is at stake in thinking about the future at the intersections of anthropology and history. Hers is a common, even favorite, ethnographic confession: this is what I expected . . . yet this is what I found. But it uniquely illustrates the tension among the modes of anticipatory thinking and their relation to the past that I have only very briefly sketched out here. For, at the point of retrospection demanded by her act of writing, two visions appear. She may see the unfolding of her future expectation as no less than perfect—a fulfillment and indication of her true progress, the photograph representing the culmination of skill and giving credit for years of hard-earned knowledge. Or, she may see, in a flash that redeems the photograph from its flat authority and produces an uncanny encounter with the past, herself as historical subject. She pursues the latter, a future other than perfect, and "arrives" still, but strangely, literally, at the beginning, of a history that the chapters yet to be read will tell.

NOTES

1. See, for example, the highly influential work of Reinhart Koselleck, *Futures Past: On the Semantics of Historical Time* (2004 [1979]).
2. First two emphases mine.
3. Kittler defines *discourse network* as "the network of technologies and institutions that allow a given culture to select, store, and process relevant data" (1990, 369). *Technologies* in the sense he uses here definitely include, though are not limited to, those of mechanical reproduction.
4. Of course I am referring to Marcel Mauss's *The Gift: The Form and Reason for Exchange in Archaic Societies* (1990 [1950]), but my interest in the temporal dimension of the gift owes much to Jacques Derrida's radical rereading of Mauss's study. See *Given Time: I. Counterfeit Money* (Derrida 1992).

5. I thank Sally Humphreys for this phrase, and for her constructive criticisms of this essay in its earlier draft form.

6. This is to paraphrase Lacan, who understands the future perfect to be the tense that best describes the temporality of the speaking subject: "I identify myself in language, but only by losing myself in it like an object. What is realized in my history is not the past definite of what was, since it is no more, or even the present perfect of what has been in what I am, but the future anterior of what I shall have been for what I am in the process of becoming" (1977, 86).

Part 2 ❧ Unsettling Knowledge

9   Julie Skurski

Past Warfare: Ethics, Knowledge, and the Yanomami Controversy

Contemporary reflections on the production of scholarly knowledge tend to take for granted the institutional groundings, professional alliances, and material resources involved in establishing and sustaining the academic disciplines. While in recent decades various "culture wars" have brought into question a wide range of disciplinary premises, the tendency in these debates has been to focus on methodological and epistemological issues independently of the concrete cultural framings and fields of power within which the disciplines are organized. Even as such challenges have helped give rise to new interdisciplinary programs, objects of study, and ethics regulations, the disciplining effect of academic practices has tended to solidify the lines between differing conceptions of knowledge and ethics within and between the sciences and humanities.

These concealed boundaries became visible at the University of Michigan in the course of an extraordinary set of events surrounding the publication of *Darkness in El Dorado: How Scientists and Journalists Devastated the Amazon* (2000), by Patrick Tierney. The controversy it provoked challenged established research assumptions and professional alignments, making visible differing conceptions of scientific knowledge and the hierarchies of power in which they were embedded. This controversy and the efforts of the Anthrohistory Program to shift the terms within which it was framed suggest how a transdisciplinary approach contributes to understanding the unseen relations on which disciplines are sustained and to posing questions that challenge dominant conceptions of the ends and ethics of knowledge.

Tierney's book claimed that renowned scientists and anthropologists from elite institutions had endangered the lives and violated the dignity of Amazonian indigenous peoples by means of unethical and exploitative research practices. These claims shook the U.S. academy in the fall of 2000 and sparked an international controversy that spiraled through the press, professional associations, and universities, dividing and confounding scholars and disciplines. The acrimonious debate raised issues of the ethics of research, the politics of knowledge, and the nature of science. Significantly, these issues were inseparably intertwined with debates over the personalities and careers of two major figures implicated by the book: geneticist and physician James Neel and anthropologist Napoleon Chagnon. These researchers had conceived and directed the projects lying at the center of the controversy, and they had done so while they were faculty members at the University of Michigan.

At the University of Michigan, the administration responded to the book's allegations by making a rapid and decisive intervention into a controversy that from the outset had national and international dimensions. Circumventing the channels of open discussion, provost Nancy Cantor issued statements that went far beyond refuting the book's erroneous allegations concerning the researchers' use of a measles vaccine. Rather, the documents defended the ethics and intellectual content of Neel's and Chagnon's body of work in their entirety and condemned Tierney's whole book as flawed and biased. The administration's statements also dismissed the arguments and integrity of Chagnon's U.S. critics and ignored the opinions of anthropologists and officials from Brazil and Venezuela.

Despite the fact that the administration bypassed established academic procedures by assuming for itself the authority to decide on a contested academic matter, preempting discussion, there were no public objections to these procedures. In fact, faculty from several departments worked behind the scenes to help research and write the provost's statements. These documents asserted they were based on research conducted by unnamed members of various departments and schools, including anthropology and medicine. This was essential for legitimating the statements as reflections of expert opinion rather than as primarily expressions of the legal concerns of the university.

The Anthrohistory Program communicated to the provost its concerns about the intellectual and ethical implications of the administration's statements and proposed a colloquium series on the controversy intended to open up discussion more broadly concerning the politics of knowledge and the ethics of research. The three-part series, "Science, Ethics, Power: The Production of Knowledge and Indigenous Peoples" (March–April 2001), focused on the Tierney controversy but also addressed the role of the university as an intellectual arena and as a node within a global network of unequal relations. It sought to place scholarly production within this broader set of relations and to submit to critical analysis the disciplinary premises that help shape the production of knowledge.

As a result of the colloquium and Anthrohistory's proposal that the university change its position, the provost issued a strikingly different statement. It dropped its scathing critique of Tierney's book and blanket defense of Neel and Chagnon, and affirmed that the university should serve as a forum for the open discussion of ideas. While Anthrohistory's initiative did not resolve the complex issues at stake, it did help transcend the narrow limits of a polarized debate and develop a space that increased the opportunities for creating ethically responsible knowledge.

This essay explores the unfolding of these events and what they reveal about constraints exerted by the often invisible bonds that link the production of scholarly knowledge, disciplinary formations, and institutional power. It discusses the issues that the Anthrohistory Program raised, the premises on which they were based, and the transdisciplinary perspective from which they emerged. It suggests that this perspective defines the reflexive and critically engaged practice that anthrohistory seeks to make its own.

Lineages of Controversy

Tierney's book manuscript alleged that scientists, in pursuit of their own careers and with indifference to the life and dignity of the subjects of their investigations, had subjected the Yanomami Indians of Venezuela and Brazil to unethical and possibly lethal research practices. As a result of these allegations, a debate concerning research among the Yanomami, long simmering within the American Anthropological Association, boiled over into the public arena and splattered onto the pages of major newspapers across the world. It landed as well in the e-mail boxes of anthropologists around the globe, for a confidential e-mail to officers of the AAA by Terence Turner (Cornell) and Les Sponsel (University of Hawai'i), anthropologists active in indigenous rights, was leaked to the public and took on a life of its own. Anthropology as a profession, their message warned, was in danger of serious damage to its reputation with the forthcoming publication of the book and of prepublication excerpts in *The New Yorker* magazine (October 9, 2000). As a result, even before the book was out, charges, refutations, and countercharges from differing camps began to fly. The most inflammatory, and quickly disproved, claim accused geneticist James Neel of provoking a measles epidemic among the Yanomami in 1968 by using a flawed vaccine so as to further his study of genetic variation. (This was removed before the book's publication.)[1]

While its allegations were less dramatic, the book's accusations had a direct impact at the University of Michigan, particularly in the Department of Anthropology and the Medical School. The book asserted that during the epidemic Neel's team had not adequately aided native villagers who were facing deadly disease and social destruction. It also argued that Neel's teams collected blood samples from Yanomami villagers without their informed consent during several expeditions. The blood continued to be stored in U.S. research institutions and was still used by researchers, thus violating Yanomami religious beliefs that all the bodily remains of the deceased should be properly disposed of by their family.

While the charges concerning Neel's research and the measles epidemic drew the greatest attention, in fact Tierney's book addressed at much greater length criticisms of Chagnon's extensive body of work, including his field methods, ethics, and theories. Chagnon's critics had long asserted that his acknowledged manipulative techniques to obtain secret genealogical information and trading of manufactured goods in exchange for blood samples, as well as his staging of conflicts for films, had in effect promoted rivalries and divisions in Yanomami villages. Thus the Yanomami violence that he described, they argued, was actually partly a consequence of Chagnon's actions. His representation of them as the iconic "fierce people," popularized and circulated in the media in Brazil and Venezuela, had a material effect on their lives, making them yet further objects of denigration, neglect, and violence.[2]

Why did Tierney's book strike a chord at this particular time? After all, much of the critical material in Tierney's massively documented but weakly argued book had long been available. Beyond the appeal of the exotic and the image of victimized indigenous people that the book tapped into, it resonated with the bitter history of nonconsensual medical experiments on minorities, the rise of indigenous rights movements, and critiques of first world exploitation of third world countries. In particular, it played into anxieties concerning metropolitan academic production that had been ignited by multicultural, postcolonial, and feminist critiques of Western thought, the results of which had shifted the terms of discussion concerning scientific authority and ethical responsibility. Thus we can see *Darkness in El Dorado* as a touchstone for debates that preceded its publication and that extended well beyond questions of academic expertise, including the sensitive issues of researchers' professional relationships with their subjects, their responsibility toward the communities they study, and the unexamined disparities of power that underlie much research.

The controversy brought to the surface debates over science and culture that had shaped the academic and political terrain in the United States for several decades. The earlier "culture wars" and "science wars" informed and formed the terms along which lines were drawn, institutional investments were evaluated, and ethical-political consequences defined. These past wars were evoked and drawn on in this battle over the "warlike" Yanomami and those who represent them.

Battlegrounds at the University of Michigan

James Neel (1915–2000), doctor and geneticist, was a highly recognized figure in the biomedical field who had deep roots at the University of Michigan, where he began teaching in 1948. A pioneer in the study of human population genetics and founder of the Department of Human Genetics (1956), his career at the University of Michigan and his international research projects had established him as a leading figure in the scientific community.[3] Notably, he was a pioneer in the study of genetic change and naturally occurring genetic variability. With funding from the Atomic Energy Commission, he studied genetic mutations among Japanese victims of the atomic bomb and subsequently directed multidisciplinary biomedical research projects on Brazilian and Venezuelan Amazonian indigenous peoples.

Neel's AEC-funded projects in the Amazon collected biological materials, genealogies, and demographic information so as to study genetic mutation and diversity in isolated tribal groups (Neel et al. 1970). The kinship practices and environmental adaptations of these groups were believed to provide clues to early human evolution and genetic selection. His evolutionary interests led him to sociobiological theories that were reflected in his argument that "dominant males" who were headmen had superior abilities ("index of innate abilities") and were thus able to acquire a greater number of wives and offspring, spreading their genes more widely than other males (1980).

During the Amazon projects, Neel was a mentor to Chagnon, a recent University of Michigan Anthropology PhD and faculty member. As part of Neel's team, Chagnon carried out research on demography, primitive warfare, and kinship, and shared Neel's concern for understanding the social mechanisms and genetic components involved in reproductive success. His long-term participation with Neel's projects, not widely known in the anthropological profession, was foundational for his subsequent research among the Yanomami. He continued his work with them during the rest of his career at the University of California at Santa Barbara (UCSB) as the director of research projects. However by 1995 he had met with antagonism from differing sectors in Venezuela and was prohibited from returning to Yanomami territory. He then sought to collect blood samples illicitly among Yanomami in Brazil and to circumvent Venezuelan restrictions by allying with an entrepreneur and the president's mistress to create a private biosphere that would grant them access to the Yanomami and to the gold in their territory (Albert 2005a, 115; Coronil 2001, 266).

Chagnon's earliest monograph, *Yanomamo: The Fierce People* (1968), was based on material gathered as part of Neel's expedition. This book branded the Yanomami as "fierce" and placed Chagnon on the anthropological map through its use in undergraduate courses throughout the country. Over the course of decades and several editions (the subtitle was later dropped), this personal and lively ethnography, in which Chagnon recounted everything from his revulsion toward certain Yanomami practices to the deceptive techniques he used to obtain secret genealogical information, became the most widely used ethnography in the United States (an estimated three million copies were sold).[4]

From his initial focus on the dynamics of village fusion and primitive warfare, Chagnon shifted to the sociobiological study of evolutionary mechanisms, documenting forms of male competition that were hypothesized to result in genetic advantage for dominant men, or a wider distribution of their genes. In an article in the journal *Science* that drew great attention, including in the Brazilian press, Chagnon argued that Yanomami male leaders exhibited qualities of "fierceness" (his disputed translation of *waiteri*), as measured by their having "killed" (his contested translation of *unokai*) another person. As a result of being "fierce," dominant men gained greater access to women (a larger number of wives) and thus had a higher number of offspring than other men (1988).[5] He concluded that fierceness, as expressed through violence, led to greater success in fathering children, providing an evolutionary genetic advantage for fierce men.

For both researchers, the Yanomami, the least contacted and most numerous (estimated 15,000) of Amazonian native peoples, represented "primitive man" as he had existed for hundreds of thousands of years. Regarded as untouched by modern disease and civilization and as constituting a genetic "virgin soil" population, the Yanomami seemingly provided scientists with a rare and vanishing opportunity to study mankind at an early stage of social evolution, which facilitated the study of genetic inheritance and the biological effects of norms concerning marriage and "mating." Such tribal groups were regarded as examples of basic human nature as it existed prior to the establishment by civilized institutions of organized social constraints and hierarchies.

These researchers held the view, widely shared at that time, that primitive people provided a window back in time, a way of studying "pre-civilized" or "savage" man living under conditions that allowed natural and social selective mechanisms to function. The Yanomami were not regarded, as Fabian has argued more broadly for anthropology, as coevals of modern society but as remnants of a past that helped explain the origins of the modern present (1983).[6] The sociobiological agenda of these researchers cast the Yanomami primarily as a population that provided resources for the advancement of science, rather than as a people whose views and interests were to be taken into account by scientists (Coronil 2001; Geertz 2001; Sahlins 2000).[7]

From Primitive Warfare to Science Wars

Long an icon of primitive warfare, the Yanomami were now placed at the center of the revived "science wars" between interpretive and objectivist approaches to science. In this polarized conflict, defenders of the objectivist view, while acknowledging there were biomedical ethical issues at stake, presented this as a clash between science and antiscience (Hill 2000; Hurtado et al. 2001). They warned that politicized attacks on science would further endanger vulnerable indigenous people, as third world governments used the critiques to legitimate establishing barriers to scientific research by foreigners, to the detriment of indigenous health and the advancement of science. Critics of this instance of the objectivist approach, in turn, denied attacking science per se but rather a particular understanding of science as a neutral enterprise, outside the play of social meanings. They decried what they saw as a disjunction between objectivist research projects, often biomedical, and concern for the interests and health of the people studied (Albert 2005a, 112–18).

The view that objectivist science tended to operate with indifference to social and ethical implications, raised by the erroneous charge that Neel's measles vaccine was responsible for Yanomami deaths, built on a history of medical studies and projects that targeted U.S. minorities and third world peoples and were conducted without their informed consent or knowledge. These instances included the infamous Tuskegee Syphilis Study (Jones 1981), AEC radiation studies (Welsome 1999), and the forced sterilization of Puerto Rican women in the 1950 and 1960s (Briggs 2002, 143). The Tuskegee case was a landmark because of the institutional racism it revealed and the legal and ethical regulations it prompted, leading to the establishment of Institutional Review Boards (IRBs) in 1974 for the approval of research with human subjects.

Questions concerning the integrity of Chagnon's work had been raised for over a decade within the AAA. His representations of the Yanomami as warlike and his argument that men who killed had greater reproductive success circulated in the Brazilian press and were used by powerful landed and mining interests to argue that the warlike Yanomami should be confined to small reservations and access to their extensive terrain should be given to investors who would promote "development" (Martins 2005). The Brazilian Anthropology Association sent a statement to the AAA in 1988 objecting to Chagnon's representation of the vulnerable Yanomami as fierce and to his failure to refute publicly the misuse of his ideas (Carneiro da Cunha 1989).[8] This was not an academic matter, they argued, for when gold miners massacred Yanomami and miners' incursions into their territory brought ecological destruction and virulent strains of malaria and other diseases, the Brazilian state, in complicity with mining interests, failed to protect them.[9] Thus the concept that the Yanomami were violent and constituted a danger to modern society helped legitimate the structural and personal violence to which they were subjected.

The University of Michigan Arms a Response

Given this background, the controversy had potentially significant legal and ethical implications for the Medical School and the university.[10] The Office of the Provost quickly convened a confidential fact-finding commission to investigate the book's allegations, and the commission speedily issued two draft statements. Prior to the provost office's final report (November 13, 2000), these drafts (September 27, October 31) circulated on the Internet and were cited in the press, but there were no mechanisms for discussion or feedback. The statements vehemently refuted the charges concerning the measles epidemic, backed the integrity of Neel's and Chagnon's work, and rejected in scathing terms the conclusions of *Darkness in El Dorado* as a whole. This was a significant intervention, given the university's prestige and the measures under way in Brazil and Venezuela to investigate the issues.

The Office of the Provost's final report hinted at the administration's initial sense of urgency and mobilization of resources.

> We immediately convened a team of senior administrators, research staff, and scholars to begin an internal inquiry. These individuals spent hundreds of hours over the course of several weeks conducting a careful and thorough review.... This effort involved people from across the university; supporting research was conducted by the offices of the Executive Vice President for Medical Affairs, Vice President for Research, and General Counsel, and by the Medical School and Department of Anthropology.

It should be noted that in the Department of Anthropology meetings at that time there was no discussion of the department's participation, which included the employment of anthropology graduate students to conduct research for the commission. This silence reflected the screen placed around the proceedings and the identity of the commission's participants.

The Office of the Provost's statement asserted, "The University of Michigan takes allegations of impropriety in research very seriously" and claimed that its commission had conducted a "fair and proper peer review" in contrast to the "sensationalized public discussion in the headlines and over the Internet." The commission evaluated the claims made in the Turner-Sponsel e-mail and in the book concerning the measles vaccine, but it went much further. It addressed the overall procedures of the 1968 expedition and the integrity of Neel and Chagnon, Chagnon's research ethics and representations of Yanomami culture in his later work, and the motives of his critics. The report concluded:

> The evidence uncovered by our review supports the conclusion that the claims are false. We are satisfied that Dr. Neel and Dr. Chagnon, both among the most distinguished scientists in their respective fields, acted with integrity in conducting their research, and that their medical care of the Yanomami and their attempts to halt the spread of a pre-existing measles epidemic through vaccination were humane, compassionate, and

> medically appropriate.... We believe that Mr. Tierney did not consult important original source material that was readily available for review. Analysis of that material and other material from persons familiar with the expeditions, the measles outbreak, and the measles vaccine refutes the allegations. The serious factual errors we have found call into question the accuracy of the entire book as well as the interpretations of its author. (Cantor 2000c)

This document's conclusions were based on certain acts of omission and silencing. They did not acknowledge anthropological sources that historicize the disruptive impact of colonialism, trade goods, epidemics, and settler violence on the Yanomami (Ferguson 1995), or those that critique Chagnon's narrow translation of key terms such as *waiteri* and contextualize Yanomami understandings of illness, death, spirits, and the body (Albert 1985, 1989; Ramos 1987; Albert and Ramos 1989). On the contrary, the statement argued for the continuity between contemporary Yanomami conflicts and pre-Columbian forms of indigenous warfare in South America, and it uncritically cited sources, ranging from Spanish conquerors to nineteenth-century naturalists, to substantiate the characterization of the Yanomami as essentially violent.

> Warfare among Indian groups in South America goes back a minimum of 3,500 years. Abundant archaeological data show raiding, including the saving of trophy heads, throughout the pre-Hispanic periods called Chavin, Moche, Chimu, Wari, and Inka. Warfare also was reported by the Spanish conquerors of the sixteenth century A.D.... Our first report about these people is from the mid-1800s, by Moritz Schomburgk (1847–1848) ... These and many other accounts, too numerous to mention here, make the claim that Yanomami violence began with Chagnon's arrival obviously false" (Cantor 2000b).

As further proof, it asserted that the Yanomami refer to themselves as *waiteri*, or fierce; "What Chagnon did was translate the term into English" (Cantor 2000b). Yet the translation of Yanomami terms had been debated earlier in anthropological publications, as noted above. Albert and Ramos had analyzed the complexities of translating *waiteri*, whose meanings include brave, humorous, and assertive, and *unokai*, which does not mean that an individual is a literal "killer" of another but is in a state of shared ritual pollution relating to a death that may have spiritual or physical origins (Albert 1989; Ramos 1987; Albert and Ramos 1989).

As with any official document, factors including discursive conventions, legal considerations, and differences of power among participants establish limits on the possibility of gaining insight into the largely opaque process of producing the provost's report. Moreover, there were informal limits on efforts to inquire into the procedures, composition, and agenda of the provost's commission even after the report's completion. Nevertheless, two documents written by Kent V. Flannery, professor of archaeology and member of the Academy of Sciences, provide a degree of insight into the agenda of the commission. They suggest that personal and theoretical loyalties were deeply intertwined, and that neo-Darwinian logic prevailed.

Flannery (n.d.) privately sent a "Memo to the Neel family" that included the subcommittees' drafts prior to revision by legal counsel. His aim, he wrote, was to reassure the family that "James Neel will be cleared of all impropriety, and will be revealed as the victim of a personal vendetta."[11] He later published a letter, "Hypocrisy in El Dorado," in *Anthropology News* (May 2002) in which he reasserted the theory of the vendetta as the explanation for the actions of Chagnon's and Neel's critics. He lauded scientists on the University of Michigan commission who had dismissed as hypocritical Turner and Sponsel's claimed concern for Yanomami welfare, along with their denial that the El Dorado controversy was in fact "tainted by personal animosity, hatred of biological models, or jealousy born of laboring for years in Chagnon's shadow" (2002).

> *The evidence uncovered by our review supports the conclusion that the claims are false. We are satisfied that Dr. Neel and Dr. Chagnon, both among the most distinguished scientists in their respective fields, acted with integrity in conducting their research, and that their medical care of the Yanomami and their attempts to halt the spread of a pre-existing measles epidemic through vaccination were humane, compassionate, and medically appropriate.*
>
> &— OFFICE OF THE PROVOST STATEMENT ON *DARKNESS IN EL DORADO*, NOVEMBER 13, 2000

The Epistemology of the Battlefield

By casting the controversy as a feud among individuals competing for prestige and power, the unpublished draft of the provost's statement, included in Flannery's memo to the Neel family (n.d.), in effect reproduced a neo-Darwinian framework. But it did not reduce the conflict to raw competition among self-interested individuals, for the opposing figures were presented as belonging to different moral orders; they were in a battle between objective truth and moralizing invention that constituted a threat to the very foundations of scientific knowledge. This Manichaean framing is reflected in the structure of the provost's public statements, built on the opposition between false allegations and true facts between irresponsible critics and ethical scientists (e.g., Cantor 2000b).

Linking the personal to the theoretical and political, the unedited draft asserts that the feud reflected a schism within anthropology between those "who believe in a scientific paradigm and those who do not." It cast "science" and "anti-science" as opposed endeavors, citing Robert Benter's definition: "Science," it stated, is "objective, quantitative, extrapersonalized, and based on proof and consensus; 'anti-science' is subjective, qualitative, personalized, moralistic, and based on individual authority with no accommodation of contrary views" (Flannery n.d.).

In making this argument, the draft drew on the binary contrast between scientific and moral models that Roy D'Andrade (Department of Anthropology, University of California at San Diego) had proposed in a scathing critique of postmodernist and postcolonial trends in anthropology (1995). Based on his framework, the report classified Sponsel and Turner as belonging to the moral model camp and offered the following evidence of their antiscience position: Sponsel's "agenda seems to be the promotion of a 'more nonviolent and peaceful world,' a world he believes is 'latent in human nature'"; Turner "is known for especially ferocious dedication to the rights of threatened indigenous people" and "claims a moral high ground because he was named to two AAA committees concerned with the Yanomami and human rights." Like other such "extreme moralists," it asserted, they denounce and demonize their opponents rather than engaging in scientific debate. It concluded that the actual targets of *Darkness in El Dorado* are "science, genetics, and neo-Darwinian theory, as exemplified by Neel and Chagnon" (Flannery n.d.).

Science, Ethics, Power

As noted above, the Anthrohistory Program questioned the administration's decision to evaluate Tierney's book and faculty members' work and the manner in which it carried out this evaluation. As David W. Cohen, professor of history and anthropology, later observed at the colloquium, "This seems, for a university, a highly specious intervention in on-going scholarly and public discussions."[12] In the opinion of a wide range of scholars, the University of Michigan statements not only conflated individuals with theoretical positions and parts of the book with the whole, it excluded the opinions of dissenting scholars and preempted debate at the University of Michigan even as investigations continued in the United States and abroad.[13]

In response to this restriction of debate, the program's directors proposed a colloquium series that would open up discussion. Recognizing that the issues raised in this controversy were being taken seriously outside and within the university, Provost Cantor, in a notable shift, gave the colloquium generous support. Nevertheless, there was resistance from within the Department of Anthropology to supporting the colloquium. In a departmental meeting some faculty objected that the invited speakers did not represent both sides of the controversy and that vocal critics of Chagnon had been included.[14] The department withheld its name from the broad list of the colloquium's supporters, and few anthropology faculty members attended the sessions, although the Chair of Anthropology, Conrad Kottak, was on the first panel.

As intended, the colloquium series did expand discussion within and beyond the university. The central issues it addressed included the goals of knowledge production, the relationship between researcher and subject, conceptions of scientific research, the ethics of writing, international disparities of power in academic arenas, colonial and imperial relations and their impact on research subjects, and the agency and voice of indigenous people. The three-part series included speakers representing positions disregarded by the University of Michigan statements: Alcida Ramos, Terence Turner, and Brian Ferguson.

The colloquium series, which drew a large audience from a variety of fields, addressed broad issues of the university's changing role in national and international arenas.[15] The initial session, "The Politics of Representation," featured Alcida Ramos (University of Brasilia), a noted ethnographer and indigenous rights activist, who highlighted national differences in cultural politics as well as the impact of disparities of power within and among nations. "In Brazil as in other Latin American countries, professional anthropologists take on ... the social responsibility to both respect and defend the rights of our research subjects, particularly indigenous peoples" (2001). Inequalities of power, she noted, inflect relations among Brazilian and U.S.

scholars and institutions, shaping the evaluation of claims made by scholars in Brazil according to the U.S. norm of value-free science and setting limits as to who can be heard within the scientific community.[16]

Michael Kennedy (Department of Sociology, University of Michigan) argued that such disparities underline the need to assess what it means to be a global university, to evaluate differing kinds of "knowledge politics," and to consider how research at the University of Michigan might "transcend the cultural politics of the American state and nation" by engaging with the needs and concerns of peoples who were research subjects (Coronil et al. 2001b).[17]

"The Ethics of Inquiry" session addressed the history of scientific research projects among the Yanomami as well as changes in conceptions of ethical norms and indigenous rights. In his address, Terence Turner expressed regret for the harm that his leaked e-mail had caused, but he also argued that the critics of Tierney's book had themselves ignored the ethical problems it raised and had erroneously conflated criticisms of specific scientific practices with an attack on science itself. This resulted in the misplaced claim that science was under siege, and in attacks on individuals rather than in empirically based discussions of research practices and ethics (Turner 2001b). Turner's new study of Neel's archived papers on the disputed 1968 expedition provided evidence, he asserted, that Neel's project, despite good intentions, followed protocols and pursued goals that placed Yanomami welfare in a secondary position (2001b).

Despite these unresolved tensions between sociobiology's and historical anthropology's approaches to the issues, Kay Warren argued, the colloquium was helping move the debate beyond the notion of science versus politics and bring attention to the perspectives from which claims to science are made and the varied ethical considerations they bring into play.

In "The Uses of History" session Brian Ferguson (Department of Anthropology, Rutgers University) challenged the notion that the Yanomami are a warlike people, arguing that conquest and colonialism had long subjected them to violence and disruption through a variety of indirect means, including the circulation of Western goods and assaults on indigenous lands and labor, that reshaped relationships among neighboring groups and between indigenous peoples and colonizing agents. Disputing the scientific versus moral models division, Ferguson argued that empirically based work focused on material conditions presented a scientific alternative to sociobiology's theory of primitive warfare.

On the basis of the evidence the colloquium provided, the director of the Anthrohistory Progream requested that the provost withdraw the university's statement on Tierney's book. In response, the provost, in collaboration with Coronil, issued a new statement on the controversy. Though unheralded and unassumingly titled "May 29, 2001, update regarding 'Darkness in El Dorado,'" this document represented a reversal of the preceding report (Cantor 2001). It acknowledged that the colloquium presentations, together with government and professional reports and academic publications, had demonstrated there was a scholarly consensus that Tierney's book, despite its errors, had raised fundamental questions concerning the ethics of research.

> These are complex questions that do not yield simple or definitive answers. Yet, as communities of scholarship, universities have appropriate means for examining these difficult issues, such as class discussions, interdisciplinary colloquiums, and academic publications. In addition, scholarly associations, through their ethics committees and special task forces, also provide mechanisms for investigating these questions.[18]

Although the Office of the Provost did not retract or comment on the original report, which in all likelihood remained the university's position in the eyes of much of the public, the process of discussion culminating in the colloquium had shifted the terrain on which boundaries were drawn from a pinnacle of power.[19]

Knowledge as Struggle

The Anthrohistory Program brought a transdisciplinary approach to a polarized conflict mired in a complex tangle of theoretical disagreements, disciplinary norms, administrative procedures, personal/professional loyalties, and institutional interests. In part by virtue of its nondepartmental and interdisciplinary status, the program was able to raise questions that jostled settled boundaries and upset the quotidian politics of mutual avoidance and forgetting that had made possible the administration's unchallenged response to Tierney's book. The ensuing discussions, at once disquieting and engaging, questioned how scholarly expertise is organized, and they challenged claims to value neutrality that obscure and reinforce disparities of power. The knotty issues raised around the Yanomami controversy were of course not resolved, but the discussions that the colloquium drew on and prompted were marked by the recognition that efforts to develop knowledge in more equitable, collaborative, and responsible terms is a shared responsibility and an ongoing struggle. An example had been set by Brazilian anthropologists who, in conjunction with indigenous leaders, redefined informed consent for indigenous communities as a continuing process of negotiation in which the communities become active participants in consenting to research and in defining how they may benefit from it, through measures ranging from rights advocacy to contributions to medical facilities (Albert 2005c, 220–27).[20]

In this instance of disciplinary battles and embattled disciplines, anthrohistory, understood as a reflexive practice that challenges naturalized boundaries, helped bring attention both to broad issues concerning the ends of knowledge and to the concrete effects and possibilities entailed in academic work. The colloquium series spoke to scholars across the conventional boundaries of topic, region, and discipline that often confine discussion. It also questioned a gap that typically separates observers from observed, particularly across hierarchies of class, ethnicity, and nation. This gap was painfully alive at the University of Michigan, as the Yanomami were present not only as subjects of debate but in the form of blood samples obtained without their consent and kept against their will in its laboratories and at other institutions.[21]

> *The University of Michigan, as a major university with global responsibilities, can best respond to the issues raised by Tierney's book by promoting their discussion through regular academic channels. Our discussions at Michigan have helped place the examination of these controversial issues within a scholarly and constructive framework directed at evaluating the impact of research sponsored by U.S. universities among peoples anywhere in the world and ensuring that priority be given to their welfare.*
> — OFFICE OF THE PROVOST, MAY 29, 2001, UPDATE REGARDING *DARKNESS IN EL DORADO*

As this controversy brought out, there have been recurrent claims for their return by Yanomami communities, and for researchers, whose careers benefit from the cooperation of their research objects, to contribute to improving the conditions of indigenous people in forms ranging from advocacy to redistribution (Albert 2005b).[22] The question of how to negotiate the conflicting demands of those within and far outside the academy refuses simple solutions, but it is being addressed in some instances.[23] Yet the blood that flows through research and goes into the making of scholarly texts, as Eiss's chapter in this volume compellingly evokes, has to be acknowledged in our struggles to fashion forms of knowledge that undermine the comfortable boundaries that hierarchically separate those who seemingly produce knowledge and those who provide them with materials from which to fashion it.²⁴

NOTES

1. Borofsky's book *Yanomami: The Fierce Controversy and What We Can Learn From It* (2005) provides the most complete and fair-minded account of the controversy as it played out among anthropologists from various subdisciplines. Borofsky provides an analysis of the issues, resources for students, and perhaps most important, a discussion of Yanomami perspectives. The book is linked to Public Anthropology website's Community Action project designed to involve undergraduates in discussing and taking action on pressing contemporary issues (http://www.publicanthropology.org/).

2. See, for example, Albert 1989; Albert and Ramos 1989; Albert 2005a, 2005c; Carneiro da Cunha 1989; Ferguson 1995; Shapiro 1976; Turner 1994.

3. Neel was a member of the American Academy of Sciences since 1963, recipient of the National Medal of Science, and founding member of the American Society of Human Genetics. See his obituary in the *American Journal of Human Genetics* (Weiss and Ward 2000).

4. Borofsky cites sources that claim this book is the best-selling ethnography in history (2005, 39). At the time of the controversy, the book was still used widely in introductory anthropology courses.

5. This article proved highly controversial. The French anthropologist Bruce Albert and Brazilian anthropologist Alcida Ramos, both ethnographers of the Yanomami in Brazil, critiqued Chagnon's argument on ethnographic and theoretical grounds, taking issue with the translation of its central terms and with its assertion that Yanomami were particularly violent (Albert 1989; Albert and Ramos 1989).

6. See Gaynor's statement in Coronil et al. 2001b.

7. On the views of Yanomami representatives, see Kopenawa Yanomami 1991; AAA El Dorado Task Force 2002; Borofsky 2005.

8. While Chagnon published a rejoinder to the letter in *Anthropology News* (1989), it refused to publish the Brazilian Anthropology Association's reply to him, a slight recalled during the Anthrohistory colloquium.

9. Brazilian miners massacred sixteen Yanomami at Haximu in 1993. Bruce Albert led an investigation for Brazilian authorities (Albert 2005c, 215–16), as did Terence Turner for the AAA.

10. Colleagues of Neel were indignant these charges were made when Neel could not defend himself, since he died in February 2000.

11. According to Flannery, "approximately 20 persons—physicians, epidemiologists, geneticists, biological anthropologists, ethnologists, ethnohistorians, archaeologists, documentary film specialists, and eyewitnesses to James Neel's and Napoleon Chagnon's field work, are working together to figure out why such hideous allegations would be made about them in the media" (n.d.).

12. See his presentation at the Anthrohistory colloquium, "Toward a Portrait of the University as Author of the Text," on the absence of standards by which such an investigation should be undertaken and proceed (Coronil et al. 2001b).

13. The AAA appointed the El Dorado Task Force to investigate the book's charges; Fernando Coronil, Director of the Anthrohistory Program, was on the task force, and the Venezuelan government and the Federal University of Rio de Janeiro in Brazil undertook their own investigations.

14. Efforts by the colloquium organizers to invite University of Michigan supporters of Neel and Chagnon's position to participate on the panels met with little success. Randolph Nesse, professor in the Department of Psychiatry and the Institute for Social Research, and a supporter of Neel, did speak on the second panel.

15. The Anthrohistory website provided related documents and links as reference for discussion (http://www.umich.edu/~idpah/SEP/sepmenu.html).

16. In response to the Tierney measles allegations, Bruce Albert organized a fact-finding commission in Brazil to study the Neel expedition. Its report found the measles vaccination claims by Tierney to be false and irresponsible. Yet it also concluded that Neel's project had procedural and ethical failings and that Tierney's book, "despite its serious documentary and conceptual failures . . . has made possible a more profound discussion reflecting upon the ethics of research among indigenous populations and minorities in general." The U.S. media and the AAA ignored this report (Lobo et al. 2000).

17. Kennedy pointed out that the University of Michigan had just made a large commitment to the Life Sciences Initiative that placed ethics and values at the core of its mission, yet there had been no debate around "the geopolitical ethics of the life sciences."

18. For the full statement, see Coronil et al. 2001.

19. It should be noted that the initial provost's statement continues to be cited by supporters of Chagnon (e.g., in Wikipedia entries).

20. See also Albert and Gomez 1997. For a nuanced discussion of ethics in anthropology, including this case, see Fluehr-Lobban 2003.

21. Yanomami blood samples are still kept at the National Cancer Institute and a smaller amount at Pennsylvania State University. To the alarm of Yanomami advocates, they could be used to develop DNA that could be commercialized, as had occurred with other Brazilian indigenous groups, without the consent of the individuals nor with any benefit to them or their communities (Albert 2005c). In 2006, following a request by the Attorney General of Roraima State, Brazil, and Public Anthropology student letters, high-level administrators of the National Cancer Institute and of Penn State agreed to return the blood to Brazil. However this has not occurred as of this writing and the Public Anthropology campaign has intensified (see http://www.publicanthropology.org/Yanomami/ 09-Fall/background.htm).

22. The El Dorado Task Force of the AAA, after much internal discord and membership critique, released its final report in 2002. It included the results of an unprecedented gathering of Yanomami village representatives in the Venezuelan

Amazon, attended by task force members, in which demands for a reciprocal relationship with researchers and criticisms of the long-standing asymmetrical relations characterizing most biomedical and anthropological research were clearly set forth (AAA 2002: http://www.aaanet.org/edtf/index.htm).

23. U.S. anthropological norms specify a narrow notion of ethics focused on the individual, and the pursuit of more equitable relations with collectivities often meets with obstacles. However, the Brazilian NGO Pro-Yanomami Commission, as well as the Public Anthropology project, have raised funds to contribute to Yanomami medical care.

24. See Coronil's essay in this volume on the concrete ethics of struggle.

10 ❧ *Shannon Lee Dawdy*

Disaster Preparedness

Anthropology and history—those are things I read, I thought, and I did until 2005. In the fall of 2005, as I drove the streets of my field site and adopted home of New Orleans soon after the floodwaters of Katrina had receded, I began to feel, to see, and to enact anthrohistory. This is a retrospective observation. At the time, I didn't know what the hell I was doing. I thought I was observing. I knew I was trying to find a way to help, a way to apply my peculiar expertise. I was looking for an opening where I could insert my best intentions and heal this corner of the world to which I am very attached. Even to transform it for the better. But this essay isn't about "applied" work, rather it is about the way in which our work applies itself to us—how it shapes our immediate perceptions and emotions, our inner experiences. This internalization in turn motivates our actions and our careers out in the world. This chapter is an attempt to capture the affective phenomenology of transdisciplinary fieldwork.

Although sentiments and emotions had begun to be an object of study for me before the storm, my interest intensified as I struggled to understand the waves that washed through me via a personal and near-apocalyptic experience. Hurricane Katrina and its aftermath has moved me to ask, What is the role of emotion in our scholarship and how does our scholarship shape our emotions? Because we are conditioned to hear this as a rather feminine-sounding question, I think we have irresponsibly skirted the issue as somehow trivial.

In offering a preliminary and impressionistic response here, I hope to avoid belaboring the reader with a narcissistic tale of "I, I, I . . ." I do *not* mean this as another chapter in 1980s-style self-reflexivity. It is not simply that such exercises are now out of fashion, but rather I want to understand the "we" that is formed by training in anthrohistory rather than the "I" of my own personal history. I want emotions to be taken seriously as a force in our work and to understand how our training shapes our experiences in similar ways. I want to understand the ways in which I "did not own my own thoughts," to paraphrase Joan Scott on E. P. Thompson (Scott 1991).

Or, perhaps better for the purpose here, "did not own my own emotions" due to ways in which my experience was filtered through the fabric of my education.

For many of the contributors to this volume, I suspect we imagine our assignment as a sort of return to the hearth. My effort here is no different. In fact, I recently reread Joan Scott's "The Evidence of Experience" (1991), an article assigned in one of the first classes I took in the Doctoral Program in Anthropology and History at the University of Michigan. You could say that here I am turning in a very late response paper. But it is a response provoked by a recent dramatic event. I reached back to this pivotal article of Scott's looking for help. I want to comprehend the "authority" my experience seemed to lend for the several academic and public audiences who soon inundated me with requests to speak on the disaster.

I also want to make clear how the way I experienced Katrina was far different from that of most Gulf Coast residents. Besides the obvious fact that I had not evacuated (I had in fact left a month earlier to return to Chicago), other differences came from the language, thoughts, and knowledge of anthrohistory that informed my perceptions. And, to my surprise, informed my emotions. In this way, I was *experiencing* anthropology and history—not as objects, nor precisely as professional activities, but as ways of living in the world. The form and content of these academic practices have become internalized, structuring forces that shape my subjective day-to-day existence. Further, if I had been immersed in only one of these fields, my reactions would have been wholly different, and a bit imbalanced. I have come to think that the dual focus of anthrohistory produces, in its way, something as unfashionable as bifocals. That is, wisdom. In New Orleans, I initially felt pushed and pulled by all that I was witnessing, researching, and participating in. But within a few weeks, I could see the historical cycles of disaster and rebuilding that make hope inevitable. At the same time, as each new political wrinkle of the disaster unfolded, my contemporary horror at the rending of a community's social fabric was keenly informed by an anthropological sensibility that values the unique, the expressive, and the local. History alone may have resigned me to radical rupture. Anthropology alone may have immobilized me with a furious urge to preserve the ethnographic present of August 28, 2005. Together, these disciplinary perspectives gave me the conviction that change should be directed by local interests and the belief that a balance between tradition and innovation in rebuilding could improve the quality of life for New Orleanians in their own terms. I was prepared for this disaster by the peculiar transdisciplinarity of anthrohistory, with a perspective that balances somewhere between necessary patience and useful outrage.

To make this a little more visual and visceral, I will describe three examples of my experiences in post-Katrina New Orleans, with the emotions they provoked and the disciplinary frames that shaped the experience. As an anthropologist, I had been trained to keep a journal of my experiences in the field, writing down whatever occurred to me, whether it seemed important at the time or not. Without that learned practice, I would have less to present here, and to digest upon reflection. Memories fill in the rest. They are memories composed of images, sensations, and sentiments, as well as thoughts that crossed my mind at odd intervals.

To set the setting, I have been doing research and professional work in history, archaeology, and preservation in New Orleans since 1994. This background qualified me in the eyes of colleagues at the Louisiana Division of Archaeology to serve as their liaison to the Historic Preservation Section of the Federal Emergency Management Agency (FEMA), a role I took on full time between early October and late December 2005. The job description was vague, but the best way to describe my role is that I was there to be a research resource for FEMA and a policy consultant for the state. I was physically "embedded" within FEMA's New Orleans area office. The first half of my time there was spent going out with their staff and other consultants on "reconnaissance" surveys of New Orleans, driving city block by city block to assess damage to "historic resources" (the terms in quotes are FEMA language). The second half of my stay consisted largely of attending city planning meetings and researching and writing policy recommendations. I will narrate my experiences and their attendant emotions in the order in which I experienced them.

As I switched hats from FEMA field office, to cemetery, to archive, I adjusted frames: an ecological frame fraught with presentist worry, a longue durée calmness about the cycles of disasters in the city, a political ethnographer's fascinated horror with the innards of "Homeland Security," an archaeologist's longing for preservation and aesthetic distinction, and a New Orleanian's macabre sense of irony. Somewhere between the apocalyptic tableaux on the streets and my computer screen filled with historic maps that predicted a cycle of biblical flooding followed by rebirth and renewal, my belief in transdisciplinarity was renewed. Frequent frame-switching was the only way that I could comprehend the enormity and complexity of the event. My knowledge of this place, its history, and the creative ways in which my teachers taught me to think (about communities, about politics, about processes of social transformation) were resources that gave me momentary, and much-needed, clarity in a disaster zone where naked people wandered disoriented through once-familiar neighborhoods, where streets disappeared under piles of debris from houses, cars, and trees, and where the senses were overwhelmed by a cloud of molecules from mold spores, decaying flesh, and the dust of demolition. My need for wisdom, an inner calm to weather an external storm, was satisfied by a rhythmic swing in perspective from the near to the far, from the anthropological to the historical. A passion for my research and my field site called me to New Orleans; this passion was in turn renewed by the intensity of experience.

Homeland Security: Terror

Before I even arrived in post-Katrina Louisiana, one of the first things I learned about FEMA was that it is one of the many federal agencies that have been brought under the umbrella of the post-9/11 U.S. Department of Homeland Security. For nearly four weeks after agreeing to come down, I waited in Chicago for the paperwork that would make me eligible for compensation to cover travel expenses. I became nervous that my past fieldwork in Cuba (though legal) had put a red flag on my file as far as George W. Bush's administration was concerned. But nothing so intriguing explained the delay, rather just bureaucratic wheel-spinning. Finally, the papers did arrive and I drove down to the new FEMA headquarters in Baton Rouge. Once there, I drove around and around a massive, abandoned department store with boarded-up windows that corresponded to the address I had been given. As I circled around the rambling structure that filled two city blocks with generations of architectural add-ons dating from the 1900s to the 1990s, I reflected how ironic it was that FEMA headquarters was located in the Maison Blanche building (French for "White House"), the name of the local family-owned mercantile empire that thrived there until its demise in 2000 due to globalization and Clinton-era buyouts. As I drove around that now faceless, boarded-up building surrounded by crack houses and currency exchanges, I marveled at how economic decay seems to set in as fast as wood rot in the South, where the only enduring infrastructure seems to be the string of roads threading together old plantations and petrochemical plants. I was about to go around the building a second time when I finally saw two armed sentries in National Guard uniforms at an entrance. They informed me I could not enter until I had an ID badge. They sent me to another location to get one.

I then drove to a small building on the other side of town, eventually arriving (without the benefit of a marked street address) at what appeared to be a former medical building. It was a 1960s modernist building sitting on raised pillars, with a parking lot beneath. The only entrance into the workspace of the building was through a tiny two-person elevator that made the one-story trip. But on this first visit, I didn't ride. The plainclothes officers, who made no effort to hide their gun holsters, told me I needed to have an appointment. I returned to my temporary home at a friend-of-a-friend's house and made repeated phone calls until I finally got through to make an appointment.

When I arrived in the late afternoon, I entered the elevator with curiosity and some smug annoyance at such a pompous bureaucracy. While probably many of the contractors and new employees entering the security clearance and human resources center had similar thoughts, I also reflected upon how redolent this serpentine system was of Spanish colonialism, a throwback to Baton Rouge's history as a post in Spanish Florida. This bit of scholarly nostalgia was reinforced, with some bemusement, at the fact that I had to wait for three hours to be handed a stack of papers one-inch thick upon which I had to enter and reenter the same information over and over again: name, address, social security number, date of birth, employment, date, and signature. There was no computer in sight. When I got to the last two pages, I realized they were "processing" me incorrectly as some sort of GIS technician. When I took my stack back to the nice lady who had handed them to me, and explained as patiently as I could that this was not my expertise or job description, she explained just as patiently that I must be mistaken. Just sign the papers. My annoyance turned to palpitating alarm when she then said, "Now we will swear you in. Raise your right hand." She then asked me to repeat a series of statements which caused newsreel images of the darkest chapters of U.S. national history to play in my head: the Tuskegee Experiment, McCarthyism, the Rosenberg Trial, the Cuban Missile Crisis, Vietnam, the Twin Towers. The oath I took was this:

> I, Shannon Dawdy, do solemnly swear that I will support and defend the Constitution of the United States against all enemies, foreign and domestic; that I will bear true faith and allegiance to the same; that I take this ob-

ligation freely, without any mental reservation or purpose of evasion; and that I will well and faithfully discharge the duties of the office on which I am about to enter. So help me God.

I remember feeling at the time a mixture of fear and wild wonder. How could the federal government enlist my inner thoughts and feelings? I was willing to give them 84 hours a week (FEMA hours in the emergency response period), to be separated from my family for much of the next three months, and to lend all the meager professional expertise I had, but this abstract demand seemed unreasonable and frankly, beyond the call of this particular duty. What crime was I committing if my allegiance to the U.S. state was tinged with "mental reserve"? What methods did they have for ascertaining that I am by nature skeptical of the moral purity of political institutions? Or worse, that as an atheist I had just perjured myself? With a thirty-second act of banality, I had compromised my own beliefs and feelings due to the expediency of disaster and the adrenaline-fueled urge to respond. After the swearing in, I felt a sense of dread, like I had just walked into a Faustian machine. The door shut behind me before I realized where I was. I then understood, from the inside out, how panic and terror could recruit even the most conscientious objectors.

The day was ending, so I had to leave and return the next day to complete the clearance process. On the way back, I made some calls to my contacts at FEMA to inquire about the ill-fitting job description. A bureaucratic mistake, of course. Tomorrow I would have to start over again once they got it figured out.

I returned to the security building the next day and had a déjà vu experience with the paperwork, minus the swearing-in (apparently the oath is not specific to job description). I was then directed to a large, adjacent room to wait for a background check and fingerprinting. I realized then why they had selected a former medical building as it was apparently going to be a long wait, and there were nearly two dozen people ahead of me in a large, comfortable waiting room. The security personnel (who I suspect were FBI employees) had set up a television connected to a DVD player. Spider Man was playing. I noted that the short stack of DVDs next to the television all had a similar theme, of heroes saving the world: Batman, Pearl Harbor, Star Wars. It made me uncomfortable when I realized that the environment I had entered was so tightly controlled that these films had no doubt themselves passed through some sort of clearance process. The result seemed to be a clumsy attempt at indoctrination. I looked around and became depressed as almost every person in the room had their eyes glued to the set. At least judging by facial expression, not one of them seemed to share my cynicism. Only one woman was distracted, trying to get her cell phone to work, although I knew our signals were blocked inside the building. My stomach fluttered for a moment when I realized no one except two FEMA colleagues whom I had never met face-to-face knew where I was. Then I chided myself for not bringing any reading material and resentfully started watching the movie, with nothing else to do.

As the movie ended, I got up to look for a bathroom. I peeked around a corner and looked into a room set up with dozens of desks and computers, with a few scattered people working the terminals. I was startled by a baritone voice behind me saying too urgently, "Where are you going, ma'am? You're not allowed back there." I turned to find a large, muscular man dressed in black frowning at me officiously. "I was just looking for a place to piss," I said with more than a little adolescent annoyance at his unnecessary authority. "It's around the other way," he responded, pointing. I went off, hoping I had embarrassed him as much as he had embarrassed me. I couldn't help thinking now what sort of activities were taking place on the other side of the building, where I had set off the alarm. As I returned to my seat I noticed that they had restarted *Spider Man* rather than make another selection. I began thinking of my colleague Joe Masco's work on federal bureaucracy, secrets, and nuclear research (Masco 2006). "This is great material for Joe." I was filled with a mixture of curiosity and contempt.

Finally, my name was called and I went into a small room with cameras and scanners. A woman took my hand and asked me to roll the palm across the bed of the scanner. She checked the results and asked me to do it again. She then guided me in doing the same with the pad of each of my five fingers. And then the same process for the other hand. After this, I was sent back to the waiting room. They would call me when my clearance went through and then I would be photographed for the FEMA ID card. All of this struck me as odd and alarming when all I thought I'd be doing was the innocuous work of advising FEMA on where archaeological sites were located in New Orleans. Never had I felt like such a criminal suspect.

At dinner that night, I shared my thoughts with an academic acquaintance, remarking that the United States had become something of a police state. He asked why this bothered me. He was making plans to visit New Orleans, saying that he was looking forward to just walking around, enjoying the architecture without having to watch his back, now that so much of the criminal element had been washed away. This colleague's training is not in anthropology or history. It is in a field that perceives humans as masses of predictable numbers. He calculates risk. While he was feeling safer, our conversation turned my earlier sensations of dread and fear into a cold, slow terror of our present times. History will judge us harshly for our inaction in the face of such insanity. As I tried vainly to fall asleep that night, I kept thinking of Hannah Arendt's *Banality of Evil* (1994 [1963]). My knowledge of her work, of the psychological history of the Holocaust as understood through her philosophical acuity, gave weight and depth to my fear. Without that understanding of history, I might have been able to sleep as soundly as my quantitative colleague.

Holt Cemetery: Despair

When I finally acquired my identification badge, it read "local hire." This status meant that I was a temporary contractor hired from the local disaster zone. It meant that I was excluded from some meetings and decisions. And it meant that, unlike the regular FEMA employees and semiregular out-of-state contractors, I was ineligible for per diem reimbursements. The absurdity of this policy became apparent when I arrived in New Orleans a week later and began being reunited with familiar faces—other "local hires" from the historic preservation community. There were people who had lost their homes and most of their worldly possessions to Katrina, as well as their jobs. Undamaged rental housing was virtually nonexistent or taken over by real estate speculators. My local colleagues were doubling up with friends and relatives, or paying the same exorbitant hotel prices as FEMA employees, but without reimbursement. Meanwhile, nonlocal FEMA employees stayed in 4-star hotels and eagerly sampled each newly reopened restaurant, paid for by the federal budget. The victims of the disaster were those aided the least by FEMA employment. While on one level I knew that it was impossible for such a massive system such as Homeland Security to operate rationally, I nevertheless felt a creeping resentment toward impersonal forces and occasional flushes of pure anger fueled by sleep deprivation and an abysmal menu of frozen food, ready-to-eat meals given out by Red Cross, food service hamburgers, and protein bars.

It was mid-October. New Orleans had just been reopened to residents, but it was a ghost town. The activity that took up the greatest amount of my time in the early weeks was "windshield" surveys of the city's twenty-one historic districts. Along with fellow embedded consultants and FEMA historic preservation specialists, I drove street by street, taking photos and making notes on damaged, endangered, and significant historic sites. It was a process of slow, intense triage that felt aimless and unreal. The ultimate goal of this activity was vague and seemed to shift erratically with managerial whim. FEMA had not yet decided what to do about New Orleans's historic properties, but taking stock of its architectural and archaeological inventory was something to do to fill the time. It was presumed that such information would be useful at some future date. The National Historic Preservation Act is intended to prevent or mitigate the effects of actions taken by the federal government. But as far as FEMA was concerned, Hurricane Katrina was a natural disaster, not a federal action. Although one of FEMA's responsibilities is to assist local governments with getting their essential services (and thus essential buildings) up and running again, the agency has no legal mandate to repair damage to privately owned properties, no matter how historically or culturally significant.

Our surveys through abandoned neighborhoods reminded me of the reconnaissance missions and compulsive intelligence gathering that characterize modern colonialism, which I learned about first through the writing and teaching of Ann Laura Stoler and Nicholas Dirks. This sense of parallelism was intensified as I became more familiar with FEMA's institutional culture, which is deeply suspicious of local expertise. I felt betwixt and between. Culturally I was in many ways a local, but professionally I was expected to act as a member of an occupying force. However briefly, I was getting a taste of what a true "subaltern" experiences. That is, not using the term in the resentful language of failed revolutionaries and idealistic graduate students, but in its original colonial definition, as an officer ranking just below the decision makers. Subaltern agents were usually recruited from the local population and were ambivalent collaborators betwixt and between two worlds, stricken with Homi Bhabha's (1994) political hybridity.

On an emotional plane, I began to realize how even those Iraqis who had welcomed the U.S. invasion in 2003 and worked with would-be "liberators" (in the Katrina case, would-be "rescuers") could be turned against the occupying government and become its most strident opponents. I found myself, along with other New Orleanians, referring back to Reconstruction, calling FEMA representatives and the swarm of contractors who followed them "carpetbaggers." Against the bombed-out backdrop of post-Katrina New Orleans, I understood perhaps for the first time the interiority of Reconstruction that surpassed, and undermined, political hope in the South. Posttraumatic anger coming from an experience of war, or warlike devastation, mixed with a feeling of impotency and a sense of betrayal by a paternal authority is a bitter recipe. Early in the Civil War, New Orleans peacefully surrendered to the Federals. Although there were certainly powerful interests invested in slavery, most historians agree that prior to occupation and Reconstruction, antiwar and antislavery sentiment ran high in New Orleans. But a year later, residents were embittered and embattled with occupying General Benjamin Franklin Butler, whom they nicknamed "The Beast" for his high-handed command.

Time and again I witnessed small, competent local companies and consulting outfits being passed over for local jobs in favor of large national firms having standing contracts with the federal government. Neither cost nor expertise seemed to govern hiring decisions. In my luggage, I had packed James C. Scott's *Seeing Like a State* (1998), which had been recommended to me by Fernando Coronil as a relevant approach to political modernity that I had been struggling to understand in my work on French colonial New Orleans. In the few spare minutes I had to read over coffee or before I went to bed, I avidly absorbed descriptions of my own experience. A giant cookie-cutter of policy and modernism was being pushed into the bleeding landscape of my peculiar and historically stubborn city. A new source of fear came from the predictions threatened by Scott's analysis of Stalin-era agricultural reform or East African resettlement initiatives. Massive, impersonal, inflexible policies implemented by seemingly well-meaning bureaucracies that ignored local knowledge produced human tragedies that compounded over generations. Was this the future of New Orleans under post-Katrina "Reconstruction"? That autumn, Scott's work did not so much inform my thinking as inform my fears and induce insomnia.

Still, "staying busy" is a very effective coping mechanism, at least for the short term. I continued with the surveys. I and some like-minded colleagues would occasionally stop to talk to returning residents. Some were in shock, numbly moving damaged items from their houses and businesses, often inefficiently, one at a time, as if the process itself mattered more than the goal of cleaning up. Clearing, gutting, and restoring just a single structure—each a disaster in its own right—was a daunting task, the end of which was hard to foresee. And the means to accomplish it (insurance, FEMA assistance, labor, basic materials) not yet assured. Those who moved more quickly, or had more help, were of two opposite types: the first brusque and angry or tinderbox depressed, and the second bearing a humorous fatalism and modest hope. In addition to these laboring residents, we saw (and smelled) many dead pets on the surveys. We saw triage graffiti painted on nearly every facade. Some read "DOA." On one day in late October we began our grim survey of the Lower Ninth Ward, unquestionably one of the most devastated neighborhoods in the city, but we were pulled back the next day. A body had been found. They brought the dogs and recovery teams back to make a second pass. I don't think I was the only one who shared a macabre fascination with what seemed like newly anointed sacred ground.

Reminders of death were everywhere, yet I kept busy and kept moving along with others. Although I had shed new tears with each news report from New Orleans in the days after the storm when I was still in Chicago, my eyes had stayed dry and focused since arriving in Louisiana. It was only while I surveyed a place of the long dead that I lost control of the emotions I had been trying to keep out of my professional head. It was not

FIG. 10.1. Holt Cemetery, New Orleans. Photo by Shannon Dawdy.

until I made a quiet visit to one of my formerly favorite places in New Orleans that I broke down.

Holt Cemetery sits in the west-central portion of the city near City Park in an area given over to a patchwork of several religious and fraternal cemeteries. Holt Cemetery is the city's pauper cemetery, formerly operated by Charity Hospital and now owned by the city. It is the resting place for the most impoverished New Orleans residents, including many of its musicians. Most of the families who bury their loved ones in Holt do not have the resources to buy a formal headstone, much less one of the city's famous whitewashed vaults. Instead, the rough, below-ground graves (often backfilled with recycled dirt full of older, forgotten human remains and artifacts) are distinguished by homemade markers made of carved wood, found objects, poured concrete, or garden statuary. Votive objects such as candles, plastic flowers, lawn chairs, toys, Mardi Gras beads, and offerings of food and drink were commonly placed upon graves. It was colorful. It was improvisational. It was rooted in the historic folk traditions of New Orleans. Holt Cemetery, more than anything, expressed the unique aesthetic of the city's residents and their charming regard for one another, even in the all-too-common face of poverty, violence, and tragedy.

On an overcast All Saints' Day (November 1), I stood on the edge of the cemetery and looked out. Normally on this day New Orleans families would be visiting their graves, cleaning weeds, repainting, straightening markers, and redecorating as they liked. The first thing I noticed was that no one was there. I and the friend who had accompanied me were the only visitors. As I began to walk the bumpy surface of the aisles, I saw that the storm had washed the color away. There were barely a handful of graves still in possession of their markers, votive objects, or decorations. Markers were broken and scattered, as were the wooden frames that outline many of the graves. As we walked, we found that some of this material had been washed against the back fence, which was leaning and about to collapse. I was speechless. I tried for a moment to explain to my friend what was missing, as he had never visited Holt before. But I couldn't gather up an adequate description of the loss. I numbly stumbled back to the caretaker's shed and sat on the stairs and cried. I felt utter despair. It was an anthropological despair. I realized that the unique beauty of New Orleans is fragile and ephemeral. It is not embodied (or at least not embodied very well) in the hundreds of historic buildings we had already surveyed. It is embodied in people who enliven the connection between the past and the present with an unpredictable verve. They were gone. They had not made it back. And they might not ever be back. At that moment, I felt a rupture with the past that seemed irreparable and world-ending. Americanist anthropology was founded with the mission of rescuing "dying" cultures from modernity. It is a mission that, despite complications coming with maturity, it has never entirely abandoned. At the very least, it strives to recognize the local and critically analyze the global. Even on the cusp of the twenty-first century, New Orleans culture had in so many ways rejected modernity that the anthropological mission had seemed quaintly misplaced. But with one catastrophic event, it (I) seemed, in fact, to have arrived too late.

It did not help that a day earlier I had learned that a strict reading of the regulations governing federal historic preservation policy eliminated cemeteries from consideration. As sites, they were ineligible for assistance. In my role within FEMA, there was nothing I could do for Holt and the lives connected to it.

Maps: Hope

The despair I felt at Holt has not entirely left me, just as the despair that New Orleanians first felt when watching their neighbors stranded on rooftops or upon returning to their mold-encrusted silent houses has not yet left them (nor will it ever entirely, I suspect). As people say there, the disaster is ongoing. I predict it will go on for decades. My longue durée view of the future is informed by a longue durée view of the past.

Once the windshield surveys were complete, or I had done all I felt I could do to help on this particular front, my FEMA activities switched to research. One of the projects I undertook was to collect and digitize as many historic maps of New Orleans as possible and to plot these into a Geographic Information System database. The idea was to create a database that visually layered different eras of the city's history in order to quickly identify high potential areas of archaeological and historical significance. In this project, I felt more in my element. As an archaeologist and urban historian, I knew maps and their potential. I spent many hours researching and downloading maps from the U.S. National Archives, the French National Archives, and local repositories. I made appointments and visited libraries and institutions such as the Historic New Orleans Collection, Tulane University, and Louisiana State University. I consulted with archivists and fellow historians who were overwhelmingly generous and helpful. I spent just as many hours working with FEMA colleagues to figure out how to convert these old maps into a usable and cost-effective database. Using the first version of the database, we were able to achieve a satisfyingly simple and helpful goal: to draw zones of archaeological probability based upon known previous occupations and contemporary disturbances. This accomplished, I felt some hope that my time was not entirely wasted, at least for preserving the older and less visible elements of New Orleans history.

But beyond that, the more I immersed myself in the maps, the more I was reminded of how frequently New Orleans had been nearly wiped out by disaster. Fires destroyed the old French town. Floods and yellow fever struck throughout the eighteenth and nineteenth centuries. And hurricanes, of course, too. Some of the maps charted these disasters. We have maps that show the "fire line" of the 1788 and 1794 fires. We have maps that show half the present area of the city inundated after the crevasse, or levee break, of 1849, echoing the flood zones of Katrina. Many of us following Katrina had used Google Earth and FEMA-distributed satellite imagery to help us absorb the immense scale of the disaster or, in a different mode, to look up the address of a friend's house (or our own) to try to estimate the water level at its high point.

But more revealing, and encouraging, was not what these individual maps of particular disasters documented but rather what emerged in the overlays, as we placed them one on top of another in chronological order. What we saw was that each major disaster was followed by a major growth spurt in the city's history, as well as some redesign of the landscape. Yet architectural traditions and even the city's street grid—its physical grammar—had remained little changed since the late eighteenth century. Despite several major disasters (some on the scale of Katrina), the city had recovered. And despite the redesigns and new growth that followed, a cultural persistence gave shape to the innovations. The process of my research and an immersion in the historical documents gave me an immense burst of hope, much more so than the speeches of politicians or pundits. It is a hope informed by history that tempers my despair with the present. I have hope, but I know that rebirth will take time. We will have to measure the recovery of New Orleans in decades, not months or years. And it will never be the same place again. But it will still be a unique place. And it will be connected to its past, but connected in some new ways.

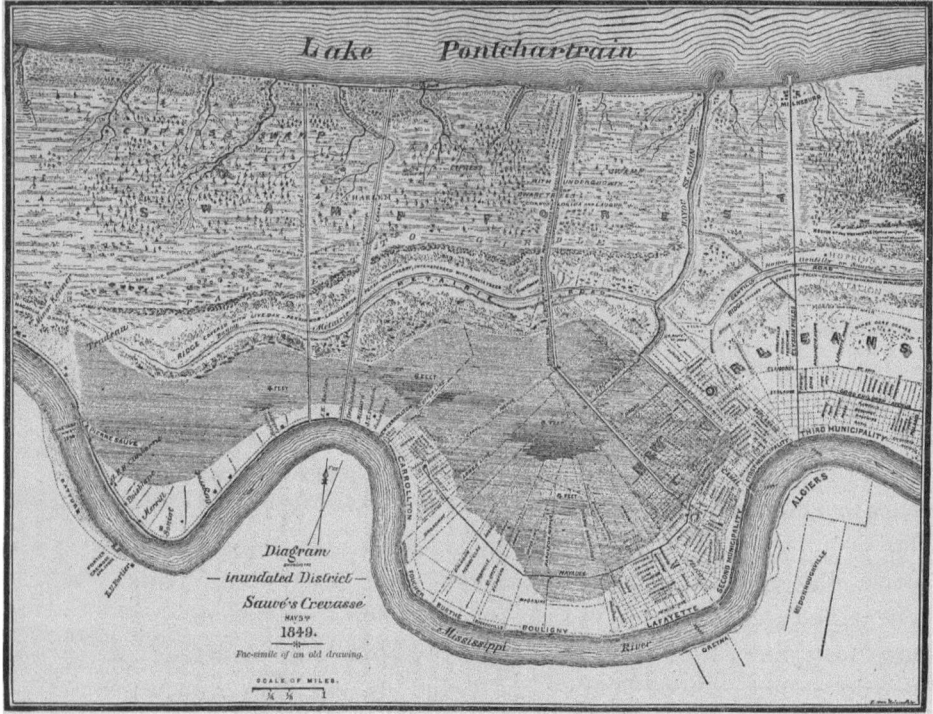

FIG. 10.2. 1849 map of New Orleans, depicting flooding in 1831

I have come to believe, and to be immensely grateful, that my transdisciplinary training has given me two old-fashioned gifts (at least in some small measure): wisdom and passion. Precisely because I am accustomed to code-switching between two disciplines, I feel better equipped to ignore the petty neuroses of either one. Precisely because I feel that I can rightfully claim to be immersed in both time (history) and place (anthropology), I am rooted to my field site and inspired by almost limitless possibilities for exploring it. I do not feel hindered by specialization. I can follow the questions that excite me and employ a diverse array of methods to answer them.

But as I hope I have also shown, we may adapt the modes of anthrohistory so thoroughly, constantly sifting experience through a critical and comparative longue durée, that we can't turn the training off. It not only gives us the tools to analyze and process the diverse types of data we collect, but anthrohistory fundamentally changes our worldview and way of being such that our most interior experiences of thought and emotion are affected. We experience the field and the archive differently. We are anthropologically suspicious of historical canons and institutions while at the same time historically skeptical about the exceptionalism of the ethnographic present. For those practicing anthrohistory, the past and the present are seen as more tightly interwoven and repetitive than either parent discipline tends to see. This bifocalism makes new realities come into focus, potentially provoking distinct emotional responses—such as in my Katrina case those of cold terror, despair, and hope. This may be the marker of a discipline unto itself. Perhaps a discipline creates a particular interiority and mode of perception more than it produces a particular academic product.

11 ❧ Zareena A. Grewal

Reclaiming Tradition

The Retrieval of Tradition

June 5, 2009. As a candidate, President Barack Obama promised to address the world's 1.5 billion Muslims from a "major Islamic forum" at the outset of his presidency. Obama's Cairo address was framed as a (renewed) bid for the Muslim hearts and minds that had been the "other" front in Bush's War on Terror, in order to signal that Americans were not (or, no longer) "at war with Islam." Minutes after President Obama's motorcade passed by en route to the Cairo University auditorium where he would deliver his address, government pickup trucks swarmed the historic Sultan Hassan Mosque, where the president had just enjoyed a tour. Security had been high for weeks in Cairo, with mass jailings and "disappearings" in the weeks leading up to President Obama's visit. Due to the near successes of global, populist Islamist movements to unseat various regimes since Egypt's independence from colonial rule, devout Muslims have been treated as a suspect population by the state, subject to random and unprovoked harassment and jailings. I observed such harassment regularly during my fieldwork in Cairo, Amman, and Damascus in 2002–3 among religious intellectuals. They were often persecuted despite the fact that many of them were apolitical and those with links to the Muslim Brotherhood or other political groups were *not* militants.

The Egyptian government officers perched on the shoulder of the road on this day were not on a security detail, nor did they arrest anyone. They began to collect the flowers and potted greens that had lined the streets and the mosque, apparently intended only for Obama (Aadil 2009). Onlookers watched in dismay but without surprise as the fragrant plants in the beds of government trucks were driven off in the haze of exhaust fumes; some mumbled that Mubarak could have waited at least for Obama's address to begin, while others wondered aloud if the brand new prayer rugs padding the marble floors of the mosque would be taken away as well and the tattered, worn ones returned. Only one piece of the story was out of the ordinary, at least for me. An American in Cairo was jailed too, without charges and without warning, and, like the jailed Egyptians, the American, a Muslim American religious seeker, was unceremoniously released on the Obamas' departure.

At any given time of the year, but especially in the summer, the intellectual urban centers of the Muslim Middle East attract dozens and sometimes hundreds of Muslim student-travelers from the West, primarily from the United Kingdom, France, Canada, and the United States. Muslim youth who have grown up in the West travel east to cities such as Cairo because they seek out a particular kind of religious and spiritual education; they want to "retrieve" the tools of their tradition, a tradition they feel remote from, a tradition they believe is under attack, in crisis.[1] Although diagnoses of Islam's various crises are ubiquitous (the crisis of violence, backwardness, stasis), Muslim Americans' invocations of crisis and retrieval of tradition reproduce a specific historical narrative of rupture; the crisis of Islamic knowledge is the result of the colonial and postcolonial reforms in education in Muslim societies and the subsequent marginalization and delegitimation of historical institutions of religious pedagogy and religious authority.[2]

This essay argues for a retrieval of tradition as well: the reclamation of tradition as an analytic. Scholars in the crosscurrents of history and anthropology have offered a number of important metareflections on the disciplinary histories and employments of particular categories, tracing the ways that they are alternatively sustained and abandoned, emptied and filled, ignored and seized upon in particular contexts and moments.[3] Tradition is arguably both more abstract and more concrete than the ways anthropologists use the term *culture,* and it has a disciplinary history of multiple and often theoretically incompatible referents.[4] In many ways, tradition and culture overlap as analytical categories: both resist definition and bounded referent; both are embedded in human experience in complex ways and illuminate the relationship between individuals and collectivities; both have temporal, discursive, regulatory, and contested dimensions; and, as analytical categories, both must be distinguished from their commonsense usages. Using an ethnographic vignette from my own research as a point of departure, I will provide sketches of a few scholarly approaches to tradition in order to explore the different analytical directions and political possibilities they open and close. Tradition heightens our self-consciousness about the politics of the production of knowledge and our own narrative relationships to specific traditions. By treating *tradition* as a shallow term, a "native" or lay category, particularly in the case of Islam, scholars may also become complicit in a new harmful, violent, and imperial project.

Scholars have long trained their gaze on the enormous harm and violence inflicted in the name of tradition in colonial and postcolonial contexts. This type of constructivist argument was first made famous by Eric Hobsbawm and Terence Ranger in their collection *The Invention of Tradition.* Hobsbawm argues that traditions "which appear or claim to be old are often quite recent in origin and sometimes invented" (1983, 1). This volume sparked a large body of scholarship that takes as its primary task the debunking of historically baseless claims and ideological rhetoric referencing tradition in service of political projects, particularly in regard to analyses of nationalism. Contemporary Islamists regularly invoke the authority of tradition as they make claims to political power. Constructivists, in turn, render their tradition claims suspect, demonstrating, for example, that a theocratic nation-state with a singular Shariah law is a radical departure from the classical structure of the Islamic caliphate and the plurality of historical Islamic law. These interventions can be important, both intellectually and politically, but they lose their analytical force when they employ the false binary of modern/traditional and reduce Islam to a ruse or a mask for the social, political, and economic agendas of Muslim actors.[5]

Tradition references the past; however, its relationship to the past is not natural but discursive, constituted by continuities as well as discontinuities. Constructivists rarely apply the same degree of suspicion in reverse to claims of newness, ruptures, discontinuities, such as those of programmatic "liberal" reformers of Islam, whose invocations of *ijtihad* are often invented breaks with tradition.[6] Rejections, critiques, dismissals, or disavowals of tradition, whether from feminists or Islamists, are as much a part of the narrative of the past, the present, and the future as claims of continuity, and thus are still located within tradition because they remain meaningful links to the past, even as they are oppositional and critical. When "normal" tradition is conceived of as an unthinking conformity to the past that opposes reason, argument within tradition can only be represented as exceptional, as a problem, a rupture in the flow of tradition. In contrast to this impoverished understanding of tradition, Alasdair MacIntyre places argument and reason at tradition's center such that debate itself becomes a testament to the health and coherence of a tradition (MacIntyre 1980). Coherence does not require agreement, consensus, or uniformity, only a common vocabulary. It is not the heterogeneity of Muslim Americans but the dizzying range of authority claims in U.S. mosques that generates a sense of crisis, an increasing sense of alarm over the perceived *incoherence* among Muslims. The sheer variety of modes of legitimacy that abound in American mosques is often interpreted by Muslim Americans to mean that there is no longer a universal language of authority, nothing that binds the incredibly diverse body of Muslim Americans to a standard or measure they all recognize as authentic. On any given issue, from the interpretation of a particular verse to social inequities among worshippers, proponents of each side engage their coreligionists by invoking a wide range of logics: religious, pragmatic, political, and so on.[7] Epistemological crises force subjects inhabiting a tradition to consider the possibility of the end of tradition and to rethink the future's relationship to the past and present through the medium of a new narrative that more adequately orders experience (MacIntyre 1984). In the case of Muslim Americans, that new narrative pivots on the Muslim east as an archive of tradition.

A Class in the Twelfth Century

> Fawzia wears a long, navy blue overcoat of georgette in the afternoon heat of July when the sun is so powerful that it seems to make even the flies in Damascus dizzy. Her white scarf, pressed and starched, conceals every hair, with the ends characteristically looped and tucked in at the neck. The overcoat and the neatly tied and tucked scarf are a kind of uniform for many Syrian women who are part of a popular women's faith movement, the Qubaysiyat, women who pass Fawzia by in the winding alleys of the old city and exchange secretive smiles and murmured greetings of peace.
>
> Despite her clothes, Fawzia never manages to fully blend in, to pass. In the tiny shops, her posture and her shoes betray the dollars and the U.S. passport in her purse long before her broken Arabic has a chance to. Fawzia is a "Cali girl" with no real interest in visiting her parents' homeland, Bangladesh. "Islam is too cultural there," she explains. "It's too mixed in with Hinduism. You can't even learn real Islam there."
>
> Instead, Fawzia came to Damascus to study Islam. Every morning, except on Fridays, Fawzia has a lesson in the art of melodious Qur'anic

recitation, mastering the strict rules of cadence and rhythm. After her Syrian teacher leaves, Fawzia spends the afternoon memorizing new chapters and practicing her recitation by recording her own voice and checking it against cassette tapes of internationally renowned reciters, in the hopes that she will earn an *ijaza,* linking her in a long chain of teachers and students that goes back to the Prophet himself, and giving her the authority to teach recitation students back in the United States. One evening a week, Fawzia attends a religious lecture given by her Qubaysiya *anisa:* a charismatic, middle-aged, white, American ex-pat who has taken Western student-travelers like Fawzia as her charge, overseeing their recitation lessons. The *anisa* opens her class with group-singing of English songs with "Islamicized" lyrics; her lecture topics cover a range of issues related to spiritual purification, complete with assignments such as supererogatory prayers and exercises to develop patience or manage anger, regimens Fawzia performs meticulously. At night, Fawzia reads books in English that came to Damascus in her suitcases: Rumi's poetry, Muhammad Asad's Qur'an commentary, and al-Ghazzali's *The Alchemy of Happiness.* Fawzia loves al-Ghazzali best; although she reads him in English, she dreams of knowing him in Arabic.

"He was an intellectual and a poet and he dealt with the West in his own way, in his own time by wrestling with Western philosophy. He didn't just reject philosophy wholesale, but he also didn't just accept stuff because Aristotle said so. He didn't just critique them like any Joe Schmoe; he became an expert himself. Half the time, Muslims now don't even know whether or why we [are] for or against certain things.

"I take [al-Ghazzali] as a model in a way of how to deal with engaging with the West but still preserving Islam. I respect him for being a man of action as well as a man of words."

Ghazzali came to Damascus in 1095. He left his family, his prestigious academic position, his entire life behind to search for a truth beyond his books and fame and wealth. He was a wandering mystic crisscrossing the desert, a simple ascetic cleaning the bathroom in the Umayyad Mosque on his knees, a humble teacher lecturing in the *zawiyah,* a lonely seeker locked away in the minaret of the mosque with his solitude and his hopes of being transformed.

Fawzia is in Damascus in 2002. As she makes her way to the mosque, through tiny, irregular streets of cobblestone, past haggling merchants and children sipping cola through straws out of clear, plastic sandwich bags, Fawzia longs for a different time, for al-Ghazzali's Damascus. Every Friday, on her way to the Umayyad Mosque, she closes her eyes and runs her fingers against crumbling walls, imagining that she is on her way to sit at the feet of her teacher and hear his seminal Damascene work, *The Revitalization of the Religious Sciences,* from his own lips, in the sunlit corner of the mosque that has since been named after him.

Discursive Analyses of Tradition (and Ideology)

In order to analyze Fawzia's account and the transnational, pedagogical networks she participates in, as well as phenomena such as the global "Islamic reawakening," one requires analytical tools that are at once fluid and deterritorialized, precise and magnifying. In my own work, the category of tradition allows me to draw together a diverse spectrum of Muslims in the United States and in Egypt, Jordan, and Syria for analytic purposes while maintaining the integrity of their differences.[8] Examining the complex workings of pedagogical networks such as the Qubaysiyat provides clues into the ways transnational formulations inform spatial, historical, and religious imaginaries that may transcend narrow nationalisms or, in this case, the concerted efforts by the state, in the name of security, to break the ties that link American mosque communities to Muslim networks beyond U.S. borders. For Fawzia and many of the American student-travelers, their ethnic heritage does not determine their destinations for religious education; they see their project of "carrying Islam" in relation to the *ummah,* the global community of believers as well as their diverse U.S. mosque communities. Through word of mouth in university student groups, e-mail discussion lists, and references from Muslim American religious leaders, these young people establish contacts with scholars overseas and other young people in the same endeavor.

However imaginative or subversive transnational identities may be, they should not be read triumphantly: transnational identities are still constituted by exclusions, constructions of difference, and limits, sometimes even national ones. Much of the rhetoric of American student-travelers like Fawzia is soaked in particularly American Orientalist tropes that often stubbornly persist despite their arrival in Muslim societies quite different from the Islamic east they have idealized, such as the "denial of coevalness" that undergirds Fawzia's construction of Damascene Arabs as living fossils (Fabian 1983). Fawzia links the contemporary crisis of Islam onto the private faith crises and public debates of the twelfth-century figure al-Ghazzali. As she derides the incoherence of her contemporary coreligionists (for not knowing what they believe or why), she offers al-Ghazzali's mastery of Aristotelian logic, his refutation of rival philosophers, and his pious training as a kind of hope and instructive example. Reproducing the trope of the ancient Greek roots of Western civilization, Fawzia equates Aristotle with "the West," a category he preceded by thousands of years, but not in the name of the nation; she makes this claim in order to project her own sense of crisis, that Islam is and has been under onslaught from "the West," back through the ages. A constructivist analysis of Fawzia's rhetoric might detail and debunk such anachronisms and claims based on tenuous links to historical record by dutifully juxtaposing her words against those of a serious scholar, such as the eminent historian Marshall Hodgson (1974) who argues, quite convincingly, that as a tradition Islam inherits Aristotelian philosophy as much if not more than "the West" does.

Constructivist analyses interrogate tradition claims: why al-Ghazzali and why now, what genealogy, what context, against what or whom are Fawzia's claims made? These questions are compelling and important. Despite all the allusions to Islam's universalism, Fawzia's pedagogical goals are animated in part by a mythic narrative of American exceptionalism, reproduced in tandem with her Arab peers and teachers; the American *ummah* is exceptional, distinguished by its wealth, resources, diversity, talent (due to the brain drain), political privilege, and vision, and, therefore, the agenda for the global *ummah* ought to be set by American Muslims, at least once they are properly trained. These kinds of territorializing claims about the (American) future of Islam can be strikingly unreflective and explicit, while others are more implicit. For example, Fawzia and her peers often sing the song "I Can Show You Islam" with their *anisa,* adapted from the Disney film *Aladdin*'s "A Whole New World," a score criticized for being replete with racist, anti-Arab lyrics!

Yet one limitation of the constructivist approach is that it foregrounds historical authenticity as the primary frame for engaging tradition, such that tradition is usually only of scholarly interest insofar as it is a *mis*representation of the past. In reaction to constructivist arguments, some theorists of tradition reject the basic line of questioning premised on degrees of historical authenticity. Rather than argue for a more rigorous analytical conceptualization of tradition, scholars working in an antihistoricist mode pare down the category of tradition further, taking a kind of nominalist stance toward tradition. Richard Handler and Joyce Linnekin (1984) argue in favor of such an approach; they isolate tradition's paradox of preservation and the ways it inevitably alters or reconstructs that which it intends to fix. They argue that since authentic tradition is defined in the present, all "genuine" traditions (in Fawzia's case, al-Ghazzali) are "spurious," and all "spurious" traditions (Disney's *Aladdin*) are "genuine." Despite often being cast as preservation, they argue, tradition is always new and always invented because authenticity is always defined in the present.

Since authenticity, historical and otherwise, implies a standard (or multiple standards) by which to judge information or behavior, the nominalists, as a gesture of their scholarly suspension of (religious) judgment and rejection of authenticity, define Islam as whatever is labeled Islam by their Muslim subjects (islams instead of Islam), such that islam in each instance is unique and the terms *traditional* and *new* are interpretive rather than descriptive. A nominalist will concern herself not with the historical al-Ghazzali or the historical Aristotle but with reading (in Geertz's sense) what al-Ghazzali, Aristotle, the landscape of Damascus, the score of *Aladdin,* and so forth *mean* to Fawzia (and others in her pedagogical network). In other words, Fawzia's "symbolic needs" in the present constitute tradition, constitute islam.

This flattening of tradition as an analytical category obscures more than it reveals. The representation of Islam as a totality of fragments on a horizontal axis fails to correspond to actual religious discourses (which are never even and always enmeshed in networks of power) and masks the very heterogeneity of Muslims it is intended to capture. The diversity and heterogeneity of Muslims is not proof of the absence of a coherent tradition, rather it is simply proof of the absence of homogeneity. Ordinary Muslims like Fawzia are at least as conscious of the diversity of interpretation and practice of Islam as academics are, evinced here by her dismissal of her Bangladeshi coreligionists, yet she is theologically invested in the *idea* of a single Islam, and, therefore, in engaging and persuading other Muslims to come around to her view of things. In other words, the move to isolate the "islam" of a group, a movement, a village, or one individual's islam as a sui generis disciplinary object obscures the relational, contested, communal quality of tradition. Fawzia's beliefs about the beliefs of others are her *own* beliefs; her dream of getting an *ijaza* pivots on her investments in being recognized as an authority by *other* Muslims. What is left out of nominalist accounts is not merely the "background information" contextualizing the Qubaysiyat as a movement or Damascus as an Islamic intellectual center, but, more important, the multiple and competing mainstreaming and marginalizing processes by which Muslims assign stigma and prestige. Fawzia's mapping of "real" Islam onto the Arab world and marking of Bengali (but not Syrian or American) culture as pollutants of Islam is one such example.

The nominalist approach is rooted in a scholarly misrecognition of orthodoxy as a fixed body of opinion that moves through time like a brittle object or a coercive instrument rather than as a discursive (and dynamic) relationship of power. Anticipating this scholarly skittishness associated with the category of orthodoxy, Talal Asad defines orthodoxy not as a body of opinion at the "heart" of Islam but as a distinctive "relationship of power. Wherever Muslims have the power to regulate, uphold, require, or adjust *correct* practices, and to condemn, exclude, undermine, or replace *incorrect* ones, there is the domain of orthodoxy" (Asad 1986, 15). Orthodoxy in this sense is not simply derived from foundational texts; rather the relationships of power that constitute orthodoxy are sustained, animated, or undermined by the deployments of foundational texts as well as a whole host of extratraditional nodes of power, such as petrodollars, the Internet, racial formations, and so on. Some scholars have mistakenly read Asad's ethnographic prescription for documenting the constitution and reconstitution of orthodoxy by Muslims as his analytical employment of a "native" category of orthodoxy that references a singular, text-based transhistorical body of beliefs and practices. Asad's prescription regarding the line-drawing exercise of orthodoxy is ethnographic; it is neither theological nor descriptive in the nominalist sense. The debates Fawzia has with her coreligionists about where and how darkly those lines of inclusion/exclusion are drawn happen in particular constellations of power and resistance, in which Fawzia's American passport, her dark skin, her broken Arabic, her Qubaysi uniform, her gender, are all signs.

> *In every era the attempt must be made anew to wrest tradition away from a conformism that is about to overpower it.*
> ❦ WALTER BENJAMIN 2007 (1955), 255

Constructivist and antihistoricist/nominalist lines of questioning neglect other angles of inquiry, such as the temporal qualities of tradition. The individual and collective interpretive relationships to the past, present, and future that constitute tradition redirect our scholarly attention in important ways. Hannah Arendt locates the trinity of religion, authority, and tradition in a constant collision course between the past and the future (1961). She argues that the past presses forward rather than pulling us back, and instead the future pushes us back into the past. Her formulation of time as contingent rather than linear is compelling because it captures the sense among the Muslim American subjects of my research of an imminent crisis of Islam on the horizon and highlights the overlap of different temporalities, highlighting the ways tradition organizes memory and desire despite the very different patterns of desire and forgetfulness encouraged by the social forces of global capitalism. Muslim student-travelers' engagements with different moments in their tradition move them through different clocks, a heterotemporality distinct from Fawzia's troubling imagined time travel. For example, I chart the coexistence of various, overlapping chronometries in the journeys of the American student-travelers, the multiple measures of time constituted by particular interactions with power. I examine the intersections between "worship time," which divides the day into units of prayer and heralds the Day of Judgment, the "mystical time" of the students of Sufism, who pursue the experience of timelessness, and "progressive time," measured in places like Damascus by "catching up to the West," changes in technology, transformations in the work "day," and the pressures of a global capitalist economy.

In the process of retrieving tradition as an analytic, we must strive against flattening the category of ideology, or the ideological dimensions of tradition, what Michael Oakeshott (1991) termed "abridgements of tradition." Veena Das (2008) points, insightfully, to the ways our scholarship has predispositions toward particular analytical strategies and against others. Reflecting on how her previous work on violence was an obstacle to her more recent research on religion, she concludes that the energy and time she spent thinking and writing about religious violence depleted her ability to analyze issues relating to the religious aesthetic of life because she could only see religion flatly, as a flight from the ugly realities of political projects animated by religious ideologies. Our challenge is to remain alert to the tension between tradition and ideology, without privileging one category over the other. Ideological claims may be constituted by constructions of the past as simple, but the claims themselves ("The personal is political," "*Shariah* is eternal," etc.) are as complex and wide-ranging as tradition claims. To my mind one of the most important differences between ideology and tradition is not the objective relation to a historical reality (although that is hardly irrelevant) but rather the binding qualities of authority that link the past, present, and future. In contrast, inventions of tradition do not carry this kind of weight or exert this pressure, which is what makes them ideological "abridgements." Handler and Linnekin's criticism of the project of historical verification has merit since historical fictions may be deeply meaningful, but to argue that anything called tradition *is* tradition is too crude, for indeed, as the constructivists illustrated, there *are* invented traditions that construct the past as a simple ideological source of symbols, ideas, and languages that can be interpreted and drawn upon to legitimate political projects. There are also tradition claims that are *not* ideological, and that also deserve our serious scholarly attention. The question in the selective transmission of tradition, as in law, is not whether the determinations of relevance are contingent on time and culture because, of course, they are; rather, the more interesting line of inquiry is to examine what constitutes likeness, difference, and relevance in different moments (Schauer 1987, 596). Handler and Linnekin's treatment conflates all forms of tradition and invented traditions, circumventing the investigation of likeness and difference, relevance and irrelevance, that constitute the transmission process.

In order for tradition to have analytical dexterity, we must develop more rigorous conceptualizations of the ideological dimensions of tradition. The central weakness of Handler and Linnekin's thesis is that in their zeal to undermine the constructivists they take the constructivist argument to an extreme conclusion that Hobsbawm himself never made: that *all* tradition is merely ideology. Just as legal fictions operate in law, a tradition is not required to have absolute transparent reflexivity. After all, in the context of a religious debate, one's claims are only enhanced by the illusion that tradition is a simple movement of a body of static beliefs and practices through time, the unbroken chain of Fawzia's teachers. There are always elements of tradition that are uncritically taken for granted just as there are always anticritical employments of tradition that deny the creativity in the transmission process. For example, the Qubaysiya teachers are reticent to admit that their criteria for *ijaza* in Quranic recitation reflect the needs and lifestyles of their students, such that the complete memorization of the Quran is no longer a condition for certification. The dynamic process of the transmission of tradition—the evaluation, amplification, suppression, refinement, and assessment of elements of the past and the present—allows the subjects inhabiting tradition to unite their veneration for a sacred past with a healthy skepticism about its relevance for the present and future without violating tradition (Pocock 1989, 268–69). Of course, their selections are always subjective, but this does not mean that they are "free" choices. The authority of tradition is constituted by expectations, demands, pressures, and limits that restrict one's freedom or ability to act in self-interest, but in a way that feels natural, or authentic, to the self; this is what distinguishes it from mere persuasion or from coercion and force.

Tradition/Detraditionalization

"Just cause you're paranoid, doesn't mean you're not being followed . . ." However skeptical we might be of Muslim Americans' diagnoses of Islam's crises, this quote from one student-traveler resonates with a harsh, political reality. I have been arguing that the most influential scholarship on tradition has emphasized the discursive qualities of tradition, however, to very different analytical and political ends. There is also a growing body of derivative scholarship on tradition with a much more troubling set of premises and political aims, in the name of "free" choice. In 2003, the Rand think tank released a report, *Civil Democratic Islam: Partners, Resources, and Strategies,* cautioning the State Department and then President Bush that although fringe Islamic militant groups came under closer scrutiny after September 11, 2001, the more *dangerous* threat to U.S. interests and global democracy came from the "traditionalist" Muslim masses. Although these "traditionalist" Muslims are moderates and *not militants*, according to Rand, the authority they grant revelation and Islamic law belies their antimodernism; even when their hearts and minds seemingly get the "right" or "Enlightened" answers (in stances against polygamy, for example) they get them from the "wrong" source, that is, tradition (Benard 2003).[9] This argument in favor of an accelerated detraditionalization builds on an earlier Rand report's "net-war" thesis. They advised the U.S. defense to adopt various models of military strategy, thinking like a street gang, swarming like pirates, communicating like Wal-Mart, fighting like the Mongols, whose outnumbered "hordes" created the largest continental empire in history (Arquilla and Ronfeldt 2001). Since the future will likely be wholly different from the past, U.S. defense strategists must embody the "detraditionalized" ability to detach from any worldview and the "freedom" to choose any framework, such that the past is irrelevant except as a storehouse of potentially usable, available modalities. History becomes *merely* a source, a kind of toolbox that evokes Lévi-Strauss's conception of bricolage.[10]

If tradition implies certain meaningful kinds of temporal links to the ways we remember the past and anticipate the future in the present, the detraditionalized bricoleur approach to history is to make do with "whatever is at hand," transforming random elements into tools or, in this case, weapons. Tools are only defined by their potential use, collected and retained randomly, representing a set of actual and possible relations (Lévi-Strauss 1966) such that disparate historical examples, corporate logics, and strategies are leveled to an even plane of detachment. Of course, not all Americans share such a detached view of the Mongol occupation of Baghdad; the Muslim Americans I encountered in Egypt, Syria, and Jordan on the eve of the 2003 U.S. invasion of Iraq remembered the Mongol occupation as the deepest cut into the Islamic tradition, threatening its very existence, bleeding rivers black from the ink of destroyed libraries. For me, this was perhaps the most compelling reason to try to rethink and reclaim the category of tradition as an analytical tool. In this limited space, I have only gestured at the story of why tradition dropped out of our analytical toolboxes, but as Rand and others herald a major transformation in the ways we understand history and experience time, the need for scholarly examinations of these processes becomes more pressing. The argument for a recuperation of tradition as an analytic should not be confused with one that posits that academia ought to be a "shelter" or "safe haven" for an embattled tradition or religion (Islam), or that our research ought to promote the interests of our (politically vulnerable, Muslim) subjects. My argument is that reclaiming tradition creates a transdisciplinary space where important differences are not collapsed under the weight of scholarly habits, a space for us to make visible the tensions between alternative, competing visions of the past and the future.

NOTES

1. Cairo is a particular magnet for American Muslim student-travelers primarily because of the lively world of religious education it offers *outside of* official institutions like Al-Azhar (discredited by many lay Muslims precisely because it was absorbed by the state), and although such unofficial pedagogical activity is quasi-illegal in Egypt, it is also readily available.

2. For a similar argument from a professional historian, see Bulliet 2004.

3. Examples include Patrick H. Hutton's reflections on memory in *History as an Art of Memory* (1993), David William Cohen, Stephan F. Miescher, and Luise White's introduction to the volume *African Words, African Voices* (Cohen et al. 2001), particularly their section titled "The Strange Career of the African Voice," and Paul Eiss's elegant essay in this volume on the category of *el pueblo*.

4. Tradition should not be reduced to a euphemism for culture or subculture, or simply as the temporal element of culture as Kroeber uses it in his classic definition of tradition as the "internal handing on through time" of culture traits (1948, 11). In the 1940s, the schema of dividing Islam into "Great" and "Little" traditions was first introduced in order to differentiate between the textual canon of religious elites in Islamic urban centers and the "popular" practices of the urban and rural masses, but this framework ultimately reproduces the binary oppositions of oral/literate, rural/urban, local/universal, and syncretic/authentic. Historical anthropologist Talal Asad (1986), in his now classic and oft-cited literature review "The Idea of an Anthropology of Islam," first redirected scholarly attention away from finding the right scale of analysis to formulating the right concepts, specifically a more rigorous conceptualization of tradition, as a set of discourses connected to an exemplary past and to interpretations of foundational texts that Muslims draw on in their ordinary lives.

5. Many scholars, for example, read the Islamic resurgence as evidence of the failure or inability of Muslim societies to modernize fully. Interestingly, other scholars explain the renewed interest in Islam (in quasi-functionalist terms) as a means for these societies to complete their transition to modernity, or as a poorly disguised form of (Arab) nationalism. Underlying both types of analyses is the assumption that the postcolonial Muslim world is a hybrid of tradition and modernity. These types of analyses represent Islamism as an inexplicable historical development by attempting to tease out causal explanations, rather than trying to make it understandable by demonstrating what constitutes Islamism in particular social, historical contexts (Asad 1993).

6. For example, Irshad Manji's best-selling *The Trouble with Islam: A Muslim's Call for Reform of Her Faith* (2003) is replete with baseless claims of newness, "reform" that breaks with her invented history of Islam, and (mis-)representation of Islamic tradition. For a deconstruction of Manji's argument, see Al-Ariss 2007.

7. Muslim American communities are often divided on the question of who should lead their mosque. These debates often include questions of cultural authority and authenticity, as in whether an "imported" religious scholar educated in prestigious Eastern religious institutions would be better able to lead than a black American convert without formal religious training but who has an intimate understanding of American society.

8. Most of the scholarship on Muslim Americans treats them as discrete national, ethnic, or racial groups, what I have elsewhere called the "village effect." I argue that scholars who work in American mosque communities rely too heavily on demographic variables in selecting subject samples, perhaps as a practical concession to the incredible diversity of Muslim Americans. This artificial, territorial-

izing isolation of Muslim Americans creates the illusion of discrete, ethnic "villages" that are often more representative of the methodological habits of academics than of the lived experience of the often diverse and overlapping mosque communities in the United States.

9. For a collaborative response from a diverse set of Muslim American scholars, see Louay Safi's report *Blaming Islam* (2006). For a critical reading of the report, see Saba Mahmood's article "Secularism, Hermeneutics, and Empire: The Politics of Islamic Reformation" (2006).

10. Lévi-Strauss's original usage of the term was applied to myth, not history. I borrow the application of the term to history from Talal Asad.

12

Impressions: An Interval

This shipwreck of fragments, these echoes, these shards of a huge tribal vocabulary, these partially remembered customs . . . they are not decayed but strong.
—DEREK WALCOTT (1998, 70–71)

To all appearances, the artist acts like a mediumistic being who, from the labyrinth beyond time and space, seeks his way out to a clearing.
—MARCEL DUCHAMP (1959, 77)

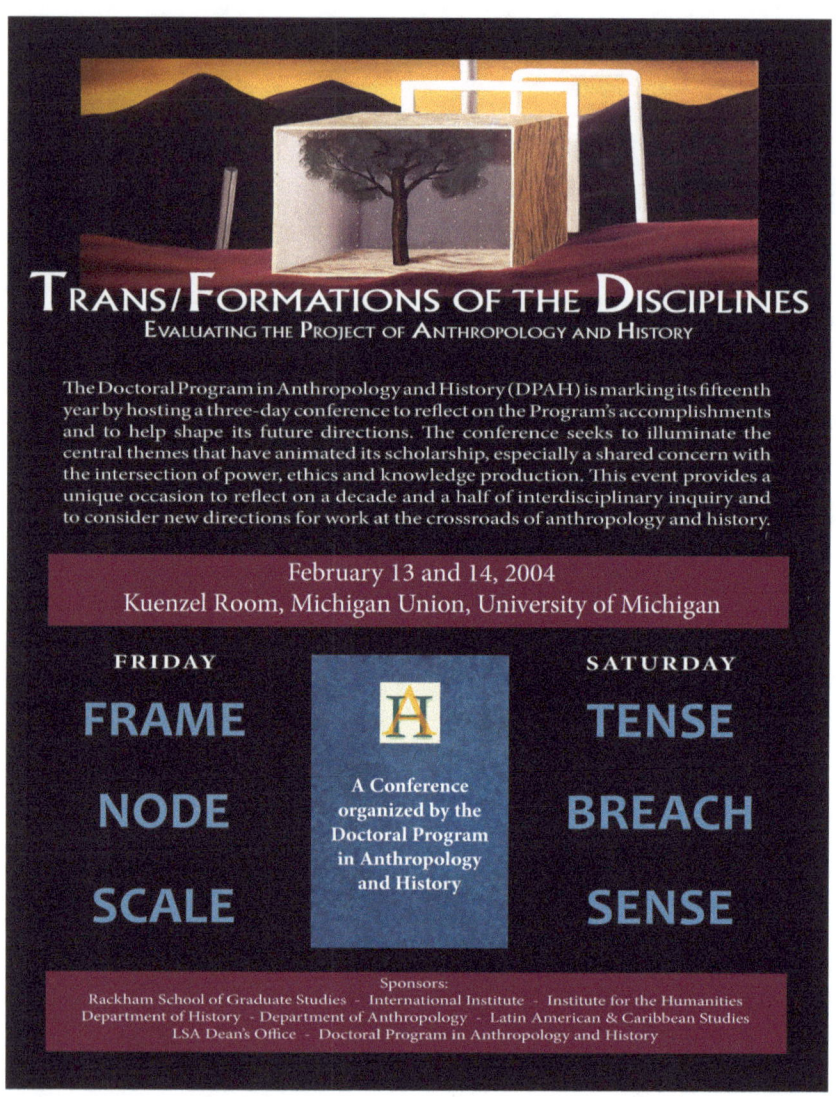

FIG. 12.1. Conference poster "Trans/Formations of the Disciplines," February 2004. René Magritte, *Le Parc du Vautour* (1926). Copyright 2010 C. Hersovici, London / Artist Rights Society (ARS), New York. "Each element is about confinement."

FIG. 12.2. Katsashuki Hokusai (1760–1849), *The Great Wave at Kanagawa* (from a Series of Thirty-six Views of Mount Fuji, ca. 1829–32). Japan. Edo period. Polychrome woodblock print; ink and color on paper, 10 1/8 × 14 15/16 in. Published by Eiudo. H. O. Havemeyer Collection, Bequest of Mrs. H. O. Havemeyer, 1929. Copyright The Metropolitan Museum of Art, New York / Art Resource, NY.

> The critical position of the (Anthrohistory) (P)rogram has been made possible—indeed, necessary—because of the bulk and durability of what counts as mainstream, conventional, and discipline-specific academic knowledge production. Figuratively, Anthrohistory has been like the evanescent foam on the tip of a wave that emerges at and from the interaction of strong uninterrupted winds, large open bodies of water (with tides, in the case of oceans) and their varied sea-beds . . .
> —DAVID PEDERSEN, THIS VOLUME

FIG. 12.3. José Guadalupe Posada, *Don Quijote* (ca. 1895–1913). Zinc etching.

This engraving by the Mexican artist Posada was used to announce the Anthrohistory Program's 2001 colloquium series "Science, Ethics, Power: Controversy over the Production of Knowledge and Indigenous Peoples" (see Skurski, this volume). Moving beyond the controversy over Patrick Tierney's problematic book, *Darkness in El Dorado,* the series addressed the geopolitical and ethical dimensions of knowledge production in connection with anthropological and biomedical research among the Yanomami and other indigenous peoples.

FIG. 12.4. Tshimbumba Kanda Matulu, *Lumumba in Buluo Prison* (1974). Tropenmuseum, Amsterdam, collection number 5867-44.

Why do I still fight? Because I am alive.
🍂 DAVI KOPENAWA (1991), BRAZILIAN YANOMAMI SPOKESPERSON

This rendering of an imprisoned and tortured Patrice Lumumba on the eve of Congo's independence was painted by Tshibumba Kanda Matulu in the 1970s as one of a series of 101 paintings depicting a history of Congo. The anthropologist Johannes Fabian (1996) encouraged this project of a painterly history as an exercise in the elaboration of popular history. The image presages the Congo leader's last confinement, torture, and execution on January 17, 1961, at the hands of the former colonial power Belgium, its Western allies, and this alliance's clients in Katanga and Leopoldville. In one of his last letters, drafted in prison for his third wife Pauline, Lumumba wrote, "History will one day have its say; it will not be the history taught in the United Nations, Washington, Paris, or Brussels, but the history taught in the countries that have rid themselves of colonialism and its puppets" (De Witte 2001, 185).

FIG. 12.5. Paul Klee, *Angelus Novus* (1920). Copyright The Artist Rights Society, New York / VG Bild-Kunst, Bonn.

A Klee painting named "Angelus Novus" shows an angel looking as though he is about to move away from something he is fixedly contemplating. His eyes are staring, his mouth is open, his wings are spread. This is how one pictures the angel of history. His face is turned towards the past. Where we perceive a chain of events, he sees one single catastrophe which keeps piling wreckage upon wreckage and hurls it in front of his feet. The angel would like to stay, awaken the dead, and make whole what has been smashed. But a storm is blowing from Paradise; it has got caught in his wings with such violence that the angel can no longer close them. This storm irresistibly propels him into the future to which his back is turned, while the pile of debris before him grows skyward. This storm is what we call progress.

—WALTER BENJAMIN, WRITING FROM PARIS IN THE LATE 1930S (2007 [1955], 257)

FIG. 12.6. Sarah Wyman, *Blanket* (2008). Copyright Sarah Wyman.

We are constantly engaging with the past. When we gaze up at the night sky or peer through a telescope, some of the light that we see may be from stars that have been extinguished for billions of years. Accounting for this vision is not simply a matter of a time-space continuum, however. A certain mindfulness toward simultaneity is also required. Different time-moments constitute the skyscape, and the objects we are closest to do not necessarily appear most clearly. . . . One must also consider the intensity and strength of certain bodies in relation to one another. Strong memories can trump more recent ones in their power and sway, and the clarity of their vision in both detail and impact. So too, the brightness of stars is ever and always relational. Without other celestial bodies to compare them to, we would have no way of determining either their place or size, nor their significance in the universe.

—MONICA EILEEN PATTERSON, THIS VOLUME

FIG. 12.7. Philippe Petit between the Twin Towers (1974). Copyright AP Photo / Alan Welner, August 7, 1974.

I will negotiate a moment of my life between the two towers. . . . My world, if you look at it and even more so if you accompany [me] to the backstage of it, is basically the world of a poet or a writer who decided to write in the sky. . . . My childhood from 6 to 16 was made of those encounters with art, with theater, writing, poetry, and painting . . . all this I mixed up and all this I put on the wire.

—PHILIPPE PETIT (2008)

FIG. 12.8. Deborah Howard, *Labyrinth* (1999). 60 × 40 in., acrylic on paper. Copyright Deborah Howard.

Beneath English trees I meditated on that lost maze: I imagined it inviolate and perfect at the secret crest of a mountain; I imagined it erased by rice fields or beneath the water; I imagined it infinite, no longer composed of octagonal kiosks and returning paths, but of rivers and provinces and kingdoms. . . . I thought of a labyrinth of labyrinths, of one sinuous spreading labyrinth that would encompass the past and the future and in some way involve the stars.

—JORGE LUIS BORGES (1962B)

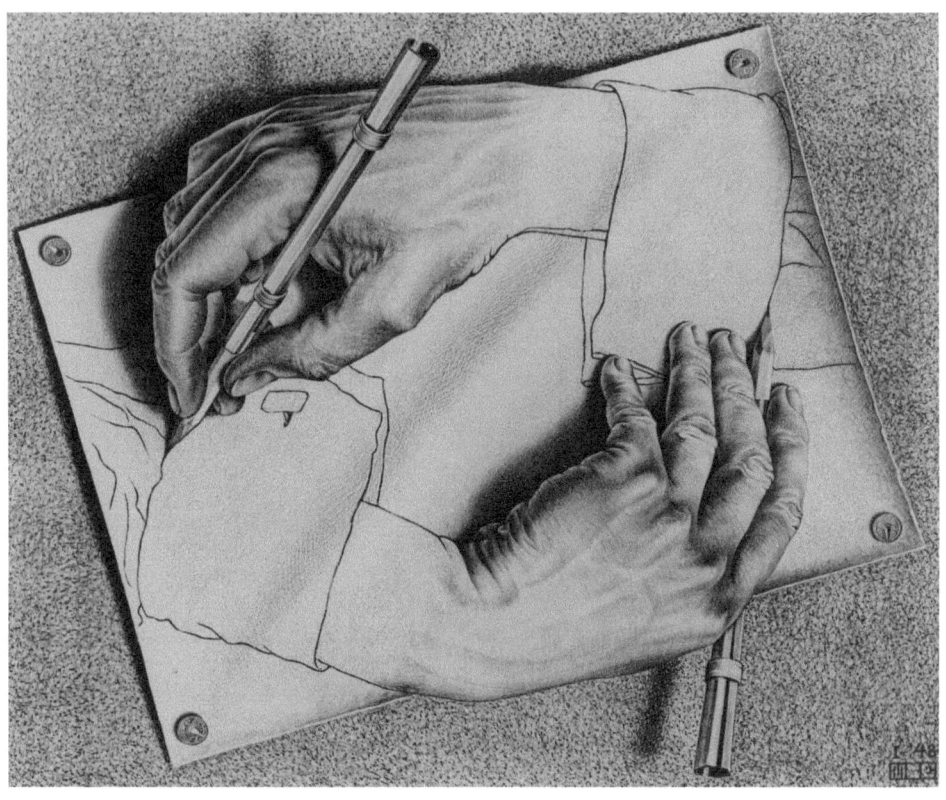

FIG. 12.9. M. C. Escher, *Drawing Hands* (1948). Copyright 2009 The M. C. Escher Company-Holland. All rights reserved. www.mcescher.com.

> Perhaps sociologists carry around buried deep within them some sense of what solidarity is or what constitutes the mystery of our social, collective existence; and perhaps political scientists have a vague inkling of what a democratic form of life might feel like ... from a certain perspective, one can imagine a sense of the phantom nature of each and every discipline.
> —THOMAS C. WOLFE, THIS VOLUME

13 ❧ Mandana E. Limbert

The Miracle of History: Temporality and Uncertainty in Southern Arabia

On July 23, 1970, Qaboos bin Said al-Bu Saidi, the only son of the sultan of Muscat and Oman, Sultan Said bin Taimur al-Bu Saidi, overthrew his father, in a (nearly) bloodless, palace coup d'état. Soon after Qaboos's return to Oman from his English education, and probably because Sultan Said bin Taimur was concerned about his own fate, Sultan Said placed his son under strict confinement (most people say house arrest) in the palace in Salalah, the capital of Oman's southern region of Dhofar. In the evening of July 23, a small group of Qaboos's supporters stormed Said bin Taimur's quarters. Said bin Taimur shot himself in the foot, surrendered, and that was the end of Said bin Taimur's nearly forty-year reign. The Royal Air Force flew the now former sultan to Bahrein, where he was treated for his podiatric injuries. He then made his way to England, where he lived the rest of his years (he died in 1972) at the Dorchester hotel in London. In the meantime, the son, the new sultan, inaugurated what has come to be understood as a new era in modern Omani history. And, indeed, the new era in Oman has a distinct name, *al-Nahda,* the (time of) renaissance, renewal, or rebirth.

This event is understood in Oman and by the foreign scholarship on Oman as *the* turning point in Omani history. With the coup, Oman, it is often said, suddenly changed from being "medieval" to "modern." To be sure, much has changed in Oman since the 1970 coup d'état. Common and oft-repeated statistics note that between 1970 and 1980, the number of modern schools increased from 3 to 363, the kilometers of asphalt roads increased from 6 to 12,000, and the number of hospitals increased from 1 to 28. And, yet, much of this has had to do with the availability of oil wealth beginning from 1967, rather than simply a change in rule. Similarly, while the impetus for the coup is often understood as emerging from Qaboos's recognition that the country "needed development," in fact, the catalyst seems to have been the expansion of the Marxist rebellion (that was centered in southern Dhofar) to Oman's northern regions, where the majority of the oil fields are located.

In this chapter, I emphasize not so much the disjuncture between official representations and personal memories of the coup, its impetus, and effects, although certainly these exist. Rather, this chapter explores the cultivation and articulation in both state and personal discourses of mystery and surprise in understandings of Oman's history and future. It is by attending to anthropology *as* history, that is, the presence of "history" in everyday life, and what this means, that nonteleological narratives about the past and present become evident. Rather than simply a linear trajectory of progress, which the state also propagates at times, history—from the past and into the future—is more often understood, and cultivated to be understood, as a process of mysteries, miracles, surprises, and possible reversals. While most states, and especially authoritarian ones, as Paul Eiss (2002) has pointed out, presume to hold the power of knowledge over a deferred utopian future, other states and their development discourses, I suggest, also encourage mysteries, miracles, surprises, and uncertainties. Omnipotent certainty gives way to a more restrained (albeit no less overdetermined) and circumspect trajectory.

Temporalities of Surprises, Rather than Trajectories of Certainties

Rather than a set stage in a teleology of progress spurred on by a coup d'état (or even oil wealth) that has either succeeded or failed, the present in Oman is often understood as temporary and the future unknowable, bleak, or, for the optimistic, redemptive. Such senses of temporariness and uncertainty raise multiple questions, not only about the specificities of temporal understandings in Oman, as I will discuss shortly, but also about scholarship on discourses and policies of development more broadly. In particular, in response to the modernization theorists of the 1960s and 1970s, theorists of development in the 1990s especially encouraged scholars to consider the ways that "development" has often been experienced as a failure (Escobar 1995; Ferguson 1994, 1999; Gupta 1998; Li 2007; Pigg 1992). Beyond the literature on development, scholars also pointed to the optimism characteristic of classic discourses of nationalism, what Anderson has called the "future perfect" and Herzfeld has argued is central to "monumental time."[1] While these analyses have brought to life contradictory experiences of development and nationalist sentiments, they have also limited our understandings of the complexities of development discourses and policies as well as "official" narratives that do not follow neat teleological models of progress. Indeed, the Omani case offers insight into a developmentalist state that presents a different temporal trajectory and sense of modern knowability, one that presumes an end (with its limited oil supplies and mortal sultan) and encourages surprises, mysteries, and uncertainties rather than an unlimited, knowable, and progressive future. In Oman, and perhaps other oil-rich states, rather than a utopia, the future portends to be a dystopia, where oil reserves are depleted and the golden age of the present has evaporated. Similarly, the present—with its "surprise" of oil wealth and mystery about origins and history—is understood as more of an anomaly, and an opaque one at that. Far from producing a less powerful state, such uncertainties further solidify the necessity of "trusting" state power and wisdom: no outcome is certain, but one must trust that the state, in having the best interest of its citizens, will provide for the most secure future.

It should be noted that in Oman temporal uncertainties about prosperity are accompanied and enhanced by uncertainties about succession as well as the potential revival of a theocratic regime. The sultan is, of course, mortal, but he is also without an heir. Furthermore, Oman's past form of theocratic government, based on Ibadism (a third distinct branch of Islam after Shi'ism and Sunnism), remains an imagined, and in some cases hoped for, future; it is a "preserved possibility." Unlike in Shi'ism and Sunnism, in Ibadi political philosophy, the leader of the Muslim community need not be

> *"From now on, I'll describe the cities to you," the Khan had said, "in your journeys you'll see if they exist." But the cities visited by Marco Polo were always different from those thought of by the emperor.*
>
> ITALO CALVINO 1972, AS CITED IN HUYSSEN 2008, 1

either a direct descendant or a member of the tribe (the Quraysh) of the Prophet Mohammad, opening the way to a more profane and accessible form of religious governance. Similarly, unlike Shi'ism or Sunnism, in Ibadism, the theocratic state is understood to exist in one of four conditions of manifestation and can, depending on particular political and religious contexts, shift from one to the other, making transition into and out of theocratic rule relatively more available than in most interpretations of Shi'ism and Sunnism.[2] Therefore, while current revivalist discourses in Oman intersect at times with transnational Islamist movements that demand social piety and that call for the establishment of an

Islamic state, the language of revival in Oman more often draws from memories and understandings of local history and political philosophy: the last Ibadi Imamate lasted from 1913 to 1955 and is part of the living memory of older Omanis. In fact, at the beginning of 2005, thirty-one Omanis were arrested, convicted, and then pardoned for plotting to reinstall the Ibadi Imamate state.[3]

Understandings of historical trajectories bring together ideologies of development and religious doctrine, as well as the oil industry. Indeed, soon after my arrival in Oman, I recognized widespread uncertainty about Oman's prosperity and future. This uncertainty, however, not only emerged from the experiences of the unevenness and failures of development (and the modernity that this development signals), which certainly exist and which I have examined elsewhere, but also in the sense of fleeting, undeserved, and sudden wealth as well as the recognition, encouraged by national proclamations and initiatives, that oil resources are limited. Oil reserves, state-run sources have been telling Omanis for at least twenty years, will be depleted in twenty years, a constantly forward-moving and, for many, threatening horizon.

Turning Points and Sinking Archives

Beyond the basic details of Oman's turning point, not much more has been known publicly about the coup, a coup that is understood to have completely transformed the country. In 2007, John E. Peterson, an American military historian who was hired by the Omani military to write its history, published *Oman Insurgencies,* which has given some more facts about conversations leading up to the coup as well as details of the actual event. Based on decades of experience in Oman and with unparalleled access to and interviews with countless Omani (and British) officials, Peterson's text is the most comprehensive account of the country's military history, including the coup, in either Arabic or English. Nevertheless, Peterson still notes that the details of the coup are based on an "official version" (Peterson 2007, 239) but enriched with more information drawn from oral sources. Peterson pieced together more, albeit still minimal, details from a variety of sources.

The main question for many people about the coup centers on British involvement. Most people familiar with the country's late twentieth-century history commonly acknowledge the coup's British backing, or at least recognize the possibility of British backing. However, the main question continues to be whether the coup was directly British organized, or whether the young Qaboos looked to the British for potential support. Certainly, considering that Qaboos had been sent to the British military academy at Sandhurst and had worked in England to learn administration and accounting, and given the "close relationship" between Britain and Oman, British involvement in the coup is hardly surprising. And, certainly, it is also not particularly surprising that the degree of British involvement in the coup has remained shrouded in mystery; the sultan's legitimacy would surely be questioned should it be widely publicized that the British installed him. Although this particular question—of British involvement—is understandably unknown, general aura of mystery about the coup both remains, and perhaps is cultivated by, the state. Given that so much has been riding on the shift in power from the old regime to the new regime in Oman, the fact that the events leading up to and surrounding July 23, 2007, continue to be shrouded in mystery is striking.

The "origin myth" of Oman's modernity is, instead, described in school textbooks, for example, as simply one of genealogy: there was a father, and then there was a son. Rather than a history of violence and possible turbulence, smooth transitions are the most common shift in rule in Oman. Furthermore, the current sultan's legitimacy rests, in part, on his genealogy. And, as "proof" of both the date and the coup's authenticity, Qaboos's first official speech is reproduced as an appendix to many texts about Oman's late twentieth-century history. This kind of documentary fetishization, as Karen Strassler (2008) notes, helps solidify the sense that history *can* be authenticated, even while, at the same time, uncertainties about legitimacy continue to proliferate.

The lack of details surrounding the coup is also reaffirmed in the annual celebrations of Oman's national day, which is (supposedly) meant to mark the transformation in rule. The day of the emergence of the new state, however, has also been changed: from July to November. Rather than the actual day of the coup, Oman's national day celebrations have been held, since 1973, on Sultan Qaboos's birthday. Certainly, given Oman's summer heat (averaging about a hundred degrees Fahrenheit in the shade), it is understandable that an outdoor event with dignitaries, Omanis and non-Omanis, would be more comfortable in November, rather than July. However, shifting the date that marks Oman's emergence into modernity from the coup to the sultan's birthday also has the effect of deemphasizing the political underpinnings of the shift of regime. This new date emphasizes instead the "natural" genealogical transition from father to son.

It is not only the details of the coup (and its annual celebration) that have remained shrouded in silence or mystery. Oman's national archives, I was told many times during my visits and stays in Oman, have been destroyed. "They disappeared in a ship that sank off Oman's coast," I was told on numerous occasions, somewhere between Salalah, the capital of the southern Dhofar region where Qaboos was held under house arrest, and Muscat, the nation's capital. This does not mean, of course, that documents about state history are impossible to find: some are available in London, at the India Office Library and at the Public Records Office.[4] And, other official documents were scattered in the 1970s into the various ministries, as the new state attempted to come to terms with the management of land, water, police, and mosques under the new bureaucratic order. On the one hand, it may seem that the recalcitrance of the state to open its archives to foreign researchers is understandable. Indeed, why would a state allow researchers to sift through its dirt? On the other hand, would the state not work to shape a sense of its omnipotence through the very establishment, and organization, of archives? What is one to make of states that claim that these archives do not exist or present obviously implausible tales?

Mystery Oil and Mystery Sons

While the reproduction of a single speech is meant to authenticate Oman's modern origins and a sunken-ship theory of archives makes unavailable documentary proof of much of official history, it is the continued uncertainty about Oman's future that truly affirms a state of surprise and mystery: both in terms of the country's limited supply of oil and in terms of rule. The Omani state has been projecting a twenty-year supply of oil, for at least twenty years. At the same time, Sultan Qaboos is popularly recognized to have no heir, and after a near-fatal car accident in 1995, his mortality became a widespread, although not morbid, concern. Here, I focus on the question of the sultan's heir and the mystery surrounding plans for his successor.

In November 1996, the government, in a surprise move, issued a "constitution," providing measures for the period after the sultan's demise. I had just moved to Bahla, the oasis town in interior Oman where I was conducting fieldwork, several months before and was living with my hosts in their house within the walls of the old town. I was in my upstairs room one afternoon, taking notes from my morning conversations and waiting for everyone to conclude their afternoon prayers, when there was a furious knock at my door. Knocks at my door were generally much more tentative and from much lower on the door frame, as they were usually from one of the children coming to call me downstairs to join the family. But as the knock was somewhat more forceful and much higher on the door frame, I instinctively threw on a head scarf, which I had been asked to wear during my time in Bahla, and went to the door. To my surprise, one of the older sons of my landlord was standing there. In this religiously conservative household, it was extremely unusual for an adult male to come to my door. We were both suddenly very uncomfortable.

Agitated, Majid suddenly and without the perfunctory salutations said, "Have you heard? There has been a coup, the government has changed!" Like most people in Bahla at the time, my hosts did not have satellite television or access to the Internet. Their (and my) main source of "news" was from national television, radio, and newspapers, as well as from rumors that flew all over the country, from the town of Salalah in the south to Muscat and the Jebel Akhdar Mountains, through family, mosques, the local market, and women's neighborly visiting groups. International radio news supplemented national news. But as Oman is hardly the focus of much international coverage, local and national events had to be gleaned from other sources. Apparently, the afternoon programming of cartoons had been abruptly cut short. An official newscaster made a statement that a very important message was to be announced by the government. In a country where "nothing happens," this kind of announcement probably fueled thousands of instant stories. Indeed, the announcement was so unusual that it propelled Majid to jump in his car, drive from his own house in one of the new suburbs of Bahla to his father's house, over horribly rutted dirt roads within the old walls of the town, and come knock on my door. We hurried downstairs, where everyone was gathered solemnly and seriously around the television, which had suddenly transformed from a source of background noise and entertainment for children into a source of serious information that might determine their collective fates. My landlord, also in unusual fashion, stood almost directly in front of the television, with his hands clasped behind his back, waiting for new information.

It soon became clear that there was no coup. Majid had been so excited about "any news" that this unusual interruption had clearly fed his imagination about the implications of the announcement. Indeed, it seems that Majid had so anticipated some sort of end to the current state of things that he had preempted it. Instead, the television newscaster announced that the government was propagating a constitution, the first in the nation's history, and that this constitution was going to provide, among other things, provisions for the eventuality of the sultan's demise.[5] The constitution was going to be called, according to the newscaster, "the white book" and was going to be made available to the public the next day. The next day, when the national newspapers printed articles about the white book, the "mystery" of the future was only partially resolved. Although the constitution consists of eighty-one articles in seven chapters, covering topics from "Principles Guiding State Policy" and "Public Rights and Duties" to the Oman Council and the judiciary, it was on the particular question of succession—article 5—that many conversations in Bahla focused. In addition to clarifying the branch of the al-Bu Saidi dynasty that would rule,[6] it was also announced that the sultan had written the name of his intended successor in a sealed and secret envelope and that the envelope would be opened at his death. The successor would have to be approved by the Council of Ministers, an appointed advisory body to the sultan. In the eventuality that an agreement could not be reached, the military would take control of the government until a decision was reached. Thus, on the one hand and at least in theory, the line of succession was clarified. On the other hand, the name of the future sultan, hidden in a sealed and secret envelope, fueled further mysteries and, not surprisingly, conversations.

One evening, a week after the constitution was made public, as I was sitting in the family room with my hosts after dinner, we began discussing the provisions for the future as laid out by the new constitution. Usually limiting his references to the sultan to unadulterated praise, my landlord added, "Only God knows what will happen. Maybe Qaboos has a son. We did not know that his father, Sultan Said bin Taimur, had a son. So perhaps Qaboos bin Said also has a son too." On the one hand, this comment was perhaps one of the more "hopeful" suggestions I had heard over the week of speculation. The words were geared at continuity and made in the face of no evidence that the sultan did in fact have an heir. On the other hand, the comment rested on the acceptance of mystery, surprise, and uncertainty. Omanis had not known that Sultan Said bin Taimur had a son, so it was likely that they did not know whether Sultan Qaboos bin Said had a son: the continuity of mystery. Rather than rejecting the state's production of mystery in its secret-envelope succession policy, my landlord was creating his own new mystery: a secret son.

Conclusions

Reinhart Koselleck, in numerous writings, has emphasized a shift, especially since the eighteenth century, in historical consciousness from a kind of messianic temporality to a linear and progressive one. For Koselleck, messianic history involves, however, a certainty: salvation. Messianic time differs from "modern time," for Koselleck, in that with modern time, the future "is thought to be open and without boundaries. The vision of last things or the theory of the return of all things has been radically pushed aside by the venture of opening up a new future: a future which, in the emphatic sense of the notion, is totally different from all that passed before" (2002, 120). Koselleck further associates this sense of a "new future" with the notion of progress, whereby the "horizon of sameness" gives way to the open and whereby progress can happen, when there is planning.

In Oman, it seems, none of these processes are at play. Or, rather, it seems that these processes are intersected with a series of other temporal (and political) sensibilities, sensibilities that are not only shaped by an oil industry that predicts limited oil reserves (see Limbert 2008) but also that resonate with expectations of a returned theocratic state as well as distinctive claims about God's unique hold on the future. Rather than optimism (as in nationalism) or a knowability associated with the "messianic," pessimism and the unknowable dominate senses of historical trajectories. Indeed, the messianic pertains to the distant future, not the near future, as Jane Guyer (2007) notes, and it is in the near future, or almost possible near future (as in theocratic rule), as well as the recent past and the present that mystery, surprise, and uncertainty prevail. And, further, as suggested, it is only God who can legitimately make claims about the future.

Indeed, with the fetishization of the coup and its "natural" chronology as well as the fixation in Oman over the future—when oil is depleted and the sultan has passed away—it is as though historical consciousness (including a sense of the future) is at once overdetermined and yet considered unpredictable. The challenge of working in the intersection of anthropology and history is not only to be attuned to resonances of the past in the present or of "cultures" in the past but also to the shifting notions and senses of time that are embedded in people's relationships to the past and future. Time, in other words, is not a pregiven ground on and through which "history" matters for anthropologists; it is temporality that must link the two disciplines.

NOTES

1. See Anderson (2003) for his reflections on what would happen to nationalism with a shift from optimism to pessimism.

2. For some English-language studies of Ibadism, see Ennami 1972; Hoffman 2004; Lewicki 1971; al-Maamiry 1980; Wilkinson 1987.

3. Although the thirty-one people who were arrested were found guilty and sentenced to prison terms ranging from ten to thirty years, the sultan pardoned them and they were freed.

4. Until 1947, Oman's records were under the auspices of the Government of India. With Indian independence, diplomatic records pertaining to Oman began to be managed through the Foreign Office in London (via the Aden Protectorate, rather than the Bushire Residency on the Iranian side of the Persian Gulf).

5. For an analysis of the constitution, or "Basic Law," see Siegfried 2000.

6. According to the constitution, the future sultan had to be a male descendant of Sayyid Turki bin Sa'id (r. 1871–88), effectively disqualifying the descendants of both the Zanzibari branch and any imamate past of the al-Bu Saidi dynasty.

14 ❧ Kerry Ward

The Politics of Burial in Post-Apartheid South Africa

> Even the dead will not be safe from the enemy if he wins.
> —WALTER BENJAMIN (2007 [1955])

The examination of what it means to be "human" in multiple contexts over time and space is at the heart of anthrohistorical approaches to the production of knowledge. As Anupama Rao and Steven Pierce argued in "Discipline and the Other Body," "To the extent that the liberal individual has become the presumed subject of contemporary human-rights discourse, it is useful to historicize the process by which histories of the 'human' have intersected with and helped constitute the liberal paradigms of rights and responsibilities" (2006, 3). One aspect of historical debates over defining the human is whether or not this definition applies to the dead. In English, there are specific commonly used words for describing a dead person: cadaver, corpse, dead or deceased body, and human or mortal remains. These terms are separate from those usually applied only to animals, like carcass or carrion. Uniquely, struggles over the humanity of the dead can only be conducted, not by the person or people in question, but on their behalf by the living who appropriate their voice. Burial rites and rights invoke claims to cultural practices that reveal the power relations in society. David William Cohen and E. S. Atieno Odhiambo explored this most eloquently in the six-month legal case of conflicting claims over the body and burial of prominent Kenyan lawyer Silvano Melea (S. M.) Otieno where conflicting claims over the right to bury S. M. involved complex productions of knowledge about ethnicity and nationhood, custom and religion, culture and modernity, countryside and city, as well as understated issues of class and gender. This case was decided in May 1987, ultimately, not in the vocal and engaged court of public opinion, but in a Nairobi courtroom, thus reinforcing the state's own right to adjudicate whose claims would prevail in the name of the rule of law (Cohen and Odhiambo 1992). Burying the dead constitutes "a historical process that has consistently redefined the 'human' through political projects of control and governance" (Rao and Pierce 2006, 3).

The politics of burial as political struggle has a long history in South Africa, and illuminating these struggles through specific events over the course of several centuries highlights how various levels of state actors have used control over the dead in order to make claims over governance of the living. Connecting these microevents that flared up into public controversies throws light onto the various facets and parties involved in the struggle over burial sites. These events are not new, but in post-apartheid South Africa they have taken on a particular form of "heritage struggle" over the meaning of nationalism, democracy, neoliberal economic development, and the politics of remembrance and memorialization.

In the 1880s, Cape Town's Muslim community was involved in a protracted struggle against the closure of their inner city cemetery by the city council and the British colonial state. Representatives of the Muslim community invoked their right to bury their dead according to the rites of their religion. The city council countered that their prohibition was in the name of progress through the nineteenth-century metaphors of "hygiene," aimed at the prevention of epidemics and the promotion of "public health." In the 1980s, during the death throes of apartheid, the Nationalist government used state of emergency powers to ban the public burials of people killed by state and political violence using claims of a "total onslaught" against the state that had to be fought using a "total strategy." Protestors invoked the moral obligation of a Christian state to allow people to bury their dead according to their beliefs, while the state denied these rights on political grounds, further generating the symbolic value of funerals as expressions of mass political protest. In both these cases, a century apart, religious communities defied the law and dared the state to deny them the right to bury their dead as a violation of their human rights. Mamphela Ramphele, partner of antiapartheid activist Steve Biko who was murdered by the police in 1977, observed, "The political theater enacted in funeral rites of a fallen hero [became] an occasion to make a statement about his position in history, the invincibility of the 'struggle' . . . and the inevitability of the ultimate price that has to be paid for freedom."[1]

The politics of funerals, burial, and cemeteries have become even more complex in post-apartheid South Africa as democratically elected governments at local, provincial, and national levels negotiate with citizens demanding their human rights to bury and memorialize the dead according to their religious and cultural rites. In contemporary South Africa contestation over burial sites, heritage issues, development policies, religious rites, and human rights have become a touchstone of competing claims to land and the obligations of the state to its citizens and more broadly the state's legitimacy based on its defense of human rights. In all of these struggles over the dead, it is impossible to categorize "the people" or "the state" as singular or unified entities. This echoes Paul Eiss's examination (in this volume) of concepts and claims about *el pueblo* as "the people" in Mexico since the nineteenth century. "In every case, *el pueblo* [the people], or perhaps better, the *idea* of *el pueblo*, emerged as a reified counterpart to what Abrams called the idea of the state, a mythical unitary social object for that mythical unitary political subject."

As in the past, burials and graves in South Africa have also become symbolic events and sites of national heritage. The people being memorialized have changed, but their symbolic significance remains as powerful and as contested by people representing multiple social and political constituencies. This is the case both for individuals who are identified as prominent figures in the evolution of the South African nation and in the recovery of unknown people who died during the colonial and apartheid eras as well as the present. The metaphor for the South African nation coined by Archbishop Desmond Tutu, the "Rainbow People of God," during the darkest days of the final struggle against the apartheid state has been reified in the new national motto, "unity in diversity." The public perception of South Africa as a "Rainbow Nation" has endured as a political ideal, and this lays open multiple claims of cultural and religious rights to be protected by the state as the human rights of its citizens (Tutu 1994). It is sometimes argued by politicians that the politics of burial is a remnant of past inequalities and that resolving this issue is one of the post-apartheid state's responsibilities toward its citizens. "As you all know," eThekwini mayor Obed Mlaba said in his opening address to the Cemeteries and Crematoria Conference in July 2004, "the legacy of apartheid's evil lives on very much in the matter of burial sites."[2] But the politics of burial is very much alive. Individuals, communities, and representatives of various state organizations continue to invoke the right to burial rites, sometimes as an act of national reconciliation, other times as an act of protest against the present government. Municipalities struggle to deal simultaneously with cemeteries filled beyond capacity, often due to the high mortality rate of the AIDS pandemic, and soaring land values prompted by the economic growth of inner cities. Burial sites and cemeteries have once more become targets for public health and development issues of the neoliberal state apparatuses that justify their actions through invoking the common good of the nation.

Cape Town is one of the crucibles for these complex politics of burial in contemporary South Africa, and as the "Mother City" burial sites can be traced back in layers of precolonial, colonial, and postcolonial rule stretching over four hundred years. The aims and implementation of neoliberal economic policies occasionally clash with individuals and community groups who feel neglected by these policies and articulate this alienation through claiming to represent the dead in terms of their burial sites. There have been several instances where uncovered burial sites have been the focus of disputes over land ownership and appropriate use. This was the case in 2003 when an inner city block on Prestwich Street being cleared for a luxury apartment building uncovered a burial ground. The unearthing of these graves generated competing claims by various community groups, private investors, and state departments over what should be done with both the human remains and with the land.

Inner city development and international tourism in Cape Town have stimulated a real estate boom that has priced even the most modest inner suburban housing out of the financial reach of most South Africans. As with most major world cities, disparities of wealth in Cape Town continue to increase. The city is partly being priced out of the reach of the locals as the housing market is inflated by foreign absentee landlords buying property at advantageous exchange rates for holiday accommodation and investment. Given the history of apartheid and forced removals in Cape Town, there have been varied and continued demands by previously dispossessed communities for land restitution. As Nick Shepherd and Noeleen Murray (2007, 5) have suggested, the forms of the apartheid city are the template for struggles over post-apartheid spatial issues around land: how it is developed; who can afford it; who profits from it; what is built where; which projects are given municipal, provincial and national government endorsement and support; and how decisions to build are made. All of these issues create tensions between various state bodies and the private sector, government and citizens, institutions and communities, which in turn interact in complex and shifting alliances and antagonisms.

These frictions naturally reverberate around issues of the contested history of apartheid, but also have longer echoes in the history of slavery and dispossession of indigenous peoples at the Cape. Economic development and nation-building projects sometimes call into question the words of the 1955 Freedom Charter. The founding document of the liberation struggle and of the new national constitution is invoked directly or implicitly by both the state and protesters against the state as each lays claim to representing the people.[3] What are the choices made between preserving graves and building luxury apartments for tourists? Who determines the "value" of land and its uses—the state, the people, or the market? These issues came to the fore in debates over what became known as the Prestwich Place burial site upon which a multimillion dollar luxury apartment building, The Rockwell, was built. But conflicts over burial sites have longer echoes in Cape Town. They include competing claims over the Muslim burial ground known as the Tana Baru and over the kramat shrines that dot the landscape of the city and surrounding mountains.

These claims intersect with the heritage of slavery in South Africa and how it is being memorialized. This is simultaneously a regional issue over competing claims in the Western Cape and a nation-building project issue. It involves the politics of South Africans who were racially classified as "colored" under apartheid. The heritage of slavery as part and parcel of colonialism in South Africa is especially important to those who feel that affirmative action initiatives by all levels of the post-apartheid government have not resulted in improved housing, economic opportunities, government employment, and access to higher education.

An anthrohistorian ... seeks to assemble and read a range of fragments in [the] quest for a more intimate engagement with [the] past: [using] stories, old journal entries, ... newspaper articles, photographs, fantasies, scars.

⁊● MONICA EILEEN PATTERSON, THIS VOLUME

But of course, the situation is more complicated than that, as it is overlaid by differences in and between religious communities in Cape Town. The perception lingers, and is articulated around specific issues including heritage and burial sites, that historical injustices have intensified because the nonracial democratic African National Congress (ANC) national government has not been able to deliver on its promises for a better life for all South Africans, nor has the non-ANC Cape Town City Council or Provincial Government.

In May 2003, a property developer, Ari Estathiou of Styleprops Ltd., was excavating a city block in preparation for building The Rockwell when a large number of skeletons were unearthed. The developer, in accordance with South African heritage law, contacted the South African Heritage Resource Agency (SAHRA) and halted construction.[4] Estathiou contracted archaeological consultants, Archaeology Contracts Office

(ACO) affiliated with the Archaeology Department at the University of Cape Town, to assess the site and exhume the human remains. The archaeology project was led by Dr. Antonia Malan and the Cultural Sites Resources Forum (CSRF). Far from being an "accidental discovery," this whole area of Cape Town was well known by various interested parties, including generations of city councilors, property developers, inner city residents, and academic historians and archaeologists as the location of various burial grounds dating from the precolonial era to the mid-nineteenth century when the ground was first built upon. It was not the first time that human remains had been unearthed in the area and had been the study of archaeological investigation.

However, the site was not commonly known by the general public as a built-over burial ground, nor were there any physical markers indicating that this was the case, even though residents or ex-residents of the area knew about the graves, or the ghosts, that inhabited the area. In this regard, Prestwich Place was similar to countless other built over city burial sites.[5] Nevertheless, the area was clearly marked in early representations of the city as the informal burial ground (Shepherd 2007, 3–4). This was the first clash of perceptions regarding the site, as some people knew about it and others did not. The developer had to begin a period of investigation and public consultation regarding the site, and the CSRF was contracted to manage this, all to comply with South African heritage law. The site was fenced off but still clearly visible to the public, and as the CSRF began exhuming the site, revealing multiple layers of bodies buried over generations, these bones could be seen by the public as they passed by the site. This, in turn, prompted public complaints, community mobilization, and media attention.

The first public meeting, called by the CSRF on July 29 at St. Stephen's Church in central Cape Town, drew a crowd of about one hundred, representing the developer, state and city officials, heritage workers, NGO and community activists, Christian and Muslim religious leaders, members of the public, academics, and the press. Of course, these categories aren't mutually exclusive. Antonia Malan moderated the discussion by the CSRF and SAHRA representatives, allowed the developer's interests to be outlined, and called for an open debate regarding the heritage issues and the importance of the site in terms of its potential for South African history and especially the history of indigenous, slave, and underclass people who lived in the Cape settlement. Responses from the floor ranged from members of the public genuinely concerned about the respect for the cultural and religious rights of the dead to outright hostility and accusations of racism and "grave robbing" that were aimed at closing off further discussion.⁶

I attended these meetings as an "anthrohistorian" in the process of revising my history dissertation on Indian Ocean forced migration in the Dutch East India Company (ca. 1652–1795) and my longer-term interest and involvement in heritage and community issues around slavery in Cape Town. Upon reflection, I am reminded of seminar discussions at Michigan over David Cohen's "The Combing of History." Invoking an early paper he wrote on the "production of history" Cohen writes: "A question central for historians, anthropologists, and others [including anthrohistorians and archaeologists] becomes 'what is the fate of expert knowledge of the past as members of the crafts or guilds of the historical disciplines recognize, or are forced to recognize, the immense power created as people popularly process the past outside the work of the guild?'" (1994, 4). There was no consensus on perceptions or analysis of these events and their significance.

Nick Shepherd subsequently characterized the Prestwich Place issue as a "fiercely contested public campaign [that] pitted pro-exhumation heritage managers, archaeologists, and property developers against an alliance of community activists, spiritual leaders, and First Nation representatives" (2007, 3). Shepherd and Ernsten have also characterized the conflict as a clash of disciplines, with the "relative openness on the part of the discipline of history to engage with prevailing social and political contexts" (2007, 222). This representation of diametrically opposed lobbies, which Shepherd describes as employing "rival languages of concern," compresses the complexities and nuances of what took place in the controversies surrounding the issue. Disciplines do not engage, their practitioners do, and in this case there were many and varied people who were involved and who cannot be neatly dissected along lines of expertise, identity, or affiliation. Shepherd and Ernsten, both archaeologists, opposed the exhumations and have argued for opening a space within the critique and production of knowledge in their discipline. "We associate archaeology with a radical—a prying—'will to knowledge,' every excavation a mini-enactment of the Enlightenment injunction to know, to uncover. Prestwich Street makes the argument for an alternative kind of archaeology: an archaeology of silence, of secrecy, of closure (rather than disclosure)" (2007, 224).

Dorothy Hodgson, in this volume, has sensitively explored the ethical dilemmas of the distinct disciplines of history and anthropology in terms of research and knowledge production in her academic career. The Prestwich Place case raises these ethical issues among a number of experts in their involvement in, and representation of, this particular situation (including this essay). My peripheral position in this case involved "witnessing" the various public events that took place during my short research trip to Cape Town in 2003. My reflections on this experience deeply resonate with one of Anu Rao and Steven Pierce's conclusions, that "the anthrohistorian is always ethically entangled with her research—not as objective critic but as witness" (Rao and Pierce, this volume). During one public open forum at the burial site itself, I pointed out that there were severe limitations to what historians could find in the archives regarding the individual identity of people buried in unmarked graves in Cape Town during the early colonial period, and most probably at this site. This supported what had already been reported by Antonia Malan and other historians and historical archaeologists that records (that I had not personally examined) indicated that the site had been used as a general burial ground for the poor and indigent and was therefore not racially, culturally, or religiously distinctive in terms of human remains or burial practice.

My statement about the limitations of the archival record contradicts one of the popularly held beliefs about archives: that if only one looks hard enough, there will be documentary evidence, and it is therefore a failing or a withholding of expert knowledge if the sought-after proof cannot be located. Historians of slavery, archivists, and educators living in Cape Town have since the 1980s made tremendous efforts to make the archives accessible to the public, and written guides to family history research have resulted in a boom for genealogical research on family origins of slavery (Worden 2009, 23–40).[7] Explaining these limitations of expert historical knowledge production has often been at the starting point of my engagement with people's firmly held notions about the past and the nature of the archives. In some cases the powerful desire for connections with dead ancestors have resulted in "dream evidence" being offered as valid alternatives to written or oral forms of historical evidence, thus fundamentally challenging the forms of knowledge production about the past by internalizing them as psychic premonition (Worden 2009, 35–36). At Prestwich Place, Belinda Silbert experienced psychic connections, relating to a reporter various stories about how individuals had been buried at the site. These stories, and the corresponding press coverage that they received, gave voice to the desires for direct connections with and knowledge about who was buried at Prestwich Place (Wheeder 2006, 77).[8]

Julian Jonker's examination of the ethical and juridical issues in the Prestwich Place exhumations presents a subtle exploration of the issues around the remembrance of the dead in South African history. "The debates about the graves should be seen as invoking ethico-juridical questions about memory, forgetting, and memorialisation. These are questions that are potent in the collective consciousness of a nation still preoccupied with transition, reconciliation, and transformation" (2005, 9). The cultural and political (but not economic) core of the Prestwich Place issue, according to Jonker, was the claiming of ancestors and of descent from those buried at the site, and who gets to determine what happens to the human remains. The "Vermillion Accord on Human Remains" of the World Archaeological Congress has evolved into a First Code of Ethics that sets in place a global obligation to cooperate with indigenous people, particularly in regard to the collection and treatment of indigenous human remains.[9] The archaeologists involved in Prestwich Place operated under this code of ethics and argued that in exhuming and examining the bones they intended to identify who these people were and where they came from—all in the name of contributing to national heritage and memorialization of the colonial underclasses, including indigenes and slaves. Legally, the issue about exhumation rested on whether or not "direct descendents" of those buried could be found. This was impossible at Prestwich Place because the graves were unmarked. The issue was posed as one of ethics, through claims of "ancestry," that people in these graves had been the ancestors of all those who make up the underclasses of Cape Town, particularly of those with slave ancestry, and even more specifically, colored Capetonians (Jonker 2005, 4–40). Yet the community organizers who mobilized around Prestwich Place failed to attract much public support (49). Claims to speak for the dead legitimated by claims over history did not resonate with the public despite attention to the issue in the media.

In the case of Prestwich Place, representatives of various state bureaucracies ultimately determined the rights of the dead. The possibility that development of the site would be prevented was not a realistic scenario, and this was articulated by city and provincial officials whose pronouncements ultimately had the force of law. As Abdulkader Tayob has pointed out in a related case, expert knowledge in terms of the legal procedures and mechanisms that underpinned the developer's and the City Council's position trumped the public mobilization of opinion and opposition as a means of halting the development (Tayob 2007, 188–89). Public claims for the site to be made a permanent memorial were ethically powerful but economically unsustainable. Instead, the municipal and national governments found a compromise solution that did not disrupt the neoliberal economic imperatives of development, particularly tourism-driven development in Cape Town, which incorporates nation-building imperatives of "the rainbow people" and of a multicultural slave past as part of gaining support and legitimacy for its agenda. These various state interests in consultation with community activists and museums decided upon a language of claiming common ancestry and heritage for all Capetonians. This meshes with the way in which the City Council and Chambers of Commerce promote Cape Town's history of slavery as one of the most visible and marketable elements of the heritage industry in the city. In fact, the national and provincial government website "Cape Gateway" frames the city's history in relation to slavery. "Cape Town was built by slaves and is a slave site in its own right. This little-known fact compounds the obscurity of what remains of our slave heritage today. The city was once bursting with slaves."[10]

Twenty sites are listed in the registry of the city's slave heritage, including the memorial garden at St. Andrews Square, where an ossuary has been built for the reinterment of human remains exhumed from Prestwich Place. A visitor's center on the site contextualizes the memorial, although this interpretation has been contested by community groups.[11] "The City, together with the South African Heritage Resources Agency, the District Six Museum, the Prestwich Place Project Committee, and Heritage Western Cape, has . . . forged a partnership to facilitate an appropriate process to honor these ancestors of the city."[12] Claims to common ancestry resolved the Prestwich Place issue in a way that fulfilled intertwined economic, cultural, heritage, and tourism goals. Prominent on the website for the Cape Town Partnership[13] is the proud declaration: "In April 2008, a blessing of the site by multi-denominational faith leaders was held and, in May 2008, the remains were transferred to their new burial site by a human chain of interfaith leaders, archaeologists and members of the community." This is also the policy of the Cape Town Partnership, an alliance of the City of Cape Town, South African Property Owners Association, and the Cape Town Chamber of Commerce and Industry (and other "stakeholders") which include "using history and memory to build a tolerant and inclusive sense of local identity for citizens throughout Cape Town, through the cultural and heritage resources of the Central City."[14]

But Cape Town's much longer history of competing claims over sites of the dead was not to be resolved so neatly. In 1886 the recently passed Public Health Act had been used to justify the closure of the Tana Baru, the main inner city Muslim cemetery. Members of the Muslim community defied this order, claiming that Islamic burial rites necessitated that the body of the deceased be carried in procession to the grave. The proposed relocation of the city cemetery to a site over seven miles away was objected to on religious grounds. Over three thousand Muslims attended an "illegal" burial of a child (understood as the most innocent of human beings) in the Tana Baru resulting in state opposition that in turn generated several days of rioting. The issue was resolved with the closure, but preservation, of the Tana Baru and a new Muslim cemetery within a few miles of the city center (Esack 1988, 474; Bickford-Smith 1995, 455).

The preservation of the Tana Baru was once more in question during the 1980s, and protests by Muslim community groups were presented on both religious and heritage grounds. The kramats (tombs) in the Tana Baru and other areas of Cape Town have been sites of remembrance, religiosity, and resistance for generations.[15] There are ongoing struggles about the memorialization of the dead and the rights of the dispossessed to sites of burial—and, ultimately, to the land. The development of the Oudekraal Estates on the slopes of Table Mountain that disturbed kramats on the site went ahead despite vocal and sustained protests by religious, community, and academic groups about the desecration of the site. As Jonker points out, developers and governmental agencies that endorsed the development couched their project in terms of a "site of cultural significance" rather than the "violation of tombs" (Jonker 2005, 44). The desecration of tombs would be difficult to justify in ethical terms but the state as the democratic representatives of the arbitrator of sites of cultural significance could legally decide when a site was not significant enough to preserve.

Most recently, the Muslim burial site, the Tana Baru, on land that is part of the Bo-Kaap (the suburb that under apartheid was known as the Malay Quarter) is again at the center of a dispute. In 2000 the Minister of Arts, Culture, Science, and Technology, Dr. B. S. Ngubane, attended the opening of the "Gateway to the Tana Baru Cemetry." The significance of the Tana Baru cemetery was framed in both national and sectarian terms as being worthy of preservation. "Their history is worthy of preservation, not only by their descendants, the Cape Muslims, but by all South Africans, irrespective of religious persuasion."[16] However, the commercial value of the land in the Bo-Kaap has increased over tenfold in the last twenty years, and Bo-Kaap families who own title deeds in the area of the Tana Baru have attempted to develop the land. Protests by the Tana Baru Trust, the Bo-Kaap Civic Association, and other community groups led to the Muslim Judicial Council (MJC) issuing a fatwa that bans any construction in the area. The conflicting parties in this case have continued to fight back. "The MJC fatwa against land sales and housing construction has been countered with three pro-development Islamic rulings, one from Cairo's Azhar University, a leading Islamic authority."[17] The Bo-Kaap Civic Association claimed that the Tana Baru has "been declared waqaaf (in communal custody)" but SAHRA representatives have counterclaimed that "even though the site is of great significant value, the private land owners have certain rights too."[18] Moreover, the Cape Town City Council may be sued for restitution claims based on the council having auctioned land in the area under the apartheid Group Areas Act during the 1960s.

However, in an earlier case, where the St. Cyprian's School bordering the Tana Baru wanted to develop part of "their" land that disrupted unmarked graves, and had been granted legal permission to do so from the City Council, a compromise with the Cape Mazaar Society was reached after public deliberations that allowed both development and memorialization. Abdulkader Tayob, a community activist and religious studies academic, has analyzed this case and his involvement in it through the recognition of different sites for the production of knowledge, protest, and claims, concluding that these processes are evidence of a "vibrant democracy": "My experience in this project has left me with the impression of a robust and open debate in the public sphere about a disputed site. All the niceties of democratic tolerance were dropped as parties expressed their deepest fears and anxieties over a process that angered and frustrated them. Here democracy was expressed in the willingness to speak out openly and clearly about an issue. The dispute ignored divisions of class, power, and sophistication." Tayob makes the point that democracy is created and sustained through open debate and peaceful resolution to disputes. Yet his own analysis reveals how the expert knowledge of architects, developers, and lawyers outmaneuvered public protest in order to achieve the ends of the school and City Council, albeit with a recognition and accommodation of community cultural and religious concerns and practices (2007, 183–88).

In the Tana Baru, which formed part of the same larger colonial burial site area on the outskirts of town that included Prestwich Place, many of the people buried are identifiable by name. Three kramats of great historical and religious significance are on this site, all from the eighteenth-century period of Dutch colonial rule: Tuan Sayeed Alawie, a banished religious prisoner; Tuan Nuruman, an ex-slave and Muslim leader; and Tuan Guru, a political prisoner of the Dutch East India Company who opened the first madrasah in Cape Town during the 1790s. The religiosity of the Tana Baru is beyond any dispute, as is its historical and cultural significance. Yet the state, through its heritage body, will not rule out the economic development of the site in terms of the commercial value of the land. The kramats of the Tana Baru are part of a "circle" of kramats in the Western Cape. The kramat of Sheikh Yusuf of Makassar was declared a national monument with great fanfare by President Thabo Mbeki. But the land on which Sheikh Yusuf's kramat is built is located above the dunes of Macassar Beach on the Cape Flats and is not yet commercially valuable, unlike the Tana Baru and Oudekraal.

The kramat of Tuan Matarah (Sheikh Sayed Abduraghman Motara), an eighteenth-century political prisoner of the Dutch, has been, and will continue to be, sacrosanct. It is located on Robben Island, which was destined to be protected as a national monument and center for the memorialization of the struggle against apartheid as a site of the shared heritage of the South African nation.[19] Robben Island was also declared a national monument in 1996 and a UNESCO World Heritage Site in 1999.

There is no danger of "The Island" coming under the control of property developers, and the state is committed to the preservation and maintenance of the land as an ecological and historical national monument. Indeed, it is seen as a desecration of the memory of the nation to even think of Robben Island in terms of the commercial value of the land. Other sites and resting places of the dead will continue to be fought over, and these struggles will include struggles between memory and forgetting, and the meaning of land value, property rights, religious rights, and heritage issues. These struggles will be interpreted and mediated by the municipal, provincial, and national governments, and within these levels of government by the heritage bodies and the various departments responsible for the implementation of economic policy.

The echoes of the dead can be also heard in the politics over sites of heritage, remembrance, and memorialization in the rest of the country. In Pretoria (the nation's administrative capital) the Voortrekker Monument, built in the early days of apartheid as the premier site celebrating Afrikaner nationalism, has as its central focus point a cenotaph as the symbolic grave of the Voortrekkers who died during the Great Trek. It also has a Garden of Remembrance where people can pay to have their ashes buried in an engraved niche in the exterior stone wall.[20] The Voortrekker Monument has been counterbalanced, literally and figuratively, by "Freedom Park," a new monument to the nation under construction on an opposite hill. This monument was designed "as a response to the need identified by the Truth and Reconciliation Commission for symbolic reparation to those who have died in struggles . . . [and] is thus based on the South African nation's reconciliation process as well as the advancement of the various rights entrenched in the constitution from a heritage perspective." Surrounding the Sikhumbuto (place of remembrance) is the Wall of Names with the names of those who "paid the ultimate price during the eight conflict events that shaped South Africa's historical consciousness." The spiritual center of this new national monument is Isivivane, which has an eternal flame that "represents the unknown and unsung heroes and heroines who lost their lives in the struggle for humanity and freedom."[21]

Benedict Anderson has shown how central this kind of monument is to imagining the nation. "No more arresting emblems of the modern culture of nationalism exist than the cenotaphs and tombs of Unknown Soldier. The public ceremonial reverence accorded to these monuments precisely because they are either deliberately empty or no one knows who lies inside them, has no true precedent in earlier times. . . . Yet void as these tombs are of identifiable mortal remains or immortal souls, they are nonetheless saturated with ghostly national imaginings" (1991, 9). In South Africa nationally significant memorials include both these anonymous and symbolic sites of remembrance as well as areas where the dead are remembered by name as part of a collective national history. It is ironic that individual slave names, because slaves were registered as property, are easily recoverable from the archives, whereas the names of indigenous people killed in precolonial and colonial wars were not recorded, and they remain largely anonymous. Freedom Park attempts to bridge the gap between symbolic anonymous and individually identifiable remembrance, but it also elevates "leaders" as extraordinary individuals in national memory.

One of the great heroes of the liberation struggle, Govan Mbeki, father of President Thabo Mbeki, was well aware of the tension between exalting individuals above the unknown masses in the politics of burial and remembrance. Known affectionately as "Oom [Uncle] Gov," Mbeki died in August 2001 at his home in the Eastern Cape. His will decreed that he be buried in the neglected Zwide township cemetery rather than the well-maintained "Heroes Memorial" of the liberation struggle or the desegregated Forrest Hill cemetery in Port Elizabeth in order to draw attention to the dilapidated state of the site that contains the graves of many ordinary political activists.[22] Govan Mbeki's funeral was a national commemoration and nation-building event with attendant media, and he realized that his own funeral was an opportunity to continue his activism as someone who had devoted his life to fighting for the implementation of the ideals of the Freedom Charter. Mbeki knew that the presence of his grave in the township cemetery would force the ANC-controlled municipality or other state bodies to upgrade the site not only for his own grave but for those of his poor dead comrades. Having spent a lifetime struggling for human rights against the apartheid state, Mbeki continued to fight literally beyond the grave for all South Africans' democratic right to a decent burial and place of remembrance in post-apartheid South Africa.

NOTES

1. Mamphela Ramphele 1996, 107.
2. Cemeteries and Crematoria Conference Opening speech by eThekwini Mayor Councillor Obed Mlaba, Durban, July 15, 2004. www.ethekwini.gov.za/durban/government/mayor/mayor/speech.html (accessed February 1, 2008).
3. The Freedom Charter. Adopted at the Congress of the People, Kliptown, on June 26, 1955. www.anc.org.za/ancdocs/history/charter.html (accessed September 12, 2007).
4. SAHRA replaced the National Monuments Council as the statutory body that manages national heritage sites.
5. For a sensitive analysis comparing Prestwich Place with the African Burial Ground in New York City, see Finnegan 2006.
6. Zenzile Khoisan, quoted in Shepherd 2007, 8.
7. For an earlier exploration of these issues see Ward and Worden 1998.
8. Michael Wheeder was instrumental in organizing the Hands of Prestwich Street Ad Hoc Committee, which later reorganized as the Prestwich Place Project Committee.
9. See The World Archaeological Congress Code of Ethics at www.worldarchaeologicalcongress.org/site/about_ethi.php (accessed September 14, 2007).
10. Cape Gateway: easy access to government information and services. "Places of Slave Rememberance in the Western Cape" www.capegateway.gov.za/eng/pubs/public_info/P/82884/3 (accessed September 10, 2007).
11. City of Cape Town, "Spatial development," vol. 1 (February 2007), 24–25.
12. City of Cape Town, "Spatial development," 25.
13. Cape Town Partnership. http://www.capetownpartnership.co.za/pro

grammes/publicspaceforpubliclife/standrewssquare.html (accessed September 1, 2009).

14. Cape Town Partnership, "Cape Town Partnership: A Profile," November 2006, 11.

15. Davids 1985; and http://www.capemazaarsociety.com (accessed September 10, 2007).

16. Dr. B. S. Ngubane, "Speech by the Minister of Arts, Culture, Science and Technology, Dr B S Ngubane at the Official Opening of the 'Gateway to the Tana Baru Cemetry,'" Longmarket Street, Cape Town, January 14, 2000. www.info.gov.za/speeches/2000/000201401p10001.htm (accessed September 10, 2007); and Davids 1985.

17. Marianne Merten, "Muslim Council issues fatwa against property development," Mail and Guardian online. www.mg.co.za (accessed July 1, 2005).

18. Merten, "Muslim Council issues fatwa" www.mg.co.za (accessed July 1, 2005).

19. Robben Island Museum. www.robben-island.org.za/departments/heritage/heritage.asp (accessed September 14, 2007).

20. www.voortrekkermon.org.za (accessed January 14, 2008).

21. www.freedompark.co.za (accessed January 29, 2008).

22. "Oom Gov fights bias from beyond the grave," Mail and Guardian online, September 4, 2001. www.mg.co.za (accessed January 6, 2008).

9/11/2001

9/11/1973

9/11/1906

15 🔖 Oana Mateescu

Losing the Phenomenon: Time and Indeterminacy in the Practice of Anthrohistory

During the night of July 23, 1950, around forty peasants from the village of Bârseti (Vrancea County, Romania), armed with firearms and other weapons, took control of the local police office, the village council, and the post office and detained several key communist officials as well as the most well-known communist party members in the village, whom they picked up from a dancing party.[1] Toward morning, they made phone calls or sent messengers to several neighboring villages, where similar gatherings were supposed to take place simultaneously. They found out that the other groups had dispersed at dawn, without taking any kind of action. Further south, in the village of Nereju, hundreds of people (some say three hundred, others four hundred), armed with pitchforks, axes, clubs, automatic rifles, and pistols, gathered in a mountain meadow. They waited for a sign—the noise of a plane, the voice of a messenger, or the light of a fire—in order to begin fighting. The signal never came, and so they left, planning to meet again.

The next day, *Securitate* (former Romanian secret police) units arrived in the region, and there began several months of hunting and terror until all the participants in these events were found, to be arrested or, in case of resistance, executed on the spot. Most of the villagers involved had run away to hide in the mountains, but they were either discovered by the *Securitate* patrols or they turned themselves in willingly, after hearing that their relatives at home were relentlessly questioned and tortured. By late November, 308 people had been apprehended, and they were put on trial in July 1951, the majority of them being sentenced to long prison terms (from ten to twenty-five years).[2] By 1964 they had all been released, except those who had died in prison. Their families suffered house arrest, humiliation, abuse, and the confiscation of property.

Locally, these events are ambivalently referred to as *chermeza* (from *Kermesse*), a revel or merry celebration held outdoors with music and dancing.[3] Subsequent accounts, those of *Securitate* files and of historians after 1989, speak of "counterrevolution" or "terrorist and subversive activities" and of "anticommunist resistance," respectively. *Securitate* investigators and researchers as well as former participants agree that the events had been planned for months beforehand to result in a synchronized insurgency in all the highland villages of Vrancea, with the idea of triggering revolt in other counties and finally, if possible, overthrowing communism in Romania. Furthermore, these accounts also agree that the immediate cause of the July events should be traced to the nationalization of forest properties in 1948 and the confiscation of locally owned lumber saws.[4] Life in the highland villages of Vrancea was based on the communal ownership of forests, lumber being the main commodity traded in the lowland towns in exchange for cereals and other products.[5]

One name, Victor Lupşa, crops up again and again in all these accounts. He was the organizer, the leader, the colonel, the liar, the spy, and the traitor. Lupşa appeared in Vrancea County in late 1948, living as a fugitive in the mountains, and he proceeded to organize and coordinate the activities of groups of people from different villages, offering hope, advice, and instruction. After the July events, he disappeared. The archives of the former *Securitate* suggest that he managed to hide in the mountains until 1955, despite the assiduous searches going on for him. Apparently, he surrendered or was captured in 1955 and was executed for his participation in the *chermeza* in 1956 (Bric 1998; Dobrincu 2006). But as the former *Securitate* was never in the business of producing historical truth, it is difficult to take this as a purely factual, disinterested, and complete account.[6]

> Nobody can say whether he was a *Securitate* agent or an honest man. Almost all who knew him were full of doubts.[7]
>
> Whatever he was, I can't say. He pretended to be a colonel. He said he had been in Yugoslavia, since '47, I don't remember exactly, and that he returned to organize people against communists. That's what he told us, but we can't know the truth. He didn't have any relatives in these parts.[8]

In different circumstances and to different people, Victor Lupşa was or might have been many things: he was bald, slim, and had a lame leg, he had a wife and kin in his native village (Zagon, Covasna county), he was deeply religious, he liked to keep written records, he was involved in money fraud, he lacked training and organizational skills, he was a good organizer, he was trained in Yugoslavia in guerrilla tactics, he was in contact with Americans, he was a lumber merchant, a colonel, an honest man, a pathological liar, a leader of anticommunist resistance, a *Securitate* agent, a coward. Victor Lupşa remains an unknown.[9]

Doing Anthrohistory

My goal here is not to set the historical record straight but rather to examine the kind of work that goes into making history. A good historian might uncover a less ambiguous story by sticking closely to the trail of files from the archives of the former *Securitate* (e.g., Dobrincu 2006). But seeing that I can lay claim to the position of an anthrohistorian (at least in virtue of my training and institutional affiliation), I could perhaps get away with exploring just how ambiguity and indeterminacy are produced and made into resources constitutive of a history.[10]

In the course of my dissertation research on the reconstitution of communal forests in the highland region of Vrancea, I heard numerous stories about, and came across various documentary traces of, the failed insurgency in 1950. Contemporary accounts of these events are marked by ambivalence, continually oscillating between potentially contradictory versions of failure. This indeterminacy is actively generated by people whose knowledge practices are fully entangled with the ways in which events unfolded and were investigated at the time. In this essay, I use the situated epistemologies of the "practical historians" (Garfinkel 2002; see also Livingston 1987) of these events as well as some ethnomethodological insights to discuss the prospective and retrospective features of anthrohistorical ways of knowing.

Participants and witnesses of the events in July 1950 are concerned with making what they see as an instance of failure into a still storyable event. Recounting revolves around the question of betrayal, which is a useful device for making sense of what happened as well as for keeping at bay the retrospective settling of meanings and accounts. Was Victor Lupşa a genuine revolutionary acting in good faith to help orchestrate an insurrection that constituted an inevitable course of action for the villagers from Vrancea, threatened as they were in their livelihood by the nationalization of forests? Was he an agent of the *Securitate* whose specific mission was to set up a loyalty test, that is, to ascertain the extent of villagers' allegiance to the new communist regime by inciting them to rebel, thereby deceiving them into an action unlikely to succeed that would ultimately prove destructive?

Situated Knowledge and the Production of Indeterminacy

These questions only indicate the high points of a whole spectrum of doubts and uncertainties surrounding the events of 1950, the role of Lupșa, and implicitly of those who trusted and followed him. They are also the questions that become undecidable, just as they come into the focus of local historical knowledge. In the process of knowledge production, former participants and witnesses relied on a whole array of procedures for the generation, evaluation, and contestation of evidence. Many of these procedures were hopelessly intertwined with the investigative work carried out by *Securitate* agents in the aftermath of the revolt as well as with the specific features of the various sites in which evidence could be obtained and interpreted.

Knowledge practices were part and parcel of people's involvement in the organization of the July events: the selection of trustworthy "recruits," the management of secrecy and avoidance, the surreptitious collection of firearms, the setting-up of secure methods of communication, and the formulation of instructions and goals were all achieved in an uncertain environment where the exchange of words, and even glances, had to be closely monitored. Doubts loomed large while they were on the run, hiding in the mountains and depending on the goodwill of other villagers for food and protection, as well as information on the relatives and families sequestered in the village.

During interrogation or in the courtroom, they had to deal with deliberately misleading questions, prehistoricized accounts prepared by *Securitate* agents in the form of "forced declarations," slips of the tongue, and, last but not least, fear of death under torture. The interrogatory setting was especially permeated by uncertainty: one could not know if and how much the others had confessed or if the *Securitate* interrogators simply used alleged confessions as bait. Rumors and accounts seeped through the walls of prison cells as well, but given that virtually anyone could have been a planted informer, the questions and answers of other prisoners were necessarily suspect. For those who made it back to their villages after serving their terms, there followed monthly sessions with the *Securitate* officers assigned to supervise them, as well as intense conversations and disputes with fellow insurgents in addition to other villagers who had developed their own theories in the intervening years. There was also pain, confusion, humiliation, and ridicule. And finally, after 1989, there were testimonies at the Association of the Former Political Prisoners (AFPP), public debates at the village council on the reconstitution of the communal forests, and interviews with journalists, historians, and ethnographers whose questions reflect the timeliness of a grand anticommunist narrative.

I will give a brief illustration of such situated knowledge practices, as they are woven through the texture of the events they are meant to illuminate. A former participant from Nereju, whom I will call Radu, reports his discussion of the question of Lupșa's innocence at a meeting of the AFPP. He reviews his association with Lupșa, the circumstances of their initial meetings, and the facts he knew from Lupșa himself as background to "the decisive proof." Radu's proof is built as follows: Lupșa was insistent on making written records after each meeting of the organization, which he placed in glass bottles, sealed with wax, and buried at an unknown location. Had he been a covert agent of the *Securitate*, those records should have surfaced during the interrogation and at the trial as incriminating evidence. This is not to say that Radu's interrogators lacked evidence: apparently they knew he had provided Lupșa with weapons and clothing on a specific occasion, that he had carried an automatic pistol on the night of July 23, and that he and several others had been charged with a particular mission, to detain the chief of the forestry office and to take over the local agricultural cooperative. However, "nobody found his writings. Nobody knows what Lupșa and I did together. They [the *Securitate* interrogators] didn't know what Lupșa and I had talked about."[11]

Radu is not perturbed by the agents' knowledge of his actions—after all, they might have obtained that information from other prisoners who were "too stupid" or who simply caved in under torture and confessed—as long as knowledge that was particular to his relationship with Lupșa was missing. For instance, Radu believes he had enjoyed Lupșa's special trust because of his experience in World War II as a paratrooper trained for undercover missions behind the front, which made him uniquely qualified for the secret operations required for the organization of the insurgency. Such details of his shared relationship with Lupșa never made it into "the file" (the prosecution's statement at the trial), and their absence exonerates Lupșa in Radu's view. However, Radu's "interactional method of proof" (Miyazaki 2004, 82) discounts the fact that neither his *Securitate* interrogators nor the prosecution were interested in obtaining evidence of what made his relation to Lupșa meaningful, but simply the facts that indicated the criminal nature of his actions. The knowledge he gained then, as well as its retrospective account now, was produced in response to specific questions designed to enable the successful organization of the interrogatory or courtroom setting.

For many other participants, the *Securitate*'s swift intervention the next day after the July events indicated prior information about their activities. While everyone involved was arrested and convicted, Lupșa's disappearance after July 23 and his absence at the trial seemed to point him out as "the informer" or "the traitor."[12] At the very least, his absence made him suddenly suspect and unbalanced people's previous understanding of the events. "Almost all who knew him were full of doubts." These doubts persisted for decades, and they remain vivid now, despite the expert assurances of journalists or historians after 1989.

Questions about Lupșa are disconcerting; they make people shift, shrug, sigh, and fidget. This is not necessarily because of forgetting or a reluctance to verbalize certain kinds of knowledge. It is rather because instead of answers, they have too many questions of their own. What is perhaps left unspoken is that many people would prefer to leave the issue undecided, insofar as to settle the Lupșa issue is another step toward settling the meaning of the *chermeza*.

> *"My memory is full of holes,"* people say casually, nonchalantly, not wishing to dwell on the matter.... *If it isn't indispensable, what's the use of tiring oneself, driving oneself crazy in the effort to fill that hole, why waste one's time? But what it has left behind it here, this opening, this disjointed, dislocated breach, makes everything reel, the hole must absolutely be filled in, it must at all costs come back, embed itself here once again, take its full place...*
> ❧ SARRAUTE 1997, 18

If they were indeed the dupes of a well-trained *Securitate* agent, their misplaced trust brought immense suffering to themselves, their kin, and fellow villagers. Moreover, this was a costly mistake that effectively canceled the chances of a successful insurgency. Not only did they fail to recover the forests confiscated by the communist regime, but they spent long years in prison and returned home to a different world where they were seen as "enemies of the people" or, at best, as misguided fools who prepared for insurrection as they would for an outdoors party (*chermeza*). If Lupșa was not a traitor, then how does one explain the dimensions of failure? How to account for the fact that they did imagine they could intervene successfully against a regime backed by Soviet troops, when they had only pitchforks and guns left over in the mud of the forest by retreating Germans in World War II? How to explain that they had wanted to believe Lupșa's promises of American intervention, "atomic bullets," and aircraft defense?[13]

As a *locally* occasioned history, the *chermeza* persists in virtue of the questions made undecidable by the situated generation and contestation of knowledge. In this sense, indeterminacy is the practical achievement of people whose methods for evidencing claims concerning historical knowledge are constitutive features of the events they describe. By such methods, they try, as best as they can, to be true to the events they experienced.[14] The construction of either version of failure entails not simply an ethical stance but also a deeply visceral process of knowledge making. Coming to know that Lupșa was or was not a traitor is a way of knowing oneself and others as the bearers of historical potentialities, as the vectors of actions that could, and sometimes did, introduce a swerve in the flow of the past.

Time and Accountability

It would be simple to argue that the device of Lupșa's betrayal stands for a refusal to confront the past and to accept responsibility for failure. It is possible to talk of the *chermeza* without making any mention of Lupșa and to talk in a way that explicitly suggests that failure was perhaps the best outcome, insofar as a local success would have prompted a much more aggressive military intervention by the Soviet troops stationed in Romania at the time.[15] It is also possible, in specific situations that require potent arguments, such as public debates on the restitution of communal forests or official encounters with government representatives, to fully uphold an unambiguous narrative of the *chermeza* as heroic anticommunist resistance. But the possibility of such accounts does not necessarily indicate that the meaning of the 1950 events has been settled. It does, however, offer clues about the extent to which narratives are embedded in temporally specific contexts of accountability.

The locally emergent history of the *chermeza* assembles both the temporality of the 1950 events as well as the sequence of accounts of the events produced after the fact in the interrogatory setting, the courtroom, the prison, village conversations, and disputes or interviews after 1989. As the events in July 1950 unfolded, actors were, so to speak, caught up in the production of history. They had to anticipate and respond in real time to unforeseen circumstances and to accomplish actions that revealed themselves only partially as they developed. They did not fully know they were involved in "counterrevolution" or "anticommunist resistance." As a former participant confessed, "I went to the meeting [on July 23] because my older brother told me to. I didn't know exactly what we were doing, but something had to be done."[16] In the temporality of the original events, actors did not have the benefit of hindsight, relying instead on the "in-hand intelligibility of a world 'not yet' reflected upon" (Garfinkel 2002, 153), a world they were busy producing on the spot with just the knowledge available at the time.

The sense of those actions as a "prospective achievement" fraught with uncertainty, misunderstanding, and surprise, but nevertheless realizable, can scarcely be recovered from retrospective accounts, be they produced immediately after the event or fifty years later. For instance, the assembly of three or four hundred people on July 23 appears retrospectively as unproblematic, as the following of instructions presumably given by Lupșa. But Lupșa himself was in direct contact with only a handful of people, and so the work of making the assembly possible—how such an action was made intelligible at the time, through what kinds of motives and methods—is largely lost. The unfolding coherence of events at the time is different from the already produced coherence of the retrospective telling.[17]

Retrospectively, the practical historians of the *chermeza* cannot but silence many of the endless minute contingencies that had to be met in organized anticipation at the time of the events. However, to the extent that their accounts are grounded in and keep track of the variously situated knowledge practices that made reflection possible, they remain accountable to the temporality of their own processes of memorialization and historical production. This specific accountability makes it impossible for them to find and accept invariable answers. The indeterminacy produced by the device of Lupșa's betrayal, among others, constantly undercuts the formation of a locally definitive account.[18] In doing so, it stands as a local reminder of historical fallibility, informing prospectively the repertoire and qualities of achievable actions.

Losing the Phenomenon

This discrepancy between the prospective and retrospective features of social practice is by no means a new issue for the social sciences (Schutz 1967

[1932]; Mills 1940), but some of its implications bear repeating. Let me approach the problem via Harold Garfinkel's penetrating critique of theorized accounts, which find in the world precisely the same phenomena they had already postulated (2002, 263–85). He illustrated the pitfalls of this process by reconstructing Galileo's inclined plane demonstration of the real motion of free-falling bodies. Garfinkel did not attempt the exact replication of Galileo's experiment as an already made event; on the contrary, he deliberately introduced small "inaccuracies" in the experiment so as to understand what would have been the problems faced by Galileo in his real-time endeavor to design what eventually became a successful demonstration. As Rawls (2002, 47) puts it, Garfinkel "wanted to understand what about the experiment *could go wrong*" (emphasis in original). By doing so, he took most seriously the issues involved in the recovery of a prospective achievement rather than a retrospective account (34). His key insight is that, in contrast to theorized enterprises that work backward from an already refined product, the process of discovery is always liable to "lose the phenomenon."[19]

Retrospectively, Galileo had to design an experiment that would prove something about gravity, being accountable to the existing field of scientific knowledge. This is what Garfinkel (2002, 173–75) calls "classical accountability." Prospectively, though, Galileo lost his phenomenon many times until he designed an experiment that would actually work, being "naturally accountable" to a wealth of concrete contingencies: the minute problems of measurement, timing, the resistance of various materials that made up "the phenomenal field of detail" (Garfinkel 2002, 278). Garfinkel's pedagogical reenactment preserves the indeterminacy of the original experiment, revealing the ways in which the phenomenon could have been lost as well as the sort of organized anticipation of contingency that prevented that.

Being able to lose the phenomenon, or dealing with indeterminacy, is generally essential to all kinds of practices, including everyday, ordinary doings and academic inquiries. I also think it is specifically important for the transdisciplinary and as-yet-unfolding project of anthrohistory.[20] Is anthrohistory liable to work like a theorized account rendered virtually infallible by retrospection? Is it able to lose phenomena?

> *One can participate in and share the fundamentals of the Labyrinth ... as it manifests itself. One can never see it in totality, nor can one express it. One is condemned to it and cannot go outside and see the whole.*
>
> ❧ BERNARD TSCHUMI 2000 (1975), 227

By way of critical illustration, I point to the problems of a "historical anthropology" (Shaw 2002) that is motivated precisely by a puzzle of the unexpected: the seeming forgetting of slave trade and colonialism in postcolonial Sierra Leone. This kind of functionalist false surprise about forgetting is first of all an effective and common rhetorical strategy, because, as expected, it only paves the way for a thorough excavation of memories (see also Cole 2001). It is also a device by means of which silences and things not spoken of are rather summarily treated as kinds of forgetting (Sider and Smith 1997). Last, the very use of forgetting in a transitive form—the forgetting of the slave trade—makes retrospective knowledge claims, implying that there once existed an experiential object such as the slave trade.[21] Furthermore, it would follow that such an object of forgetting can indeed be neatly mapped out on "the slave trade" as the product of scholarly periodization and synthesis.

Shaw's answer to this puzzle takes the form of an equation of practice to memory. Memory is practice insofar as it is also nondiscursive, "implicit" or "embodied," while practice is memory insofar as it has the capacity to condense and perpetuate historically patterned actions and meanings.[22] Thus, Temne ritual practices—such as techniques of divination, diviners' visionary experiences, rumors of cannibalism, and practices of witch finding—*are* memories of the Atlantic slave trade and the colonial "legitimate" trade, spanning four centuries of forgotten historical processes.

Shaw can scarcely claim a total nondiscursivity for the ritual practices she investigates; it is their mnemonic qualities that lack verbalization and need to be properly excavated by the anthrohistorian. In this context, only the observer equipped with the necessary historical knowledge can probe the temporal depth of practices and thereby identify them as "memories." Shaw does so by tracing continuities or disjunctures between the observable practices of current diviners and the accounts of past practices offered by colonial officials, missionaries, or academic historians. For instance, a current Temne practice of divination based on contracts between diviners and tutelary spirits "recapitulates" or "crystallizes" images of landlord-stranger contracts from the Atlantic slave trade, practices of intermarriage between Temne and Mande invaders, as well as colonial practices of seizure for indebtedness (Shaw 2002, 106–15). Whatever the often-invoked "recapitulation" means, it is difficult to understand how a present *practice* is constituted as the memory of variously situated and occasioned *accounts* of past observers, unless one ignores even the possibility of a "fallacy of misplaced concreteness."[23]

Nondiscursive memory is predicated on a process of embodiment that does not necessarily require the input, awareness, or even understanding of Temne actors.[24] Rather, it occurs by recursive recapitulation: memories of the Atlantic slave trade mediated experiences of colonialism, and together these mediate the experience of postcolonialism, acting as a critique of the contemporary injustices brought by neoliberalism. This alleged hidden and silent underside of practice, which has so exasperated social theorists (Turner 1994), is recovered here as an eminently passive analytic material.

It is important to note that Shaw's fieldwork in the late 1970s dealt with questions of power, knowledge, and gender in divination rituals. It was only in the early 1990s, while residing at Harvard, when she read historical sources from the fifteenth to the nineteenth centuries and acquired "the conceptual framework of historical anthropology," that she came to see rituals as memories (Shaw 2002, 43–45). It is then unfortunate that anthrohistory, retroactively applied, yields the isomorphism between theory and ethnography. Shaw seems to have found exactly what her theorized account promised: not only do ritual practices embody memories, but the memories are implicit condemnations of the postcolonial present. In a refreshingly straightforward essay, Sanders articulates this very problem, by taking up the literature on African ritual and occult practices as critiques of neoliberalism (2008, 108–9). In this context, Sanders discusses what I think is a more pervasive problem: a seductive but tautological analytic strategy by means of which anthropologists strive to produce ethnographic evidence for their own politicized sensibilities and theorized expectations. Such analytic strategy works like clockwork, being unable to lose any phenomena.

Against Retroactive Anthrohistory

The encounter between anthropology and history unfolds as a highly theorized enterprise that constantly questions and reshapes its domain. As a work of situated retrospection, the project of anthrohistory cannot but keep track of all the dialogues, exchanges, critiques, and clashes that, in fact, make up its history. But to the extent that it is (and should be) a work in progress, sometimes precariously situated in-between disciplinary boundaries, anthrohistory is also a form of anticipation, prospectively orienting the attention of its practitioners to a world where pasts and presents are still being made. Actually using anthrohistorical ways of knowing helps one tune into the uncertainties of knowledge production be they problems of transdisciplinary reflection or the resilient questions of people practically historicizing their experiences and their methods for making sense of the world.

It is a commonplace that knowledge is most often actualized retroactively. As William James (1997, 102–20; see also Latour 2008) put it, "the retroactive validating power" courses through all the knowledge acquisition pathways in a "continuous scheme" of sequential experiences. Yet the very continuity of this uninterrupted chain of experiences that makes up the practice of knowledge implies a constant real-time engagement, a process that is, and must be, liable to failure in order to preserve and fully account for the countless indeterminacies of the world. A familiar trope approximates this trajectory by the moving back and forth between theory and ethnography. My attempt here has been to tamper a while with the latter distinction in order to emphasize the usefulness of anthrohistory as a real-time practice, a method of historicizing knowledge, rather than simply a (potentially infallible) theorized account. In other words, I suggest that anthrohistorians should take delight in their liability to err and fail. Or, if this proves too disheartening, to at least keep in mind the many things that could and perhaps did go wrong until the events and practices they study finally took (theoretically) recognizable shapes. To apply anthrohistory retroactively as a self-sufficient, closed, conceptual framework is possible, but it *would* lose the phenomenon.

NOTES

1. My dissertation research in Vrancea (Romania) in 2003, 2004, and 2005–7 was funded by the University of Michigan's International Institute, the Wenner-Gren Foundation and the Social Science Research Council (IDRF). I am indebted to Dorin Dobrincu for invaluable archival help regarding the 1950 events in Vrancea, to David William Cohen, Josh Reno, Katherine Verdery, and Joseph Viscomi for useful suggestions, and to Daniel Lea for never letting me err on the side of infallibility.

2. There were also five death sentences (Dobrincu 2006). Most of those sentenced to prison were men; there were several women, and they received more lenient sentences (one to two years).

3. Former participants in the events are generally called *chermezani,* and they also refer to the events by the moniker *chermeza.* Some of my interlocutors from Nereju suggest that the name *chermeza* was derisively applied by "the commu-

nists" so as to mock the failed insurgency, while others connect it to the events in the village of Bârseşti where the insurgency coincided with a public ball organized by the communist youth union. In the rest of the paper, I follow the use of *chermeza* as it is the appellative with the widest currency in the region. I also follow my interlocutors' usage of *communism* to refer to the political regime in Romania from 1947 to 1989.

4. Soldiers who had fought on the eastern front also brought distressing stories from the Soviet Union, shaping people's expectations of the new communist regime. Hunger constituted a leitmotif of these stories, and in this context, the confiscation of forests and lumber saws was widely interpreted as the policy of a regime bent on condemning its citizens to a slow death.

5. Since the Vrancea region was a privileged object of inquiry for the Romanian interwar sociologists and historians, there are numerous works discussing the history and characteristics of local communal ownership over forests. See especially Henri Stahl 1939.

6. It is important to note that the archives of the former service have only partially been opened for research. Furthermore, *Securitate* files are records of activities that often involved the recruitment of informers, deals, and covert operations. In this sense, some of them could have been deliberately designed to ensure obscurity, especially in view of the fact that the *Securitate* was not a monolithic organization and that its various branches could (and sometimes did) pursue conflicting goals. See Lynch and Bogen 1996 for an excellent analysis of the vicissitudes of evidence in the investigation and historicization of a famous covert operation, the Iran-Contra affair.

7. Interview with former participant Simion V. Cojocaru (Bârseşti) in Anghel and Alupei (1992, 9). I use real names when referring to interviews already published by journalists and other investigators. For my own research, I refer to interlocutors by pseudonyms.

8. Interview with former participant Nicolae Burlui (Bârseşti) in Mihil (1994, 35).

9. Unlike the randomly chosen character of Alain Corbin's re-creation of a nineteenth-century clog-maker's probable life and perspective on the world (2001), Victor Lupşa is not unknown due to the absence of any kind of traces. I argue that Lupşa is made unknowable in virtue of the kinds of evidence available, the stories possible, and the implications of narrative choices.

10. I am inspired here by Kenneth Burke's work on the ambiguity of motives as a resource for (1969), and his use of "perspective by incongruity" as a method of, analysis (1984 [1937]). My understanding of the indeterminacies of situated historical production owes much to David William Cohen and A. S. Atieno Odhiambo (2004) and Michael Lynch and David Bogen (1996).

11. Interview at Nereju (Vrancea), July 20, 2006. *Securitate* files report that in September 1950 a wooden box containing Lupşa's writings was unburied at a shepherd's cote in the mountains near Nereju (Dobrincu 2006). Another set of documents was apparently retrieved upon his capture in 1955, long after the trial of 1951 (Brişcă 1998). However, I do not think these facts would affect Radu's reasoning in this case.

12. Interviews with two men and three women who participated in the 1950 events, Nereju, 2003–6. *Securitate* files claim that there was indeed an informer infiltrated in the group of insurgents at Nereju, apparently a local teacher. The alleged informer provided very sketchy information about local unrest that is only retrospectively connected by *Securitate* agents with the events in 1950. The details provided clearly indicate that it could not have been Lupșa in this case.

13. "I don't know about Lupșa, but I know they were fools who believed in Americans and other lies," said Sanda, the wife of a former participant, in a tone that suggested both pity and resentment. "Of course, the Americans never came and things stayed the same or they got worse for some of us." Sanda was newly married in 1950 and had a one-year-old baby. Her husband was imprisoned and returned home after fourteen years. They separated sometime in the late 1960s and even now are not on speaking terms. Interview with Sanda, Nereju (Vrancea), August 10, 2004.

14. It is often the case that specific kinds of repressive states—including the communist one—help to produce indeterminacy and uncertainty in the social body, and that this reinforces their power. However, my concern is with how people themselves work toward creating indeterminacy so as to indefinitely postpone the local ascription of failure. Victor Lupșa—with his potential betrayal—gives a particular figuration of failure, making up a manageable storytelling device that prevents any lapse into generic categories and keeps the story firmly rooted in a local context of accountability. Implicit here is the notion that failure is hard to recount, explain, and live with; ironically, the narrative production of indeterminacy requires just as much hard work (it is not a given state, but something that needs to be made and remade with every telling of the story of the *chermeza*). I thank the editors for helping me to clarify this point.

15. In response to one of my tendentious questions, asking him to choose among possible reasons for his involvement in the 1950 events, Radu gave the following account: "We heard this rumor in '48 that they [communists] had begun the nationalization of forests. They wanted to take our forests and people were in despair because they didn't have other means of living. And then we rose in rebellion. For the forest. And maybe our rebellion wasn't well thought out, but something good could have come out of it. Because, maybe if we succeeded here, other people would have rebelled in the lowlands and everywhere. . . . But this was the time of the Russians, and their program was that if they couldn't suppress rebellion, they came to bombard the villages and turn them into steppes. To destroy! Nobody wanted to have their villages destroyed. And so, in the end, I was content that they caught me. If I ran in the mountains, I'd have been shot." Interview at Nereju (Vrancea), July 20, 2006.

16. Interview with "Toma," Nereju (Vrancea), July 1, 2006.

17. For a slightly different take on this problem of narrative temporality, see Bauman and Briggs 1990 on the distinction between narrated events and narrative events.

18. Dwelling on the temporal incongruity between retrospective anthropological analysis and the prospective orientation of Fijian knowledge practices, Hi-

rokazu Miyazaki (2004) understands locally produced indeterminacy as the necessary impetus for action, the precondition of a practical philosophy of hope.

19. Losing the phenomenon is a constant preoccupation in Garfinkel's studies. In particular, his "tutorials" dealing with recordings of everyday actions such as rhythmic clapping in time with a metronome or the act of listening for a ringing phone try to recapture the work of anticipation that is lost in retrospective accounts, be they recordings or narratives (2002, 145–68).

20. Ian Hacking (1995, 234–57) would say that indeterminacy is as important for history and in general for the memory sciences, to the extent that newly available descriptions of actions have retroactive effects on the definition of past actions, so much so that the past itself is rendered indeterminate.

21. Jeff Coulter (1985) notes that transitive forgetting is predicated on a positive ontology, in contrast to a failure of recall or a simple "I don't remember" that remain equivocal with respect to the existence of the event or action in question. In a critique of the inherently positive valuation of memories, Johannes Fabian (2007, 77) articulates a similar insight: "Is it not inherently contradictory to use forgetting as a transitive verb, designating an action that has an object? The contradiction lies between the *negation* expressed in a forgetting whose meaning is constituted in opposition to remembering and the *affirmation* of some content that is being forgotten."

22. Both analytic gestures are more or less indebted to Pierre Bourdieu's notion of habitus as "forgotten history" bodily remembered as "second nature" (1977). See Throop and Murphy 2002 for a pertinent critique.

23. My point is that the status of these historical sources requires minimal problematization: in what sense can they be taken as descriptions of the past, and especially of a past that persists in present practices? Would they be recognizable to the Temne as accounts of their past? Birth (2008) develops this as a critique of homochronism, that is, the equation of "history, a representation of the past, with historicity, a representation of a connection to the past." But see Trouillot 1995 and Price 1998 for a sensitive treatment of multiple historical accounts. On the fallacy of misplaced concreteness, see Whitehead 1997.

24. Shaw gives little consideration to how memory practices are "always socially occasioned," as Jennifer Cole (2001, 106) puts it. Engaged in a similar project in Madagascar, Cole treats the memories of ritual practices as potentialities that require social occasioning, individual purposes and projects, and social recognition, in order to be variously actualized. The practical nature of remembering is the substantive achievement of variously situated actors, and not an inherent feature of formally designed processes of recapitulation. See also Lambek 1996.

Part 3 ❧ Questioning Discipline

16 ❧ Thomas C. Wolfe

Anthrohistory and Phantom Limb Syndrome: Transdisciplinarity in a Disciplinary World

In 1872 Silas Warner Mitchell published an article considered to be the first modern description of what he called "phantom limbs." This was the phenomenon of a person whose extremities had been amputated continuing to feel the presence of the now absent finger, toe, arm, or leg (Ramachandran and Hirstein 1998). It occurred to me that something analogous might happen to graduates of the Anthrohistory Program. Not that they face the horrific trauma of an actual amputation, but rather the brute reality of the academic marketplace is that there are very few niches where a fully hyphenated professor can find a place. In other words, being hired into some department involves the amputation of one of our hyphenated limbs: either "history" drops off into the dark green metal wastebasket in the corner of a bioanthro lab, or "anthropology" falls onto the soft carpet of a wood-paneled library lined with volumes whose spines bear titles printed in spidery *Fraktur*. And just as the vanished limb continues to exert a ghostly presence on amputees, assuring them, for example, that they are able to pick things up with a nonexistent hand, or to run a race on nonexistent legs, graduates of the program continue to feel the presence of a way of thinking that is ostensibly not there.

This metaphor is something to be cautious with, for it raises the question of just what a normal life is. Horrific accidents and events that involve the separation of limbs from bodies rupture normal life and require long processes of painful reconstruction that lead only to an approximation of the life previously led. Few amputees become bionic men and women, climbing mountains and running marathons, and even the ones that do achieve remarkable levels of functioning struggle with the existential haunting of what they lost. The amazing thing is that eventually a new normal is made, and new ways of living coalesce because of and despite what is not there. Shifted to the register of this essay, there is a way that coming to live without a hyphen has entailed coming to see more clearly the normal world of academe, and the slow and haphazard construction of a new life of practice.

In my case, I entered a Department of History, and therefore the part of my brain that continues to be active despite having little articulation in the working world is the anthropological part. I do not offer courses on the "Anthropology of" anything, nor do I see myself as "bringing" anthropological concepts and methods to my history department colleagues, as if carrying over precious nuggets of ore mined in distant hills to craftsmen eager for new material to transform. This would be carrying coals to Newcastle. The reality of contemporary history is the breathtaking diversity of its subjects and approaches. Perhaps unlike those historians in the moment of the program's birth, contemporary historians don't need anthropologists' help with anything. No, the persistence of the anthropological in my case has nothing to do with arguments over ideas, and much more to do with what might be lurking at the pedestrian core of anthropology's disciplinary identity, the question asked by one of the many policemen who appear in Monty Python sketches: "What's all this then?" The layers of such a question can be peeled off like the layers of an onion: it can be about historical causation (how did all this come into being?) and it can be about social and cultural interpretation (how are we to describe all this?). It can be about meaning (what does all this mean?) and it can be about the need for creating a little bit of order in one's life (let's figure this out so we can just get along with our lives.) So that the anthropological phantom limb in my case refers to the steady insistence on a general ethnographic orientation to (Douglas Adams's) life, the universe, and everything. Or more specifically, it means asking at all times, what is this "doing of history"? What is this collective of historians, gathered in an institution under the name "department"? Who and what are we/they, these professional historians? What do we see when we look at history in an ethnographic fashion?

> In order not to write like the Judge, I have tried to find out how the Judge wrote.
>
> ᛫ SHAHID AMIN 1995, 1

These are indeed book-length questions.[1] And while I will offer some cursory answers here, I will, toward the end, turn toward a more important task, namely, wonder how things could be different. But before moving on to this work, I should admit that this sense of the anthropological that I have given might appear to involve a little selective memory, for I have indeed reduced anthropology to something very general and abstract. Here it could be said that I may be imagining something that is not obviously there, just as an amputee might remember a hand or leg that was stronger or more muscular or more beautiful than it really was. But on the other hand, there is a way that this dim memory might also be more accurate, more useful, and more compelling, in providing us with a bodily sense of the significance of those texts, practices, and generations of lives led as disciplinary practitioners—with, in other words, a sense of the *value* of such a life. This is perhaps like a man, who, having lost his hand in an accident, acquires a new and vivid though inarticulate sense of just what it is that a hand can do. For it is as if I "remember" anthropology as a pure space of practical curiosity, grounded in the world but not quite of the world, a space, then, not "determined" by any subject matter, but rather by the brute facts of having a body that moves through the world with a tongue of language constantly darting out to taste, sample, and engage. It seems that anthropology was—is?—like this.

(And what if things were the other way around, if I had ended up in an anthropology department? What would I "remember" of history? This is indeed a challenging thought experiment, given the near black hole–like gravitational field of the specific institutional precinct I find myself in, but it might involve something about death and disappearance, about traces, and about the recommendation to love unconditionally all things that are lost. And what of other disciplines and their phantom cores? Perhaps sociologists carry around buried deep within them some sense of what solidarity is or what constitutes the mystery of our social, collective existence; and perhaps political scientists have a vague inkling of what a democratic form of life might feel like. And so from a certain perspective, one can imagine a sense of the phantom nature of each and every discipline. And yet this is hard, because our disciplinary lives are shaped not by grappling with anything phantomlike, but rather with the all-too-real processes of building buildings, institutions, budgets, reputations, and results. After all, disciplines are not judged by the sense of persons nourished there, but by the quality of the products produced there.)

So what is a group of historians living together under the administrative auspices of a college or university? They are above all a collective of producers of historical works. This is the single most important thing to understand about the ethnographic site of a department of history. This may seem tremendously obvious, but the implications of this observation are far-reaching. For these *producers* are the *persons* who constitute the everyday life of the institution; the identity of "producer of historical works" is the bedrock of the local form of being. And the institution's reproduction takes place in the course of the interactions between producers of different forms and kinds of historical knowledge.

So what is the main trait of this production collective? When we look at the actual production of faculty, we are immediately struck by the heterogeneity of the topics that receive examination. University-based historians produce an immense variety of works. In any given year the faculty of a given department might write books and articles on topics as varied as Marie Antoinette's private life, the number of failed marriages in Appalachia, the American military strategy in Indochina, the significance of a Roman inscription, the history of the city of Prague, and the lives of colonial residents of Bangkok. Their works will appear in different material genres; they will appear in scholarly and popular journals, newsletters, and magazines, and sometimes they will be the basis for television "histumentaries." Their texts might be 400-page books or 5-page articles. The fact is that a department of history is composed of an extraordinarily varied group of people, with an extraordinary diversity of backgrounds. And this is only to be expected, because becoming a historical producer involves much more than acquiring a set of skills; it requires developing oneself as a person who is involved intimately with a certain sometimes vanished and usually imaginary group of people (one's subjects). This self-development itself requires immersion in a wider group of people—the members of a subfield—who are also developing themselves in the same way; it demands acquisition of this group's way of thinking, operating, and understanding. Becoming a producer requires one to sync oneself to a specific process and procedure of production. This means that the diversity of a given department's membership goes far beyond something as superficial as their epistemological points of view. Every historical producer bundles within him- or herself instincts, dispositions, beliefs, inclinations, and so forth, that are the product of a lifetime's journey of membership in this collective.

It might be observed that this is true of all academic departments, and in one sense it is, although in another sense, each discipline marks itself as different by the possession of a different vision of itself as a site of intellectual labor. I would argue that there are peculiar and particular things about a collective of historical producers that shape departments and associations as particular kinds of institutions. This involves the way that history has absorbed the supposed cleavage between scientistic and humanistic method. In the social sciences, the origins and backgrounds and convictions of producers are not supposed to matter because researchers are assumed to absent themselves from their works; social scientists are supposed to come together solely as inquiring minds gathered over data.

In other words, one does not need to be present to the life journey of a sociologist of religion or a political scientist who studies voting behavior. And on the other side of things, in literature, cultural studies, and comparative literature departments, there is *nothing but* the personal journey of the producer. Departments named according to national literatures, like English or Spanish or Portuguese, are increasingly collections of intellectual solo-explorers and/or autobiographers, for the conviction that there is something out there called English that all English scholars examine has all but vanished. Scholarly fields like Bengal women's writing and seventeenth-century colophons and inner city literacy are like the pillars of the ruins of Greek temples, holding up a roof that doesn't exist anymore. While the methods and mythologies of science provide a centripetal pull to the social sciences, and while literature departments have been shaped by the centrifugal force of wave after wave of philosophical critique, history departments muddle on, sheltering simultaneously Science and postmodernism, positivism and poststructuralism, without ever really noticing it or thinking that this plastic, absorptive nature is anything worth talking about.

On the one hand, the diversity of historian-persons is plain to see. Personhood and scholarly fields are densely intertwined, for historical fields are projections of the success persons have had in their scholarly production. Like literature departments, then, history departments are collectivities of solitary producers. But on the other hand, history departments are unique in being a place where society stores up and keeps going something patently obvious and important, namely, History. Perhaps no other department or segment of the humanities has foundations beneath it that are this solid. When budget cuts loom and departments are examined for their future viability, administrators reach first for Anthropology or Sociology or German or Film Studies, for it is unthinkable to have a college or university without a Department of History. History survives as a self-evident part of our culture; it provides the tools for both patriotic understandings and "global citizenship." How could we locate ourselves as modern people without History?

Now these observations about the heterogeneity of historians would not be worth pausing over were a department merely a collectivity or "stable" of writers. For the social contexts within which departments exist go far beyond an occasional meeting to celebrate another publication. Departments are bureaucratic units with hefty budgets; they are organizers of curricula for students; they are mini-enterprises, collecting and disbursing money; they are granters of educational degrees; they are sites for the socialization of strangers into common purposes. In other words, departments are intensely social things that take shape above all in the course of personal interactions. Departments are of course impersonal bureaucratic creations, but their day-to-day incarnations depend on flows of personalities and moods, and above all on styles of communication. Departments, moreover, are in constant flux, as new students enter colleges and universities, and as the list of faculty expands and contracts in accordance with budgets and the literal health of the faculty themselves.

Shifting from the phrase *collectivity of historical producers* to the word *faculty* signals this other dimension of writers' lives, for there is an immense amount of work done by faculty that has nothing directly to do with historical production. Hiring, raises, leaves, admissions, internal grants, committee memberships, honors theses, grading, the life of a faculty member is a nonstop round of judgments, some made alone, others made in the context of interactions with a whole range of others. And as long as a given situation has clear standards of judgment, the grammatical correctness displayed in the language of two competing funding proposals, for example, there is no problem. But in many cases, faculty come together to judge with the issue at hand being something complex like the need to choose between four candidates for a position. In such circumstances, the ghostly collectivity of historical producers reforms, with each candidate attracting or repelling on the basis of a faculty member's idiosyncratic life journey. These are situations in which the materiality, the messiness, and the vital intractability of ideas in the production of history become the elephants in the room.

And here we note the most interesting feature of departmental life: that individual historical producers, when assembled as faculty, come to the table not simply as themselves, but as transporters and articulators of a range of invisible interests. The historian as producer possesses a cadre of allies, so that any given conflict multiplies to include far more people than those gathered. This quality of representation is sometimes banal, as when U.S. historians are understood to be speaking for the interests of all Americans, or when Europeanists are understood to be speaking for and with those creative geniuses whose works represent the high points of Western civilization. The more frequent assemblage of allies involves those people to whom one has hitched one's metaphorical and hypothetical fortune, namely, the people who have become a part of yourself, people you have written about. Thus the conversations that occur in the course of deliberation can become the scenes of assembled multitudes. These could include seventeenth-century European scientists, Chinese officials from the Ming dynasty, the persecuted Cambodian masses, the American Public, victims of fascism, Andean peasants, Roman emperors, former slaves, American consumers, Soviet citizens, and so on. A given historical producer carries with him- or herself the fact of being a representative of an issue, a cause, or a problem. In other words, what stands behind a faculty member as historical producer are the interests and allies that justify their work to a larger audience. Conflicts consist of an impasse or a standoff between groups of interests and allies.

This is probably most noticeable concerning hiring decisions, when one candidate will be recognizable to some faculty as joining the ranks of their allies, supplementing their interests, and strengthening their orientation, while another faculty member will mobilize a counterset of allies and interests with the goal of diminishing or reducing or marginalizing that work. But hiring is by no means the only moment when this representational character of faculty life appears. It also appears whenever anyone from outside the specialized world of historical production comes and asks the department to articulate what history is, or when the department has to produce promotional documents in which it has to define the meaning of History. As I said before, despite the existence of History with a capital H, there is no history apart from the individual embodiment given to history by the succession of particular historical works. Historians lead neurotic lives to some extent, being assured by many important people, from deans on up to Mayors and Governors, and yes, even Presidents, that of course History exists and is vitally important, but also knowing that no single definition of history is ever enough to encompass all the works that appear in its name. Or in other words, it exists, but is too everywhere to ever be known.

These, then, are the two problems-that-must-not-be-named, and that loom like vast shadowy umbrellas over departmental daily life: first, that disciplinary history is not constituted by ideas as much by personal convictions and social powers, and second, that instead of there being a great Temple of History situated on a sun-swept summit where feasts are held and sacrifices made, there are only shantytowns of historical complexities and contradictions that metastasize across the landscapes of global culture.

Now is there anything inherently wrong with this situation? Certainly not if one is inside it, doing one's best to make such a complicated thing work and at the same time keeping going the creative core of one's life. But if one takes a step outside one's department to seek a sense of the shape of higher education as a whole, then one might find reason to look at standard operating procedure in a new light. There are numerous such descriptions of the state of things in higher education, and here I can barely scratch the surface, but I can simply restate what many commentators have written about what is happening to the university as a site of engaged, critical inquiry.

The first point to recall is the by now banal point that the university is thoroughly of society, not set apart from it. In the words of the American philosopher John Stuhr, "it is increasingly misleading to view the university as an autonomous institution and its employees as disinterested seekers of truth. It is increasingly necessary to view the university within the context of a larger system of the production and distribution of knowledge, material resources, and power—as part of a complex, interwoven system of colleges and universities, research institutes and think tanks, the media, government agencies, and corporations" (1997, 17). The consequence of this embedding is that universities are understood to be but a particular form of enterprise, one in which consumers pay for the product of a credential that then guarantees their entry into desirable and lucrative positions within the system. Higher education has become dominated by what Stuhr calls "Edu-business," whose most disturbing effect has been the flattening of all terrains of human inquiry, so that

Minos contrived to hide this specimen in a maze,
A labyrinth built by Daedalus, an artist
Famous in building, who could set in stone
Confusion and conflict, and deceive the eye
With devious aisles and passages . . .
❧ OVID, *METAMORPHOSES*, 186

> the humanities—like leisure studies, hotel management, commercial graphic design, and of course, business administration—have become just another one of the many enterprises of these educational corporations we call universities. As such, they have become the humanities, incorporated—complete with middle management deans, associate deans, and department heads, fund-raisers, grant-writing assistants, public relations specialists, and marketing experts. All of these people watch the bottom line and count profits. They count faculty publications, course enrollments, departmental credit hours, and alumni donations. And all of these people, in committee permutations, develop strategic plans so that in the future there will be bigger numbers to count. And humanists participate in, legitimize, and strengthen all of it. (Stuhr 1997, 14)

One must say that these observations, depicting a situation emergent in the early 1990s, apply with disturbing accuracy to the situation within higher education of fifteen years hence.

The question then becomes, How do historians feel about being key employees of "the humanities, incorporated"? It might be useful to sketch out the consonance between the enterprise-based model of education and the production-oriented nature of academic history. It is not simply that there is a certain elective affinity between the administrative logic of quantification and the appearance of ever more publications written by persons who would identify their primary identity as "authors"; it is not only that there is an intertwining of interests between academic historians and the advertising and public relations departments of colleges and universities, for each uses the other, the one by writing important books that will generate yet more time off to write, the other to attract more consumers by showing the prestigious nature of the educational product they proffer.

Now let me insist that I am not saying that this logic dominates all humanities departments of every college and university across the country. But there are certainly demonstrations of this logic everywhere, as well as moments of apparent resistance to this logic. The development that Stuhr and many others note is of a perceptible movement in the direction of *reducing* all intellectual life to a process of production.

So that the questions that all this leads to are, Who might historians be if they were not primarily writers/producers? What other expression exists for the identities of historians, and what might an identity look like that attempted to rearticulate the significance of open-ended, uncertain inquiry for the creation of full persons? These questions are complex, speculative, imaginative, and cannot be separated from a number of other big questions, like, What is the purpose of education? What is the difference between formal, institutionally based education, and other kinds of learning? How is the difference that Dewey noted in the 1920s between education and simple schooling manifest in this hypertechnological age? What features should one value in the imagining and creating of community? What sorts of activities foster the growth of persons attuned to their own and others' highest potentials? How might a group of people work toward an idea of democracy as being something emergent from the ethical activities of individuals, as opposed to being the institutional manifestation of a prior model?

These questions are indeed huge, and there are many possible starting points, but the one I will mention here is the pragmatic tradition of Emerson, James, Dewey, and Rorty. These writers stress that the ongoing emergence of society is a process that should not be understood as an unfolding from models but rather should emerge in the course of finding means to expand and deepen human solidarity. Pragmatists argue that philosophy cannot prescribe human arrangements, it can only use language in new ways that open up new paths of feeling and understanding. The ultimate philosophical question becomes not What is Truth? or What is Being? but What is useful for the creation of communities in which the search for the well-being of persons is the value manifested in every social context?

Pragmatists would probably suggest that a reorientation of the humanities, and of history departments within them, might begin by suggesting that history is most useful as a way of focusing attention on our common condition of life. Historians might describe themselves first and foremost with the term *educator,* although not in the sense that most edu-businessmen would give to the term. The majority of academic historians would probably understand *educator* as a pretentious and slightly anachronistic word for *teacher,* for indeed, with the exception of the most privileged and prolific of academic authors, university-employed academics must get into the classroom to instruct students in order to receive their paychecks. Many academics would even claim the importance of teaching to their scholarly production, describing the classroom as the site where they try out new ideas on captive audiences, the students being a kind of test market standing in for the paying public beyond the gates of the university. By contrast, a pragmatic sense of the term would stress the educator as an organizer and initial designer of inquiries.

As educators, historians would build their activities from an acknowledgment of the primacy of the immediate relationships they contribute to in the day-to-day life of the college or university. They would argue that a knowledge of the past is useful for contributing to the imaginative potentials of persons to interpret and improve upon the communities they dwell within. This means more than simply bringing a "historical perspective" to things, as if some perspectives were outside history. History would be neither taught nor written as projections upon a screen, but rather history's "content" would emerge from the effort to expose and illuminate relationships in the past that would foster new ways of imagining the future. Historians would be persons who constructed situations within which students and others would learn to recognize both the general effort of persons to shape better worlds for themselves, and specific contexts of temporary developments and solutions. *Every* formal context of education like a class or program would consciously admit its relationship to broader social problems, although pragmatists would insist on a difference between their understanding of the phrase *social problems* and the usual way it appears in the media of the established inegalitarian, capitalist, consumerist order, namely, as interference in the practice of personal freedom. For pragmatists, the phrase *social problems* refers to nothing more or less than whatever constitutes obstacles to the ongoing emergence of democratic communities.

Such a view of the historian's life would imply a radical change in how we think of everyday aspects of a department's life. Concerning the perennial problem of constructing an undergraduate curriculum, if we understand history to be a vital mode of connecting with the present, then professors would not fight over issues such as what content students should know and be tested on. Such arguments depend on a narrow concept of "useful" knowledge, as if knowledge learned apart from dense exploration of its context is ever useful. Rather, professors would cooperate in an ongoing process of determining what historical terrains are most useful for students' negotiation of their own processes of becoming ethical persons. Likewise, a pragmatist reorientation of the training of academic historians in graduate programs would require the removal of those aspects of the graduate experience explicitly oriented to the task of instructing students how to join the ranks of History, Inc., and it would stress instead that graduate programs in history should be institutions where educators are formed whose particular talent is to make vanished lives meaningful *for the project of* building ethical communities. This would require a different concept of fields and subfields, of expertise and authority. It would require, for example, that we give up the idea that geography provides useful and meaningful categories for dividing up historical investigation. On the one hand, graduate training would become much more individual, for students would decide to be historians because they understood it to offer a particular kind of path for personal growth, one developed in the particular context of the classroom and in the activity of teaching. Instead of showing that students had fulfilled area distributional requirements, the evaluation process would involve faculty asking their students, Where are you in the process of understanding and making your own the values of the vocation you came here to pursue?

But on the other hand, graduate training would become much more concretely social than it is now, for the pressing connection to the present would be the constantly repeated refrain audible in all contexts. Students would not be segregated into subcohorts by areas but would actually inquire into the common resources that different terrains of the past offered for examination of certain issues. They would also note the different linguistic and cultural shapings of institutions and practices across time and space, and apply these forms to different compelling problems in their midst.

Such a reclaiming of purposeful inquiry for the construction of democratic community would not involve the disappearance of scholarship or scholarly publication. Rather, it would involve the writing of new kinds of books, books whose shape we are only beginning to imagine now. These would be texts written not by producers, but by educators, who would never treat the past as someplace to disappear into, but as a place to inquire into, fully aware that the condition of the voyage in the first place is the purchase of a roundtrip ticket.

There is much more to say about what a pragmatic revisioning of the field of history might look like. But let me begin my conclusion by making a point about the program whose trajectory is the source of the reflections in this volume. It is clearer to me now how the production of phantom limbs was in a sense intrinsic to the program from the outset, how their existence is a structural by-product of the program itself. After all, in their course of studies the program's students are only *half* socialized into the ways and means of each discipline. This might entail as a consequence a sense of inexperience or even naïveté about the way things "really work" out there where disciplines and their productions are the coin of the realm. And then upon graduation, one-half of one's "training" will be suspended as a kind of path-not-taken, as one takes one's place among the grinding gears of disciplinary reproduction. All this poses a kind of practical dilemma for the student, namely, how to cope with one's being made into both *idiot* and *savant*. And at the same time, there are urgent, practical problems to confront, such as, how to maintain the positive, enabling possibilities inherent in such "inadequate" preparation, especially as institutional logics seem to require thorough absorption of disciplinary ways of relating to oneself and to one's field. After all, any institution that dedicates itself to the intense scrutiny, criticism, and reimagining of the setting that supports it will always be suspect to some degree. This will involve learning how to manage the forces and circumstances that push the program in the direction of disciplinarity and how to guard its first priority, namely, producing new ways of enacting the world.

Whatever this one program's future, it is I think clear that these issues of phantom limbs and disciplinary identities that lay at its intellectual core is but one instantiation of a larger struggle articulated by Bruno Latour, in a 2004 effort to take stock of the ambiguous legacy of science studies in the public sphere. Latour wonders, among other things, about how humanities and social science scholars can be useful in society, given what he calls the dead end into which the tradition of critique has led them. He concludes that disciplinary production supported by rusty philosophical armature will not do, and that scholars must find their way to a sense of concern over what is really there in all its intractable complexity (Latour 2004). In retrospect, it seems that the program has also been about finding one's way from matters of fact to matters of concern.

I should conclude this wandering thought train by addressing a disconnect that the reader may be sensing between this attention to the discipline of history and the larger presence of interdisciplinarity that has appeared all over higher education in recent decades. There is much to say here, but let me restrict myself to just one point. One of the questions that (still) looms over higher education is how to address the fact that most institutions are still places where the scholars' work is conceived in the same way as it was in the twelfth century, as the work of monks in monastic cells. Interdisciplinarity might break down walls, but it still leaves the cells intact. Moreover, it does not question the authority of disciplines; rather the model seems to be that of Bloomsbury: a painter will somehow profit from sipping sherry with a poet, a novelist will be challenged and inspired by a playwright. The scholar is conceived as a creator type who will respond to different kinds of fuel for keeping the production going. This style of interdisciplinary thinking suggests that when you have exhausted all the interesting interlocutors in your field, or when your creative juices have dried up, or when you just plain feel stale, then it is a matter of taking on board another set of concepts, another vocabulary of analysis from the intellectual universe down the hall or across the campus. And while many scholars have without doubt benefited from these kinds of encounters, and while there is a kind of pleasure in entertaining the possibility that one can make oneself into a kind of polymath, into a kind of postmodern Renaissance man (*sic*), it is also the case that the embrace of interdisciplinarity across the landscape of higher education has been mostly about enabling and celebrating yet more production. We might also note that it also has enabled all sorts of monstrous hybrids to appear in the pages of journals and on the proliferating PowerPoint screens: bearskin has been grafted on to whale blubber, bees' wings onto armadillos' backs, with such fanciful creations pointed to as evidence of the wonderful productivity inherent in interdisciplinarity.

Much more attractive is the idea that crosses many of the essays in this volume, the idea of transdisciplinarity, which projects the view that thinking does not naturally emerge in the silos of disciplines, but that it travels above and across them in pursuit of associations and connections that enable not awkward hybrids but creatures of an altogether different nature. Moreover, this movement of ideas has nothing to do with production but with something much simpler, namely, an attempt to articulate a problem and diagram a response. It is not about borrowing arguments but crossing (up) communities. It seems to me that transdisciplinarity is best understood as something enacted as a form of communication and social interaction, of attention and listening, of speech and gesture. It is something that comes into being by being experienced in common, that manifests itself not in journal articles but in lives folding out toward others.

But the fact is that transdisciplinarity has yet to be made present as a form of everyday life, grounded in inquiry into common problems. It is very rare to find contexts of interactions in which people are not identified by the disciplinary skills they bring to the table, as if a common life were a building constructed by members of different trades, rather than the creative dilemmas our lives are an expression of. A life in common can only emerge from cutting against the grain of specialized knowledge and functional differentiation, and to this end, we must find a way of thinking toward the university as a space of ongoing experimentation: in the classroom, in arenas of faculty governance, and in the conferences and journals where scholarly activity is put on display. I prefer to see the Anthrohistory Program as an expression of this larger spirit of experimentation, with the phenomenon of the phantom limb, as I have sketched it here, as just a necessarily troubling aspect of the work that is to be done.

NOTES

I would like to thank my colleagues at the University of Minnesota for accepting an anthropologist in their midst.

1. They are also not new questions. Forty-five years ago Bernard Cohn published "An Anthropologist among the Historians: A Field Study," in the *South Atlantic Quarterly,* which takes even more literally than I do here the metaphor of the anthropologist traveling to the strange and distant land of the Historians. What is interesting about that article in nearly a half-century's retrospective is

both how dated it feels, and yet how current its conclusion seems. It was written in the midst of the vast expansion of higher education in the United States, both the rapid growth of disciplines and the professoriat, and one feels that Cohn has no problem generalizing an essence of history from an observation of the *research* conducted by historians. My argument here, by contrast, is that historians' research has become so varied and heterodox that such an essence no longer exists, and rather, that what they share is now constituted in their imaginary relationship to an image of history supplied not by themselves but by broader social and cultural forces that call for a never-ending stream of historical production. His conclusion, however, where he values what he calls "biculturality" over a "multidisciplinary team approach," can be read as gesturing toward what I call here the phenomenon of the phantom limb. See Cohn 1962. See also the 1996 article by his student and one of my coadvisers—and one of the founders of the program—Nicholas Dirks.

17   Anupama Rao and Steven Pierce
On the Subject of Governance*

In 1955 the leader of the largest political party in the northern Nigerian regional House of Assembly, Ahmadu Bello, made a speech insisting that many of the region's problems stemmed from an abandonment of ancient tradition. Thus, for example:

> The right traditions that we have gotten away from are the cutting of the hands of thieves, and that has caused a lot of thievery in this country. Why should we not be cutting the hands of thieves in order to reduce thieving? That is logical and it is lawful in our own tradition and custom here.[1]

British colonialism had transformed governmental practice and had radically modified the application of Islamic law. Governance and the proper practice of Islam were intertwined; colonialism had corrupted each. If Nigeria were to achieve self-government, such distortions would need to end. British officials in Nigeria and London—and southern Nigerian political opinion—were unimpressed by this romantic view of precolonial political tradition, wondering whether Bello could be dispensed with. However, Bello remained in office and politically dominated the federation through independence and until a military coup in 1966 ended Nigeria's First Republic.

Bello's invocation of tradition as a pathway to a culturally appropriate modernity was not unusual. From Julius Nyerere's African socialism to Mobutu Sese Seko's "authenticity," in many places postcolonial rulers invoked the past as a way of transcending colonialism. Bello's formulation was provocative, however, in its apparent rejection of liberal constitutional norms, which posited the equal citizenship of universal subjects and were extremely delicate about judicial reliance on violations of bodily

---

*Our essay is dedicated to the memory of Anjan Kumar Ghosh, who died on June 5, 2010. Our fellow student at Michigan during the 1990s, Anjan exemplified the spirit of interdisciplinarity and the ethical commitments associated with anthrohistory. We miss him.

integrity. "The cutting of the hands of thieves," like other forms of corporal punishment or indeed like torture, struck many observers as antithetical to the forms of democratic modernity that nationalist politics attempted to claim. Such an interpretation, however, misses the multiple paradoxes Bello and his contemporary critics were attempting to navigate as they negotiated the problematics of nationalist politics: all were centrally concerned with the difficulties of erecting the "human" as the central ethical category for democratic postcolonial governance. Whether the citizen was conceived of as a universal liberal subject or as an enfranchised member of a local ethnic or cultural community (for Bello, northern Nigerian Muslims), national independence entailed a simultaneous acceptance and disavowal of European political categories.[2] In this way Bello's seemingly conservative invocation of precolonial punishment was a more radical rejection of British political practice than his southern colleagues would tolerate. Even though many castigated his politics of indigeneity as divisive—calling it "tribalism" or "communalism," for example—and privileged a utopian future through development, the precolonial past has retained a more general significance as a place from which alternative histories and subjectivities might be fashioned. It also, and crucially, has been key in a continuing reformulation in how the "human" can be politically imagined.

As Partha Chatterjee (1993) has argued, the resignification of culture was a defining characteristic of anticolonial thought. No longer a colonial category or an object of European derision, culture became instead a sign of authenticity and the expression of nativist subjectivity. In Chatterjee's formulation, the derivative nature of anticolonial thought is indicated by the fact that both colonizers and anticolonialists imagined "culture" and "tradition" in essentially the same way. The novelty of nationalist formulations emerged primarily in a transfer of sovereignty from a colonial elite to a national one, achieved through what anticolonial nationalism claimed was an inevitable relationship between violence and politics. From the Fanonian demand for a purifying counterviolence against colonial dehumanization, to M. K. Gandhi's deeply embodied and fraught explorations of the relationship between violence and nonviolence, to Bello's advocacy for what he claimed was a return to physical disfigurement as a solution to social disorder and moral decay, violence was associated with collective ethicality and imbued with political pertinence. In this sense, then, Bello's speech is more than an idiosyncratic defense of northern Nigerian Muslims' culture. Rather, it is a particular instance of this more general search for anticolonial political community, one that retained profound colonial continuities even as it produced powerful indeterminacies in how culture, violence, and the "human" were negotiated within an anticolonial political imaginary.

The anticolonial moment of romanticizing tradition seems strangely distant today, when the failures of development, new forms of imperialism, and the global war on terror recall rather older colonial agendas even as they pose novel challenges to the project of anthrohistory. At the same time, contemporary discussions of the global South if anything anathematize culture and tradition. Non-Western cultures—and increasingly, Islam in toto—are portrayed as static impediments to modernity, development, and democracy, requiring external intervention and tutelage. Where fifty years ago, they heralded the promise of political freedom, now they appear a source of instability and intrinsic violation of human rights. Scholars today are faced with a double challenge in opposing neoimperial projects: conducted in an idiom of human rights and universal welfare, they are nearly impossible to disentangle from these urgent political imperatives. At the same time they are something more than a simple recapitulation of the colonialisms of a century ago. Both the problem of strategy and the analytic riddle of the present can be addressed by close attention to this earlier political moment, and to what has changed between then and now. What is at stake in a shift from conceiving of non-Western political societies through paradigms of culture to addressing their crises as issues of humanitarianism and cultural pathology? How do we address the political distinctiveness of the new universalism while historicizing its relationship to liberal paradigms of universality and difference produced during the last century? And how do we narrate the problematic and ahistorical ways in which nationalist politicians romanticized much earlier periods?

It would be too simple to argue that enthusiasm for decolonization has given way to skepticism about non-Western sovereignty, or to suggest that human rights has emerged as the dominant legitimator of international intervention. Rather, today's human rights discourse is the product of two partially distinct intellectual trajectories, both centrally concerned with the entailments of the "human." Both traditions have undergirded discussions of non-Western sovereignty, but only one informed the moment of decolonization. On one hand, "human rights" is a recent phenomenon, a post–World War II reaction to the horrors of the Holocaust and the need to deal with the problem of displaced persons in a context in which state sovereignty was still an ambiguous matter. On the other, a longer-term international public concerned with the suffering of non-Western "others" emerged in response to the slave trade and to a continuing series of colonial scandals—the trial of Warren Hastings, permanent settlement, the Irish question, King Leopold's Congo, to name a few. Human rights as a project of global governance and institutional capacity-building must thus be distinguished, at least heuristically, from a genealogy of the "human" as it has developed through proximity to acts of collective dehumanization (viz., slavery) *and* the cultivation of sentiment to oppose them. We focus on this latter strand of anticolonial critique, its critique of colonial dehumanization, because it clarifies the paradoxical permeability of "violence" and "the human."

Such a perspective offers a detour around the usual critique of human rights discourse, where the universality of rights is typically posited against the specificity of culture and tradition. However, the valorization or denigration of "tradition" are not opposed paradigms but instead demonstrate a continuing ambiguity within liberal projects of governance. A continuing and consistent ideological emphasis on allegedly unchanging cultural formations alternately impedes and enables particular liberal political projects, which place the issue of culture at the center of debates over governance. To the extent that populations become identified with a specific culture imagined to be discrete, the universal liberal subject is inevitably tied up with localized cultural entailments. A human is thus always already limited to her cultural identity, toward which liberal models of governance are at best ambivalent. Ultimately, this ambiguity inheres in a specifically biopolitical model of governance that is at once universalizing and dependent on ever-shifting categories of difference. Even as "culture" or "tradition" becomes an ethnographic real, a sign of nativist difference, and potentially the site of pure alterity, it also marks a point of entry for understanding social practices and political forms constitutive of the "other body."

In editing a volume on colonial violence, *Discipline and the Other Body* (Pierce and Rao 2006), we set out to explore how colonial categorization and regimes of control produced what we termed the "colonial exception." Our use of "colonial exception" was indebted to theoretical departures, especially in the work of Carl Schmitt (2005) and Giorgio Agamben (1998, 2005), which revisits the genealogy of European subject-formation as its relates to the problem of political sovereignty and its limit case of legal exception. In colonial contexts, we argued, the putative inadequacy of colonial subjects served both to violate and to protect regimes' claims to a certain liberalism. The irrational, unreasonable "native" could not be governed through rational means, justifying bodily violence and necessitating modes of governance that targeted them not as rational individuals but as collectivities bound together by "tradition." In examining these issues through the lens of a volume on comparative colonialism, we drew upon conversations in the history and anthropology of colonialism that had taken distinctive shape at the University of Michigan, under the rubric of the Doctoral Program in Anthropology and History (e.g., Dirks 1992; Cooper and Stoler 1997; Coronil 1997; Dirks 1998), even as we extended those concerns to inquire into a colonial genealogy of the "human." Our end point in this earlier work was the emergence of "human rights" as the discursive marker of this liberal ambivalence toward governing the "other," but many critical issues remained unaddressed, most notably how to understand late colonial and postcolonial transformations in governing practice. In this short chapter, we will sketch out some theoretical and methodological problems in fleshing out this problem, particularly in relation to this volume's discussions of anthrohistory as a project.

As scholars of the British Empire, and of India and Nigeria in particular, we are concerned with colonial paradoxes of political liberalism manifest in the nineteenth and early twentieth centuries, though putting aside debates internal to the development of liberal thought in this period. Although we do not discount the long history of European preoccupation with questions of humanity and difference whose sixteenth-century roots are in European contact with Amerindian communities (Muthu 2003), our focus is both more historically specific and theoretically contained. Our original concern was with the paradoxical relationship between ideologies of freedom and the justification for corrective violence that took shape in colonial contexts in the period of high imperialism, in the aftermath of slave abolition, and during a period of increased concern with the developmental narrative of "the human." By examining a moment when scholarly preoccupation with the "human" intersected with policy-centered concerns about humanitarianism and human rights, we can see how ideas of rights and protection are entangled with changing technologies of discipline and punishment. "Enlightenment in the colonies" (Mufti 2007) reflected the uneven development of humanitarianism, itself constituted by the vexed dialectic between violence and the human. An ultimate effect was the nationalist difficulty of conceptualizing both pre- and postcolonial political community.

Culture, Rights, and the Universal

Recent forms of political violence, neoliberal development and structural adjustment, and the increased mobility of capital and labor have exacerbated the ethical dilemmas of ethnographic fieldwork. Such developments have also transformed the idea of rights—especially inalienable human rights—and how they are borne out in practice. Paradoxically, as communities are rendered ever more vulnerable to catastrophe, natural and man-made, and as "life" itself seems more political and precarious, the persuasive power of human rights discourse has increased. Human rights increasingly appear to be a geopolitical universal, and at least in the abstract are accepted everywhere as a good. However, both sides of the term *human rights* require investigation: the universality implied by the *human*—transcending dichotomies such as male/female and traditional/modern—and the assumption that *rights* undergird claims of justice and equity. Clearly, the postwar reformulations of human rights and humanitarianism must be located against long-standing ethnographic concerns with rights, culture, and difference (Povinelli 2002; Scott 2003), and on a longer-term history of the suffering subject. The intersection between the three concerns brings into focus the role human rights has played to articulate claims and to regulate those articulating them. To what extent is a discourse of universal rights, derived from the traditions of nineteenth-century political liberalism, applicable to emerging technologies of violence and new mobilizations of difference—ethnic, religious, gendered, sexual? How can we remain committed to the dignity and worth of all people while remaining critical of universalism? What are the historical and cultural limits of humanitarianism?

Anthropology's long engagement with empire and its legacies is a useful point of departure for examining the question of "the human." For example, imperial and postcolonial scandals over *sati* (Sunder Rajan 1990; Mani 1998), foot-binding (Ko 2005), and genital operations (Walley 1997; Thomas 2003; Boddy 2007) find an echo in recent arguments that some cultures are "bad" for women—protecting women requires extricating them from culture and community (Okin 1999)—or conversely in claims that feminism and human rights activism are forms of Western imperialism. Both positions affirm that some cultural practices are incommensurable with human rights, and both presuppose that the only way to ensure human rights is to spread Western cultural forms around the world. At the heart of this impasse between rights and culture is the figure of the liberal individual, which has become the presumed subject of contemporary human rights discourse through intersections between histories of the "human" and liberal paradigms of rights and responsibility.

> *Yes, I can see them.*
> *Captives in groups near the shore.*
> *In slave camps.*
> *Waiting to be sold.*
> *You have grown up without knowing.*
> *You have read so many books.*
> *You have seen and compared so many sets of figures.*
> *You have traveled the routes of the slave ships.*
> *But still you do not know why the sea does not cast these corpses back up.*
> *Listen...*
> *You can enter history.*
> *But you cannot leave it.*
> ✐ FRANÇOIS WOUKOACHE IN SOW ET AL. 1995

Nowhere is the impasse around culture and rights better illuminated than by the fact that culture continues to be regarded as an impediment to modernization, justifying political intervention and cultural correction—as with the demonization of Islam and claims that the invasions of Afghanistan and Iraq were conducted in the interest of women's liberation (Abu-Lughod 2002). For behind the comforting claim that the "international community" opposes sexual violence, while criminal regimes and primitive people commit them, is the call to resuscitate empire as an efficient strategy of global governance (Ferguson 2003). And as we have seen in Abu Ghraib and beyond, governing exigencies produce uncomfortable similarities between the so-called barbarism of native practice and the acts of terror and violence used to contain them.

A domestic variant of this global problematic is the debate over multiculturalism and immigration in Europe and the United States. Charles Taylor (1994), for example, argues that the politics of identity force liberal democracies to balance the commitment to equality and universal rights against claims to cultural authenticity. As individuals and groups use symbols of ethnic, religious, sexual, and cultural belonging as markers of authenticity, they also deepen the public visibility of particularistic identities as the grounds for making claims upon the social collectivity for equal rights, on the one hand, and for tolerance and respect, on the other. For Taylor as for other communitarians, the right to recognition is a claim to the right to difference. The problem for a politics of identity thus becomes how to distinguish the recognition of difference from the perpetuation of inequality; reformist agendas must go further, distinguishing the social redistribution of political and economic opportunity from support for repugnant practice.[3]

Ironically, liberal tolerance might ultimately enable "liberal strategies of exclusion" (Mehta 1999). Moral repugnance has become a powerful defense against cultural practices such as genital operations, veiling, and polygamy, even as it becomes the legitimating grounds for political intervention, often and increasingly in the name of human rights. In these as in less extreme instances an often-articulated culturalist answer to human rights critiques is a demand to contextualize cultural practices on their own terms: with sufficient cultural knowledge, the hope goes, liberal consensus can distinguish "good" difference from "bad." In this way, human rights discourse recapitulates the logical structure of criminal law, though the defendant is now a culture rather than an individual.

The long entanglement of liberal universalism in imperial projects thus demands viewing contemporary human rights as something more than a critique of culture (Merry 2006). Anthropological approaches offer a way to oppose careless universalism (Benedict 1943; Herskovits 1969, 1973; Boas 1988 [1940]), though there is a danger here in that ethnographic sensitivity is susceptible to distortion as a relativist straw man. How does one oppose the covert imperialism of human rights without attempting to speak for a putatively mute other? This dilemma, we suggest, can be addressed through a more careful investigation of the ways in which the subject of rights is ultimately constituted, as a subject of biopolitical governance.

The Biopolitical Subject of Rights

If it is possible to discern an overall trajectory in global paradigms of governance, subjectivity, and alterity, and if historical patterns of change are driven largely by the continual failure of governing projects and the scandals that emerge from them, academic analysts must pay careful attention to a bewildering range of concerns. One must pay careful attention to the complex history of the rise of "modern" forms of rule—the emergence of the bureaucratic state, the dispersal of power into a host of discourses and instrumentalities, and ongoing mutations of capitalism and globalization—and the emergence of a global humanitarian public. Foucault is a natural point of departure as a profound analyst of institutional power and the development of modern state bureaucracy, though too often functionalist readings elide his profound ethical engagement, understanding his historical account as simply one of all-conquering power and the circumscription of "agency," conceptualized as a kind of absolute voluntarism. To avoid this, we need to return to Foucault's continued interest in the technologies of the self, considered in regard to the development of state racism.

Foucault's account of the body as a key site of regulation and control and as material artifact of racialization and sexual differentiation showed how the body's political extensions and social entailments have radically shifted over the past several centuries. Drawing on these perspectives, one might argue that the trajectory of colonial embodiment suggests a larger political subtext to universalistic liberal claims about bodily integrity—a key assumption for contemporary human rights—even as it illuminates the technologies through which difference is inscribed upon the body of an emergent other. That is, while a human rights critique of a specific instance of bodily violation appears superficially to be structured by questions of specific acts and instances of culpability, the subject whose rights have been violated is always already inadequate. The violated subject can never be universal.

This process creates challenging theoretical and methodological dilemmas. In an abstract sense, it underlines an opposition Rey Chow (2006) has noted between Foucault's (1980) view of biopolitics as essentially productive—a command to *live*, albeit in highly particular ways—and Agamben's (1998) formulation, in which it is essentially a politics of death, a rule of law premised on the expulsion of some into the realm of "bare life." It is worth noting that some of this emerges from the very different role the state plays in the two formulations of biopolitics. Where for Foucault the state (and law more generally) was largely a repressive force and was only a small part of the complex of instrumentalities through which power was deployed, for Agamben the state is at the center of his considerations; the question of how sovereignty is achieved, the problem of disentangling the moral considerations of the *citizen* and the human bearer of "bare life" subtend his account of biopolitics.[4] That is to say, a Foucaultian account of the inadequate subject would focus on the genealogies of the discourses constituting her—how she came to be known, the evidentiary rules for describing her scientifically, the continuities and discontinuities in such discourses. Agamben, by contrast, would look upon her as a problem of sovereignty, caught in the gap between a biological human and the citizen, a gap that could threaten her very existence through counterinsurgency, social disruption, or genocide—the "native" becomes a "guerrilla," a "refugee," or simply a statistic. Here we note only that this tension between the tendency to historicize categories and to explore the manifestation of enduring social forms mirror challenges facing anthrohistory as a whole.

Implications for Anthrohistory

To the extent that the problem of the "human" is posed as a specific species of *failure,* a gap between liberal universalism and governing practice, or between behavioral norms and empirical conduct, it becomes easy to imagine that anthrohistory is simply a matter of tracking cultural change or of examining historical developments with an eye toward explaining the gap between theory and practice, between culture and the universal. However, if we remain committed to paradigms that do not reify culture as discrete, coherent, and uncontested, the evidence for our specific concerns is elusive at best. An archive for recouping such phenomena can be assembled only through careful and creative rereadings and a willingness to imagine experiential universes at odds with the dominant idioms that have received explicit record (Guha 1988; Stoler 2001; Eiss 2002).

To return to Ahmadu Bello's invocation of Muslim tradition, the ideological implications of his speech would be lost if one attempted simply to look at actual practices in precolonial northern Nigeria (or elsewhere) to evaluate how a specifically postcolonial representation of "tradition" represented (or failed to represent) historical reality. Much more interesting is the question of the kind of political community Bello's invocation of the past was meant to achieve, the creation of a polity that retained substantial continuities with the colonial state but that also enfranchised a particular (male, Western-educated, largely aristocratic) postcolonial elite. And at the same time, this notion of political community is clearly susceptible to a human rights critique, which might spectacularize the figure of a host of non-Western others—female, unfree, criminal, deviant, terrorist—as of course has happened in global coverage of contemporary Islam as a violent counterethics, from its support for the regulation of intimacy by shari'a criminal law to its incitations to martyrdom and suicide. Like other utopian imaginations of postcolonial social order, the challenge of Bello's speech is as a political performative, though not necessarily as what he *intended* to achieve. Reading the signs of this project in the archive is a challenge. Just as important (and just as difficult) is to illuminate what is at stake in the attempt to criticize this assertion of political community, to protect the rights of those it excludes. That is to say, the task of anthrohistory in this instance is to discover how the discourse of human rights installs the subject of rights as a subject of governance.

In this regard, the interdependence of governance and violence suggests that a focus on the latter may be a way to get at this elusive history. One cannot reduce the long-term genealogy of the "human" to a series of examples or object lessons in dehumanization. Rather, one must attend to particular instances or invocations of violence: the role of (colonial) violence in constituting ideologies of the partial humanity of colonial subjects, the resignification of violence as purifying activity as in Fanon's (1968, 36) account of the violent work of purification that is necessary for the emergence of a New Man "freed from the filth of the past corruption," the Gandhian turn to *self-violence* in response to social conflict, or Ahmadu Bello's invocation of traditional legal violence in the making of postcolonial political community. The relationship between violence and personhood posited in each instance is not a description of the role of violence in social life. Rather, it brings the biopolitical subject into existence in a new form—or at least it attempts to do so. Although this conclusion seems minimal in the abstract, it is more disquieting as a methodological injunction. An anthrohistory of the subject of governance must always explore the violence that constituted her, elusive or overt. In this way, the anthrohistorian is always ethically entangled with her research—not as objective critic but as witness. And in tracing patterns of remaking the humanity of peoples through processes of dehumanization, she inevitably undermines her own claims to universal subjecthood.

NOTES

1. PRO CO 554/1183 (1954–56). Political Situation in the Northern Region of Nigeria. Extract from Political Intelligence Notes of Nigeria, NR, no. 23, March 19, 1955.

2. Frederick Cooper (2008) has usefully pointed out that citizenship served variously means of articulating claims—to rights within empires, within other political formations that nonetheless were not nation-states, within nations, and in more localized communities or identities—suggesting that a closer attention to the politics of citizenship allows scholars to pose useful questions about the precise nature of particular historical contexts.

3. A useful approach in this regard is Anthony Appiah's recent (2005) sugges-

tion that a solution lies in what he terms a "rooted cosmopolitanism," or "a form of universalism that is sensitive to the ways in which historical context may shape the significance of a practice" (256). He suggests that the modal form for human interaction ought to be a position of mutual respect for difference and for a rigorous and ethically engaged commitment to dialogue across all axes of difference.

4. This, ironically, is the flip side of the difference Chow notes between Foucault's conceptualization of power as fundamentally productive and Agamben's notion of it as repressive. Agamben's subsequent (2005) elucidation of the topologies of sovereignty maintains the centrality of the state in his conceptualization of how human subjects exist—whether *inside* the state or *abandoned* by it. And in both instances, Agamben skirts around the possibility of a more expansive genealogy of the "human," one that is not organized by the telos of the Holocaust. In contrast is Hannah Arendt's (1973) prescient observation of the relationship between colonial conquest and origins of the European biopolitical state of the early twentieth century. Arendt argued that (1) colonizers were the first to essentialize racial identity and to render it a form of civic disability, thereby laying the conceptual groundwork for all modern racism; (2) governing colonies required the elaboration of bureaucratic rationality that reached its apogee in the fascist and totalitarian regimes of Europe; and finally, (3) "administrative massacres" in the colonies laid the preparatory ground for Nazism's extermination of the Jews.

18 ❧ S. C. Humphreys
Between Disciplines, After Modernity

How is interdisciplinarity possible? A discipline is a way of constructing the world to make it researchable: a paradigm, a kind of language. So the first step is to be bi- (or multi-) disciplinary. And that was the main emphasis of the plan for the Interdepartmental Program in Anthropology and History[1] at the University of Michigan in 1987: that its students, instead of relying on stereotypes (that anthropology deals with ritual, religion, "tradition," and "culture" as a separate domain of human experience; that history discovers what really happened in the past),[2] should get an insider's view of both disciplines, understanding their conflicts and tensions as well as their terminology and assumptions. Insofar as we saw anthropology and history as complementary, our interest was in the gaps and blind spots in these assumptions. Historians desired "total history" but did not always historicize their own categories of analysis or think critically about the relation between questions and "sources"; anthropologists were trying to find regularity ("culture," "structure") through short-term observation in changing situations.

Twenty years later, though bidisciplinarity is still essential, the reflexivity implied in being transdisciplinary—being able to stand outside as well as inside two disciplines—seems more important. Both disciplinary paradigms are now more energetically questioned from within, and the modern narrative time-frame in which they were constructed now looks like a part of the past out of which it was moving. Historians recognize that narratives are constructed, anthropologists recognize that the same is true of localities[3] and cultures. If the idea of a "cultural turn" still has any energy, it is in the invitation to think critically about disciplines as cultures.

A bidisciplinary training ought to equip students to criticize the unstated assumptions and fetishes of both disciplines and thus put them in an advantageous position for thinking critically about the modern university and its current inadequacies.

There is increasing recognition now that the disciplinary structure inherited from the nineteenth century no longer fits the interests and problematics of students, researchers, and funding sources (whether public or private). But the common reaction has been to deal with these issues by piecemeal tinkering (new "interdisciplinary" departments or programs of Gender Studies, Religious Studies, Comparative Literature, or new Institutes), without reconsidering the whole departmental system, let alone the category distinctions between general education, research, and professional training, or between Science and Social Science/Humanities.

> *Give me a date! you cry, to anyone who tells you about anything: I can't think about it without a date!*
>
> ✒ STEEDMAN 2007, 207

When the Anthrohistory Program began at the University of Michigan, we were still living in "modernity"[4]—though it might be argued that 1989, the year of the program's official inception, was the end of the modern period. Now, although *postmodernism* has become a familiar term, the disciplinary implications of the end of modernity are not sufficiently analyzed. History departments seem reluctant to treat the modern period as part of the past, as having ideal-typical characteristics like those attributed to antiquity or the middle ages. A well-known modern book title proclaimed *The Death of the Past* (Plumb 1969). If the past is not dead—that is, if conceptions of any part of the past, however remote, can serve as legitimating maps for action—what becomes of the modern model of linear time as stretching from remote beginnings gradually into recent history and thence to the present?

This question is particularly relevant to anthrohistory because in modern stereotypes anthropologists worked with living informants while historians studied documents. On this view, the anthrohistorian would do both, an ambition that (regrettably) excluded most of premodern history and avoided serious questions about the durée and reconfigurations of institutional and ideological structures.[5]

There is also little systematic thinking in universities about the implications of globalization for education (What should exchanges of students and faculty hope to achieve? What are the obstacles?), for problematics/research on multinationals, suprastate organizations, population movements, and so forth, or for research cooperation around the world. It is an encouraging sign that Western graduate students traveling to do research now regard local scholars as teachers and colleagues rather than as informants, but non-Western scholars are still far too often treated as having only local knowledge.

So how do I view the prospects for anthrohistory in the postmodern, global, university? My frustration with the failure of universities to rethink the modern categories and assumptions on which they have been based since the early nineteenth century has led me into an international, postmodern research project called "Modernity's Classics" that aims to criticize a range of current categorical distinctions: between Western and non-Western cultures, "cultural literacy" and critical thought, sacred and secular spheres, the "classic" and modernity. This links up to my conception of anthropology as the critical analysis of categories, above all those of the researcher's own culture (Douglas 1973). Critical anthropology depends on the capacity both to scrutinize our conceptions of the exotic and to exoticize what seems to us real—the state, power, property, technology, and so on (see Coronil 1997; Pierce 2005; Rao and Pierce, this volume). Some anthropologists do seem to be returning in this critical spirit to the eighteenth-century conception of anthropology as the theory of what it is to be human—which should include not only the interface with biology that now interests cognitive anthropologists but also the capacity to be mystified, to repress obvious elements of experience, to learn what not to know (Rebel 2005).

One aspect of this anthropology of humanness, particularly relevant to historical anthropologists, would be the analysis of conceptions of pastness.[6] The modern conception of time as linear implied that the past could no longer provide images of possible futures, but stimulated new forms of historical poetics (Rancière 1992) in which the classic and the sacred, culture, the nation, and evolution, in varying articulations, were the organizing concepts. Greek and Roman classics were positioned as ancestors of the modern West and hence read as progressive or timeless[7] and as secular substitutes for religion. Other classics (Indian, Chinese, Islamic, Judaic) were the heritage of specific cultures and/or religions, which had diverged from the track of evolution: this created tensions between cultural/religious identity and modernization (Chatterjee 1993; Wagner 2000).

Beyond these differences, however, are common modern tendencies and tensions. General belief in modern progress in science and technology implied constructing the value of the classic as spiritual rather than practical (itself a modern dichotomy).[8] A modern reconfiguration of the classic also required detaching the classic work from continuing traditions of interpretation, and those who derived authority from them (cf. Weidman 2006); the classic was constructed as belonging to a remote past recovered by new modern skills. Interpretation and commentary, in this perspective, were not a form of dialogue, and the framing and supplementation they provided were not seen as affecting the classic on which they worked. As Don Preziosi (1989) has argued for art history, multiple ways of engaging with objects from the past were replaced by a far more rigid division between creation, interpretation, and "appreciation." The classic was museumized (see also Preziosi 2003). New anthropologies of knowledge, reading, and the person were part of this process. As Preziosi emphasizes, this distancing of the past from the modern world led to museumization and the growth of academic interpretation industries positioned between the "classic" and the consumer, constructed as ignorant and passive.⁹ All too often, interpretation degenerates into providing "information" (easy to test and grade) rather than transmitting skills of critical reading, seeing, and inventive bricolage.¹⁰

> the museum: a place where you could walk through time by walking through space
>
> ❧ PREZIOSI 2003, 50

Education systems are important to anthropology because they derive from and reinforce conceptions of the person, of what it is to be a human being (and a citizen). Being human implies not only memory but elaborate and selective conceptions of time as well as space. Modern educators claimed to make their students more rational, but the gap between rationality and critical thought has been widening ever since the foundation of the Frankfurt school. Transdisciplinarity implies a critical view of the models of rational thought constructed by disciplines.

NOTES

1. Nick Dirks and I began negotiations for setting up the Anthrohistory Program in 1987. The term *interdepartmental* (which stresses administrative rather than intellectual concerns) was imposed by the university.
2. These stereotypes are still very popular among historians (Eley 2005 and Sewell 2005 present a more positive view of what "culture" contributed). Kalb and Tak (2005) distinguish "anthropological history," based on them, from "historical anthropology" as anthropological analysis with an extended time-frame. But their historical anthropology (with the exception of Rebel 2005) is not very reflexive about "history."
3. See, e.g., Randeria 2003; Kalb and Tak 2005; Çaglar 2006.
4. See, e.g., Maxwell 2007; Barnett and Maxwell 2008.
5. See Rebel 2005 on "figurations." The Michigan Anthrohistory Program mostly failed to recruit students to work on western Europe and North America. This was partly due to perceptions of the job market, but disciplinary stereotypes also played a role.

6. This goes beyond memory, myth, historical narrative, and nostalgia. See, for examples, M. Thompson 1979; Wolfe 1991, 1999.

7. Progressive if protoscientific, timeless if literary. Theology was allegedly absent; philosophy was read first as progressive, later as timeless.

8. See Humphreys 2002; Prakash 1999; also E. P. Thompson 1977 on the difficulties of the base/superstructure model in Marxism.

9. Ignorance, like knowledge, is culturally constructed. Barth 1975 still seems to be the only ethnographic study; see also Rancière 1987, and Steedman 1995 on the modern reconfiguration of childhood. We need an anthropology of ignorance.

10. De Certeau 1980. Cf. also his thought-provoking question (1982; 1986, 52), "Does one read a text as if it were lying on the couch?"

19 ❧ Dorothy L. Hodgson

The Politics of Naming: Ethical Dilemmas and Disciplinary Divides in Anthropology and History

According to Rena Lederman (2006c, 484), disciplines have become "moral orders," with their own ethical presuppositions, obligations, and concerns. Those of us who work at the intersection of anthropology and history therefore confront not just theoretical and methodological challenges, but an array of ethical ones as well: What constitutes "informed consent"? To whom are we most accountable, our research "subjects," our scholarly peers, our funding agencies? What does such "accountability" entail: A fair representation of the facts? Protection from risk and harm? A commitment to render visible the workings of power? How do (or should) our political commitments shape our ethical obligations? How do we justify our research agendas, research design, and choice of venue/language/form in which we share our results? Do we support an ethics of intervention, ethics of representation, ethics of participation, or ethics of dialogue with the people we study (Pels 1999; Cahill, Sultana, and Pain 2007)?

A key methodological difference between anthropology and history that has profound ethical, epistemological, political, and theoretical implications is the politics of naming. In anthropology, the normative methodological practice is to mask the identity of most people and places in order to "protect" them from the risks of political backlash, personal embarrassment, and other possible threats to their physical, emotional, and social security. These principles of "protection" and "risks" are enshrined in the most recent version of the discipline's Code of Ethics (AAA 1998), which emphasizes the "primary ethical obligations" of anthropologists to the "people with whom they work." These obligations, which compose what I refer to as "accountability," include "to avoid harm or wrong," "to respect [their] well-being," and "to consult actively with the affected individuals or group(s) with the goal of establishing a working relationship that can be beneficial to all parties involved." Ethical considerations are central to the training of anthropologists and the practice of anthropology; "anthropological researchers must expect to encounter ethical dilemmas at every stage of their work" (AAA 1998).[1]

Historians, in contrast, rely precisely on the practice of naming in order to conduct their research by tracing connections among people, stories, maps, and records. The "need to leave a clear trail for subsequent historians to follow" is defended in their Statement of Standards of Professional Conduct (AHA 2005). Although the issue of providing "confidentiality" to some sources is briefly noted, with direct reference to "conducting oral history interviews," the statement repeatedly emphasizes that "as much as possible . . . [historians] should also strive to serve the historical profession's preference for open access to, and public discussion of, the historical record" (AHA 2005). The "Evaluation Guidelines" of the U.S. Oral History Association similarly stress the goal of preserving and making oral history interviews available "for general use" in an accessible public archive or repository and note that only "under extreme circumstances" should interviewees "choose anonymity" (OHA 2000). For historians who work in written archives, significant responsibility for protecting people is displaced onto the archives themselves, who use such practices as "moving walls" of, say, twenty to thirty years to restrict the availability of time-sensitive documents or limit their access and use in compliance with the written requests of the patron.

Disciplinary distinctions are socially real and experienced, in part, as ethical affronts. Attention to the ethical ordering of disciplines may help trace out the complex interweaving of intellectual and moral justifications for our ways of meeting responsibilities to research subjects, and for our expectations about trust and truth-telling within specialist communities. Such attention may help also in the remaking and broadening of those communities.
LEDERMAN 2004, 8

The issue of whether or not to name research subjects entails a conflicting set of ethical and political entailments. On the one hand, as Caitríona Ní Laoire argues, the promise of anonymity or confidentiality can offer a "safe space" for people to open up, share intimate knowledge, and express critical perspectives, especially "when telling stories about the recent past, telling stories that have wider emotional resonance, and when narrators' experiences conflict with dominant narratives" (2007, 385).

On the other hand, anonymity can condemn participants to remain hidden (paraphrased from Ní Laoire 2007, 377), contribute to reproducing enduring stereotypes and assumptions about the homogeneity of certain groups of people (Bradley 2007), or defuse the potentially transformative potential of some research to challenge the status quo (Baez 2002). The decision about whether or not to name people, organizations, places, and dates is therefore not just a technical decision but engages questions of accountability, agency, power, and representation. In some cases, even when the identities of research subjects and their places were masked, the subjects felt betrayed and humiliated by the public portrayal of their private concerns (Scheper-Hughes 1979, 1982; Davis 1993). In other cases, community members have contested the anthropologist's decision to follow anthropological conventions of masking the identities of places, institutions, and people in their publications and reports (AAA 2007b, 2007c; cf. Brettell 1993). More problematically, the use of fictitious names often fuels the anthropological "sport" of revealing the "true" identities of people, places, and organizations (e.g., Hicks 1977).

These questions are even more pertinent, given recent efforts by Institutional Review Boards (IRBs, often called human subject review boards) to expand their mandate to include oral history, with related pressure for informed consent, anonymity, confidentiality, and the eventual destruction of data. While anthropologists have long had to submit their research projects for review and approval to such boards, historians who conduct oral histories are suddenly required to assess the risks of their methods for their research participants, develop informed consent procedures, and recognize that they may be forced to "block" the evidentiary trail for other scholars to follow by providing anonymity or confidentiality[2] to their research participants and even, ultimately, destroying their data after the project's completion. As Lederman (2006c, 485–86) notes, drawing on Shopes (2000):

> Oral historians have been horrified by these expectations when, in the wake of the recent bureaucratic "mission creep," they have come under IRB scrutiny. Primary research in oral history is all about creating a permanent, reconsultable archive of taped and transcribed words by named individuals whose stories are not yet part of the historical record.

The ensuing debates about the "chilling effect" of IRB regulation on oral history (Shopes 2000) and efforts to exempt oral history from IRB review since it does not seek to produce "generalizable knowledge" but only "unique perspective[s]" (Ritchie and Shopes 2003; cf. Shopes and Ritchie

2004) are clearly relevant to the collection of interviews, personal narratives, and other oral information by anthropologists.

Moreover, ethnographic research, with its distinctive reliance on participant-observation as a key method, has always posed problems for the regulatory apparatus and epistemological assumptions of IRBs. IRBs presume almost complete investigator control of the research design, process, and methods. The practice of participant-observation, however, "involves a disciplined relinquishment of control over sociotemporal contexts and conceptual frameworks of research by the researcher to his or her expert interlocutors" (Lederman 2006c, 485). The epistemological value of participant-observation is precisely its "systematic openness to contingency, particularly, its interest in exploring unexpected entailments of generated constraints" (488). In other words, "Human subjects regulations construe the researcher and the researched as having radically different kinds of agency. They are construed not simply as unequal but as incommensurable: always potentially opposed and most certainly in need of third-party mediation" (488).

In addition, accountability to IRBs entails more than just another level of bureaucratic oversight and paperwork, but a reframing, if not narrowing, of ethical questions to conform to the "actuarial perspective" of IRBs, which assess ethical practices through a risk-benefit analysis developed from biomedical research protocols and designed to satisfy university lawyers nervous about liability issues. It restructures the research relationship as a "dyadic" one between the researcher and researched, and ignores the larger power structures and inequalities that inform the research context (Pels 1999; Bradley 2007). As Philippe Bourgois (1990, 51) argues, "the ethic of informed consent as it is interpreted by human subject review boards at North American universities implicitly reinforces the political status quo. Understood in a real world context, the entire logic of anthropology's ethics is premised on a highly political assertion that unequal power relations are not particularly relevant to our research." IRBs also demand that scholars draw clear boundaries between "research" (for which IRB review and permission is required) and "daily life" (even if conversations, experiences, and events eventually produce and inform what becomes a "research project"), challenging the often blurry parameters of what constitutes ethnographic fieldwork, especially if the research is unfunded or occurs "at home" (see Lederman 2006a). The dramatic differences in self-perceived reach, application requirements, legal interpretations, and "improvisations" (Lederman 2006c, 489fn3) of IRBs at different institutions only further complicate matters (Lederman 2006b, 2006c; cf. Bradley 2007).

How, therefore, should those of us who work at the intersection of anthropology and history navigate the ethical, political, and epistemological issues raised by the disciplinary differences in this seemingly prosaic practice? Does it matter whether we are studying "up" versus "down," at home or abroad, or on topics considered of personal versus political sensitivity? What are the consequences of our "choices" for our research relationships, knowledge production, and scholarly trajectories? In this chapter, I explore my own struggles as an anthrohistorian and the experiences of others to navigate these distinct demands in our research, writing, and professional practice. To do so, I will briefly present three cases of naming dilemmas I have encountered, the principles I used to resolve them, and, where applicable, the consequences of my decision. These cases reflect not just different moments in my career, but broader changes in the theoretical, methodological, and therefore ethical concerns of anthrohistory. For this reason, the principles and priorities I have developed are not presented as universal answers but as contingent responses to specific contexts and concerns. Nonetheless, I hope the discussion moves us closer toward a transdisciplinary approach to the politics of naming.

Case 1: Links, Legacies, and Lapses

My first book, *Once Intrepid Warriors* (Hodgson 2001), explored the cultural politics of development among Maasai pastoralists in colonial and postcolonial Tanzania. Although the colonial history addressed all of "Maasailand" (a different kind of naming practice), I conducted intensive ethnographic research in three different Maasai communities to discern more recent changes, continuities, and challenges. Like many historians, I became a detective, scouring colonial and missionary archives, memoirs, and maps for the names of places and people in order to link the past and present. I countered the predictable absence of everyday Maasai in the written records by conducting extensive oral history and life history interviews, probing kinship and marriage relations, migration histories, education, and more. These interviews sought not just "truth" (in terms of Maasai renditions of historical events) but "meaning" (Maasai interpretations, perspectives, and narratives of their lives and experiences). Given the high rates of illiteracy, I primarily used oral consent procedures to describe my project, convey the promise of confidentiality, and explain their right to end the interview and refuse to answer questions at any time. Most of the interviews were taped and transcribed. In conducting the research, I confronted the complex realities of Maasai personal naming practices and multiple renditions of place-names, which were further confounded by the varied transcription and translation practices, misunderstandings, and shortcuts of colonial and postcolonial state officers, missionaries, and census takers.[3]

In writing the book, I confronted an epistemological and ethical dilemma common to most anthrohistorians studying the recent past: how to acknowledge my debt to the written and oral historical materials that provided me with the evidence I needed to make links and trace legacies without harming or embarrassing research participants. How could I negotiate the seemingly direct contradiction between the naming conventions of anthropology and history, and their underlying rationales? After much deliberation, I followed three naming principles: (1) I named places (including my three research communities) and dates; (2) I only named Maasai who were notable historical or public figures or insisted that they be named; (3) I masked the identity of all other Maasai, using pseudonyms and/or providing generic details about gender, age, residence, education, and employment where relevant. I believed that this combination of principles enabled me to "leave a clear trail" for other scholars to follow while protecting the identities of those participants who opted for confidentiality. Moreover, since the specific histories and locations of each community (including connections among them) were central to my analysis of the shifting dynamics of gender, generation, and class, masking place-names and dates would have deeply compromised my ability to present historical and contemporary data to support my conclusions. Finally, my approach met the expressed desire of community members for me to describe the complicated realities of their lives in order to challenge the enduring stereotypes that continued to shape state and donor interventions in their communities.[4] As one older Maasai man noted, "No one has ever asked us what *we* wanted for our lives."

Case 2: The Perils of "Naming Up"

In my second book, *The Church of Women* (Hodgson 2005), an ethnohistorical study, in part, of how gender had shaped the encounter between

Catholic missionaries and Maasai men and women, I faced a different set of issues. Since Catholic evangelization among Maasai only began systematically in the 1950s, relatively few Catholic missionaries had worked in my three research communities. I relied on their mission journals, newsletters, published articles, and books to complement my taped interviews, participant-observation, and conversations in order to develop a fuller portrait of their experiences and attitudes. The book focused especially on three American priests, each of whom worked in the communities in different eras, under different guidelines, employing different approaches, and was therefore easily identifiable. When they signed my informed consent form, all three agreed to be identified and to have the tapes and transcripts of our interviews deposited in their congregation's archives.

And so I named them in the book, trying, as always, to be as fair in my portraits and descriptions as I could while also being true to the interview transcripts and other research materials. The story of one priest in particular proved a challenge, as I had recorded some caustic statements and witnessed several angry outbursts during my participant-observation at church services. Ever mindful of context, I attributed some of his ambivalence, impatience, and irritation to the fact that he was tired, overworked, and at the end of his career.

Nonetheless, once the book was published and I sent him a copy, he (I will not name him again) vehemently objected to my portrayal of him. Rather than write me, however, he wrote long e-mails to the chair of my department and my editor attacking his portrayal in the book, listing some minor errors, challenging my interpretations and conclusions, and demanding that the press withdraw publication of the book (both my chair and editor supported me). When one of his confreres published a positive review of *The Church of Women* in the congregation's newsletter, he responded with a lengthy critique of the book, dripping in sarcasm and venom. After consulting with my editor and chair, I decided not to publish a rejoinder, so as not to further fuel his fury. Meanwhile, he began to track published reviews of the book, sending reviewers copies of his critiques and fiercely disputing any positive comments.

The point is that "naming up," like "studying up" (Nader 1969), can be perilous; the publication of critical conclusions or unflattering portraits of people or institutions of power can result in professional attacks, harassment campaigns, and even legal actions. In contrast to most Maasai participants, this well-educated, well-connected American priest knew how to use Google, e-mail, and his knowledge of academic hierarchies and the mechanics of the publishing industry to launch his critical offensive. Ironically (and fortunately), in this case the bureaucratic apparatus of IRBs protected me from further legal action; the priest had signed an informed consent form granting me permission to name him, and I had interview tapes and detailed field notes to substantiate my characterization of him and his work. Other colleagues, however, have faced the wrath of organizations they have studied or named in their research, enduring lengthy depositions, demands for their field notes, and expensive litigation as the organizations' lawyers have sought to challenge their allegations (see, e.g., Mosse 2006).

Case 3: In the Wake of "The Enemy"

My latest study explores the historical, cultural, social, and political dynamics of pastoralist organizations in Tanzania (Hodgson 1999, 2002a, 2002b, 2008, 2011). In this case, the political stakes of the naming dilemmas were markedly different; they involved potential backlash by the state and donors against progressive institutions instead of the personal embarrassment of priests. When I began this project in the mid-1990s, state officials were eager to discredit and even deregister these organizations. By the mid-2000s, relationships with the state were less confrontational, but most organizations were now deeply dependent on donor funding and therefore wary of challenging donor agendas. Moreover, when I arrived for a final year of research with these organizations in July 2005, I sensed a new wariness on the part of some leaders to discuss their work. Many of them were furious at another anthropologist who had interviewed them, studied their organizations, and then written several scathingly harsh critiques in which he named both organizations and activists. A program officer from a major donor agency read one of the articles, which was published in an internationally recognized journal for scholars and practitioners of development, then sent copies to the named organizations and individuals demanding a response to the scholar's allegations. I was shocked to hear even one of the calmest, most respected Maasai activists refer to this scholar as "the enemy" (*ol mangati*) in conversation. "We let him into our lives," he explained, "but then he betrayed our trust."

This activist's comments speak to the legacies of our ethical and political choices and those of others in shaping our access to certain research topics, sites, and participants. In the wake of their collective sense of betrayal by "the enemy," I strongly doubt that these activists would have allowed an unknown researcher to work with and study them. Fortunately, I was able to continue my research because of my longtime presence and long-term relationships in Tanzania. I had taught many of the pastoralist activists and leaders in the mid-1980s at the local Catholic secondary school, worked with others when I was coordinator of the local Catholic Church's development team, and circulated copies of my books and other publications over the years. Moreover, from the beginning I had positioned myself as an "interlocutor" with these activists, sharing my ideas, work, and preliminary conclusions with them in ongoing, constructive, and sometimes contentious discussions and debates in an effort to inform and shape their policies and practices, without directly aligning myself with one group or faction (Hodgson 2002a, 1045). Over the years, we had built a mutual respect and rapport.

Nonetheless, in the wake of "the enemy," I was even more acutely sensitive to the politics and perils of naming and critique (cf. Brosius 1999; Hodgson 1999). Moreover, I was very aware of the concerns of feminist scholars, among others, about the increased vulnerability of research participants with whom researchers developed long-term, friendly relations and shared personal, intimate information (e.g., Stacey 1988; Howell 2004). Navigating the path between leaving an evidentiary trail and protecting these activists and their organizations from risk seemed particularly treacherous in the context of their heightened political sensitivities, the potential consequences of my publications for the future of their organizations, and my long-term relationships with many of them.

I addressed these dilemmas by adopting a deeply conservative and protective stance. In general, although many participants gave me permission to name them, I limited naming of any kind, however seemingly innocuous, in order to minimize potential and unforeseeable risks to them. For this reason, I only named major pastoralist organizations and prominent activists who were easily identifiable and whose documents, publications, or activities I relied on to construct a history of the movement. In addition, I masked the identification of activists and organizations (including those named elsewhere) when citing interview excerpts or comments that critiqued the government, donor organizations, or specific individuals and organizations. Rather than repeat individual allegations of financial abuse or mismanagement, I bundled specific accusations to make broader claims (about, for example, the structural contradictions of "scaling up"). I believe that the practice of delinking names from critiques allowed me to present crucial evidence to support my arguments while protecting my sources from the risk of retribution and me from accusations of betrayal.

Bridging the Divide: Context, Consequences, Connections

So what do these three cases suggest about possible principles to use in navigating the ethical quandaries produced by these distinct disciplinary protocols of naming? Is it possible to bridge these divides to formulate a transdisciplinary approach to the politics of naming? As John Comaroff (1982, 144) noted years ago, "there ought to be no 'relationship' between history and anthropology, since there should be no division to begin with. A theory of society which is not also a theory of history, or vice versa, is hardly a theory at all." If, at its core, anthrohistory presumes and pursues an understanding of the world in which the social and historical are deeply intertwined and mutually constitutive, how do we overcome certain methodological obstacles to this theoretical, epistemological, and empirical vision?

First, we need to think beyond the "dyadic relationship" of researcher-researched to carefully evaluate the context of our research, by which I mean the relations of power that shape the topic itself, our relationship to the topic and people being studied, and the variable positioning of research subjects. Questions to consider include, Is the research topic on a particularly sensitive or even possibly illegal matter? Whose interests are being served by the principles of anonymity and confidentiality and IRB protocols of informed consent? Are there perhaps limits to informed consent, such as in settings of highly unequal power relations (Bourgois 1990, 51)? Who are we protecting and why? Given their range of topics and situations, anthropologists have developed and argued for an array of naming conventions. For example, in order to obtain information on international criminal networks, anthropologist Carolyn Nordstrom (2007) had to promise, like many journalists, to never reveal her sources. Conversely, Philippe Bourgois (1990) justified violating anthropological dictates to protect the privacy of his research subjects in order to publicize human rights violations in El Salvador to the media and human rights organizations. Finally, to protect the reputations of his research informants, Sjaak van der Geest (2003) not only used pseudonyms and fictitious place-names in his publications about abortion practices in a small town in Ghana, but he also published the materials under a pseudonym and tried to prevent circulation of the publications in the community.[5]

My own research has always explored the production, reproduction, and complex intersections of multiple social inequalities (including gender, ethnicity, class, and citizenship). But I have had to reflect on and revise my own naming principles as the topics have become increasingly current and politically sensitive. Naming people in the past potentially has different consequences than naming in the present, and the political stakes are different for American priests than for Maasai activists. In contrast to my first two books, my current project has a relatively shallow temporal depth (about twenty years), and many of the key actors and organizations are still active today. Fortunately, in addition to careful naming practices, the common multiple-year time lag between research and publication can provide another layer of protection to research participants by positioning their present as past and reducing the practical value of any sensitive data to donors and governments (cf. Bourgois 1990, 49).

Second, once we have traced the parameters of power that shape our research context, we need to identify, assess, and discuss the possible consequences of our naming decisions for our research "subjects," ourselves, and our scholarly peers and audiences. The potential "risks" to subjects of naming or otherwise identifying them can vary widely, from causing personal embarrassment (cf. Scheper-Hughes 1977, 1982; Davis 1993; van der Geest 2003), to undermining the political futures of organizations (Mosse 2006), to endangering people's lives and livelihoods (Bourgois 1990; Hill 1994). As is the case with most ethical dilemmas, we are usually forced to clarify our ethical priorities and privilege the needs of one group over others. The AAA Code of Ethics "does not address the fact that the contours of 'the field' for ethnographic research have changed dramatically over the past decade, so that 'the people we study' are rarely (if ever) a single group" (Hodgson 1999, 204). For this reason, "I would argue that an ethical and political stance that holds that we are equally accountable to all people masks the sometimes quite stark differences in economic, political, and cultural power that exist among these people" (213).

My decisions have clearly valued the political futures of organizations (Case 3) over the personal sensibilities of an individual (Case 2) and the risks to the most vulnerable people (usually nonelite Maasai women) in situations of exploitation and political struggle (Case 1; cf. Hodgson 1999). Moreover, throughout my years of research, I have followed the edicts of

IRBs and disciplinary codes for advance negotiation with research subjects about their wishes to be named (or not). At a minimum this has entailed using either written or oral informed-consent protocols in which I explained the possible risks and gave participants a choice. Yet in all three cases, I still preferred to use pseudonyms, even if someone wanted to be named, because of my wariness about possible unforeseen risks, hurt, and betrayal. In part this was because even though someone consented to be interviewed and knew I was continually engaged in participant-observation, they could not know what kinds of information or critical perspectives I would draw from the participant-observation to link with their interview data. Finally, in the case of Maasai activists (Case 3), in addition to opting for a very protective stance with regard to naming people and organizations, I have continually shared my preliminary findings, published and unpublished papers, and other material with them in a continued process of dialogue, debate, and transparency.

At the same time, I have tried to produce as careful and transparent a "scholarly apparatus" (AHA 2005) as possible, while doing "everything in [my] power to ensure that [my] research does not harm the safety, dignity, or privacy of the people with whom [I] work, conduct research, or perform other professional activities" (AAA 1998). I have always carefully assessed whether it is necessary to publish certain information to substantiate a claim or make an argument and, conversely, whether presenting that evidence would pose too many risks to research participants. In the course of over twenty years of research in Tanzania, I have learned many personal details about priests, pastoralists, and other people that I would never divulge because it would put them at risk of professional, legal, or even criminal action. The broader point, however, is that the politics of naming highlights a tension between the "scholarly apparatus" of history and that of anthropology in terms of their "presuppositions concerning sources" (Lederman 2006, 60). Historians, as evident from their codes and practices, rely strongly on the thick use of citations to primary sources to legitimate and substantiate their arguments and thereby establish their scholarly authority. Anthropologists, in contrast, establish their scholarly authority by "being there," and generally use their field notes as "private records or aides mémoires" rather than citing them directly as primary sources (Lederman 2004).

Of course we can never predict all the consequences of our choices. One unexpected outcome of my decision to name places and dates in my first book (Case 1) has been that it has also enabled activists to "follow the trail" and use my evidence in their claims against the government. And, having worked so hard to present "missionaries as human beings, as men with a range of talents and temperaments, of quirks and quibbles" in contrast to the "monsters caricatured by some scholarly works on missionary evangelization" (Hodgson 2005, xi), I certainly never would have predicted that at least one of them would become so enraged (Case 2).

Finally, the context in which research and writing are conducted has itself changed dramatically in the past few decades, as researchers and researched have become linked in an ever-tightening web of communication, connection, and contact. As Nordstrom quickly discovered, even when she used only her first name to protect her own identity, her sources could quickly use the "global info-net" to discover more than just her last name; "he can dip his cyber-fingers in at midnight and find out who I am, when I was born, and whether I am safe to talk to" (Nordstrom 2007). I began my research in Tanzania in the days of thin blue aerogrammes and unreliable postal services; now I communicate regularly with pastoralist activists and others through Skype, e-mail, and cellphone text messages. These cheap, easy connections can facilitate consultation over ethical dilemmas like naming but they can also compress the protective time lag between research and publication as draft conference papers and presentations are increasingly posted to the Web and accessible to anyone with an Internet connection, including, increasingly, the people we write about (Brettell 1993).

How we name ourselves matters as well. My PhD is in anthropology, I teach full-time in a department of anthropology, and my publications, research proposals, and promotions are predominantly (but not exclusively) evaluated by other anthropologists. Although I identify myself as an anthrohistorian and merge the theories and methods of anthropology and history in all that I do, my primary identification is as an anthropologist. Because of anthropology's vexed history as the "colonial science" in Africa, however, there have been times when it is far easier to identify myself as a historian.[6] For example, during a preliminary research trip to Dakar, Senegal, to explore the framework for a new comparative research project on forms of activism and organizing among women, it quickly became clear that I would have much more access and success if I described my project as a "history" of women's organizing in Senegal (which is true) than an "ethnography." History was perceived as safe, understandable, and harmless, while anthropology was intrusive, controversial, and suspect. Foregrounding my historian self over my anthropologist self necessarily shaped the kinds of questions and methods I employed and the kinds of ethical dilemmas I faced.[7] Similar self-naming dilemmas shape our decisions about which journals to publish in and how to adapt (and defend) our writing and naming practices to the journal's often disciplinary-bound conventions about citations, scholarly credibility, and the relationship of empirical data and theoretical arguments. Journals, like IRBs, funding agencies, and national research boards, serve as scholarly "gatekeepers" that can support or reject our submissions unless we conform to their ethical expectations.

In conclusion, the articulation of anthropology and history produces an array of ethical dilemmas such as the politics of naming. The code of ethics in anthropology foregrounds our obligations to the people we study, while the standards of professional conduct for historians emphasize our obligations to other scholars. The distinct concerns of anthropology and history presume and produce different kinds of relationships between the researcher and the people researched, other scholars, and regulatory regimes like IRBs. But ethical codes are always "historical facts, texts produced at certain times and places, indicators of specific historical practices and their corresponding mentalities" (Pels 1999, 113). As such, the contours and content of "ethics" and "ethical codes" are themselves subject to fierce debate, constant revision, and endless disagreement. Despite the differences between practices of naming in anthropology and history, I have suggested some common elements of a transdisciplinary approach for naming in anthrohistory: the need for informed consent (whether of individuals, institutions, or archives) as the basis for research, attention to the contexts of power shaping our research topics and relationships, considered reflection about the consequences of different naming practices for all involved in the research project, clarification of our priorities when ethical and political conflicts inevitably emerge, and the production of as transparent a "scholarly apparatus" as possible—not just for fellow scholars, but, where possible, for the people, institutions, and communities we study and work with. Every research project poses its own set of naming challenges, and the principles for their resolution depend on the context, consequences, and connections of our work. Those of us working across these disciplinary divides need to reflect carefully on these contexts and consequences, the desires of our research participants, and our obligations to our scholarly professions as we navigate the twisted political and ethical thickets of our transdisciplinary approaches.

NOTES

I am grateful to the participants in the 2007 Ann Arbor workshop for their comments, suggestions, and critiques, especially Josh Coene, Julie Skurski, David William Cohen, and Paul Eiss. Rick Schroeder also offered clarity in a moment of confusion.

1. Although the AAA is currently (2010) in the process of revising the 1998 Code, the proposed revisions do not change this definition of accountability. There is a huge literature in anthropology about ethical questions, the history of the development of ethical approaches and codes in the discipline, case studies of ethical dilemmas, and so forth. Important contributions include Hymes 1969, Berreman 1991, Pels 1999, Fluehr-Lobban 1991, 2003, Hodgson 1999, Meskel and Pels 2005, Lederman 2006b, and the debate about "objectivity versus militancy" between Andrade 1995 and Scheper-Hughes 1995. See also the online *Handbook on Ethical Issues in Anthropology* (AAA 2007a).

2. IRBs distinguish between assuring "anonymity" (where data is recorded so that there is no identifier whatsoever to link a subject's identity to his or her response) and "confidentiality" (where an identifying link does exist, but the researcher promises not to reveal the identity of the subject in any report of the study).

3. For example, men and women acquire a range of names over their lifetime, including nicknames, personal names for family use, clan names, and Christian names; names are recycled across generations; and most people are addressed by category names (*koko*, "grandmother") or gift exchange names (*pakine*, "giver of young sheep"). In terms of place-names, they included a shifting amalgam of Maasai territory names (rendered in a broad range of transcriptions), state political units, and distinct geographical features.

4. Before I began my research, I held meetings with each of the three communities to describe my research project, answer questions, and ask for permission. At every meeting, people inevitably asked, "What will we get out of your research?" During the discussion, they agreed that presenting a more accurate picture of the changing dynamics of their lives and their perspectives on change, development, the state, and so forth might better inform state and donor-initiated development projects.

5. The use of pseudonyms by anthropologists is rare, but prominent examples include Laura Bohannan writing as Elenore Bowen and Karla Poewe as Manda Cesaire.

6. The long history of "applied" involvement by anthropologists as colonial researchers, government policy consultants, development practitioners, representatives of indigenous peoples, military advisers, and now corporate researchers has provoked recurring debates (often cast in the language of moral superiority) about the relative merits (and politics and ethics) of anthropologists as academics, advocates, and/or activists. These debates have been heightened in recent years with the (re)emergence of "public anthropology" (D'Andrade 1995; Scheper-Hughes 1995; Pels 1999; Rylko-Bauer, Singer, and Willigen 2006). Histori-

ans, in contrast, have occupied a far narrower (and less controversial) range of "applied" positions in public history, museums, and government agencies.

7. The converse can be true as well. An anthrohistorian told me that in Chile it can be more controversial to position oneself as a "historian" than as an "anthropologist," because of the efforts by historians to recuperate the "truth" of the violence and repression that took place during the Pinochet years.

20 ❧ *Sonja Luehrmann*

On the Importance of Having a Method, or What Does Archival Work on Soviet Atheism Have to Do with Ethnography of Post-Soviet Religion?

During my dissertation research, I learned to appreciate the fact that archival documents cannot speak. Specifically, they cannot tell their reader that she is inappropriately dressed, that she should not also look at that other set of documents because it will mislead her, or that she is not qualified to read beyond a certain point. And they cannot ask who sent her and why she is there in the first place. Archivists, of course, can do all these things; but the ones I was dealing with in the state archives of the Republic of Marii El were reassuringly certain of the scholarly significance of my interest in 1960s Soviet atheist propaganda, requiring no other explanation than that I was writing a doctoral thesis on the topic.

In short, during my year of research in an autonomous republic in Russia's Volga region in 2005–6, the archives, where I spent between six and eight hours on most weekdays, were the place I came to relax. Outside lay the ethnographic part of my project: post-Soviet religious groups that were developing in a society partly shaped by the atheist work I was reading about in the archives. Hoping to avoid adopting the perspective of any one denomination, I was going back and forth between as many groups as I felt able to make meaningful contact with: congregations of the Russian Orthodox and four different Protestant churches, Sunni Muslims at the central mosque in the capital, and a loose network of traditionalist Mari "pagans" holding sacrificial ceremonies in villages across the republic.[1] The problem I encountered was twofold: from the point of view of the religious practitioners, visiting a place of worship to "observe" rather than participate was somewhere between strange and impossible, and visiting many different places raised grave concerns about the state of my soul and the story that I was likely to tell in the end. From the point of view of my own self-image as a researcher, I sometimes found it difficult to explain even to myself what I was doing at these different places, wandering between archival and ethnographic contexts where I often encountered vigorous criticisms of the same people with whom I had just shared a church tea or a sacrificial feast.

The rationale I repeated to myself was that I was interested in what remained of Soviet atheism within post-Soviet religion. I wanted to know if the decades of official atheism had transformed post-Soviet religious life, rather than merely representing shackles to be thrown off on the way back to how things were before. Some of the people I worked with expressed interest when I said I wanted to know about the efforts it took to rebuild religious life after the Soviet period. But their assumptions about what I was doing in their gatherings varied so much that I could hardly come up with a consistent way to explain myself to all: Protestants took me as their natural ally when I answered questions about my faith by saying that I was a Lutheran. Sometimes they assumed that when I was among them I was simply worshiping, not really doing research. Some Muslim women I met hoped that I was seeking to convert; the imam seemed to suspect that I was trying to create trouble for his congregation with the authorities in the context of Russia's "war on terror." An Orthodox priest told me that he thought "the Americans" had sent me because they wanted to find and destroy the basis of Russia's spiritual strength. Mari pagans were most used to having ethnographers around but wondered why I was not recording a specific genre of folklore or asking about a specific type of ceremony, as did most of the Russian and Finnish ethnographers they had encountered. A number of people I met in religious settings had been involved in atheist propaganda in capacities of teachers, college instructors, scholars, or party bureaucrats, and some talked about propaganda activities as sources of skills for religious work. But they still seemed to think that the relevant prehistory of their religious activities was Soviet-era repression of religious communities, not people's involvement in secular culture.

My guiding intuition was that there might be something very worthwhile in looking for connections between settings that participants considered irrelevant for one another. I found confirmation for this from the mute archival files. From them I learned that I was not alone in facing diverse groups of people and trying to come up with approaches that would be specific enough to work for each of them, and consistent enough to demonstrate the general relevance of some wider framework. The scholars and party lecturers charged with propagating scientific communism in the Soviet Union had confronted these problems under the particularly restrictive conditions of a system of doctrinary orthodoxy. In their training sessions and reports, they discussed them under the seemingly technical heading of "method." When scholars from regional centers learned to spread what was known as a "materialist worldview" among peasants and workers, or rural teachers struggled to absorb the latest findings of science, anxieties about how to work with people whose assumptions and backgrounds were widely different from one's own were often expressed as requests for guidance from superiors about method.

These archived anxieties helped me in two ways. First, certain persistent assumptions behind the concept of method—that people are similar enough to react to certain stimuli in a consistent way, and that instruction is a problem of persuasion that has universal solutions—provided some of the links between the archives and the field that I had been looking for. Second, I began to think about the forces propelling my own search for method—on what premises did I think I needed a guiding principle that would work across research contexts? Was there a way in which I could question the claims to incommensurability made by some of my interlocutors without relying on the homogenizing counterclaims of method?

Method-Talk in the Archives and in the Field

In Soviet and post-Soviet Russia, "method" constitutes such an important field of expertise that a profession is dedicated to it. The *metodist* ("methodician") is a person who might be employed by a culture palace, youth organization, library, or, during Soviet times, by a Communist Party division of agitation and propaganda, and whose expertise lies in operationalizing knowledge for behavior-changing transmission to mass audiences. Though akin to what might be called a director of programming or events manager at a cultural institution in the United States, the term *methodician* calls attention to a special reflexive expertise in developing, disseminating, applying, and evaluating ways of engaging people in educational and self-transformative behavior. "The task of the methodician is to link theory with practice," as one of my interviewees, a methodician at the Center for Folk Creativity of the republican Ministry of Culture, put it.[2]

In the vast Soviet Union, *theory* meant a constantly developing interpretation of Marxism-Leninism, and linking it with practice meant showing an audience what transformations of behavior were expected of them in particular local circumstances. Discussions of "method" in training seminars and conferences on atheist propaganda thus involved the question of how to make universal theoretical truths relevant and comprehensible in diverse contexts that were often unfamiliar to propagandists and lecturers. In the Russian usage, these debates were "methodical" (*metodicheskie*) rather than "methodological" (*metodologicheskie*); their desired outcomes were practical recipes for achieving ends whose desireability could not be questioned rather than the deeper reflection on the underlying philosophy of various approaches.

Requests for methodical guidance were a dominant theme at conferences of the Knowledge Society (*Obshchestvo "Znanie"*), founded in 1947 and known as Society for the Dissemination of Political and Scientific Knowledge until the name was shortened in 1963. The society was an organization of scholars and intellectuals engaged in popularizing political ideas as well as scientific findings (Powell 1975, 48–51). In the 1950s, the atheist section of the society disseminated stenographic transcripts of lectures by Moscow academicians to the regional divisions, as well as bringing together lecturers at unionwide seminars in Moscow. Such texts were helpful, a natural scientist from Chita in the Far East said at a seminar in 1956, but they did not answer such basic questions as how to explain to a person with a seven-year elementary school education or less "that protein, just through its chemical potentialities, could become the primary carrier of life."[3] He recounts the plight of a lecturer who attempts to deliver a lecture with a standard narrative of the progress of science, but runs into queries not anticipated in the script.

> These questions, after all, are in need of a particular methodical format [*nuzhdaiutsia v opredelennoi metodicheskoi razrabotke*] and it is here that the lecturer runs into particular problems. From Aristotle to our days the lecturer tells his story and everything works out fine, works out splendidly, here it is quite possible to bring in a certain atheist element, but the moment they start to ask you questions,—but what is protein, that is where the searching starts. Some consider it possible to say that protein consists of small particles formed by amino acids, but we have no serious methodical points of orientation.[4]

This statement shows that the concern with methodology arose in part out of the peculiar position of the popularizing lecturer toward doctrinary orthodoxy. The question about proteins came up because of the definition of life as "the form of the existence of protein bodies" that Soviet scientists borrowed from Friedrich Engels's *Anti-Dühring* as the proper materialist explanation (1962 [1878], 75). The lecturer does not challenge the definition but simply asks for guidance on how to make it make sense to a lay audience. The cautious question about a possible explanation of proteins ("Some consider it possible to say that . . .") and an earlier inquiry whether or not to use the works of a particular biologist[5] lie on the boundary between asking for information about the latest findings of science and testing the limits of the politically permissible. Both concerns could be bundled in a single question about method.

The way in which statements about method traveled from relatively more powerful centers to their peripheries shows how the formality of method helped give a sense of centrally defined direction to a variety of local undertakings. A representative from the Tatar ASSR at the 1956 seminar stated that methodical directions from Moscow were needed more than finished lecture texts, because members of the regional section had sufficient expertise to furnish the content of lectures themselves.[6] If administrative centers had the prerogative of pronouncements on the methods by which propaganda was to be conducted, this made it possible for them to control technical standards for orthodoxy while being able to rely on the knowledge and initiative of intellectuals in diverse peripheries.

What methodical directives looked like in practice demonstrates the work they did for inserting peripheral localities into a pan-Soviet framework. In 1962, the Mari division of the Knowledge Society printed 250 copies of a lecture by a historian from the republic's capital, entitled "The realization of the decisions of the March plenum of the Central Committee of the CPSU—the concern of the whole party, the whole people," for the use of lecturers in the rural districts. Interspersed in the text are bits of "methodical advice to the lecturer," all of which ask the lecturer to fill in specific local information in a pregiven format. Where the lecture text talks about the contribution of the Mari ASSR to the task of improving the provisioning of the USSR with agricultural products, the lecturer is advised to "provide data on the condition of agricultural production, the plans for 1962 and the coming years in the district, collective farm, or state farm in which the lecture will be read."[7] There are also recommendations to provide the names of local progressive workers or to give examples of the participation of the industrial enterprise or school where the lecture is delivered in agricultural campaigns.[8]

The way methodical directives were requested and delivered shows two important features of the concept of method with which the Knowledge Society operated: a method had to be appropriate to a particular audience, but should in principle be universally applicable. Universal applicability meant first of all that the method should produce the same results no matter who applied it, provided it was applied correctly. When correctly applied, a method should not only work independently of who was using it, it should also produce the same result in any audience of comparable social and educational background. The wide variety of such backgrounds within Soviet society meant that there also had to be a comparable variety of methods, but the underlying idea was still that human beings were so similar to one another that they would respond in the same way when given identical training and information.

I encountered this hope for systematic and predictable ways of influencing human behavior again in religious organizations, though in some more strongly than in others. Many of the most active members of religious groups were people who could be characterized as methodicians either by professional training or previous voluntary engagement. A Lutheran pastor had been a journalist for a factory newspaper; an instructor of Quranic reading had been in charge of organizing amateur concerts and plays for her trade union; and a Baptist Bible study leader had served as the political propagandist of her fellow child-care workers.

In at least three villages I visited, employees of the village culture club played crucial roles in organizing Mari sacrificial ceremonies. One club director used the language of Soviet cultural administration when talking about the revival of religious ceremonies in the sacred grove that had been used for secular mass festivals during Soviet times: "I asked the administration not to hold these mass events there, but, so to speak, to renew the work which was carried out [*provodilas'*] before, to clean the prayer grove." By using a verb that commonly refers to the agency of bureaucracies (*provodit'*—"carry out," "organize"), the director assimilated ceremonies to such forms of "cultural work" as mass festivals, classes offered in the club, or youth discos.

Tempted as I was to interpret enthusiasm for method as a sign of continuity between Soviet and post-Soviet times, such enthusiasm did not always have to draw on Soviet models. The clearest orientation toward method was among evangelical Protestants, who attended seminars on evangelization where they learned such things as the "three stages of fulfilling God's plan," or how to divide a society into "peoples" (*narody*), social groups that needed individualized approaches to evangelization. The first seminar was taught by a representative of the U.S.-based "Institute of Life Principles," the second by local members of a Charismatic-Pentecostal church inspired by the teachings of a Nigerian preacher who had founded a megachurch in Ukraine. Their inspiration clearly lay out-

FIG. 20.1. Architect's drawing of the cinema *MIR* (1961) in Ioshkar-Ola, USSR, built in 1961, in honor of the twenty-second party congress of the CPSU, which proclaimed communism to be within reach of the present generation. Drawing by Iu. M. Kazarinov, *Mariiskaia Pravda,* December 29, 1961, 4.

FIG. 20.2. Evangelizing concert of the Pentecostal church (2005) that owns the former cinema now. The fence was erected by church members out of security concerns but also assimilates the building to the aesthetic of other houses of worship in the city. By superimposing the fence on the original drawing, one might obtain a potential past of the *future unintentional.* 2005. Photo by Sonja Luehrmann.

side the Soviet Union, but in a similar faith in methodically reproducible personal transformations that underlies conservative Protestant social programs in North America and around the world (Erzen 2006; Sullivan 2009).

Skepticism against method, by contrast, was voiced most sharply by Orthodox clergy, although their background in Soviet cultural work was similar to that of many Protestants. For instance, when I asked an Orthodox parish priest—a former instructor of agricultural engineering—how he would explain to a person who worshiped in both Mari prayer groves and Christian churches that these were not the same thing, he said that there was no way to explain this. If someone did not see "in the heart" what stood behind the outwardly similar practices, that person could not be made to see it. Another rural priest, a former instructor of atheism at the Mari republic's College of Cultural-Enlightenment Work, answered my question whether this work experience helped him in a decisive negative, saying it only hindered his service for the church. When I asked what was most important for this service, he said that it was "to be without sin yourself." If he were without sin, he explained, his work in the parish would be easier, because "a saint can be felt from far away," and people would flock to him, not needing further persuasion.

These anti-methodical remarks bring into focus some of the assumptions underlying the idea of method in Soviet and Protestant contexts, some of which can give the anthrohistorical scholar pause in her own search for consistency. First, there is an optimism about the rapid transformability of people, based on the assumption that the key to successful learning lies in the correct process of transmission, initiated by the teacher according to acquired technique. Deep-seated characteristics, either of the teacher or of the student, are of secondary importance. This stands in opposition to the understanding voiced by the Orthodox priests, according to whom what matters is not the "how" of explaining or performing, but the "heart" of the recipient and the sinlessness of the instructor. The focus of method on "how" rather than "who" relies on a second assumption, one about essential human predictability and uniformity. Methods work across contexts because people respond to stimuli in similar ways. Specific local circumstances have to be taken into account but can be treated according to general schemata, as in the example from the lecture text that asked the lecturer to insert relevant information about the employees and production figures of the enterprise where the lecture was being held. Method thus implies assumptions about the relationship between the general and the particular that depend on a particular anthropology of essential and easily available sameness.

The Orthodox priests were also referring to generalizable disciplines, such as the life of prayer, penitence, and work that would make a person a saint. But their focus was on the slow transformations that occur within both teachers and students and make them receptive to insights that may eventually lead to salvation, rather than on techniques that anyone could employ with minimal preparation (Palmer, Sherrard, and Ware 1979–95). The priest who had been a teacher of atheism said that he regretted having received "the wrong foundation" in his education, but he obviously found it too late to make up for it after turning to Orthodox Christianity in his forties. By contrast, Protestant Christians who were former methodicians could talk at length about the way that their education had provided them with skills of public speaking and adapting content to particular audiences. Their idea of salvation as accomplished instantaneously through giving one's life over to Christ made their preconversion past morally neutral and available as a repository of skills and formative experiences (cf. Harding 1987). This moral neutrality of the past made it easier to answer a researcher's biographical questions than the Orthodox assumption that one's "foundation" mattered very much for who one was or could hope to be.

Learning (Bildung) is precisely that for which there are no proper customs; it can be acquired only through spontaneous exertion and interest, cannot be guaranteed through classes alone, be they even of the type of general studies. Yes, in truth it does not even follow exertion, but openness, the capacity to allow something intellectual to come close and to integrate it productively into one's own consciousness. . . . Were I not afraid of being misunderstood as indulging in sentimentality, then I would say that becoming learned requires love; the deficiency at issue is a lack of the capacity to love.

▰ THEODOR W. ADORNO 1971B (1962), 40; TRANSLATION BY SONJA LUEHRMANN

Looking for talk about method, then, provided me with a link between different contexts, but a link of ambiguous nature—pursuing it meant in a way adjusting to Soviet and Protestant models of the easy transformability of people and neutrality of the past, and made it harder to make meaningful conversation with interlocutors who insisted on incommensurability. However, rejecting method as just another modernist generalization that post-humanist social science should leave behind would have meant overlooking its social effects. Soviet administrative efforts had so transformed the country according to their universalist scheme that lecturers could easily plug in requisite local information into their precirculated text (cf. Scott 1998). And even Orthodox converts could only bemoan the effects of their Soviet training, not entirely escape them.

Method and the Practice of Anthrohistory

I have briefly surveyed the Soviet understanding of method, which seems to have affinities with Protestant evangelism not purely caused by biographical continuities, but by more far-flung common roots and parallel developments within the field of modernist projects of social transformation. For the purposes of this article, the point was to ask how the presuppositions underlying the methodician's search for transposable and relevant approaches helps illuminate the predicament of the researcher who seeks to include different periods and communities in her research. To be clear from the outset, one lesson I do not want to draw is one of radical particularity. Methodicians of different stripes and ideologies create and work in worlds that have something in common, and such commonalities should be within the purview of the researcher, especially perhaps when her interlocutors in the field are uncomfortable with drawing them.

The appeal of "method" in research as well as teaching lies in promising a consistency of approach that authorizes connections or contrasts between materials of different origin. The Doctoral Program in Anthropology and History has challenged students to draw such connections, both within their own research, which often spans periods accessible through different kinds of sources, and in discussions with other students whose work focuses on geographically and temporally remote topics. What makes such conversations possible, however, is more often the experience of juggling the demands and possibilities of a *variety* of methods, rather than any particular approach. When the juggling act becomes confusing, it is worth remembering the slightly comical aspect of the plea for guidance on how to correctly answer the question "what are proteins, anyway?" In such a plea, the search for method shows itself to be part of what Theodor Adorno (1971a, 75) calls "the immanent untruth of pedagogy": the fact that its task is the circulation, not production, of knowledge. The methodician, like pedagogues in a variety of other sociopolitical settings, is in no position to question the premises of scientific truth and so worries instead about how she can adapt them to particular recipients. A number of systems of pedagogy use methodical prescriptions to restrict students' and teachers' ability to question the premises of the knowledge being transmitted, be they party-sponsored education, the uniform weekly lessons studied in Seventh-Day Adventist congregations worldwide on any given Saturday (Miyazaki 2004, 88), or the ideally "teacher-proof" curricula of test preparation in contemporary U.S. schools (Collins 2003, 32).

In all these systems, standardized methods are intended to ensure the replicability of a curriculum among very different groups of teachers and students. As a researcher going back and forth between several such methodical contexts of learning, I valued the inconsistency this forced on my research as a form of freedom, and sought to respect my interlocutors' skepticism about the connections between my ethnographic and archival sites as a productive questioning of my own premises. I also recognized that my simultaneous reading of archival sources gave me a framework of comparison not shared by any of the people I was talking to in my ethnographic work. If there is any point to comparative social research, perhaps it lies in the opportunity to produce knowledge that is in some way different from what is already circulating in any of the social contexts being compared. Rather than expressing the researcher's conceit of finding the real truth through neutral comparison, responsible work across temporal or communal boundaries can help question the premises on which connections are made or denied by the researcher as well as by her interlocutors in the field.

These thoughts about the freedom of working with continually shifting premises are indebted to anthropology's sensitivity to its own peculiar relationship to a method—participant observation—which is often criticized (or praised) for not being methodically consistent at all, while helping to define anthropologists' relationships to the subjects of their research (Clifford 2005). But I am also drawing on a particular understanding of history: a view of history writing as not so much the reconstruction of a chain of causes and effects, origins, continuities, and ruptures, but as a way of tracing signs of things unfolding over time as they become visible from a particular perspective. In such a view, elements from the past do not necessarily appear as causal factors according to immutable laws but can be juxtaposed with present conditions to illuminate "their developmental, conceptual essence," to use Susan Buck-Morss's (1989, 73) interpretation of Walter Benjamin's passion for historical objects. This means that historical objects, as well as present interlocutors, can challenge a researcher's view of the present and of the pathways that connect it to the past.

For instance, one "method" I tried to apply with some consistency in order to make connections between archival and ethnographic materials was to ask religious activists with previous training or work experience in secular contexts if they found that this training was useful in their religious work, and in what ways. The answers I received varied from a Lutheran deacon's detailed enumeration of the skills of public speaking, writing, drawing of posters, and singing that he gained as a Komsomol worker and through which "God prepared me" for current work, to the brusque statement of the Orthodox priest quoted above, that the past was only a hindrance. I would probably have found these answers trivial if it was not for the echoes I heard in them of Soviet methodicians' pride in finding, compiling, presenting, and adapting information in such forms as wall displays, skits, and popular lectures. Interpreting affirmations and denials of the importance of such practical details by reference to the methodical concerns I was reading about in the archives, I began to understand the power and attraction of ideological engagement in terms of method's capacity to so preoccupy practitioners as to become an end in itself. This understanding grew out of the reflections of past and present practitioners, but few of them would be likely to agree with it wholeheartedly.

One of the points of combining a study of Soviet and post-Soviet "methodicians" might then be not to establish chains of historical causality but to place the two groups in a new relation of simultaneity in which each of them can contribute to understanding the other. One can recognize something of the pride with which a model club director in 1963 reported on her efforts to supply her collective farm with hand-painted propaganda posters in the enthusiasm with which a Baptist Bible study leader talks about the way she searches for Bible verses relating to a given topic, and learn to suspect past susceptibility to this pride and enthusiasm as the foil against which Orthodox priests now insist on the limits of lifelong transformability. Asking about the range of possible historical relationships behind such moments of similarity can be one way in which seemingly inconsistent cross-contextual research produces insight that goes beyond the remembering and forgetting through which members know their own community.

NOTES

1. Marii El, a republic of about 750,000 inhabitants, is located 500 miles east of Moscow, in the Volga region of European Russia. The Mari, who make up about 44 percent of the population, have had Russian Orthodox missions among them since they became subjects of Muscovy in the sixteenth century, but worship of Mari gods in sacred groves continued in many villages through the tsarist and Soviet periods. Approximately 6 percent of the population is Tatar, many of them Muslims. Russians and other Eastern Slavs, mostly from traditionally Orthodox families, make up almost half the population. Baptists and Pentecostals have been present in the republic since the 1940s, but current Protestant churches were either founded or significantly enlarged in the early 1990s with support from the United States and Finland, a country with which the Mari intelligentsia is forging ties through reference to the Finno-Ugric origin of the Mari language. For a more general discussion of religious life in the post-Soviet era, see Luehrmann 2005. My research in Marii El in 2003 and 2005–6 was funded by the German Academic Exchange Service, the Wenner-Gren Foundation, and the University of Michigan's International Institute and Center for Russian and East European Studies.

2. While I have found no explicit discussions of the profession of *metodist* in historical scholarship, historians have dated to the 1920s the emergence of a professional group of Soviet "festival experts," in charge of organizing both mass and small-scale events (Rolf 2006, 72). They have stressed the influence of various strands of prerevolutionary reformist cultural pedagogy, from Wagnerians (Clark 1995) to movements for workers' education (Plaggenborg 1996) and science popularizers (Andrews 2003).

3. State Archive of the Russian Federation, Moscow (henceforth GARF), f. A-561, op. 1, d. 65, l. 116 (Transcript of the All-Russian seminar meeting of the chairpersons of scientific-atheist and natural-scientific sections in the regional and ASSR divisions, January 10–11, 1956).

4. Ibid.

5. GARF, f. A-561, op. 1, d. 65, l. 82.

6. GARF, f. A-561, op. 1, d. 65, l. 168.

7. State Archive of the Republic of Marii El (henceforth GARME), f. R-737, op. 2, d. 115, l. 64 (Lecture text by A.M. Gluzman, Ioshkar-Ola 1962).

8. GARME, f. R-737, op. 2, d. 115, l. 65–66.

21 ❧ Setrag Manoukian

Wanderings beyond Codification and Desire

Wandering the zone of anthrohistory, in my long-term research on the production of knowledge in Iran, I often find myself at the crossroad between two seemingly discordant perspectives. Here they are.

States of Affairs

I feel the need to locate the book, image, or conversation I am working with. It seems relevant to describe the circumstances that accompanied and presupposed events in as much detail as possible.[1] Circumstantial information, even if it does not "explain" a book, an image, a conversation, seems anyhow to make sense of it, embedding it within a set of contingencies that highlight its particular configuration. The description and discussion of circumstances seem to appease and bring solace to the analysis. Events appear complex because they are connected to a web of circumstances out of which they emerge. To describe events as relational states of affairs, to draw connections between them and other such events, to weave genealogical lines of development: these are the tasks that will convey what these books, images, and conversations are, and why they seem relevant enough to study.

Take for example *Âsâr-i 'Ajam* (Fursat 1896), a late nineteenth-century book on the history and geography of the southern region of Iran called Fars and on its capital Shiraz. It is one of the first systematic descriptions of the remains of ancient Iran written by an Iranian scholar, related to the growing interest in the pre-Islamic past of the country that characterized the late nineteenth century. This interest amounted to a reconfiguration of ideas about the past, in parallel with European orientalist projections (Tavakoli-Targhi 2001). *Âsâr-i 'Ajam* presented the ancient past of Iran as a foreign territory that could and should be appropriated through a "scientific" approach: measures, drawings in perspective, detailed descriptions, and philological readings of the inscriptions. The book, sponsored by the governor of the region and indirectly by the shah, also marked a particular moment in the configuration of intellectual work in Iran: still connected to the court system of patronage that for centuries had been central to the production of knowledge, it also signaled shifts in the system that would soon result in the edification of a state administration of knowledge, with the nation as its central concern. While Fursat, the author of the book, wrote for the court and for science, his relocation of the remains of the past connected them with the political and social concerns of the day and made them and their study part of the construction of a new subject of knowledge: the reasoning/reasonable individual who learns and acquires information and is thus able to discern what is best for himself (not herself) and for the nation. In Fursat's work this trajectory results from the assemblage without disjuncture of both his encounters with European individuals and books as well as his encounters with mystical mentors and practices: he therefore defies the assumed fissure between Europe and Islam that historians often posit as a given. At the same time, a specific colonial trajectory is also at work in the circumstances of Fursat's life and work: the British were a significant presence in Shiraz at the time, and one of Fursat's patrons was their closest ally. In turn, technological transformations that were taking place at the time make this state of affairs even more layered and complex. And I could go on, adding more information, describing more circumstances, establishing more relations between trajectories to give a composite account.

Take for example the 1903 photograph that portrays Fursat with other poets from Shiraz (Imdad 1993, 235).[2] One can detail the biographies of the people in the photograph, their poems, and their books and reconstruct in several ways the peculiar community they constituted, at the junction between the different transformations that were happening in those years. For centuries, gatherings of poets had been a common practice in the city, connected to the system of patronage as well as to different forms of male sociality. In the beginning of the twentieth century, however, they acquired a more political bent and often included wide-ranging conversations on questions of the day as well as a different positioning in relation to the poets and writers of the past. So the construction of the reasoning/reasonable individual I mentioned above can be read in parallel with the emergence of a class of professionals, which involved a mode of production but also a certain lifestyle and posture, an aestheticized relation to the social world. This is what a description of the photograph might suggest, if one were to note the poets' different posturing in front of the camera but also reflect on their inscribed names on the picture and discuss both features as instances

FIG. 21.1. Fursat with other poets in Shiraz, Iran, 1903

of a process of identification, in turn linked to photography as a specific medium. And one could go on relating this photograph to previous or immediately subsequent ones, shot in Shiraz and elsewhere in Iran, or compare it with the Parisian photos of Verlaine and Rimbaud to add a more explicit comparative layer to the analysis.

Or take a conversation I had in 2003 in Shiraz with Mansur Ouji, a noted contemporary Shirazi poet born in 1940, in which he proceeded quite systematically to connect the different poems he had written to the political and social events of the country as well as to his life. Ouji belongs to a generation of modernists who abandoned quantitative prosody in favor of free verse, in a move that signaled a break from the past that was parallel to the discourse on "modernization" heralded by the Iranian state in the 1960s—even if the "modernity" these poets were evoking was at odds with the propaganda of the shah at the time. Through these programmatic aesthetic choices, as others of his generation, Ouji drew a line of demarcation between himself and the past, though retaining many of the tropes of classical poets. His short verses deploy poetic metaphors only to reverse their habitual meanings, or present a view of Shiraz that condenses well-established images of the city (gardens, roses, poetry itself) and attunes them to a twentieth-century sensibility. Ouji's poetry is an analytical vocabulary for emotions that distills history, politics, and culture into hermetic expressions that owe as much to European poetics (and its orientalist trajectories) as to the "gardens" of Shiraz: the poetry constructs the figure of the poet as an affective subject. All this emerged in our conversation that was marked by the declamatory style of the poet, who proceeded to define his position on the city, the nation, and beyond. "I do not frequent poetic gatherings," he insisted, and went on to comment negatively on the low quality of the poems of those who did, and the idleness of the social occasions they represent. This does not mean that Ouji is modest; on the contrary, he is a careful producer of his public image, as the conversation with me only confirmed, and his poised portraits attest.

Out of these different states of affairs, one can discuss the transformations in the imagination of the past in Iran, the ways in which, after a hundred years, the reasonable/reasoning individual has become a stylized "intellectual" who speaks to society its truth, while guarding a snobbish distance from it. One can also advance hypotheses on the social formations of knowledge in the country, discussing the relation between politics, poetry, and self-fashioning.

These books, images, and conversations have also to be connected with the circumstances that led me to encounter them, adding crucial layers to the analysis. Fursat, as other "local" Shirazi intellectuals, is the object of an intense revival in contemporary Shiraz. These recent cultural activities are aimed at constructing Shiraz as the cultural capital of Iran, a place that embodies both its pre-Islamic past as well as its poetic heritage, with all the political modulations and conflicts that such operations entail, in order to make characters and events fit either the state rhetoric of the day or alternative visions for the nation, both among Iranians in the country and abroad.

The books, photographs, and conversations I discuss and the descriptions I give of them are also connected to the particular kinds of ideas about anthropological and historical research that have been going on in the past fifteen years or so and more particularly to those that were circulating in the Doctoral Program in Anthropology and History when I was there in the 1990s. The relevance of the national imagination for the production of knowledge, the encroachments of colonialism and modernity, as well as the idea that one could carry on anthropology of written texts, that one could think in parallel about the past and the present, that poetry and photographs could be accepted material for anthropological reflection were all part of the conversation.

The trajectories that led me to Shiraz and my particular encounters and sensations should be added to these circumstances, as well as my preconceptions, my idiosyncrasies, and, most of all, the relations of power through which myself and my research were constituted: all crucial components of these states of affairs, as reflections on ethnography have underlined.

All these circumstances together have been opening up possibilities as much as they have been setting limits for my research and my thinking. I called this perspective *states of affairs* to use a fairly neutral term and underline how it is based on establishing relations and layers that locate particular fragments of ethnography and weave them into an analytical territory. It is a perspective that could be described with different keywords that refer to different or opposite approaches and "methods," some of which have recognized authors, while others are more implicitly elaborated in the practice of research: thick description (Geertz 1973), evidential paradigm (Ginzburg 1989, 1990), contextual reading, conjunctural analysis, genealogy (Nietzsche, but really Foucault), nomadology (Deleuze and Guattari 1987).[3] These mutually exclusive approaches, especially when used to think about ethnography, rather than discussed from a purely theoretical point of view, all share at some level the idea that social research works better when it devotes itself to the description and correlation of events and describes them as the product of these relations. The insistence on states of affairs goes hand in hand with a constructivist position that gives prominence to the productive activities of humans and things and conceives social reality as the com-participatory work of researchers and others.

What better way could there be than one of these states-of-affairs frameworks to give the fullest possible account of contingencies, in order to encompass the richness of their interrelations without succumbing to a monocausal view? And is this not what seems to be the path to follow among many practitioners of anthrohistory? This, many of us think, is a way of getting around the supposed totalizing hubris of social theory. It seems to offer the richly detailed kind of accounts one longs for and to respond to the ominous call to describe the "construction of" whatever one is researching.

Blocs of Sensations

At times, however, immersing myself in the notes and memories of a conversation, staring at a photograph, reading a book, or listening to a recording pushes me to attend to the sensations that these things seem to emanate or retain. This approach brings to the foreground colors, shapes, noises, and all the other elements that compose whatever one is engaging. These are elements that do not amount to any circumstantial relation and yet constitute crucial components of whatever we are engaged with, impossible to be accounted for through a discussion of states of affairs. From this point of view, books, photographs, and conversations appear as blocs of sensations, compounds of expressive elements. Blocs of sensations is a term I take from Deleuze and Guattari's (1994) discussion about art. They use the expression to define what they see as the specificity of art, as something that "preserves" smiles, colors, and movements and does so by being a compound of percepts and affects. Deleuze and Guattari describe the latter as perceptions and feelings after they have passed and are therefore beyond those who undergo them: they are beings that exceed any lived experience of them. They stand for themselves (1994, 164). This perspective can be appropriated to bear on other things and events in order to assess the specific forces they unleash, beyond the circumstances of their production. At stake here are the particular expressive possibilities and limits of the material we think through, and the effects of thoughts and affects they project.

This posture is easily shunned in social research as it might fall into one form or another of essentialism, while at the same time failing to bring forth what are considered to be the properly "social" imports of the material. Recognizing these limitations it seems to me that this approach provides an invaluable entry point into the forces that make up these events, letting them pierce through and affect whoever gets in touch with them. It is also an approach that suggests an altogether different temporality from "states of affairs": not relational positions and their power effects through time, but the unfolding of a more abstract and less measurable flow made of virtualities. From this perspective, books, photographs, and conversations are less the product of circumstances than particular monads, intensive, autonomous, and differing assemblages that aggregate and disaggregate to compose the world as we come to know it (Tarde 1999).

Take *Âsâr-i 'Ajam*. No genealogical or conjunctural analysis would account for the particular assemblage the book is. Yes, the book can be described as a historical and geographical account of the region of Fars, but it is a fragmented and multiple composite of different materials, images and words, that project a peculiar exploratory intensity, a statement that supersedes whatever genealogical location one might assign to it. Images and words weave into each other, while the narrative constantly moves from prose to poetry, discusses in the same pages Achaemenid remains and encounters on the road, dives into philosophical controversies while remembering friends and reproaching foes. The book deterritorializes whatever territory of ancient remains is meant to delineate, and it presents knowledge as an endless and constantly derailing trajectory rather than an explanation that moves from ignorance to awareness.

Or take the photograph of the poets: the piercing eyes, the smiles, the inspired looks, but also the interplay between the designs on the carpet and those on the wooden windows in the background, all in turn interlaced with the calligraphy on the photograph. They compose a decorative stage for the scene, which counterpoints the uniform coloring of the men's clothing and makes them stand out. At the same time the contrast of lighter and darker robes and head covers establishes a particular quality of the light that works by diffusion more than by juxtaposition. The lines that traverse the image also contribute to its effect: the horizontal lines of the carpet and the pool, of the first row of poets and of the lower edge of the windows; the vertical lines that from the windows descend through some of the poets; the sinuous line of the second row of poets; the converging and diverging lines of the sticks but also the sinuous line of the eyes of the poets, the line of their mouths and their beards and mustaches. The two flower vases, their shape and color reversing the cone-shaped hats of some of the poets, channel the centripetal viewpoint toward the poet Asuda's head but are off-center enough to unbalance the whole composition and impress some movement on it. All these elements contribute to compose a particular bloc of sensations, of percepts and affects. They do not "represent" or "illustrate" anything but establish a particular set of forces that make the photograph stand on its own, that "preserve" its affects, regardless of its circumstances.

Or take my conversation with the poet, his directed but abstracted look, my body on a sofa opposite to "his" armchair, the particular light of a Shirazi sunny afternoon refracted through the windows and merging with the color of the tea, immobile in the cups on the low table in front of us. The sound of his voice, a syncopated rhythm without sustain or hesitation, filling the room with its books, magazines, and 1960s modernist furniture, and at times interrupted by his bursts of laughter when retelling

Into what labyrinth, what multiplicity of heterogeneous places, one must enter in order to track down the cryptic motivation
. . .
☙ JACQUES DERRIDA 1986 (1976), xlvii

stories, mentioning people, and replying to my comments. My white notebook, his volumes and newspaper clips spread around us. These and other elements constitute the bloc of sensations of that particular event and make up the force that makes it relevant in my research. This relevance is made up of percepts and affects that do not denote so much a situation as point to a specific flow, a becoming, a series of expressive elements that framed the event and gave it its power, making it stand for itself, beyond my concerns with the poet's modernist style or his self-assertiveness, pushing me to return to it time and again to experiment with its virtual field of possibilities.

When I am confronted with such forces in conversations, books, photographs, or whatever else I encounter, there seems to me to be the need for a different kind of description, one that cannot be resolved with an invocation of the state of affairs but has to come to terms with these affective trajectories beyond the particular configurations in which they can be inserted. This I feel is a more shaky and adventurous terrain, one where established conventions in the disciplines I practice are not easily found and a more dubious and challenging endeavor is required. It is possible to impute these forces to an "it," a kernel that is phenomenological for some (see Boyer 2005 for a recent discussion), "material" for others, empty but almighty for those of a Lacanian persuasion, or ontological/ontic, as the recent success of these terms indicate. The "it" would function as a matrix, a productive machine of thoughts and affects, or as a ground, resistant to discussion but nevertheless there. Discussions around technology have also opened up many ways to think about blocs of sensations and make them socially relevant (see Kittler 1999).

However, all these perspectives go fast and reduce the virtuality of the blocs either to some circumstance or the other or to some founding principle that explains all. What I envisage is instead the possibility, and Deleuze and Guattari seem to me to be more fit than others in this regard, to pursue an approach that does not give up a description of the blocs and their effective forces and unsettles the direction in which circumstances seem otherwise to take the analysis: while Fursat's *Âsâr-i 'Ajam* is being heralded today as an early example of the emotional and political investment in the ancient empire of Iran that characterized the twentieth century and continues to this day, and while scholars who have paid attention to the book have seen it as a token of the birth of the Iranian nation and the modern Iranian individual, the book itself, as I briefly mentioned, pushes back these layers by destabilizing its own supposed cartography. And as a counterpoint to the hypothesis about self-fashioning and subject formation—rather than suggest the constitution of liberal selves through the medium of poetry, the photograph of the poets and my conversation with Ouji bring forth particular forces that deterritorialize the dominant discourses in and about Shiraz: the irony, the aestheticized posturing, the conversational lifestyle itself, can be discussed as comments and alternatives to the duties and forms of a certain politics of knowledge.

Wanderings

I have been at the crossroad. I have sketched what appear as two discordant approaches: I deliberately chose awkward terms to describe them and emphasized the difference between them in order to put their characteristics in stark relief.

However, it will not do to stand in front of them for too long. It will either result in their merging or in their fixation as polar opposites. On the one hand, one can recognize that, after all, the two approaches describe complementary endeavors: my descriptions in one of the sections above could be connected to those in the other, and the theoretical trajectories I mention could be modulated together. Moreover, one can argue, and this is indeed the case, that it is a particular set of circumstances related to current developments in anthrohistory, as well as to my own research, that pushed me to write about blocs of sensations, that made me react to what appears as a generalized contentment in relating an event to its circumstances, as if that would appease all analytical doubts. On the other hand, the difference between the two approaches could be worked up into a permanent tension, a sort of productive double bind that would strike an impossible balance while exposing the limitation of both approaches. An exercise in negative dialectics, something that those like me who inhabit the zone of anthrohistory often find congenial.

And yet I think it is time to leave the crossroad behind and venture into the unknown, toward a direction that is not so easily predictable, because it would require more ethnographic and analytical labor than this essay allows and because it would have to be discussed each time anew depending on affects and circumstances. Let me, however, wonder what some of its trajectories could be.

It would be a path of wandering and self-experimentation—the painful and patient construction of a direction out of the scattered materials at hand while being in the midst of them, swimming at sea without the leisure to step outside and look from the shore at what one is doing (Blumenberg 1997). It would be a path in which skill and expertise are made and remade depending on the matter of concern at hand rather than being an abstract set of rules by which one has to abide. An approach that I somehow find consonant with my experience in the Anthrohistory Program, where we did not practice the naive celebration of a supposed "interdisciplinary freedom," nor, as was otherwise fashionable then, pursue misconstrued reflections on one's own "identity" but were pushed toward a sustained effort to turn our states of affairs into affective potentialities to engage the world around us.

This new direction would underline how circumstances and affects could not be simply equated without attending to their specificities, nor could they be mutually exclusive. It would be a direction that does not posit an ultimate distinction between an outside and an inside, no partition between affairs and sensations, between codification and desire. Instead a new vocabulary would have to be devised that describes codification and desire as animated by the same effort, resulting in expressive formations whose intensities are themselves productive circumstances. In this task help might come from science studies and art history (see respectively Latour 2005; Didi-Huberman 2003), fields that seem particularly concerned with these intersections. As self-experimentation, however, this direction would be mostly concerned with process, with *how* to construct an account, and the works of Sebald or Perec, to quote two writers present elsewhere in this collection, might help in coming to terms with codification and desire, with photographs and living rooms. In particular one could experiment along with Perec in a modality of description that in pursuing absolute externality and neutrality (his endless lists of circumstances) achieves a powerful intensity that avoids all representation or illustration to convey the sheer force of affective states of people and things.

In my research this approach would entail foregrounding singular percepts and affects in Shirazi conversations, photographs, and books, reflecting on their expressive power without reducing them to the product of circumstances or abstracting them into some kind of solipsistic musing. I would like to use them instead to produce accounts of Iran that go beyond the dyad of nation and religion, to highlight how the production of the modern Iranian reasonable subject is linked to the ways in which certain potentialities turn into peculiar expressive forms, books, photographs, and conversations full of virtual potentials. This path of research would interrogate recent anthropological work on Islam that repositions cultural difference as disciplinary training, insisting on sensory and emotional cultivation.[4] In the preceding pages I deliberately hinted at processes of subject formation that have characterized social life in Iran in the last one hundred years and questioned their immediate and presumed directionality. It is one thing to chastise approaches that attribute events to what appear just haphazard circumstances and fail to recognize the normative constraints of moral systems, but it is something different to impute to these moral systems the production of social life and its particular blocs of sensations. A view of Iran that does not take this into account would inevitably reproduce the many already circulating stabilized views on the country and its people.

destroy all monsters began as an anti-rock band. our menagerie of words, images and sounds were an attempt to thumb our noses at the pretentious circus of rock-star bullshit and musical emptiness that filled the air-waves during the early to mid-1970s. the images that moved us then were a strange combination of film-noir, monster movies, psychedelia, thrift-shop values and the relentless drone of a crazed popular culture. our influences were a combination of audiovisual stimuli . . . our music sometimes contained a narrative or storytelling direction that was never well explored. a sense of gloom, disaster and apocalypse mixed with doses of anarchy, comedy and absurdity kept us together and were some of the major themes which colored our small scene.
❧ LOREN 1996

The direction I am envisaging would unsettle some of the epistemological ground at the intersection of anthropology and history; it would trouble what seems to have become its constitutive distinctions, such as those between field and archive, between present and past, between oral and written. The wandering path would break away from the implicit division between history-as-information and anthropology-as-theory/method that sometimes lurks behind the scenes. It would impose a rethinking of temporality to include its virtual aspects and come to terms with the fear that writing ethnographies in the present is necessarily a negation of time, while opening up to the idea that certain pasts are indeed presently becoming. It would also reconfigure the vague constructivist approach many current trends share but do not problematize. "States of affairs" approaches, for all their constructivist declarations, need an underlying "necessity" in order to stand on their feet: Giambattista Vico argued that what was true was what was made by humans in the course of history, but he could claim this position because he had a teleological idea of time grounded in the divine order of the universe.

How would all this sound? Maybe Destroy all Monsters, a 1970s antirock band from Ann Arbor, could be an apt, local example for the kind of sonorities I would like to evoke in my production.[5] The band was composed of nonmusicians who played an interchanging set of instruments and home made devices to produce a critical mass of sound that was supposed to both contrast and accompany the kinds of music that were going around then. The idea would be to destroy all the critical monsters, but not in some kind of nihilist posture, more rather like a Midwestern bricolage that would liberate unexpected forces and would unsettle received views on books and conversations. Or, to get to more recent vibrations, something akin to the current "noise" sonorities that in the last few years have made of Ann Arbor/Ypsilanti the center of a global network, masses of indistinct static out of which all of a sudden melodies emerge as intensities and experimentations.

Both Destroy all Monsters and the noise groups have undergone processes of commodification (albeit "alternative" ones) that are turning their expressive forces and the circumstances that accompanied them into market devices. Anthrohistory slogans have been marketed with more or less commercial success. But that is not the point. The point is rather to think about the kinds of desire and codifications anthropology and history have produced in the past and in the present, and whether they are best left free to wonder, and therefore nameless.

NOTES

1. There are many ways of naming these relations; here I choose to name them *circumstances* both because it is a word that is not associated with any particular current theory and because I'd like to insist on the reference to "that which stands around or surrounds: the totality of surrounding things; surroundings, environment" as the *Oxford English Dictionary* definition of *circumstance* suggests.

2. Fursat is the fourth poet from the left, in the upper row.

3. I deliberately mention widely separate frameworks not because I see them as compatible but because they have often been part of the same reading lists (of course there would be many more). Needless to say a longer discussion would call for an emphasis on their differences. Despite his staunch assertions to the contrary, in my view even Ginzburg practices a form of constructivism.

4. I am referring here to the analytical edifice that Talal Asad has been carefully and admirably constructing in the past twenty years and that is coming now

to fruition in his work and that of other anthropologists of Islam (Mahmood 2005; Hirschkind 2006). My argument is not with their work per se, but with the effects that their work projects in current anthropological discussions of Islam where many seem yet again to put aside circumstances toward an assessment of what is distinctive about Islam.

    5. http://www.furious.com/PERFECT/dam.html: as it fits their image, I have yet to hear a single note by the group. I became aware of this and other musical trajectories long after I left Ann Arbor. I think that life in the Anthropology and History Program, as it is often the case in the university, was particularly oblivious to the circumstances that surrounded it, but I do not mention this music (to which one should add at least the Once Festival 1961–66) to moralize on ivory towers and the seclusion of knowledge but rather to make the point that these are by all means "states of affairs" connected to the program, even if they have no direct relation to it (at least as far as I am aware).

Openings

22 ॐ *Fernando Coronil*

Pieces for Anthrohistory: A Puzzle to Be Assembled Together

—IN HOMAGE TO MARX'S AND BENJAMIN'S THESES ELEVEN

> There are many people adept in those diverse disciplines, but few capable of imagination—fewer still capable of subordinating imagination to a rigorous and systematic plan. The plan is so vast that the contribution of each writer is infinitesimal.
> —JORGE LUIS BORGES, "TLÖN, UQBAR, ORBIS TERTIOUS"

1 ॐ

The chief defect of all hitherto existing academic disciplines is that they conceptualize discipline as their mode of being, seldom as an object for being. Taking into account perspectives from borders and margins, since the 1980s several scholarly fields have developed critical evaluations of the history, premises, and politics of Western knowledge—its teleological narratives, disciplinary classifications, and complicity with eurocentrism, racism, sexism, elitism, and other modalities of dominative knowledge. As the offspring of these fields, anthrohistory shares with them genealogies, concerns, and products. As an academic project devoted to producing knowledge betwixt and between disciplines, anthrohistory seeks to educate scholars in anthropology and history by transgressing their limits and tending to their impact. Insofar as it is capable of subordinating imagination to a rigorous and systematic plan, it becomes a questioning discipline that undisciplines the disciplines and educates the educator. Through this critical practice, discipline is subordinated to its object.[1]

2 ॐ

Growing out of disciplines implicated in Western understandings of the world and dominion over it, anthrohistory, like kindred critical ventures, occupies an open-ended space oriented toward making sense of the world and of sense making. In its openness to possibilities, it interprets being, what was and what is, as forms of becoming. Through its recognition that what can be inhabits what is, it pursues knowledge for a world that can become home to multiple worlds.[2]

3

Of this world but not at home in it, anthrohistory resists being disciplined in existing institutions or contained by definitions. As long as this planet is not home for all, this project must roam as an exile, witnessing what has been made of it and reflecting on the work to make it habitable. For to the extent that winning entails domination, no one—not even plants—can be safe from the enemy, for who would inherit the earth's energy and care for our collective legacy? Brushing history against the brain, its task is to examine what has been recorded and uncover what has been silenced, bringing to light possible histories.[3]

4

As an ensemble of practices for examining human practices through ever-changing prisms, anthrohistory acquires form as a never-ending puzzle whose pieces are crafted and pieced together by these practices. Assembled as a labyrinth whose exits become entrances into an expanding labyrinth, its arrivals are points of departure and its answers pose new questions.[4]

5

"If a place on the map is also a place in history," any representation simultaneously encloses time and space. There is no space outside time nor time without space; together they form the medium through which our world is constituted and brought into awareness. At a specific scale, a map represents a place in space at a moment in time, whether a grain of sand or a whole country. Just as in an account of the cosmos "the paltry fifty millennia of homo sapiens" could be a single point, in a chronicle of the battle of Borodino Napoleon's head cold and the action of a "most humble soldier" could mark two significant moments. Macrohistory and microhistory are two scales of the same history. Anthrohistory seeks to produce representations of the world as fragments of an unfolding totality, itself a fragment of other totalities. Any totality is partial.[5]

6 ❧

Points on maps make a point. Like lines in a play, they become meaningful by being joined to each other by the authors and publics who join them. These lines form not just texts about the world, but the texture of the world. They represent an external reality from within it. Their truth is measured by their exactitude as models of the world they image, but it is realized by the world they help create. The point of a map defines its points. Our journey is guided by a compass; our destination defines our destiny.[6]

7 ❧

Imagine a discussion about truth in a Jorge Luis Borges story written by Italo Calvino and illustrated by M. C. Escher. In a magnificent square called "Paris 1945–2000," Jean-Paul Sartre, Claude Lévi-Strauss, and Jacques Derrida argue in French about how best to explain human history through forms of reasoning associated with "dialectical materialism," "structuralism," and "poststructuralism." Through a crack in its foundation, a path suddenly opens into a larger square called "Europe," where Kant, Hegel, and Marx animatedly discuss the nature of universal history in German while Heidegger listens. Unbeknownst to them, "Europe," their assumed center of world history, is located atop a grain of sand, minutely drawn by William Blake's mind. Trapped in a convent built upon Aztec ruins located inside this granule, Sor Juana Inés de la Cruz reflects on faith through Christian, Muslim, and Buddhist theologies. From one of the convent's secret doors, a labyrinthine path one hundred years long leads us to an elongated islet, "Saint Domingue, 1791–1820," where rebel Boukman, a slave who had learned from his African ancestors the power of spirits and plants, places his faith in Legba to battle for freedom, and Ti Noel, a freed slave oppressed under Henry Christophe's kingdom in independent Haiti familiar with Boukman's rebellion and with the Declaration of the Rights of Man and Citizen, at the end of his life comes to declare war against all masters. From a telescope 10 (500)n times more powerful than the Palomar Observatory located in a star of another universe, we could retrace all their words and deeds, backward or forward, floating as cosmic dust, long after their authors died. And if we look for certain words with care, we may be able even to find those brought together by Alejo Carpentier in a historical novel and read that in a place called *The Kingdom of this World*, where each individual life came to be valued as a precious universe, historical truth was discovered to be fundamentally practical, a matter of struggling against the forces that limit life, the source and aim of history, an elusive marvel.[7]

8

The struggle for life is the matter. We can find its germinations and ruins in fields, those expanding spaces where social activity continuously unfolds, and archives, the ever more varied containers of its readable traces and signs. Both are formed through the myriad classificatory and discriminatory procedures that shape lives and select significance. Through "fieldwork" and "archival research" the disciplines of anthropology and history construct their objects. In pursuit of its object, non-dominative knowledge excavates deep within and beyond given fields and archives. Brushing history against the brain, as if mining for life's gems, from the debris this practice of survival creates its own library, organized less as a Museum of Knowledge than as a Practical Workshop: photos, musical tapes, poems, films, field notes, books, newspapers, artifacts, kept digitally in data banks or located in crates thrown all over the floor in constant use in pursuit of knowledge for free people, who therefore will continue to struggle for aims we now can barely imagine. Honoring those oppressed in the past by standing for freedom in the present, we can perhaps envisage a future unburdened by origins, free to abandon images that sustained past struggles—a future perfect released from the burden of the past. By this novel time, images that Benjamin conjured up to inspire our struggles, whether of a dark past—"the hatred and the spirit of sacrifice" of enslaved ancestors—or of a bright future—the dream of "liberated grandchildren"—will become historical dust, the taken-for-granted soil of new social landscapes, except perhaps for a few tattered relics kept by historians or antiquarians. Recognizing in lives built amidst "wreckage upon wreckage" the stronger love that holds together what has been broken, we could then be moved by a "structure of political thought" that, in the yearning words of a historian of longing, "will recognize what has been made out on the margins; and then, recognizing it, refuse to celebrate it; a politics that will, watching this past, say 'So What?', and consign it to the dark." As our struggle is endless, the poet reminds us that "irony is the struggle to struggle."[8]

9 ❧

> Synchrony and diachrony
> Are modes of holding
> Space in time or
> Time in space. If
> all depends on
> the eyes of the beholder
> Who, What,
> holds the beholder?[9]

10 ❧

> The poetry of
> the present
> holds
> the prose of
> the future
>
> And vice versa.
> So much, as much,
> depends on
> Words as Deeds.[10]

11 ❧

It's about people making it.

NOTES*

These pieces are constructed in playful counterpoint to Karl Marx's "Theses on Feuerbach" and Walter Benjamin's "Theses on the Philosophy of History," accompanied by Fernando Ortiz's *Cuban Counterpoint.*

1

1.1. In this volume we use the terms *anthrohistory* and *anthrohistorians* because this is how we came to identify ourselves in our regular activities at the University of Michigan. As far as I know a similar term, *anthrohistorical*, was first used by Paul Friedrich in his *Princes of Naranja: An Essay in Anthrohistorical Method* (1986). Just as Juliet's *Romeo* or Quijote's *Dulcinea*, my "anthrohistory" here is an idealized, hyperreal subject; perhaps love holds not just an ideal reality, but the impetus to make it real. As in any romance, readers can treat "anthrohistory" in this text as a space-holder for a love of their own. If love of the general is realized through love of particulars—for me the central lesson of seeing the "personal" as "political"—these pieces for anthrohistory may work for other projects as well. Upon reading a draft of this paper, Javier Sanjínes, a member of a Latin American group also involved in decolonizing projects, commented that much of what I say here about "anthrohistory" applies to this group. Perhaps the core of this general project is the recognition of mutuality and reciprocity among living beings, and the ethical obligations entailed in acknowledging this collective interdependence. If we come to "work and toil for people we will never know," as Ti Noel realized at the end of Carpentier's novel *The Kingdom of This World* (1957), it is because we are sustained by the work and toil, and by the love, of others. In recognition of this entangled gift, I dedicate these pieces to the memory of Lya Imber de Coronil, my mother, Venezuela's first woman doctor who dedicated her life to public health, and to *Bellas,* for their care.

1.2. The major scholarly fields involved in the critical movement associated with intellectual turns in the 1980s are social and cultural history, cultural anthropology, linguistics, literary theory, critical geography, British and U.S. cultural studies, microhistory, feminist, gay, and queer

---

*Imagine these notes as endnotes within notes, in counterpoint with each piece. They can be read as footnotes, or as beginning notes, all at once, or next to the eleven pieces—as side notes.

studies, the German school *Kultur-Gesellschaft-Alltag,* and postcolonial and subaltern studies in their hegemonic as well as Latin American and African modalities.

1.3. I use the word *movement* following David William Cohen's suggestion that the category "social movement" serves to examine the development of "historical anthropology." Coinciding with this notion, in internal discussions among a group of scholars and activists united by a decolonizing project centering on Latin America, Walter Mignolo has argued for the value of thinking of ourselves as a "social movement" that seeks to overcome Western separations between the knowing subject and its object as well as academia and society.

1.4. My use of "borders" and "betwixt and between" here intends to suggest the potentiality inhering in liminal social spaces, as explored in the works of Victor Turner (1967), Gloria Anzaldúa (1987), and Walter Mignolo (2000), among others.

1.5. The notion of "undisciplining the disciplines" is inspired by the work of the network of Latin American scholars and activists associated with the decolonizing project mentioned above, guided by Anibal Quijano and Enrique Dussel (1993, 1998), as well as by the work of kindred thinkers, such as Boaventura do Santos (1995) and Franz Hinkelammert (2006); for a collection of essays on this topic, see the books edited on this topic by Castro-Gómez and Mendieta (1998) as well as those by Catherine Walsh (2002) and Edgardo Lander (2000).

1.6. In the 1990s the Gulbenkian commission celebrated the "opening" of the social sciences and the blurring of the disciplinary boundaries separating the social sciences, the humanities, and the natural sciences (Wallerstein et al. 1996). I think it is evident that the disciplines now are more self-aware and open; they certainly have assimilated terms and concepts from each other. Yet, professional interests, market pressures, and conservative politics, in my view, are normalizing these changes and leading to a closing of the social sciences. Michael Buroway's insightful critique of the Gubelkian report is also an indictment of the conformism affecting academic disciplines a few years after its publication (2005). Given the growing corporativization of the universities (see the January 2008 issue of *Anthropology News*), I fear that the promotion of interdisciplinarity at the present time is too often cast instrumentally as the pursuit of established objectives through the interaction among given disciplines, rather than as a genuine expansion of the horizons of knowledge through the questioning of assumptions, boundaries, and ends.

1.7. The current "privatization of knowledge" in multiple forms, including the concentration of knowledge production in research centers and universities located in metropolitan centers increasingly subjected to corporate pressures, is a general phenomenon that affects all academic programs, including anthrohistory.

1.8. Critical praxis should be distinguished from the conventional pragmatism that focuses on efficient means to achieve given ends. Marx's claim that we must prove the truth of "human thinking" through transformative practice is far from narrowly instrumental, for it entails the constant redefinition of ends through practical activity. If human beings are both the creators and creatures of their circumstances, a critical praxis entails the ongoing and mutual formation of means and ends as part of the permanent exchange between people and their circumstances. Just as "the educator must be educated," ends must be defined as well as realized by means, and means must prefigure ends. Ends and means mediate each other.

1.9. Marx's thesis eleven (1978) asserts, "The philosophers have only interpreted the world: the point, however, is to change it." As his work shows, radically interpreting the world not only is necessary for transforming it but already changes it.

1.10. Benjamin's thesis eleven argues for a view of development based on the realization of labor and nature rather than on their exploitation, as proposed by German social democracy's technocratic view of progress. Labor and nature are the twin factors that make up the comparative advantage of the global South and help structure its ongoing subordination as a region not despite but through the mediation of high modernist enclaves located in its midst and connected economically and culturally to metropolitan centers. The increasingly more evident negative effects of the global exploitation of labor and nature, as it leads to persisting poverty and inequality worldwide as well as to the destruction of the planet, may open spaces for global alliances toward alternative visions of development. This requires, as Arturo Escobar (1995) has suggested, a negation of development as commonly understood in the modern period, but also, as Enrique Dussel (1998) proposes, the pursuit of a vision of "transmodernity" that recognizes in modernity the ground upon which to construct a more just, harmonious, and plural world; transmodernity involves not a rejection of modernity, but its transformation.

2

2.1. There is a vast literature on the complicity between Western academic disciplines and Western dominion. In my view, its fundamental contribution has been to illuminate the connection between the fragmentation of the world into seemingly independent and unequal entities and the reification of knowledge into separate disciplines, each concerned with bounded units. Serious intellectual projects should challenge boundaries that blind us to the processes that have made the world at once interconnected and fragmented. Far from the egotistic "diversity" celebrated by the free market, the Zapatista ideal of a world that can hold multiple worlds is only possible under conditions of inclusive global solidarity and deep democracy.

3

3.1. The concept of knowledge in exile builds on Edward Said's work and renders homage to his memory.

3.2. The warning that not even the dead will be safe as long as the enemy remains victorious comes from Walter Benjamin's thesis six.

3.3. Much of contemporary history has been shaped by the control through networks of elites, corporations, and states of hydrocarbon energy that belong to humanity, our collective inheritance of organic life in the planet. The hidden struggle over oil and other natural resources in the making of modern history makes particularly evident that what Trouillot (1995) called the "silences of the past" extends widely into the present, defining its delusory clarity (my current book project, *Crude Matters,* centers on the exploration of the opacity of the present through research on the 2002 coup d'état against Hugo Chávez's petrostate and its aftermath).

4

4.1. The image of a labyrinth whose exits open into another labyrinth comes from Jorge Luis Borges's stories; this image inspired Jacques Derrida's deconstructive work. My use of the notion of a puzzle to be assembled together comes from Subcomandante Marcos (1997), who used it as a metaphor in an article on global capitalism published in *Le Monde;* I use it to evoke a performative epistemology and representational strategy.

5

5.1. The citation about the map comes from Adrienne Rich's "Notes toward a Theory of Location" as cited in my "Beyond Occidentalism: Towards Nonimperial Geohistorical Categories."

5.2. The citation about an account of the cosmos as "a point" is itself an unreferenced citation of a "modern biologist" in Walter Benjamin's thesis eighteen.

5.3. The reference to the need to include Napoleon's head cold and the actions of humble soldiers in accounts of the battle of Borodino comes from Carlo Ginzburg's 1993 comments on Tolstoy's *War and Peace* as an inclusive model of microhistory in "Microhistory: Two or three things I know about it."

6

6.1. This reflection about maps as metaphors for positivist science is inspired by Jorge Luis Borges's short story "On Exactitude in Science." Showing the uselessness of a map that coincides with the empire point by point, his story suggests that any representation is partial in two senses: incomplete and partisan. Its exactitude, and thus the exactitude of science, depends not on its correspondence to reality, but on its significance. If one treats maps not just as objects that represent the world but that perform representing it, their point centers on the effects of their representations—on how they connect their producers and users to the world. Critical knowledge production is not a matter of "filling gaps" so as to make representations more complete (as in much of historical and anthropological work; I owe this insight to David Pedersen), but of creating useful knowledge—producing maps that can guide us toward, and define, desirable ends.

7

7.1. This piece refers to real figures in imagined situations, except for Ti Noel, an actual character in Alejo Carpentier's *The Kingdom of This World*, a novel about the Haitian revolution centering on the life of a common man, Ti Noel, subjected to different forms of oppression under various masters during this revolutionary period.

7.2. Claude Lévi-Strauss's 1966 critique of humanism and discussion of multiple temporal scales in *The Savage Mind* paralyzed Jean-Paul Sartre's effort to write a grand theory of history in his *Critique of Dialectical Reason* (1976). In turn, Jacques Derrida undermined Lévi-Strauss's structuralism by questioning the necessarily assumed foundations of any structuralism (for illuminating discussions, see Gikandi [2005] and Young [1990]). Since any paradigm involves the acceptance, even if tactical, of unproven premises, truth lies on faith, as Sor Juana Inés de la Cruz suspected long ago.

7.3. In the First Thesis of his *Theses on the Philosophy of History*, Benjamin criticizes the determinism of historical materialism, yet in the others he endorses an open-ended historical materialism; Sartre's struggle to reconcile these two viewpoints was deeply affected by Lévi-Strauss's critique of his humanism and eurocentrism.

7.4. The notion that one can see the universe in a grain of sand comes from William Blake (1982), but it derives from medieval theology and cosmologies of nature. Extrapolating from an insight by Nicos Poulantzas (1978: 14) on nation-state formation, this piece suggests that any point anywhere at any scale (a grain of sand, a square, a nation, an island, a convent) involves the territorialization of a history and the historicization of a territory. Treating such concepts as the "universe" and a "grain of sand" as metaphors for the relationship between wholes and parts, in a discussion of Cuban historiography I suggested that in order to see the universe in a grain of sand one must also see a grain of sand in the universe (2003). Yet this programmatic assertion leaves uncharted the hard analytical task of integrating different temporal and spatial scales and finding adequate modalities for representing such visions.

7.5. The image of recovered histories from another star comes from Calvino's *Mt. Palomar* (1985), with gratitude to Genese Sodikoff who brought his stories to my attention and whose own work on Madagascar, by connecting footprints of laborers in forest preserves to the workings of global capital, shows the complex interweaving of parts and wholes at different scales as well as the possibility of developing an exemplary narrative to represent this process.

7.6. The notion of multiple universes comes from recent work by physicists on the nature of reality. The figure of 10 to the 500th degree mentioned here represents the number of solutions allegedly credited to string theory—the theory that one metalaw applies to the "multiverse," an entity composed of zillions of universes within which ours is only a granule. It will probably be a while before the social sciences will feel at home in Einstein's relative world. At that future time, Bakhtin's "chronotrope," inspired by Einstein, will be seen as a pioneering ancestor, but at least for a while, Newton's notion of absolute space and time probably will continue to define our earthly three-dimensional reality.

8

8.1. The goal of challenging what he called "non-dominative knowledge" comes from Edward Said's sustained critique of the complicity between power and knowledge.

8.2. Critical of German social democracy's notion of progress for being forgetful of past struggles, Benjamin proposed that struggles for a better future should be guided not by images of "liberated grandchildren" but by "hatred" or the "spirit of sacrifice" (Thesis Twelve; my thanks to Janam Mukherjee for clarifying my reading of Benjamin). In light of the failure of the revolutions of 1848, Marx invoked a poetics of the future as a guide to radical change. A poetics of the present informs Ortiz's work on Cuba, as well as Derek Walcott's notion that the love that puts together a broken vase is stronger than the love that created it (1998). Despite their differences, there is an intimate affinity among Benjamin's call to recognize the struggles of the past, Walcott's appreciation of love in the present, Marx's poetics of the future, and Caroline Steedman's desire to free the present from the burden of the past.

8.3. My word *ruin* here is itself a ruin taken from dialogues with Javier Sanjinés, Ann Stoler, and Nicholas Dirks, as well as from Trouillot's 1995 evocation of Haiti's Sans Souci (both the palace and Jean Baptiste Sans Souci), Benjamin's image of the wreckages of history, and Volnay's recognition of imperial spoils in *Les Ruines, ou Méditations sur le Révolutions des Empires*.

8.4. A vision of the past as a piling of "wreckage upon wreckage" comes from Benjamin's Thesis Nine. The quote about transcending the past (ending with a provocative "So what") comes from the conclusion of Steedman's extraordinary account of working-class longing, *Landscape for a Good Woman*.

8.5. A conception of "struggle" as a quotidian disposition defines an ethical-political position that seeks to find plenitude within history, not outside it. Wrestling against what holds people down may guide scholarly work away from narrow careerism, detached curiosity, antiseptic scientism, abstract aestheticism, or a value-free social science restricted to evaluating means, not ends. If "rationality" is to have any connection with reason, then ends, not just means, have to be subjected to reasonable scholarly examination, rather than exiled to the realm of personal preferences. As Rolph-Trouillot argues in *Silencing the Past* (1995), representations of the horrors of the past lack "authenticity" if they do not engage the horrors of the present. Yet, as Dan Birchok writes me from the midst of his mine-filled fieldwork, "But at the same time, a certain kind of constructive unpurposefulness is also an important part of this endeavor. Too much purpose ruins the opportunities to draw new maps. Perhaps too much purpose is what makes it so difficult to subordinate imagination to a plan (to paraphrase your opening quote)." Perhaps the realization that the blood of the world is on our pages—my reading of Paul Eiss's article in this volume—would enable us to connect plan and freedom, purpose and imagination in writing our pages.

8.6. The citation about the irony of struggling to struggle comes from Joshua Edwards's "Small Islands Are Largely Themselves, Aphorisms &Poems (Erasures)," a paper/poem presented in my seminar "What's Left in Latin America," University of Michigan, Winter 2007.

9

9.1. From its origins to the present, anthropology has confronted the complex problem of integrating different units of analysis at different scales. Perhaps a symptom of the difficulty of relating them to each other is a tendency to define these units as if they were self-contained and to examine them in terms of such binaries such as past and present, diachrony and synchrony, events and structure, society and culture, the material and the ideal, the global and local, and other such polarities. This tendency is present in both British and U.S. anthropology, for instance, in discussions of "social structure and social organization" (Raymond Firth), "process and structure" (Max Gluckman), structure and contingency in "social dramas" (Victor Turner), and "culture" and "society" as treated in the United States by major figures (e.g., Boas, Benedict, Mead, Schneider, Geertz, and Sahlins). While Sahlins's early work, with its focus on material production, privileges "society," his later work treats "culture" as a determining structure; it seems to argue that events make history, but under cultures not of their own choosing. William Sewell (2005) treats Geertz as a theoretician of synchrony, and Sahlins as a theoretician of the "event," yet in both cases structures explain events but are not explained by previous events; in this respect, history remains a mystery.

It is revealing that one of the most influential anthropologists of the twentieth century centered his work on the rejection of "history." For Claude Lévi-Strauss, structures define primitive or "cold" societies, events modern or "hot" societies. In the former, events are turned into structures; in the latter, structures generate events. By freezing history, cold societies reveal the logic of "savage thought," but this thought turns out to be not a particular mode of thinking but the transhistorical structures of a universal Mind. Given the fundamental ahistoricism of his structures, in a pioneering critique of Lévi-Strauss, Octavio Paz (1967) referred to his work as Kantianism without a subject or a transcendental objectivism. Attempts to introduce a temporal dimension in these structures, as in Piaget's genetic structuralism, reveal the difficulty of overcoming the subject/object duality once this duality is posited as a starting point, as with Kant. The reification into polarities of the distinctions between subject/object and diachrony/synchrony was insightfully challenged rather early in the twentieth century in Russia by Volosinov and Bakhtin, who focused their critique on Saussure's agentless structuralism and Vossler's and Humboldt's voluntaristic subjectivism. As Raymond Williams (1989) noted, their work had little impact on Western social thought, which in an unfortunate fateful turn has come to be framed by the reified polarities defined by Saussure.

The ideas expressed here in poetic verse benefited by the sensibility of Christina Lazaridi and Nomi Stone; my gratitude.

9.2. While mainstream anthropology has often treated "history" (as what happened) as a messy force that disorders "culture," historians since the 1980s, affected by the linguistic turn, have treated "culture" (as an analytical construct of the Geertzian variety) as a meaningful system that helps examine difference not just among different societies separated by space, but of the same society at different times.

9.3. Marxists interested in historical change, less prone to restrict social agency to individuals (except for analytical Marxists who favor methodological individualism), have focused on the connection between "objective" conditions and "subjective" meaning (Sartre) or on the relation among different "structures" or "instances of society" (Althusser). In Sartre's grand historical narrative, totality is an encompassing and evolving historical process defined by universal politics; in Althusser's grand structuralism, totality is a hierarchical system discerned by science. In both cases, even if at any one point historical outcomes can result from individual agency or be dominated by superstructural instances, it is the economy—or the principle of value—that "in the last instance" asserts itself in time, that is, that determines the direction of history.

9.4. Dipesh Chakrabarty (2000) has recently expanded his compelling critique of historiography by making a distinction between the time of History and the times of God and exploring the workings of different historicities in different social formations. His discussion reflects a productive tension of South Asian Subaltern scholarship between finely grained historical studies and sharp categorical distinctions between the West, as the home of modernity, and the rest, as the home of difference. A view of capitalist modernity—narrated in the time of history—as a heterogeneous global process shows how diverse historicities and agents are frequently entangled in the same region, even in the home of capital, making it possible, for instance, for Mr. Henry Ford to organize his River Rouge factory according to the logic of capital and yet to claim that God "runs his business." For a lucid argument about capitalism as a heterogeneous formation—as "a 'one' that is a 'many'"—that builds on a critical engagement with the work of David Harvey and Dipesh Chakrabarty, see the work of Vinay Gidwani (2008). In my own work I have sought to examine capitalism as a global process that takes different forms in distinct locations and to view modernity as involving the counterpointal formation of its dominant and subaltern modalities. This view of modernity as a partial totality always in the making allows for the examination of forms of negation and difference not subsumed by capital or defined in relation to it.

9.5. The body of work that Sherry Ortner (1984) famously discussed as practice theory sought to resolve the structure/event conundrum through the analysis of the practical interactions of social agents. Yet the tendency to view society as a sum of self-constituted parts, rather than as a constantly changing ensemble of mutually formed relations, inhibits even interactional perspectives from grasping the ongoing formation of the interacting agents. For instance, while Eric Wolf famously argued for an interactional view and criticized conceptions of societies as "billiard balls"—as bounded units clashing with each other—his own work presented global capitalism as a self-fashioned overwhelming ball that crushed other societies. The "West" has been shaped not just by capitalist social relations but by a cosmological order that privileges a metaphysics of external relations among independent individuals, often related to each other through the figure of the contract and seen as motivated by relentless pursuit of personal gain. This worldview is so hegemonic that it renders it difficult to imagine different social logics as well as alternative social orders.

9.6. Here this holding together of the knower and the known treats the Heisenberg "uncertainty principle" as a norm not just about knowing but about caring.

10

Many of the notes of other pieces apply to this piece, particularly 9.2–5. As these notes explain, "poetry of the future" refers to Marx's notion of desired futures in the *18th Brumaire of Louis Bonaparte*. In *The Great Transformation*, Karl Polanyi (1944) suggests that unknown futures are first imagined by poetry, not prose. Yet, for Bakhtin, prose, as the medium of heterogeneous voices, not poetry, holds the potential of change through dialogue among diverse subjects. But perhaps the political use of poetry under Stalin affected his conception of poetry as monological. As the poetry of Whitman and Neruda make evident, poetry, like prose, can imaginatively express not just a single authorial voice but the diverse voices of a multiple humanity.

Bibliography

Aadil, Shima. 2009. The government removes flowers and decorations thirty minutes after Obama's departure from Sultan Hassan. *AlMasry AlYoum.* http://www.almasryalyoum.com/article2.aspx?ArticleID=213802 (accessed June 9, 2009).

Abrams, Philip. 1988. Notes on the difficulty of studying the state. *Journal of Historical Sociology* 1:58–89.

Abu-Lughod, Lila. 2002. Do Muslim women need saving? Reflections on cultural relativism and its others. *American Anthropologist* 104:783–90.

Adorno, Theodor. 1971a. Tabus über dem Lehrerberuf. In *Erziehung zur Mündigkeit,* ed. Gerd Kadelbach, 70–87. Frankfurt am Main: Suhrkamp.

Adorno, Theodor. 1971b. Philosophie und Lehrer. In his *Erziehung zur Mündigkeit,* ed. Gerd Kadelbach, 29–49. Frankfurt am Main: Suhrkamp, 1971.

African National Congress. The Freedom Charter: Adopted at the Congress of the People, Kliptown, on 26 June 1955. African National Congress. http://www.anc.org.za/ancdocs/history/charter.html.

Agamben, Giorgio. 1998. *Homo sacer: Sovereign power and bare life.* Stanford: Stanford University Press.

Agamben, Giorgio. 2005. *State of exception.* Chicago: University of Chicago Press.

Alam, Muzaffar, and Sanjay Subrahmanyam. 2004. The making of a Munshi. *Comparative studies of South Asia, Africa, and the Middle East.* Special issue, *Forms of knowledge in early modern South Asia* 24:61–72.

Albert, Bruce. 1985. Temps du sang, temps des cendres: Représentation de la maladie, système rituel et espace politique chez les Yanomami du Sud-est (Amazonie Brésilienne). PhD diss., University of Paris X.

Albert, Bruce. 1989. Yanomami "violence": Inclusive fitness or ethnographer's representation? *Current Anthropology* 30:637–64.

Albert, Bruce. 1990. On Yanomami warfare: A rejoinder. *Current Anthropology* 31:55–62.

Albert, Bruce. 2005a. Round one: Reflections on *Darkness in El Dorado;* Questions on bioethics and health care among the Yanomami. In *Yanomami: The fierce controversy and what we can learn from it,* ed. Robert Borofsky, 110–19. Berkeley: University of California Press.

Albert, Bruce. 2005b. Round two: Biomedical research, ethnic labels, and anthropological responsibility; Further comments. In *Yanomami: The fierce controversy and what we can learn from it,* ed. Robert Borofsky, 157–76. Berkeley: University of California Press.

Albert, Bruce. 2005c. Round three: Human rights and research ethics among indigenous people; Final comments. In *Yanomami: The fierce controversy and what we can learn from it*, ed. Robert Borofsky, 210–13. Berkeley: University of California Press.

Albert, Bruce, and G. Goodwin Gomez. 1997. *Saúde Yanomami. Um manual etnolinguístico*. Belém: Museu (Collection Eduardo Galvno).

Albert, Bruce, and Alcida Rita Ramos. 1989. Yanomami Indians and anthropological ethics. *Science* 244:63.

Alexander, Jeffrey C. 2004. Rethinking strangeness: From structures in space to discourses in civil society. *Thesis Eleven* 79:87–104.

Alsberg, P. A. 1991. *Guide to the archives in Israel*. Vol. 1, *The Israel state archives*. Jerusalem: Israel Archives Association.

American Anthropological Association. 1998. Code of Ethics of the American Anthropological Association. http://www.aaanet.org/committees/ethics/ethcode.htm (accessed August 28, 2007).

American Anthropological Association. 2002. *Papers of the American Anthropological Association El Dorado Task Force*. http://www.aaanet.org/edtf/index.htm.

American Anthropological Association. 2007a. *Handbook on Ethical Issues in Anthropology*. http://www.aaanet.org/committees/ethics/toc.htm (accessed August 28, 2007).

American Anthropological Association. 2007b. Case 5: Anonymity declined. In *Handbook on ethical issues in anthropology*. http://www.aaanet.org/committees/ethics/case5.htm (accessed August 28, 2007).

American Anthropological Association. 2007c. Case 6: Anonymity revisited. In *Handbook on ethical issues in anthropology*. http://www.aaanet.org/committees/ethics/case6.htm (accessed August 28, 2007).

American Historical Association. 2005. Statement of standards of professional conduct. http://www.historians.org/pubs/Free/ProfessionalStandards.cfm (accessed August 28, 2007).

Amin, Shahid. 1995. *Event, metaphor, memory: Chari Chaura, 1922–1992*. Berkeley: University of California Press.

Amis, Martin. 1991. *Time's arrow or the nature of the offence*. London: Jonathan Cape.

Anderson, Benedict. 1991. *Imagined communities: Reflections on the origin and spread of nationalism*. London: Verso.

Anderson, Benedict. 2003. Untitled position paper. University of Victoria, Asian Nationalism Project. http://web.uvic.ca/~anp/Public/Posish_Pap/Anderson.pdf (accessed July 27, 2010).

Andrews, James. 2003. *Science for the masses: The Bolshevik state, public science, and the popular imagination in Soviet Russia, 1917–34*. College Station: Texas A&M University Press.

Anghel, Valeriu, and Silviu Alupei. 1992. Mișcarea de rezistență națională împotriva comunismului "Vlad Țepeș al II-lea." Revolta de la Bârsești-Vrancea. *Tinerama* 24–30:8–9.

Annin, Peter. 2006. *The Great Lakes water wars*. Washington, DC: Island Press.

Anzaldúa, Gloria. 1987. *Borderlands: The new Mestiza—la frontera*. San Francisco: Spiters-Aunt Lute.

Appadurai, Arjun. 2000. Grassroots globalization and the research imagination. *Public Culture* 12:1–19.
Appiah, K. Anthony. 2005. *The ethics of identity*. Princeton: Princeton University Press.
Arendt, Hannah. 1961. *Between past and future*. New York: Penguin Books.
Arendt, Hannah. 1973. *The origins of totalitarianism*. New York: Harvest Books.
Arendt, Hannah. 1994. *Eichmann in Jerusalem: A report on the banality of evil*. New York: Penguin Classics.
Ariss, Tarek al-. 2007. The making of an expert: The case of Irshad Manji. *Muslim World* 97:93–110.
Arquilla, John, and David Ronfeldt. 2001. *Networks and netwars: The future of terror, crime, and militancy*. Los Angeles: Rand Corporation.
Asad, Talal. 1986. The idea of an anthropology of Islam (Occasional Papers Series/Center for Contemporary Arab Studies). Washington, DC: Georgetown University Press.
Asad, Talal. 1991 [1993]. *Genealogies of religion: Discipline and reasons of power in Christianity and Islam*. Baltimore: Johns Hopkins University Press.
Asad, Talal. 2000. Muslims and European identity: Can Europe represent Islam? In *Cultural encounters: Representing "otherness,"* ed. Elizabeth Hallam and Brian V. Street, 11–27. New York: Routledge.
Asad, Talal. 2003. *Formations of the secular: Christianity, Islam, modernity*. Stanford: Stanford University Press.
Austen, Ralph A., and Jonathan Derrick. 1999. *Middlemen of the Cameroons rivers: The Duala and their hinterland, c. 1600–c. 1960*. New York: Cambridge University Press.
Axel, Brian Keith, ed. 2002. *From the margins: Historical anthropology and its futures*. Durham: Duke University Press.
Baez, Benjamin. 2002. Confidentiality in qualitative research: Reflections on secrets, power, and agency. *Qualitative Research* 2:35–58.
Barker, Holly M. 2004. *Bravo for the Marshallese: Regaining control in a post-nuclear, post-colonial world*. Belmont: Wadsworth.
Barnett, Ronald, and Nicholas Maxwell, eds. 2008. *Wisdom in the university*. London: Routledge.
Barth, Fredrik, ed. 1969. *Ethnic groups and boundaries: The social organization of culture difference*. Boston: Little, Brown.
Barth, Fredrik. 1975. *Ritual and knowledge among the Baktaman of New Guinea*. New Haven: Yale University Press.
Barthes, Roland. 1981. *Camera lucida*. New York: Hill and Wang.
Bataille, Georges. 1988 [1954]. *Inner experience*. Trans. Leslie Ann Baldt. Albany: State University of New York.
Bauman, Richard, and Charles L. Briggs. 1990. Poetics and performance as critical perspectives on language and social life. *Annual Review of Anthropology* 19:59–88.
Becker, Howard. 1940. Constructive typology in the social sciences. In *Contemporary social theory*, ed. Harry E. Barnes, Howard Becker, and Frances Bennett Becker, 17–46. New York: Appleton-Century.

Becker, Howard. 1956. *Man in reciprocity: Introductory lectures on culture, society, and personality.* New York: F. A. Praeger.
Bellos, David. 1986. *Oulipo: A primer of potential literature.* Lincoln: University of Nebraska Press.
Benard, Cheryl. 2003. *Civil democratic Islam: Partners, resources, strategies.* Los Angeles: Rand Corporation.
Benedict, Ruth. 1943. *Race: Science and politics.* New York: Viking Press.
Benjamin, Walter. 2007 [1955]. Theses on the philosophy of history. In *Illuminations: Essays and reflections,* ed. Hannah Arendt, trans. Harry Zohn, 253–64. New York: Schocken Books.
Berger, John. 1979. *Pig earth.* New York: Pantheon Books.
Berger, John. 2001. *The shape of a pocket.* New York: Vintage Books.
Berreman, Gerald D. 1991. Ethics versus "realism" in anthropology. In *Ethics and the profession of anthropology: Dialogue for a new era,* ed. Carolyn Flueher-Lobban, 38–71. Philadelphia: University of Pennsylvania Press.
Bhabha, Homi. 1994. *The location of culture.* New York: Routledge.
Bhasker, Roy. 1997 [1975]. *A realist theory of science.* London: Verso.
Bickford-Smith, Vivian. 1995. Black ethnicities, communities, and political expression in Late Victorian Cape Town. *Journal of African History* 36:443–65.
Birth, Kevin. 2008. The creation of coevalness and the danger of homochronism. *Journal of the Royal Anthropological Institute* 14:3–20.
Blake, William. 1982. *The complete poetry and prose of William Blake.* Anchor Books: New York.
Blalock, Hubert M. 1967. Middleman minorities. In *Toward a theory of minority-group relations,* 79–84. New York: Wiley.
Blalock, Hubert M. 1982. *Race and ethnic relations.* Englewood Cliffs: Prentice-Hall.
Bluestone, Barry, and Bennett Harrison. 1982. *The deindustrialization of America: Plant closing, community abandonment, and the dismantling of basic industry.* New York: Basic Books.
Blumenberg, Hans. 1997. *Shipwreck with spectator: Paradigm of a metaphor for existence.* Cambridge: MIT Press.
Boas, Franz. 1988. *Race, language, and culture.* Chicago: University of Chicago Press.
Boddy, Janice. 2007. *Civilizing women: British crusades in colonial Sudan.* Princeton: Princeton University Press.
Bonacich, Edna. 1973. A theory of middleman minorities. *American Sociological Review* 38:583–94.
Borges, Jorge Luis. 1962a. Death and the compass. In *Ficciones,* trans. Anthony Kerrigan, 129–41. New York: Grove Press.
Borges, Jorge Luis. 1962b. The garden of forking paths. In *Ficciones,* trans. Helen Temple and Ruthuen Todd, 89–101. New York: Grove Press.
Borges, Jorge Luis. 1964. The library of Babel. In *Labyrinths: Selected stories and other writings,* ed. Donald A. Yates and James E. Irby, 51–58. New York: New Directions.

Borges, Jorge Luis. 1975. Of exactitude in science. In *A universal history of infamy*, 139–42. London: Penguin Books.
Borofsky, Robert. 2005. *Yanomami: The fierce controversy and what we can learn from it.* Berkeley: University of California Press.
Bourdieu, Pierre. 1977. *Outline of a theory of practice.* Cambridge: Cambridge University Press.
Bourgois, Philippe. 1990. Confronting anthropological ethics: Ethnographic lessons from Central America. *Journal of Peace Research* 27:43–54.
Boyer, Dominic. 2005. *Spirit and system: Media, intellectuals, and the dialectic in modern German culture.* Chicago: University of Chicago Press.
Boym, Svetlana. 2001. *The future of nostalgia.* New York: Basic Books.
Bradley, Matt. 2007. Silenced for their own protection: How the IRB marginalizes those it feigns to protect. *ACME: An International E-Journal for Critical Geographies* 6:339–49.
Bretell, Caroline, ed. 1993. *When they read what we write: The politics of ethnography.* Westport, CT: Bergin and Garvey.
Briggs, Charles L., and Clara E. Mantini-Briggs. 2001. Perspectives on Tierney's *Darkness in El Dorado. Current Anthropology* 42:269–71.
Briggs, Laura. 2002. *Reproducing empire: Race, sex, science, and U.S. imperialism in Puerto Rico.* Berkeley: University of California Press.
Bric, Adrian. 1998. Victor Lupa (1921–1956). *Arhivele Totalitarismului* 19–20: 223–25.
Brosius, J. Peter. 1999. On the practice of transnational cultural critique. *Identities* 6:179–200.
Buck-Morss, Susan. 1989. *The dialectics of seeing: Walter Benjamin and the Arcades Project.* Cambridge: MIT Press.
Bulliet, Richard. 2004. *The case for Islamo-Christian civilization.* New York: Columbia University Press.
Burawoy, Michael. 2005. Provincializing the social sciences. In *The politics of method in the human sciences,* ed. George Steinmetz, 508–26. Durham: Duke University Press.
Burke, Ersie. 2006. Francesco Di Demetri Litino, the Inquisition and the *Fondaco dei Turchi. Thesaurismata* 36:79–95.
Burke, Kenneth. 1962. *A grammar of motives.* Berkeley: University of California Press.
Burke, Kenneth. 1984 [1937]. *Attitudes toward history.* Berkeley: University of California Press.
Çaglar, Ayse. 2006. Hometown associations, the rescaling of state spatiality and migrant grassroots transnationalism. *Global Networks* 6:1–22.
Cahill, Caitlin, Farhana Sultana, and Rachel Pain. 2007. Participatory ethics: Politics, practices, institutions. *ACME: An International E-Journal for Critical Geographies* 6:304–18.
Calhoun, Craig, ed. 2007. *Sociology in America: A history.* Chicago: University of Chicago Press.
Calvino, Italo. 1979. *Invisible Cities.* London: Pan Books.

Calvino, Italo. 1985. *Mr. Palomar.* San Diego: Harcourt Brace Jovanovich.
Calvino, Italo. 1988. *Six memos for the next millennium.* Cambridge: Harvard University Press.
Cantor, Nancy. 2000a. Statement regarding the book "Darkness in El Dorado" (September 27). http://www.umich.edu/news/index.html?Releases/2000/Sep00/r092700b.
Cantor, Nancy. 2000b. Statement regarding the book "Darkness in El Dorado" (October 31). http://www.umich.edu/news/index.html?Releases/2000/Oct00/r103100a.
Cantor, Nancy. 2000c. Statement regarding the book "Darkness in El Dorado" (November 13). http://www.ns.umich.edu/Releases/2000/Nov00/r111300a.html.
Cantor, Nancy. 2001. May 29, 2001, update regarding the book "Darkness in El Dorado." http://www.vpcomm.umich.edu/archive/darknupd.html.
Cape Gateway. Places of slave remembrance in the Western Cape. Government of South Africa, provincial government of the Western Cape, City of Cape Town. http://www.capegateway.gov.za/eng/pubs/public_info/P/82884/3.
Cape Mazaar Society. Guide to the Kramats of the Western Cape. Cape Mazaar Society. http://www.capemazaarsociety.com.
Cape Town Partnership. Cape Town Partnership: A profile, 2007. Cape Town Partnership. http://www.capetownpartnership.co.za.
Carneiro da Cunha, Manuela. 1989. Letter to the editor. *Anthropology Newsletter* 30:3.
Carpentier, Alejo. 1957. *The kingdom of this world.* New York: Farrar, Straus and Giroux.
Cassidy, Tanya M. 2000. "Race to the park": Simmel, the stranger, and the state. *Irish Communications Review* 8:14–20.
Castro-Gómez, Santiago, and Eduardo Mendieta, eds. 1998. *Teorías sin disciplina: Latinoamericanismo, postcolonialidad y globalización en debate.* Mexico City: Miguel Angel Porrúa.
Celan, Paul. 1967. *Atemwende.* Frankfurt am Main: Suhrkamp.
Chagnon, Napoleon. 1968. *Yanomamo: The fierce people.* New York: Holt, Rinehart, and Winston.
Chagnon, Napoleon. 1988. Life histories, blood revenge, and warfare in a tribal population. *Science* 239:985–92.
Chagnon, Napoleon. n.d. Letter to the editor. *Anthropology Newsletter* 3:24.
Chakrabarty, Dipesh. 2000. *Provincializing Europe.* Chicago: University of Chicago Press.
Chatterjee, Partha. 1993. *The nation and its fragments.* Princeton: Princeton University Press.
Chow, Rey. 2006. Sacrifice, mimesis, and the theorizing of victimhood (a speculative essay). *Representations* 94:131–49.
City of Cape Town. Spatial development framework newsletter, February 2007. City of Cape Town. http://www.capetown.gov.za.
Clark, Katerina. 1995. *Petersburg: Crucible of cultural revolution.* Cambridge: Harvard University Press.

Clifford, James. 2005. Rearticulating anthropology. In *Unwrapping the sacred bundle: Reflections on the disciplining of anthropology*, ed. Daniel A. Segal and Sylvia J. Yanagisako, 24–48. Durham: Duke University Press.
Cohen, David William. 1994. *The combing of history*. Chicago: University of Chicago Press.
Cohen, David William. 2009. Unsettled stories and inadequate metaphors: The movement to historical anthropology. In *CLIO/ANTHROPOS: Exploring the boundaries between history and anthropology*, ed. Andrew Willford and Eric Tagliacozzo, 273–94. Stanford: Stanford University Press.
Cohen, David William, Stephan F. Miescher, and Luise White. 2001. Introduction: Voices, words, and African history. In *African words, African voices: Critical practices in oral history*, ed. David W. Cohen, Stephan F. Miescher, and Luise White, 1–30. Bloomington: Indiana University Press.
Cohen, David William, and E. S. Atieno Odhiambo. 1992. *Burying SM: The politics of knowledge and the sociology of power in Africa*. London: James Currey.
Cohen, David William, and E. S. Atieno Odhiambo. 2004. *The risks of knowledge: Investigations into the death of the Hon. Minister John Robert Ouko in Kenya, 1990*. Athens: Ohio University Press.
Cohen, Jeremy D. 2003. Cultural and commercial intermediaries in an extra-legal system of exchange: The practicos of the Venezuelan Littoral in the eighteenth century. *Itinerario* 27:105–24.
Cohn, Bernard S. 1962. An anthropologist among the historians: A field study. *South Atlantic Quarterly* 61.
Cohn, Bernard S. 1987. *An anthropologist among the historians and other essays*. Delhi: Oxford University Press.
Cole, Jennifer. 2001. *Forget colonialism? Sacrifice and the art of memory in Madagascar*. Berkeley: University of California Press.
Collins, James. 2003. Language, identity, and learning in the era of "expert-guided" systems. In *Linguistic anthropology of education*, ed. Stanton Wortham and Betsy Rymes, 31–60. Westport: Praeger.
Comaroff, John L. 1982. Dialectical systems, history and anthropology: Units of study and questions of theory. *Journal of Southern African Studies* 8(2): 143–72.
Connell, R. W. 1997. Why is classical theory classical? *American Journal of Sociology* 102:1511–57.
Constable, Olivia Remie. 2003. *Housing the stranger in the Mediterranean world: Lodging, trade, and travel in late antiquity and the Middle Ages*. New York: Cambridge University Press.
Costantini, Massimo. 1996. Le strutture dell ospitalità. In *Storia di Venezia dalle origini alla caduta della serenissima, vol. V: Il Rinascimento: società ed economia*, ed. Alberto Tenenti and Ugo Tucci, 881–911. Rome: Istituto della Enciclopedia Italiana.
Cooper, Frederick. 2005. *Colonialism in question*. Berkeley: University of California Press.
Cooper, Frederick. 2008. Possibility and constraint: African independence in historical perspective. *Journal of African History* 49:167–96.

Cooper, Frederick, and Ann Laura Stoler, eds. 1997. *Tensions of empire: Colonial cultures in a bourgeois world*. Berkeley: University of California Press.
Corbin, Alain. 2001. *The life of an unknown: The rediscovered world of a clog maker in nineteenth century France*. New York: Columbia University Press.
Coronil, Fernando. 1996. Beyond Occidentalism: Towards non-imperial geohistorical categories. *Cultural Anthropology* 11:51–87.
Coronil, Fernando. 1997. *The magical state: Nature, money, and modernity in Venezuela*. Chicago: University of Chicago Press.
Coronil, Fernando. 2000. Towards a critique of globalcentrism: Speculations on capitalism's nature. *Public Culture* 12:351–75.
Coronil, Fernando. 2001. Perspectives on Tierney's *Darkness in El Dorado*. *Current Anthropology* 42:265–66.
Coronil, Fernando. 2003. Epílogo: El universo en un grano de arena, un grano de arena en el universo. *Sociedad, cultura y vida cotidiana en Cuba, 1878–1917*, ed. José Amador. Havana: Centro Marinello.
Coronil, Fernando. 2004. Latin American postcolonial studies and global decolonisation. In *Postcolonial literary studies*, ed. Neil Lazarus, 221–41. London: Cambridge University Press.
Coronil, Fernando, and Colloquium Speakers. 2001. The production of knowledge and indigenous peoples. *Journal of the International Institute* 9:6–7, 26–27. http://hdl.handle.net/2027/spo.4750978.0009.104.
Coser, Lewis A., ed. 1965. *Georg Simmel*. Englewood Cliffs, NJ: Prentice-Hall.
Costantini, Massimo. 1996. Le strutture dell ospitalità. In *Storia di Veneza dalle origini alla caduta della serenissima, vol. V: Il Rinascimento: societa ed economia*, ed. Alberto Tenenti and Ugo Tucci, 881–911. Rome: Istituto della Enciclopedia Italiana.
Coulter, Jeff. 1985. Two concepts of the mental. In *The social construction of the person*, ed. K. J. Gergen and K. E. Davis, 129–44. New York: Springer.
D'Andrade, Roy. 1995. Moral models in anthropology. *Current Anthropology* 36:399–408.
Das, Veena. 2008. If this be magic. In *Religion: Beyond a concept*, ed. Hent de Vries, 259–82. New York: Fordham University Press.
Davids, Achmat. 1985. *The history of the Tana Baru*. Cape Town: Committee for the Preservation of the Tana Baru.
Davie, D. Grace, et al. 2001. Reimagining South Africa and the political imagination of South Africans. Conference organized by African History graduate students at the University of Michigan, January 13.
Davis, Dona L. 1993. Unintended consequences: The myth of "the return" in anthropological fieldwork. In *When they read what we write*, ed. Caroline Brettell, 27–35. Westport, CT: Bergin and Garvey.
Deane, Grant B., and M. Dale Stokes. 2002. Scale dependence of bubble creation mechanisms in breaking waves. *Nature* 418:839–44.
de Certeau, Michel. 1980. *L'invention du quotidien I. Arts de faire*. Paris: Gallimard.
de Certeau, Michel. 1982. Lacan: une ethique de la parole. *Le Débat* 22:54–69.
de Certeau, Michel. 1986. *Heterologies: Discourse on the other*. Trans. Brian Massumi. Manchester: Manchester University Press.

de Certeau, Michel. 1988a. *The practice of everyday life.* Trans. Stephen F. Rendail. Berkeley: University of California Press.

de Certeau, Michel. 1988b. *The writing of history.* Trans. Tom Conley. New York: Columbia University Press.

Deleuze, Gilles. 1997. *Essays critical and clinical.* Trans. Daniel W. Smith and Michael A. Greco. Minneapolis: University of Minnesota Press.

Deleuze, Gilles, and Felix Guattari. 1987. *A thousand plateaus: Capitalism and schizophrenia.* Minneapolis: University of Minnesota Press.

Deleuze, Gilles, and Felix Guattari. 1994. *What is philosophy?* New York: Columbia University Press.

Derrida, Jacques. 1986 [1976]. Foreword. In *The Wolf Man's magic word: A cryptonymy,* by Nicolas Abraham and Maria Torok, trans. Nicholas Rand, xi–il. Minneapolis: University of Minnesota Press.

Derrida, Jacques. 1992. *Given time. I, counterfeit money.* Trans. Peggy Kamuf. Chicago: University of Chicago Press.

De Witte, Ludo. 2001. *The assassination of Lumumba.* Trans. Ann Wright and Renée Fenby. New York: Verso.

Didi-Huberman, Georges. 2003. *Images malgré tout.* Paris: Minuit.

Dirks, Nicholas, ed. 1992. *Colonialism and culture.* Ann Arbor: University of Michigan Press.

Dirks, Nicholas. 1996. Is vice versa? Historical anthropologies and anthropological histories. In *The historical turn in the human sciences,* ed. Terrance McDonald, 17–51. Ann Arbor: University of Michigan Press.

Dirks, Nicholas. 1998. *In near ruins: Cultural theory at the end of the century.* Minneapolis: University of Minnesota Press.

Dobrincu, Dorin. 2006. Rezistena armat anticomunist din Vrancea. Organizaia "Vlad epe II" (1949–1950). *Colloquium politicum* 1:1–40.

Dolgon, Cory. 1999. Soulless cities: Ann Arbor, the cutting edge of discipline; Postfordism, postmodernism, and the new bourgeoisie. *Antipode* 31 (2): 129–62.

Douglas, Mary. 1975 [1973]. *Implicit meanings.* London: Routledge.

Dube, Saurabh, ed. 2007. *Historical anthropology.* New York: Oxford University Press.

Duchamp, Marcel. 1959. The creative act. In *Marcel Duchamp,* ed. Robert Lebel, 77–78. New York: Paragraphic Books.

Dussel, Enrique. 1993. Eurocentrism and modernity. *Boundary* 2:65–76.

Dussel, Enrique. 1998. Beyond Eurocentrism: The world system and the limits of modernity. In *The cultures of globalization,* ed. Frederick Jameson and Masao Miyoshi, 8–31. Durham: Duke University Press.

Eco, Umberto. 2005. *The mysterious flame of Queen Loana.* Orlando: Harcourt.

Edward, Joshua. 2007. Small islands are largely themselves, aphorisms and poems (erasures). Paper/poem presented at the seminar "What's Left in Latin America," Winter 2007, in Ann Arbor, Michigan.

Eiss, Paul. 2002. Redemption's archive: Remembering the future in a revolutionary past. *Comparative Studies in Society and History* 44:106–36.

Eley, Geoff. 2005. *A crooked line: From cultural history to the history of society.* Ann Arbor: University of Michigan Press.

Engels, Friedrich. 1962. Anti-Dühring. In *Werke*, by Karl Marx and Friedrich Engels, vol. 20, 5–303. Berlin: Dietz.

Ennami, Amr K. 1972. *Studies in Ibadism (al-Ibadiyah)*. Tripoli: University of Libya Press.

Erzen, Tanya. 2006. *Straight to Jesus: Sexual and Christian conversions in the ex-gay movement*. Berkeley and Los Angeles: University of California Press.

Esack, Farid. 1988. Three Islamic strands in the South African struggle for justice. *Third World Quarterly* 10:437–98.

Escobar, Arturo. 1995. *Encountering development: The making and unmaking of the Third World*. Princeton: Princeton University Press.

eThekwini Online. Cemeteries and Crematoria Conference opening speech by eThekwini Mayor Councillor Obed Mlaba, Durban, July 15, 2004. eThekwini Municipality: City of Durban. http://www.ethekwini.gov.za/durban/government/mayor/mayor/speech.html.

Fabian, Johannes. 1983. *Time and the other: How anthropology makes its object*. New York: Columbia University Press.

Fabian, Johannes. 1996. *Remembering the present: Painting and popular history in Zaire*. Berkeley: University of California Press, 1996.

Fabian, Johannes. 2007. *Memory against culture: Arguments and reminders*. Durham: Duke University Press.

Fallers, Lloyd. 1955. The predicament of the modern African chief: An instance from Uganda. *American Anthropologist* 57:290–305.

Fanon, Frantz. 1968. *The wretched of the earth*. New York: Grove Press.

Feldman, Ilana. 2005. Everyday government in extraordinary times: Persistence and authority in Gaza's civil service (1917–1967). *Comparative Studies in Society and History* 47:863–91.

Feldman, Ilana. 2007a. The Quaker way: Ethical labor and humanitarian relief. *American Ethnologist* 34:689–705.

Feldman, Ilana. 2007b. Difficult distinctions: Refugee law, humanitarian practice, and political identification in Gaza. *Cultural Anthropology* 22:129–69.

Feldman, Ilana. 2008. *Governing Gaza: Bureaucracy, authority, and the work of rule (1917–67)*. Durham: Duke University Press.

Feldman, Ilana. 2009. Gaza's humanitarianism problem. *Journal of Palestine Studies* 38:1–16.

Ferguson, James. 1994 [1990]. *The anti-politics machine: "Development," depoliticization, and bureaucratic power in Lesotho*. Minneapolis: University of Minnesota Press.

Ferguson, James. 1999. *Expectations of modernity: Myths and meanings of urban life on the Zambian Copperbelt*. Berkeley: University of California Press.

Ferguson, Niall. 2003. *Empire: How Britain made the modern world*. London: Allen Lane.

Ferguson, R. Brian. 1995. *Yanomami warfare: A political history*. Santa Fe: School of American Research Press.

Finnegan, Erin. 2006. Buried beyond Buitengracht: Interrogating cultural variability in the historic "informal" burial ground of Prestich Street, Cape Town. M.Phil diss., University of Cape Town.

Flannery, Kent V. 2002. Hypocrisy in El Dorado. *Anthropology News* 43(5): 3.
Flannery, Kent V. n.d. Memo to the Neel family. http://www.nku.edu/~humed1/darkness_in_el_dorado/documents/0167.htm.
Fluehr-Lobban, Carolyn, ed. 1991. *Ethics and the profession of anthropology: Dialogue for a new era.* Philadelphia: University of Pennsylvania Press.
Fluehr-Lobban, Carolyn. 1999. Comment on Peter Pels, "Professions of duplexity." *Current Anthropology* 40:119.
Fluehr-Lobban, Carolyn, ed. 2003. *Ethics and the profession of anthropology: Dialogue for ethically conscious practice.* 2nd ed. Walnut Creek: AltaMira Press.
Foucault, Michel. 1980. *The history of sexuality, Volume 1, An introduction.* New York: Vintage.
Foucault, Michel. 1984. Nietzsche, genealogy, history. In *The Foucault reader*, ed. Paul Rabinow, 76–100. New York: Pantheon Books.
Freedom Park. A heritage destination. Freedom Park Corporation. http://www.freedompark.co.za.
Friedrich, Paul. 1986. *Princes of Naranja: An essay in anthrohistorical method.* Austin: University of Austin Press.
Furnivall, J. S. 1944. *Netherlands India: A study of plural economy.* New York: Macmillan.
Fursat Shîrâzî, Muhammad Nâsir. 1896. *Asâr-i 'ajam.* Bombay: Matba'-i Nâdirî.
Garfinkel, Harold. 2002. *Ethnomethodology's program: Working out Durkheim's aphorism.* Boulder: Rowman and Littlefield.
Geertz, Clifford. 1960. The Javanese Kijaji: The changing role of a cultural broker. *Comparative Studies in Society and History* 2:228–49.
Geertz, Clifford. 1973. *The interpretation of cultures.* New York: Basic Books.
Geertz, Clifford. 1983. Blurred genres: The refiguration of social thought. In *Local knowledge: Further essays in interpretive anthropology,* 19–36. New York: Basic Books.
Geertz, Clifford. 1988. Being there: Anthropology and the scene of writing. In *Works and lives: The anthropologist as author,* 1–24. Stanford: Stanford University Press.
Geertz, Clifford. 2001. Life among the anthros. *New York Review of Books* 8:18–22.
Gidwani, Viney. 2008. *Capital interrupted: Agrarian development and the politics of work in India.* Minneapolis: University of Minnesota Press.
Gikandi, Simon. 2005. Poststructuralism and postcolonial discourse. In *The Cambridge companion to postcolonial literary studies,* ed. Neil Lazarus, 97–119. London: Cambridge University Press.
Ginzburg, Carlo. 1989. Clues: Roots of an evidential paradigm. In *Clues, myths, and the historical method,* trans. John Tedeschi and Anne Tedeschi, 96–125. Baltimore: Johns Hopkins University Press.
Ginzburg, Carlo. 1990. *Myths, emblems, clues.* London: Hutchinson Radius.
Ginzburg, Carlo. 1993. Microhistory: Two or three things I know about it. *Critical Inquiry* 20: 10–35.
Grafton, Anthony. 1997. *The footnote: A curious history.* Boston: Harvard University Press.

Greene, Molly. 2000. *A shared world: Christians and Muslims in the early modern Mediterranean.* Princeton: Princeton University Press.
Guha, Ranajit. 1988. The prose of counter-insurgency. In *Selected subaltern studies,* ed. by Ranajit Guha and Gayatri Chakravorty Spivak, 45–86. New York: Oxford University Press.
Gupta, Akhil. 1998. *Postcolonial developments.* Durham: Duke University Press.
Guyer, Jane. 2007. Prophecy and the near future: Thoughts on macroeconomic, evangelical, and punctuated time. *American Ethnologist* 34:409–21.
Hacking, Ian. 1995. *Rewriting the soul: Multiple personality and the sciences of memory.* Princeton: Princeton University Press.
Handler, Richard, and Joyce Linnekin. 1984. Tradition, genuine or spurious. *Journal of American Folklore* 97:273–90.
Harding, Susan Friend. 1987. Convicted by the Holy Spirit: The rhetoric of fundamental Baptist conversion. *American Ethnologist* 14:167–81.
Harvey, David. 1990. *The condition of postmodernity: An enquiry into the origins of cultural change.* Cambridge, MA: Blackwell.
Head, Randolph C. 1990. Religious boundaries and the inquisition in Venice: Trials of Jews and Judaizers, 1548–1580. *Journal of Medieval and Renaissance Studies* 20:175–204.
Herskovits, Melville. 1969. *The new world negro: Selected papers in Afro-American Studies.* New York: Minerva Press.
Herskovits, Melville. 1973. *Cultural relativism: Perspectives in cultural pluralism.* New York: Vintage.
Herzfeld, Michael. 1991. *A place in history: Social and monumental time in a Cretan town.* Princeton: Princeton University Press.
Herzfeld, Michael. 1997. *Portrait of a Greek imagination: An ethnographic biography of Andreas Nenedakis.* Chicago: University of Chicago Press.
Hicks, George. 1977. Anonymity and scientific accuracy: The problem of pseudonyms. *Human Organization* 36:214–20.
Hill, Jonathan D. 1994. Alienated targets: Military discourse and the disempowerment of indigenous Amazonian peoples in Venezuela. *Identities* 1:7–34.
Hill, Kim. 2000. A statement by Kim Hill. http://www.psych.ucsb.edu/research/cep/eldorado/kimhill.html.
Hinkelammert, Franz J. 2006. *El sujeto de la ley: El retorno del sujeto reprimido.* Caracas: Fundación Editorial El Perro y la Rana.
Hirschkind, Charles. 2006. *The ethical soundscape: Cassette sermons and Islamic counterpublics; cultures of history.* New York: Columbia University Press.
Hobsbawm, Eric. 1984. Introduction: Inventing tradition. In *The invention of tradition,* ed. Eric Hobsbawm and Terence Ranger, 1–14. New York: Cambridge University Press.
Hodgson, Dorothy L. 1999. Critical interventions: Dilemmas of accountability in contemporary ethnographic research. *Identities* 6:201–24.
Hodgson, Dorothy L. 2001. *"Once intrepid warriors": Gender, ethnicity, and the cultural politics of Maasai development.* Bloomington: Indiana University Press.
Hodgson, Dorothy L. 2002a. Introduction: Comparative perspectives on the in-

digenous rights movement in Africa and the Americas. *American Anthropologist* 104:1037–49.
Hodgson, Dorothy L. 2002b. Precarious alliances: The cultural politics and structural predicaments of the indigenous rights movement in Tanzania. *American Anthropologist* 104:1086–97.
Hodgson, Dorothy L. 2005. *The church of women: Gendered encounters between Maasai and missionaries.* Bloomington: Indiana University Press.
Hodgson, Dorothy L. 2008. Cosmopolitics, neoliberalism, and the state: The indigenous rights movement in Africa. In *Anthropology and the new cosmopolitanism: Rooted, feminist, and vernacular perspectives,* ed. Pnina Werbner, 215–30. Oxford: Berg.
Hodgson, Dorothy L. 2011. *Being Maasai, becoming indigenous: Postcolonial politics in a neoliberal world.* Bloomington: Indiana University Press.
Hodgson, Marshall G. S. 1974. *Venture of Islam: Conscience and history in a world civilization.* Chicago: University of Chicago Press.
Hoffman, Valerie J. 2004. The articulation of Ibd identity in modern Oman and Zanzibar. *Muslim World* 94:201–16.
Howell, Jayne. 2004. Turning out good ethnography, or talking out of turn? Gender, violence, and confidentiality in Southeastern Mexico. *Journal of Contemporary Ethnography* 33:323–52.
Hume, Douglas W. n.d. *Darkness in El Dorado:* The anthropological niche of Douglas W. Hume. http://www.nku.edu/~humed1/index.php/darkness-in-eldorado.
Humphreys, S. C. 2002. Classics and colonialism: Towards an erotics of the discipline. In *The strangeness of gods,* 8–51. Oxford: Oxford University Press.
Humphreys, S. C. 2004. *The strangeness of gods.* Oxford: Oxford University Press.
Hurtado, Magdalena, Kim Hill, Hillard Kaplan, and Jane Lancaster. 2001. Disease among indigenous South Americans. *Anthropology News* 42:5–6.
Hutton, Patrick. 1992. *History as an art of memory.* Hanover: University Press of New England.
Huyssen, Andreas, ed. 2008. World cultures, world cities. In *Other cities, other worlds: Urban imaginaries in a globalizing age,* 1–23. Durham: Duke University Press.
Imdâd, Hasan. 1993. *Anjumanha-yi adabî-i shîrâz: Az avâkhir qarn-i dahum tâ imrûz.* Iran: Intishârât-i "Ma."
James, William. 1997 [1909]. *The meaning of truth.* New York: Prometheus Books.
Jameson, Frederic. 1991. *Postmodernism, or, the cultural logic of late capitalism.* Durham: Duke University Press.
Jasanoff, Maya. 2005. *Edge of empire: Lives, culture, and conquest in the East, 1750–1850.* New York: Knopf.
Jones, James H. 1981. *Bad blood: The Tuskegee syphilis experiment.* New York: Free Press.
Jonker, Julian. 2005. The silence of the dead: Ethical and juridical significances of the exhumations at Prestwich Place, Cape Town, 2003–2005. M.Phil diss., University of Cape Town.

Kalb, Don, and Herman Tak, eds. 2005. *Critical junctions: Anthropology and history beyond the cultural turn.* New York: Berghahn.
Kantrowitz, Barbara, and Bill Turque. 1987. Black protest campus racism. *Newsweek* (April 6): 30.
Keane, Webb. 2003. Self interpretation, agency, and the objects of anthropology: Reflections on a genealogy. *Comparative Studies in Society and History* 45:222–48.
Kittler, Friedrich. 1990. *Discourse networks 1800/1900.* Trans. Michael Metteer with Chris Cullens. Stanford: Stanford University Press.
Kittler, Friedrich. 1999. *Gramophone, film, typewriter. English.* Stanford: Stanford University Press.
Kittler, Friedrich, and John Johnston. 1997. *Literature, media, information systems: Essays, critical voices in art, theory, and culture.* Amsterdam: G+B Arts International.
Ko, Dorothy. 2005. *Cinderella's sisters: A revisionist history of footbinding.* Berkeley: University of California Press.
Kopenawa, Davi. 1991. Interview with Davi Kopenawa Yanomomi. http://www.aaanet.org/committees/cfhr/rptyano5.htm (accessed Oct. 2, 2009).
Koselleck, Reinhart. 2002. *The practice of conceptual history: Timing history, spacing concept.* Palo Alto: Stanford University Press.
Koselleck, Reinhart. 2004. *Futures past: On the semantics of historical time.* New York: Columbia University Press.
Kramer, Paul A. 2006. *The blood of government: Race, empire, the United States, and the Philippines.* Chapel Hill: University of North Carolina Press.
Kroeber, A. L. 1948. *Anthropology.* New York: Harcourt, Brace.
Lacan, Jacques. 1977. *The four fundamental concepts of psycho-analysis.* New York: Norton.
Laclau, Ernesto. 2005. *On populist reason.* London: Verso.
Lambek, Michael. 1996. The past imperfect: Remembering as moral practice. In *Tense past: Cultural essays in trauma and memory,* ed. Paul Antze and Michael Lambek, 235–54. New York: Routledge.
Lander, Edgardo, ed. 2000. *La colonialidad del saber: Eurocentrismo y ciencias sociales: Perspectivas latinoamericanas.* Buenos Aires: Consejo Latinoamericano de Ciencias Sociales/Unesco.
Latour, Bruno. 2004. Why has critique run out of steam? From matters of fact to matters of concern. *Critical Inquiry* 30:225–48.
Latour, Bruno. 2005. *Reassembling the social: An introduction to actor-network-theory.* Clarendon Lectures in Management Studies. Oxford: Oxford University Press.
Latour, Bruno. 2008. A textbook case revisited: Knowledge as a mode of existence. In *The handbook of science and technology studies,* ed. Edward J. Hackett, Olga Amsterdamska, Michael Lynch, and Judy Wajcman, 83–112. Cambridge: MIT Press.
Lederman, Rena. 2004. Towards an anthropology of disciplinarity. *Critical Matrix* (Princeton) 15:60.

Lederman, Rena, ed. 2006a. *AE* forum: IRBs, bureaucratic regulation, and academic freedom. Special section, *American Ethnologist* 33 (4): 477–548.
Lederman, Rena. 2006b. Introduction: Anxious borders between work and life in a time of bureaucratic ethics regulation. *American Ethnologist* 33:477–81.
Lederman, Rena. 2006c. The perils of working at home: IRB "mission creep" as context and content for an ethnography of disciplinary knowledges. *American Ethnologist* 33:482–91.
Lefebvre, Henry. 1995. *Introduction to modernity*. Trans. John Moore. New York: Verso.
Lévi-Strauss, Claude. 1966. *The savage mind*. Chicago: University of Chicago Press.
Lewicki, Tadeusz. 1971. Ibadiyya. In *Encyclopedia of Islam*, new ed., 648–60. Leiden: E. J. Brill.
Li, Tania M. 2000. Articulating indigenous identity in Indonesia: Resource politics and the tribal slot. *Comparative Studies in Society and History* 42:149–79.
Li, Tania M. 2007. *The will to improve: Governmentality, development, and the practice of politics*. Durham: Duke University Press.
Limbert, Mandana. 2008. Depleted future: Anticipating the end of oil in Oman. In *Timely assets: The politics of resources and their temporalities*, ed. Elizabeth Ferry and Mandana Limbert, 25–50. Santa Fe: SAR Press.
Livingston, Eric. 1987. *Making sense of ethnomethodology*. London: Routledge.
Lobo, Maria Stell, Karis Maria Pinho Rodrigues, Diana Maul de Carvalho, and Fernando Sergio Viana Martins. 2000. Report of the medical team of the Federal University of Rio de Janeiro on accusations contained in Patrick Tierney's *Darkness in El Dorado*. Trans. Catherine Howard. http://www.tamu.edu/anthropology/UFRJFinal.html.
Luehrmann, Sonja. 2005. Recycling cultural construction: Desecularisation in post-Soviet Mari El. *Religion, State, and Society* 33:35–56.
Lynch, Michael, and David Bogen. 1996. *The spectacle of history: Speech, text, and memory at the Iran-Contra hearings*. Durham: Duke University Press.
Lynd, Robert S. 1939. *Knowledge for what? The place of social science in American culture*. Princeton: Princeton University Press.
Lyotard, Jean-Francois. 1984. *The postmodern condition: A report on knowledge*. Trans. Geoff Bennington and Brian Massumi. Minneapolis: University of Minnesota Press.
Maamiry, Ahmed Hamoud al-. 1980. *Oman and Ibadhism*. New Delhi: Lancers.
MacIntyre. Alisdair. 1980 [1977]. Epistemological crisis, dramatic narrative, and the philosophy of science. In *Paradigms and revolutions: Appraisals and applications of Thomas Kuhn's philosophy of science*, ed. Gary Gutting. Notre Dame: University of Notre Dame Press.
Mahmood, Saba. 2005. *Politics of piety: The Islamic revival and the feminist subject*. Princeton: Princeton University Press.
Mahmood, Saba. 2006. Secularism, hermeneutics, empire: The politics of Islamic Reformation. *Public Culture* 18:323–47.
Mail and Guardian. 2001. Oom Gov fights bias from beyond the grave. Mail and Guardian online. http://www.mg.co.za (accessed September 4, 2001).

Malinowski, Bronislaw. 1922. *Argonauts of the Western Pacific: An account of native enterprise and adventure in the archipelagoes of Melanesian New Guinea*. London: Routledge.

Malinowski, Bronislaw. 1989. *A diary in the strict sense of the term*. Stanford: Stanford University Press.

Mani, Lata. 1998. *Contentious traditions: The debate on Sati in colonial India*. Berkeley: University of California Press.

Manji, Irshad. 2003. *The trouble with Islam: A Muslim's call for reform in her faith*. New York: St. Martin's Press.

Manno, Antonio. 1995. *I mestieri di Venezia: storia, arte e devozione delle corporazioni dal XIII al XVIII secolo*. Cittadella: Biblos.

Marcos, Subcomandante. 1997. La 4e guerre mondiale a commencé. *Le Monde diplomatique* (August): 4–5.

Marx, Karl. 1978. Theses on Feuerbach. In *Marx and Engels reader*, ed. Robert C. Tucker, 143–46.

Martins, Leda. 2005. On the influence of anthropological work and other ethical considerations. In *Yanomami: The fierce controversy and what we can learn from it*, ed. Robert Borofsky, 110–19. Berkeley: University of California Press.

Masco, Joseph. 2006. *The nuclear borderlands: The Manhattan Project in post–Cold War New Mexico*. Princeton: Princeton University Press.

Mauss, Marcel. 1990 [1950]. *The gift: The form and reason for exchange in archaic societies*. Trans. W. D. Halls. New York: W. W. Norton and Company.

Maxwell, Nick. 2007 [1984]. *From knowledge to wisdom*. London: Pentire.

Mehta, Uday Singh. 1999. *Liberalism and empire: A study in nineteenth-century British liberal thought*. Chicago: University of Chicago Press.

Merry, Sally Engle. 2006. *Human rights and gender violence: Translating international law into local justice*. Chicago: University of Chicago Press.

Merten, Marianne. 2005. Muslim Council issues fatwa against property development. Mail and Guardian online. http//www.mg.co.za (accessed July 1, 2005).

Meskell, Lynn, and Peter Pels, eds. 2005. *Embedding ethics*. Oxford: Berg-Wenner-Gren Foundation.

Metcalf, Alida C. 2005. *Go-betweens and the colonization of Brazil, 1500–1600*. Austin: University of Texas Press.

Mignolo, Walter. 2000. *Local histories/global designs: Coloniality, subaltern knowledges, and border thinking*. Princeton: Princeton University Press.

Mihăilă, Ruxandra. 1994. "În 1948 ne-au luat muntele . . ." Răscoala țărănească din Munții Vrancei—23 iulie 1950. Destinuirile participanilor I. *Memoria* 11:35–45.

Mills, Charles Wright. 1940. Situated actions and vocabularies of motive. *American Sociological Review* 5:904–13.

Minkov, Anton. 2004. *Conversion to Islam in the Balkans: Kisve Bahasi petitions and Ottoman social life, 1670–1730*. Leiden: Brill.

Minow, Martha. 1998. *Between vengeance and forgiveness: Facing history after genocide and mass violence*. Boston: Beacon Press.

Mitchell, Lisa. 2009. *Language, emotion, and politics in South India: The making of a mother tongue*. Bloomington: Indiana University Press.

Mitchell, Timothy. 1988. *Colonising Egypt*. Berkeley: University of California Press.

Miyazaki, Hirokazu. 2004. *The method of hope: Anthropology, philosophy, and Fijian knowledge.* Stanford: Stanford University Press.
Montouri, Alfonso. 2008. Forward: Transdisciplinarity. In *Transdisciplinarity: Theory and practice,* ed. Basarab Nicolescu, ix–xvii. Cresskill, NJ: Hampton.
Mosse, David. 2006. Anti-social anthropology? Objectivity, objection, and the ethnography of public policy and professional communities. *Journal of the Royal Anthropological Institute* 12:935–56.
Motte, Warren, Jr. 1986. *Oulipo: A primer of potential literature.* Lincoln: Nebraska University Press.
Mufti, Aamir. 2007. *Enlightenment in the colony: The Jewish question and the crisis of postcolonial culture.* Princeton: Princeton University Press.
Muthu, Sankar. 2003. *Enlightenment against empire.* Princeton: Princeton University Press.
Nader, Laura. 1969. Up the anthropologist: Perspectives gained from studying up. In *Reinventing anthropology,* ed. Dell Hymes, 284–311. New York: Pantheon Books.
Nash, Gary, Charlotte Crabtree, and Ross E. Dunn. 1997. *History on trial: Culture wars and the teaching of the American past.* New York: Alfred A. Knopf.
Neel, James V. 1980. On being headman. *Perspectives in Biology and Medicine* 23:277–94.
Neel, James V., W. R. Centerwall, and N. A. Chagnon. 1970. Notes on the effects of measles and measles vaccine in a virgin soil population. *American Journal of Epidemiology* 91:418–29.
New York Times. 1987. Sarah G. Power, 52, Dies in 8-Story Fall: Michigan U. Regent. March 26, section D, 27.
Ngubane, Dr. B. S. 2000. Government of South Africa. Speech presented at the official opening of the Gateway to the Tana Baru Cemetary, January 14, in Cape Town, South Africa. http://www.info.gov.za/speeches/2000/000201401 p1001.htm.
Nietzsche, Friedrich. 1984. *Dithyrambs of Dionysus.* Trans. R. J. Hollingdale. Redding Ridge, CT: Black Swan Books.
Nietzsche, Friedrich Wilhelm. 1989. *On the genealogy of morals.* New York: Vintage.
Ní Laoire, Caitríona. 2007. To name or not to name: Reflections on the use of anonymity in an oral archive of migrant life narratives. *Social and Cultural Geography* 8:373–90.
Nordstrom, Carolyn. 2007. What the highwayman knew. *Chronicle Review* 53:B10.
Nordstrom, Carolyn, and Antonius C. G. M. Robben. 1995. *Fieldwork under fire: Contemporary studies of violence and survival.* Berkeley: University of California Press.
Nowotny, Helga. The potential of transdisciplinarity. *Interdisciplines* http://www.interdisciplines.org/interdisciplinarity/papers/5.
Oakeshott, Michael. 1991 [1962]. *Rationalism in politics and other essays.* Indianapolis: Liberty Fund.
O'Brien, Jay, and William Roseberry, eds. 1991. *Golden ages, dark ages: Imagining the past in anthropology and history.* Berkeley: University of California Press.

Ohnuki-Tierney, Emiko. 1991. *Culture through time: Anthropological approaches.* Stanford: Stanford University Press.
Okin, Susan Moller. 1999. *Is multiculturalism bad for women?* Princeton: Princeton University Press.
Oral History Association. Evaluation Guidelines. http://alpha.dickinson.edu/oha/pub_eg.html (accessed January 8, 2008).
Ortiz, Fernando. 1995. *Cuban counterpoint: Tobacco and sugar.* Durham: Duke University Press.
Ortner, Sherry B. 1984. Theory and anthopology since the sixties. *Comparative Studies in Society and History* 26(1):126–66.
Ovid. 1955. *Metamorphoses.* Trans. Rolfe Humphries. Bloomington: Indiana University Press.
Palmer, G. E. H., Philip Sherrard, and Kallistos Ware, ed. and trans. 1979–95. *The Philokalia: The complete text compiled by St Nikodimos of the Holy Mountain and St Makarios of Corinth.* 4 vols. London: Faber and Faber.
Park, Robert E. 1928. Human migration and the marginal man. *American Journal of Sociology* 33:881–93.
Patterson, Monica Eileen. 2009. Constructions of childhood in apartheid's last decades. PhD diss., University of Michigan.
Paz, Octavio. 1967. *Claude Lévi-Strauss o el nuevo festín de Esopo.* Mexico City: Joaquín Mortiz.
Pedersen, David. 2009. Keeping it real: Semiotic practice and fateful temporality in William Sewell's *Logics of History. Social Science History* 32 (4): 567–77.
Pels, Peter. 1999. Professions of duplexity: A prehistory of ethical codes in anthropology. *Current Anthropology* 40:101–36.
Pemberton, John. 1994. *On the subject of "Java."* Ithaca: Cornell University Press.
Perec, Georges. 1969. *La disparition.* Paris: Les Lettres Nouvelles.
Perec, Georges. 1973. *La boutique obscure: 124 rêves.* Paris: Denoël.
Perec, Georges. 1988. *W, or the memory of childhood.* London: Collins Harvill.
Perec, Georges. 1993. The doing of fiction. Kaye Mortley, pers. comm., August 1981.
Perec, Georges. 1997. *Species of spaces and other pieces.* London: Penguin Books.
Perec, Georges, and Robert Bober. 1995 [1980]. *Ellis Island and the people of America.* Trans. Harry Mathews. New York: New Press.
Peterson, John E. 2007. *Oman insurgencies.* London: Saqi Books.
Petit, Philippe. 2008. Interview. James Marsh, Simon Chinn, Michael Nyman, J. Ralph, and Philippe Petit. 2008. *Man on wire.* Los Angeles: Magnolia Home Entertainment.
Piaget, Jean. 1998 [1974]. L'épistémologie des relations interdisciplinaires. In *Internationales Jahrbuch für interdisziplinäre Forschung,* ed. Kalus Düwel and Sean Nowak, 154–72. Berlin: Walter de Gruyter.
Pierce, Steven. 2005. *Farmers and the state in colonial Kano: Land tenure and the legal imagination.* Bloomington: Indiana University Press.
Pierce, Steven, and Anupama Rao, eds. 2006. *Discipline and the other body: Correction, corporeality, colonialism.* Durham: Duke University Press.
Pigg, Stacy. 1992. Inventing social categories through place: Social representations

and development in Nepal. *Comparative Studies in Society and History* 34:491–513.
Plaggenborg, Stefan. 1996. *Revolutionskultur: Menschenbilder und kulturelle Praxis in Sowjetrussland zwischen Oktoberrevolution und Stalinismus*. Cologne: Böhlau.
Plumb, J. H. 1969. *The death of the past*. London: Macmillan.
Pocock, J. G. A. 1989 [1971]. *Politics, language, and time: Essays on political thought and history*. Chicago: University of Chicago Press.
Polanyi, Karl. 1944. *The great transformation: The political and economic origins of our time*. New York: Farrar & Rinehart.
Pollan, Michael. 2006. *The omnivore's dilemma: A natural history of four meals*. New York: Penguin Books.
Portelli, Alessandro. 1990. *The death of Luigi Trastulli, and other stories: Form and meaning in oral history*. Albany: State University of New York Press.
Poulantzas, Nicos. 1978. *State, power, socialism*. London: New Left Books.
Povinelli, Elizabeth. 2002. *The cunning of recognition: Indigenous alterities and the making of Australian multiculturalism*. Durham: Duke University Press.
Powell, David E. 1975. *Antireligious propaganda in the Soviet Union: A study of mass persuasion*. Cambridge: MIT Press.
Prakash, Gyan. 1999. *Another reason: Science and the imagination of modern India*. Princeton: Princeton University Press.
Pratt, Mary L. 1992. *Imperial eyes: Travel writing and transculturation*. New York: Routledge.
Press, Irwin. 1969. Ambiguity and innovation: Implications for the genesis of the culture broker. *American Anthropologist* 71:205–17.
Preziosi, Donald. 1989. *Rethinking art history: Meditations on a coy science*. New Haven: Yale University Press.
Preziosi, Donald. 2003. *Brain of the earth's body: Art, museums, and the phantasms of modernity*. Minneapolis: University of Minnesota Press.
Price, Richard. 1998. *The convict and the colonel*. Boston: Beacon Press.
Quijano, Anibal. 1997. Colonialidad del poder, cultura, y conocimiento en América Latina. *Anuario Mariateguiano* 9:113–22.
Ramachandran, V. S., and William Hirstein. 1998. The perception of phantom limbs. *Brain* 121:1603–30.
Ramos, Alcida Rita. 1987. Reflecting on the Yanomami: Ethnographic images and the pursuit of the exotic. *Cultural Anthropology* 2:284–304.
Ramos, Alcida Rita. 1998. *Indigenism: Ethnic politics in Brazil*. Madison: University of Wisconsin Press.
Ramos, Alcida Rita. 2001. About ethics in ethnographic research. *The Journal of the International Institute*. Ann Arbor, MI (Fall): 7.
Ramos, Alcida Rita. n.d. *Sanumá memories: Yanomami ethnography in times of crisis*. Madison: University of Wisconsin Press.
Ramphele, Mamphela. 1996. Political widowhood in South Africa: The embodiment of ambiguity. *Daedalus* 125: 99–117.
Rancière, Jacques. 1987. *Le maître ignorant*. Paris: Fayard.

Rancière, Jacques. 1991. *The ignorant schoolmaster: Five lessons in intellectual emancipation*. Ed. Kristin Ross. Stanford: Stanford University Press.

Rancière, Jacques. 1992. *Les noms de l'histoire*. Paris: Seuil.

Rancière, Jacques. 1994. *The names of history: On the poetics of knowledge*. Trans. Hassan Melehy. Minneapolis: University of Minnesota Press.

Randeria, Shalini. 2003. Cunning states and unaccountable international institutions: Legal plurality, social movements, and rights of local communities to common property resources. *Archives Européennes de Sociologie* 44:27–60.

Rao, Anupama, and Steven Pierce. 2006. Discipline and the other body: Humanitarianism, violence, and the colonial exception. In *Discipline and the other body: Correction, corporeality, colonialism*, ed. Steven Pierce and Anupama Rao, 1–35. Durham: Duke University Press.

Rawls, Anne Warfield. 2002. Introduction to *Ethnomethodology's program: Working out Durkheim's aphorism*, by Harold Garfinkel, 1–64. Boulder: Rowman and Littlefield.

Rebel, Herman. 2005. Figurations in historical anthropology: Two kinds of structural narrative about long-duration provenances of the Holocaust. In *Critical junctions: Anthropology and history beyond the cultural turn*, ed. Don Kalb and Herman Tak, 72–87. New York: Berghahn.

Reyerson, Kathryn. 2002. *The art of the deal: Intermediaries of trade in medieval Montpellier*. Leiden: Brill.

Richter, Daniel K. 2001. Native voices in a colonial world. In *Facing east from Indian country: A native history of early America*, 110–50. Cambridge: Harvard University Press.

Riley, Dylan. 2009. The historical logic of *Logics of History*: Language and labor in William H. Sewell Jr. *Social Science History* 32 (4): 555–65.

Ritchie, Donald A., and Linda Shopes. Oral history excluded from IRB review. http://alpha.dickinson.edu/oha/org-irb.html (accessed January 8, 2008).

Robben, Antonius C. G. M., and Jeffrey A. Sluka, eds. 2007. *Ethnographic fieldwork: An anthropological reader*. Oxford: Blackwell.

Robben Island Museum. http://www.robben-island.org.za.

Robinson, David. 2000. *Paths of accommodation: Muslim societies and French colonial authorities in Senegal and Mauritania, 1880–1920*. Athens: Ohio University Press.

Rolf, Malte. 2006. *Das sowjetische Massenfest*. Hamburg: Hamburger Edition.

Rony, Fatimah Tobing. 1996. *The third eye: Race, cinema, and ethnographic spectacle*. Durham: Duke University Press.

Roseberry, William. 1989. *Anthropologies and histories: Essays in culture, history, and political economy*. New Brunswick: Rutgers University Press.

Rothman, E. Natalie. 2006. Becoming Venetian: Conversion and transformation in the seventeenth-century Mediterranean. *Mediterranean Historical Review* 21:39–75.

Rothman, E. Natalie. 2011. *Trans-imperial subjects: Boundary markers of the early modern Mediterranean*. Ithaca: Cornell University Press.

Roy, Arundhati. 1998. The end of imagination. *Guardian*. August 1:1.

Ruggiero, Guido. 2001. The strange death of Margarita Marcellini: *Male*, signs, and the everyday world of pre-modern medicine. *American Historical Review* 106:1141–58.

Rylko-Bauer, Barbara, Merill Singer, and John Van Willigen. 2006. Reclaiming applied anthropology: Its past, present, and future. *American Anthropologist* 108:178–90.

Safi, Louay. 2006. *Blaming Islam: Examining the religion-building enterprise.* Detroit: Institute for Social Policy and Understanding.

Sahlins, Marshall. 2000. Jungle fever: Review of *Darkness in El Dorado. Washington Post,* December 10.

Said, Edward W. 1993. *Culture and imperialism.* New York: Knopf.

Said, Edward W. 2000. *Reflections on exile and other essays.* Cambridge: Harvard University Press.

Sakai, Naoki. 1997. *Translation and subjectivity: On "Japan" and cultural nationalism.* Minneapolis: University of Minnesota Press.

Sanders, Todd. 2008. Buses in Bongoland: Seductive analytics and the occult. *Anthropological Theory* 8:107–32.

Sandford, Victoria, and Asale Angel-Ajani, eds. 2006. *Engaged observer: Anthropology, advocacy, and activism.* New Brunswick: Rutgers University Press.

Santos, Boaventura de Sousa. 1995. *Toward a new common sense: Law, science, and politics in the paradigmatic transition.* New York: Routledge.

Sarraute, Nathalie. 1997. *Here.* New York: George Braziller.

Sarte, Jean Paul. 1976. *Critique of dialectical reason: Theory of practical ensembles.* Trans. Alan Sheridan-Smith; ed. Jonathan Rée. London: NLB.

Schauer, Frederick. 1987. Precedent. *Stanford Law Review* 39: 571–605.

Scheper-Hughes, Nancy. 1977. *Saints, scholars, and schizophrenics: Mental illness in rural Ireland.* Berkeley: University of California Press.

Scheper-Hughes, Nancy. 1982. Preface to the 1982 paperback edition. *Saints, scholars, and schizophrenics: Mental illness in rural Ireland,* v–xii. Berkeley: University of California Press.

Scheper-Hughes, Nancy. 1995. The primacy of the ethical: Propositions for a militant anthropology. *Current Anthropology* 36:409–20.

Schmitt, Carl. 2005. *Political theology: Four chapters on the concept of sovereignty.* Chicago: University of Chicago Press.

Schutz, Alfred. 1967 [1932]. *The phenomenology of the social world.* Trans. George Walsh and Frederick Lehnert. Evanston: Northwestern University Press.

Scott, David. 2003. Culture in political theory. *Political Theory* 31:92–115.

Scott, James L. 1998. *Seeing like a state: How certain schemes to improve the human condition have failed.* New Haven: Yale University Press.

Scott, Joan W. 1991. The evidence of experience. *Critical Inquiry* 17:773–97.

Sebald, Winfried Georg. 2001. *Austerlitz.* New York: Random House.

Sewell, William H., Jr. 2005. *Logics of history: Social theory and social transformation.* Chicago: University of Chicago Press.

Sewell, William H., Jr. 2009. Response to Steinmetz, Riley, and Pedersen. *Social Science History* 32 (4): 579–93.

Shapiro, Judith. 1976. Beastly or manly? Letter to the editor. *Time Magazine.* May 31, 107(23):forum.
Shaw, Rosalind. 2002. *Memories of the slave trade: Ritual and the historical imagination in Sierra Leone.* Chicago: University of Chicago Press.
Shepherd, Nick. 2007. Archaeology dreaming: Post-apartheid urban imaginaries and the bones of the Prestwich Street dead. *Journal of Social Archaeology* 7:3–27.
Shepherd, Nick, and Christian Ernsten. 2007. The world below: Post-apartheid urban imaginaries and the bones of the Prestwich Street dead. In *Desire lines: Space, memory and identity in the post-apartheid city,* ed. Noëleen Murray, Nick Shepherd, and Martin Hall, 215–32. New York: Routledge.
Shepherd, Nick, and Noëleen Murray. 2007. Introduction: Memory and identity in the post-apartheid city. *Desire lines: Space, memory and identity in the post-apartheid city,* ed. Noëleen Murray, Nick Shepherd, and Martin Hall, 1–18. New York: Routledge.
Shopes, Linda. 2000. Institutional review boards have a chilling effect on oral history. *Perspectives.* American Historical Association newsletter. http://www.historians.org/perspectives/issues/2000/0009/0009vie1.cfm (accessed January 8, 2008).
Shopes, Linda, and Don Ritchie. 2004. An update on the exclusion of oral history from IRB review. http://alpha.dickinson.edu/oha/org_irbupdate.html (accessed January 8, 2008).
Sider, Gerald, and Gavin Smith. 1997. Introduction. In *Between history and histories: The making of silences and commemorations,* ed. Gerald Sider and Gavin Smith, 3–30. Toronto: University of Toronto Press.
Siegfried, Nikolaus. 2000. Legislation and legitimation in Oman: The basic law. *Islamic Law and Society* 7:359–97.
Silverman, Marilyn, and P. H. Gulliver. 1992. Historical anthropology and ethnographic tradition: A personal, historical, and intellectual account. In *Historical anthropology through Irish case studies,* ed. Silverman and Gulliver, 3–74. New York: Columbia University Press.
Simmel, Georg. 1950. The stranger. In *The sociology of Georg Simmel,* ed. Kurt H. Wolff, 402–8. Glencoe, IL: Free Press.
Skaria, Ajay. 1999. *Hybrid histories: Forests, frontiers, and wildness in Western India.* Delhi, New York: Oxford University Press.
Sow, Samba, Birame Faye, Awa Sene Sarr, Babacar Diene, Fabienne Loriaux, Sidiki Bakaba, N'Gone Fall, and François L. Woukoache. 1995. *Asientos.* Rotterdam: P.B.C. Pictures.
Sperber, Dan. 2003. Why rethink interdisciplinarity? *Interdisciplines.* http://www.interdisciplines.org/interdisciplinarity/papers/5.
Sporn, Barbara. 1999. *Adaptive university structures: An analysis of adaptation to socioeconomic environments of US and European Universities.* Higher Education Policy Series 54. London: Jessica Kingsley.
Stacey, Judith. 1988. Can there be a feminist ethnography? *Women's Studies International Forum* 11:21–27.
Stahl, Henri H. 1939. *Nerej—Un village d'une region archaique.* 3 vols. Bucharest: Institut de Sciences Sociales de Roumanie.

Steedman, Carolyn Kay. 1986. *Landscape for a good woman: A story of two lives.* New Brunswick: Rutgers University Press.
Steedman, Carolyn Kay. 1995. *Strange dislocations: Childhood and the idea of human interiority, 1780–1930.* Cambridge: Harvard University Press.
Steedman, Carolyn Kay. 2007. *Master and servant.* Cambridge: Cambridge University Press.
Steinmetz, George. 2009. *Logics of History* as a framework for an integrated social science. *Social Science History* 32 (4): 535–53.
Stoler, Ann Laura. 2001. Tense and tender ties: The politics of comparison in North American history and (post) colonial studies. *Journal of American History* 88:831–64.
Stoler, Ann Laura. 2009. *Along the archival grain: Epistemic anxieties and colonial common sense.* Princeton: Princeton University Press.
Stoler, Ann Laura, and Karen Strassler. 2000. Castings for the colonial: Memory work in "New Order" Java. *Comparative Studies in Society and History* 42:4–48.
Stonequist, Everett V. 1961. *The marginal man: A study in personality and culture conflict.* New York: Russell and Russell.
Strassler, Karen. 2008. Material resources of the historical imagination: Documents and the future of the past in post-Suharto Indonesia. In *Timely assets: The politics of resources and their temporalities,* ed. Elizabeth Ferry and Mandana Limbert, 215–42. Santa Fe: SAR Press.
Stuhr, John. 1997. *Genealogical pragmatism.* Albany: State University of New York Press.
Subrahmanyam, Sanjay. 2005. *Explorations in connected history: From the Tagus to the Ganges.* 2 vols. Oxford: Oxford University Press.
Sullivan, Winnifred. 2009. *Prison religion: Faith-based reform and the Constitution.* Princeton: Princeton University Press.
Sunder Rajan, Rajeswari. 1990. The subject of Sati: Pain and death in the contemporary discourse on Sati. *Yale Journal of Criticism* 3:1–23.
Swedenburg, Ted. 1995. *Memories of revolt: The 1936–1939 rebellion and the Palestinian past.* Minneapolis: University of Minnesota Press.
Tanner, Jacob. 2004. *Historische anthropologie zur einführung.* Hamburg: Junius Verlag.
Tarde, Gabriel. 1999. *Monadologie et sociologie.* Paris: Institut Synthélabo.
Taussig, Michael T. 1986. *Shamanism, colonialism, and the wild man: A study in terror and healing.* Chicago: University of Chicago Press.
Taussig, Michael T. 2006. *Walter Benjamin's grave.* Chicago: University of Chicago Press.
Tavakoli-Targhi, Mohamad. 2001. *Refashioning Iran: Orientalism, occidentalism, and historiography.* Houndmills: Palgrave.
Taylor, Charles. 1994. *Multiculturalism: Examining the politics of recognition,* ed. Amy Gutmann. Princeton: Princeton University Press.
Tayob, Abdulkader I. 2007. On a knife-edge or in the fray: Managing heritage sites in a vibrant democracy. *Desire lines: Space, memory, and identity in the post-apartheid city,* ed. Noëleen Murray, Nick Shepherd, and M. Hall, 183–94. New York: Routledge.

Thomas, Lynn. 2003. *Politics of the womb: Women, reproduction, and the state in Kenya.* Berkeley: University of California Press.
Thompson, E. P. 1977. Christopher Caudwell. *Socialist Register* 14:77–140.
Thompson, E. P. 1994. *Persons and polemics.* London: Merlin Press.
Thompson, Michael. 1979. *Rubbish theory.* Oxford: Oxford University Press.
Throop, C. Jason, and Keith M. Murphy. 2002. Bourdieu and phenomenology: A critical assessment. *Anthropological Theory* 2:185–207.
Tierney, Patrick. 2000. *Darkness in El Dorado: How scientists and journalists devastated the Amazon.* New York: Norton.
Tilly, Charles. 1984. *Big structures, large processes, huge comparisons.* New York: Russell Sage.
Trouillot, Michel-Rolph. 1995. *Silencing the past: Power and the production of history.* Boston: Beacon Press.
Tschumi, Bernard. 2000 [1975]. The architectural paradox. In *Architectural theory since 1968,* ed. K. Michael Hays, 214–29. Cambridge, MA: MIT Press.
Turner, Stephen. 1994. *The social theory of practices: Tradition, tacit knowledge, and presuppositions.* Cambridge: Polity Press.
Turner, Terence. 1993. Anthropology and multiculturalism: What is anthropology that multiculturalists should be mindful of it? *Cultural Anthropology* 8:411–29.
Turner, Terence. 1994. The Yanomami: Truth and consequences. *Anthropology Newsletter* 35:46, 48.
Turner, Terence. 2000. Imminent anthropological scandal. http://members.aol.com/nymIIIIIII/darkness_in_el_dorado/documents/0055.htm.
Turner, Terence. 2001a. Eugenic ideas in James Neel's conception of "Primitive Society." Paper presented at the University of Michigan Colloquium "Science—Ethics—Power: Controversy Over the Production of Knowledge and Indigenous Peoples." http://www.umich.edu/~idpah/SEP/sep_te.html.
Turner, Terence. 2001b. The Yanomami and the ethics of anthropological practice. Occasional Paper of the Center for Latin American Studies Program in Ithaca, NY. http://www.anth.uconn.edu/gradstudents/dhume/darkness_in_el_dorado/documents/0497.htm.
Turner, Terence. 2005a. Round one: Ethical issues arising from Patrick Tierney's *Darkness in El Dorado* and the ensuing controversy. In *Yanomami: The fierce controversy and what we can learn from it,* 147–56. Berkeley: University of California Press.
Turner, Terence. 2005b. Round two: Anthropological responsibilities, scientific ethics, and the ideology of "science": What do we owe the Yanomami? In *Yanomami: The fierce controversy and what we can learn from it,* 198–209. Berkeley: University of California Press.
Turner, Terence. 2005c. Round three: New light on the darkness: New evidence and new readings in the Tierney/Neel/Chagnon controversy. In *Yanomami: The fierce controversy and what we can learn from it,* 270–81. Berkeley: University of California Press.
Turner, Victor W. 1967. *The forest of symbols: Aspects of Ndembu ritual.* Ithaca: Cornell University Press.

Tutu, Desmond. 1994. *The rainbow people of God: The making of a peaceful revolution*. New York: Doubleday, 1994.
University Record. 1987. Special edition. Ann Arbor, MI, March 25, 1987:1.
Urban Padoan, Lina. 1990. *Venezia e il "foresto." Situazioni avventure, "meraviglie," quando anche i re alloggiavano in locande: hosterie, locande e alberghi dal XIII al XIX secolo*. Venice: Centro internazionale della grafica.
U.S. Army Corps of Engineers and the Great Lakes Commission. 2000 [1999]. *Living with lakes: Understanding and adapting to Great Lakes water level changes*. Detroit: U.S. Army Corps of Engineers.
van der Geest, Sjaak. 2003. Confidentiality and pseudonyms: A fieldwork dilemma from Ghana. *Anthropology Today* 19:14–18.
Vellela, Tony. 1987. Racism on campus: Assault on black students at Columbia latest in growing trend. *Christian Science Monitor* (March 26):3.
Voortrekker Monument and Nature Reserve. Vortrekker Monument Group. http://www.voortrekkermon.org.za.
Wagner, Rudolf. 2000. *The craft of a Chinese commentator*. Albany: SUNY Press.
Walcott, Derek. 1998. The Antilles: Fragments of epic memory. In *What the Twilight Says: Essays*, 65–85. London: Faber and Faber.
Wallerstein, Immanuel et al. 1996. *Open the social sciences: Report of the Gulbenkian Commission on the restructuring of the social sciences*. Stanford: Stanford University Press.
Walley, Christine. 1997. Searching for "voices": Feminism, anthropology, and the global debates over female genital operations. *Cultural Anthropology* 12: 405–38.
Walsh, Catherine, Freya Schiwy, and Santiago Castro-Gómez, eds. 2002. *Interdisciplinar las ciencias sociales*. Quito: Universidad Andina/Abya Yala.
Ward, Kerry, and Nigel Worden. 1998. Commemorating, suppressing, and invoking Cape slavery. In *Negotiating the past: The making of memory in South Africa*, ed. Sarah Nuttall and Carli Coetzee, 23–40. Cape Town: David Philip.
Weidman, Amanda. 2006. *Singing the classical, voicing the modern: The postcolonial politics of music in South India*. Durham: Duke University Press.
Weiss, K. M., and R. H. Ward. 2000. Obituary. James V. Neel, M.D., PhD. (March 22, 1915–January 31, 2000): Founder effect. *American Journal of Human Genetics* 66:755–60.
Welsome, Eileen. 1999. *The plutonium files: America's secret medical experiments in the Cold War*. New York: Dial Press.
Wheeder, Michael Ian. 2006. The palaces of memory: A reconstruction of District One, Cape Town, before and after the Group Area Act. M.A. thesis, University of the Western Cape.
White, Hayden. 1987. *The content of the form: Narrative discourse and historical representation*. Baltimore: Johns Hopkins University Press.
White, Richard. 1991. *The middle ground: Indians, empires, and republics in the Great Lakes Region, 1650–1815*. New York: Cambridge University Press.
Whitehead, Alfred North. 1997 [1925]. *Science and the modern world*. New York: Free Press.

Wilkerson, Isabel. 1990. U. of Michigan fights the taint of racial trouble. *New York Times* (January 15):12.
Wilkinson, John C. 1987. *The imamate tradition of Oman.* Cambridge: Cambridge University Press.
Willford, Andrew, and Eric Tagliacozzo, eds. 2009. *CLIO/ANTHROPOS: Exploring the boundaries between history and anthropology.* Stanford: Stanford University Press.
Williams, Raymond. 1973. *The country and the city.* New York: Oxford University Press.
Williams, Raymond. 1977. *Marxism and literature.* Oxford: Oxford University Press.
Williams, Raymond. 1989. *The politics of modernism.* Ed. Tony Pinkney. London:
Wilson, Bronwen. 2003. Reflecting on the face of the Turk in sixteenth-century Venetian portrait books. *Word and Image* 19:38–58.
Wilson, Richard A. 2001. *The politics of truth and reconciliation: Legitimizing the post-apartheid state.* Cambridge: Cambridge University Press.
Wolf, Eric R. 1956. Aspects of group relations in a complex society: Mexico. *American Anthropologist* 1958:1065–78.
Wolf, Eric R. 1982. *Europe and the people without history.* Berkeley: University of California Press.
Wolf, Eric R. 1994. Perilous ideas: Race, culture, people. *Current Anthropology* 35:1–12.
Wolfe, Patrick. 1991. Should the subaltern dream? "Australian Aborigines" and the problem of ethnographic ventriloquism. *Comparative Studies in Society and History* 33:197–224.
Wolfe, Patrick. 1999. *Settler colonialism and the transformation of anthropology: The politics and poetics of an ethnographic event.* London: Cassell.
Worden, Nigel. 2009. The changing politics of slave heritage in the Western Cape, South Africa. *Journal of African History* 50:23–40.
World Archaeological Congress. The World Archaeological Congress code of ethics. World Archaeological Congress. http://www.worldarchaeologicalcongress.org/site/about_ethi.php.
Yanomami Davi Kopenawa. 1991. Interview by Terence Turner. http://www.aaanet.org/committees/cfhr/rptyano5.htm.
Young, James. 1993. *The texture of memory.* New Haven: Yale University Press.
Young, Robert. 1990. *White mythologies: Writing history and the West.* New York: Routledge.

Contributors

CHANDRA D. BHIMULL is an assistant professor in the Department of Anthropology and the African American Studies Program at Colby College. She is the author of "The Dimensions" in the journal *Small Axe* and is currently completing a book about airline travel in the Atlantic World.

DAVID WILLIAM COHEN is a professor emeritus of Anthropology and a professor emeritus of History, College of Literature, Science, and the Arts, University of Michigan. He is the author of numerous publications, among them *The Risks of Knowledge* (with E. S. Atieno Odhiambo) and *The Combing of History*.

FERNANDO CORONIL is Presidential Professor at the Graduate Center of City University of New York and a professor emeritus of Anthropology and a professor emeritus of History, College of Literature, Science, and the Arts, University of Michigan. He is the author of *The Magical State: Nature, Money, and Modernity and Venezuela* and numerous articles on politics, postcolonialism, and social theory.

DEIRDRE DE LA CRUZ is an assistant professor in the Departments of History and Asian Languages and Cultures at the University of Michigan. She is currently completing a book on apparitions of the Virgin Mary in the Philippines, from the mid-nineteenth century to the present.

SHANNON LEE DAWDY is an assistant professor in the Department of Anthropology at the University of Chicago. She is the author of several publications, including *Building the Devil's Empire: French Colonial New Orleans*.

PAUL K. EISS is an associate professor of Anthropology and History at Carnegie Mellon University. He is the author of *In the Name of El Pueblo: Place, Communities, and the Politics of History in Yucatán* and numerous articles in such publications as *Cultural Anthropology* and *Comparative Studies in Society and History*.

CONTRIBUTORS

ILANA FELDMAN is an assistant professor of Anthropology and International Affairs at George Washington University. She is the author of *Governing Gaza: Bureaucracy, Authority, and the Work of Rule, 1917–67* and numerous articles in journals such as *Cultural Anthropology, American Ethnologist,* and *Comparative Studies in Society and History.*

ZAREENA A. GREWAL is an assistant professor in the Departments of Religious Studies and American Studies at Yale University and a documentary filmmaker. Her research focuses on Islam in the Middle East and in the United States, engaging themes of memory, transnationalism, and community.

DOROTHY L. HODGSON is a professor in the Department of Anthropology at Rutgers University. She has authored several publications, including *Once Intrepid Warriors: Gender, Ethnicity, and the Cultural Politics of Maasai Development* and *The Church of Women: Gendered Encounters between Maasai and Missionaries.*

S. C. HUMPHREYS is a professor emeritus in the Departments of Classics and History at the University of Michigan. She is the author of several books and articles, including *Anthropology and the Greeks* and *The Strangeness of Gods.*

MANDANA E. LIMBERT is an associate professor in the Department of Anthropology at Queens College and the Graduate Center of the City University of New York. She coedited *Timely Assets: The Politics of Resources and Their Temporalities* and is the author of *In the Time of Oil: Piety, Memory, and Social Life in an Omani Town.*

SONJA LUEHRMANN is an Izaak Walton Killam Postdoctoral Fellow in the Department of Anthropology at the University of British Columbia. She is the author of *Alutiiq Villages under Russian and U.S. Rule* and currently completing *The Promise of Method: Atheism and Religion on the Middle Volga.*

SETRAG MANOUKIAN is an assistant professor in the Institute of Islamic Studies and the Department of Anthropology at McGill University. He is currently completing *The City of Knowledge: History and Culture in Contemporary Shiraz.*

OANA MATEESCU is completing her Ph.D. in the Doctoral Program in Anthropology and History at the University of Michigan. Her dissertation is entitled *Memory, Proof, and Persuasion: Re-creating Communal Forests in Postsocialist Romania.*

EDWARD MURPHY is an assistant professor of History and Global Urban Studies at Michigan State University and is affiliated with the Center for Latin American and Caribbean Studies. The author of *Historias poblacionales: hacia una memoria incluyente,* he is currently completing *A Home of One's Own: The Urban Politics of Propriety in Chile, 1960s to the Present.*

MONICA EILEEN PATTERSON recently completed her Ph.D. in the Doctoral Program in Anthropology and History at the University of Michigan. She is the author of several publications, including "Youth Struggle" and "Reconciliation as a Continuing and Differentiated Process," and is currently the postdoctoral fellow at the Center for Ethnographic Research and Exhibition in the Aftermath of Violence at Concordia University in Montreal.

DAVID PEDERSEN is an assistant professor in the Department of Anthropology at the University of California at San Diego. He has published widely in such journals as *Public Culture* and *Cultural Anthropology* and is completing a book manuscript, *American Value,* on transnational migrant life between El Salvador and the United States.

STEVEN PIERCE teaches African history at the University of Manchester. He is the author of *Farmers and the State in Colonial Kano: Land Tenure and the Legal Imagination* and with Anupama Rao is coeditor of *Discipline and the Other Body: Correction, Corporeality, Colonialism.* He is currently completing a book manuscript entitled *A Moral Economy of Corruption: State Formation and Political Culture in Northern Nigeria.*

ANUPAMA RAO is an associate professor in the Department of History at Barnard College. She is the author of *The Caste Question: Dalits and the Politics of Modern India* and *Discipline and the Other Body: Correction, Corporeality, Colonialism* (with Steven Pierce), in addition to numerous articles on caste, gender, and the politics of untouchability.

E. NATALIE ROTHMAN is an assistant professor of History at the University of Toronto. The author of *Trans-Imperial Subjects: Boundary-Markers of the Early Modern Mediterranean,* she is completing *The Dragoman Renaissance: Diplomatic Interpreters and the Making of the Levant.*

JULIE SKURSKI is Distinguished Lecturer in Anthropology at the City University of New York Graduate Center. She is the author of several publications, including *States of Violence* (with Fernando Coronil). She is currently completing *Civilizing Barbarism: Nationhood, Masculinity, and Mestizaje in Early Twentieth-Century Venezuela*.

KERRY WARD is an associate professor of World History at Rice University. She is the author of *Networks of Empire: Forced Migration in the Dutch East India Company*.

THOMAS C. WOLFE is an associate professor of History at the University of Minnesota and is affiliated with the Department of Anthropology, Institute for Global Studies, and the School of Journalism and Mass Communications. He is the author of *Governing Soviet Journalism: The Press and The Socialist Person after Stalin*.

Index

academia, 12, 16–18, 21, 26, 32, 227–38, 253
Adorno, Theodore, 282
affect, 25–26, 29, 72–76, 140, 289, 291–95. *See also* emotion
Agamben, Giorgio, 243, 248, 251
American Anthropological Association, 123, 128, 132
    Code of Ethics, 257–59, 267–68, 271
Anderson, Benedict, 182, 190n1
    Imagined Communities, 204
anthrohistory, 4, 14–15, 18, 21, 25–26, 28–33, 49, 64–65, 81, 83, 85, 92, 154, 218–19, 225–27, 252, 301–3, 306
Anthrohistory Program (Doctoral Program in Anthropology and History at the University of Michigan), 4–6, 9–10, 17, 20–21, 23–24, 27, 29–31, 49–50, 53–54, 58, 62, 173, 252–53, 282
    in the 1990s, 289–90, 295–57
    and the Yanomami controversy, 121–25, 132–36, 172, 174
anthropology, 3, 11–18, 24–29, 49–50, 53–54, 57, 59–60, 65, 81, 257–60, 262, 268–71, 296, 313–14
    in Africa, 269
    and cultural intermediaries, 74
    and culture in the 1950s, 73
    origins of Americanist, 152
    and the "plural society" paradigm, 74
anticipation, 28–29, 111–15, 218, 222n19
apartheid, 63, 90–96, 191–205
Appadurai, Arjun, 55, 57
archaeology, 197
    and the First Code of Ethics, 199
archive, 38–39, 41–42, 45, 83, 86, 198
    archival fetish, 39

Palestine/Israel, 97–104
Arendt, Hannah, 164–65
    Banality of Evil, 147
art history, 255
Asad, Talal
    "The Idea of an Anthropology of Islam," 169n4
    on orthodoxy, 164
atheism, 145
    Soviet, 273–76, 280–71
Auschwitz, 83, 87–88
authenticity, 162–63, 169n7, 240–41, 246, 313

Bakhtin, Mikhail, 312, 314, 316
Barthes, Roland: *Camera Lucida,* 112–13
Bello, Ahmadu, 240–41, 249
Benjamin, Walter, 176, 191, 283, 301–12
biopolitics, 248
"blocs of sensations," 29, 290–97
body, the, 243, 248
Borges, Jorge Luis, 95n6, 111, 179, 301, 303, 309–10
Brazil, 121–39
bureaucracy
    in Gaza, 98–99, 105–6
    and Institutional Review Boards, 259–60
    in post–Katrina New Orleans, 144–46
burial politics, 191–207

Calvino, Italo, 32–33, 303, 321
Cantor, Nancy, 122–23, 128–39
capitalism, 309, 315
    in early modernism, 75
    as global power structure, 78n24

Carpentier, Alejo: *The Kingdom of This World*, 310
Chagnon, Napoleon, 122–33, 147–48
    Yanomamo: The Fierce People, 126
Chakrabarty, Dipesh: *Provincializing Europe*, 315
Chatterjee, Partha: *The Nation and Its Fragments*, 241
Cheney, Lynn, 60
childhood/children, 81–96
Cohen, David William, 132–33, 307
    The Combing of History, 85, 197
    with E. S. Atieno Odhiambo, *Burying S.M.*, 191
colonialism, 54, 57, 217–18, 243–44
    British, 240
    and the concept of "culture," 111
    and ethnicity, 74
    as global power structure, 78n24
    New World, 64, 134
    and the Ottoman Empire, 69
    in Southeast Asia, 73
colonial studies, 53–54
Communism
    in Romania, 209–12
    in Soviet Union, 274
comparison
    in social research, 19, 283
conservatism, 60–61
"contact zones," 72–73
    and Mary Louise Pratt, 67
    in sixteenth-century Venice, 68, 74–76
Cooper, Fred, 53, 250n2
Coronil, Fernando, 6, 44, 53, 138n13
cultural turn, the 34, 52–53, 252. *See also* interpretive turn, the
culture, 241–49, 254, 314
    as analytic category, 74, 157
    in anthropological theory, 78n24, 78n26
    and anticolonial thought, 241–42
    on Eric Wolf, 74
    and rights, 245–57

Daniel, E. Valentine, 10, 53
decolonization, 242

Deleuze, Gilles: *What Is Philosophy?*, 291, 293
democracy, 167, 202, 233
Derrida, Jacques, 303, 311
Destroy All Monsters, 297–98
development, 182–84, 201–3, 261, 308
Dirks, Nicolas, 53, 244, 255n1
discipline and disciplinarity, 15–17, 20, 24–25, 27, 31–32, 49, 53–54, 65, 83, 225–27, 236–38, 252–53, 257–72, 301, 307, 309
Doctoral Program in Anthropology and History at the University of Michigan (Anthrohistory Program), 4–6, 9–10, 17, 20–21, 23–24, 27, 29, 38, 49–50, 53–54, 58, 62
dreams, 22, 33, 84–85, 304
evidence, 198
Duchamp, Marcel, 171
Dussel, Enrique, 308

economics
    and "marginal trading peoples" theory, 74
    and "middleman minority" theory, 74
    and the "plural society" paradigm, 74
Eley, Geoff, 51–58, 60
    A Crooked Line: From Cultural History to the History of Society, 52
emotion, 81, 86–88, 234, 288–97
    in academic research, 140–41, 145–48, 150–55
    desires, 85
    emotive category of childhood, 91, 93
    feeling, 83, 86
Enlai, Zhou (first premier of the People's Republic of China), 56
Ernsten, Christian: "The World Below," 196, 197
Escher, M. C., 180
ethics, 20–23, 257, 312
    American Anthropological Association Code of (1998), 257–59, 267–68, 271
    American Historical Association

(2005) Statement of Standards of Professional Conduct, 258, 268
archaeology code of, 199
and Institutional Review Boards, 259–60
and personhood, 235
and research, 121–39, 197–99
in the sciences vs. humanities, 121
U.S. Oral history Association "evaluation Guidelines (2000), 258
ethnography, 40, 126, 218–19, 290
everyday, the, 11, 82, 108, 182, 216, 227, 235
exhibition, 113
expertise, 24, 275

Federal Emergency Management Agency (FEMA), 26, 142–48, 150–53
feeling, 26, 29
See also affect; sentiment
Ferguson, Brian, 133–34
field, the, 38–39, 44–45
field notes, 40–41, 45–46
field work, 39–40, 44–46, 57, 91, 273
Flannery, Kent V., 131
forgetting, 91, 135, 165, 213, 217, 222n21
Foucault, Michel, 247–48
fragments, 9 (text box), 14, 41, 81, 83, 93, 171, 195, 303
France
French Revolution, 56
and the Ouvroir de litérature potentielle (OuLiPo), 82
Furnivall, John Sydenham, 74, 78n21
Fursat, 287–88, 292
Âsâr-i 'Ajam (1896), 286–87, 291–93
future, the, 29, 110–17, 304, 312, 316

Galileo, 216
Gaza, 28, 97–108
Geertz, Clifford, 12, 41, 163, 290, 313
al-Ghazzali, *The Alchemy of Happiness*, 160–63
Ginzburg, Carlo, 48–49, 297n3, 310

globalization, 63
governance, 240–51
Guattari, Felix: *What Is Philosophy?*, 291, 293
Guyer, Jane: *Prophesy and the Near Future*, 110

Handler, Richard: "Tradition, Genuine or Spurious," 162–63, 166
Heritage Foundation, 60–62
higher education. *See* academia
historical turn, the, 57
history, 3, 11–18, 24–29, 49, 52–54, 59, 65, 81, 89, 226–37, 252, 257–59, 268, 296, 313–14
in Africa, 269
of childhood, 86
Hobsbawm, Eric: *The Invention of Tradition*, 158, 166
Hodgson, Dorothy
The Church of Women (2005), 262–64
Once Intrepid Warriors (2001), 261–62
Holocaust, 82–88, 95
Homeland Security, U.S. Department of, 143, 147
human, the, 191–92, 241–42, 244–46, 250, 255
human rights, 92
debates in South Africa, 191–93
humanitarianism, 244–45
humanities, 229, 232–34, 237, 307

imagination, 86, 89, 234, 301, 313
imperialism, 57
informed consent, 124, 128, 136, 259–61, 264, 266–70
Institutional Review Boards, 128, 259–60, 264, 266–68
interdisciplinarity, 3, 11–13, 16–18, 25, 57–59, 64, 237–38
intermediaries, cultural, 24
in sixteenth-century Venice, 67–69, 73–76
interpretive turn, the, 53. *See also* cultural turn, the
Iran, 286–96

Islam, 156–70
  and anthropology, 296
  Ibadism, 183–84, 190n2
  law and tradition, 240–41, 249
  Qubaysiyat, 159–66
  in South Africa, 192, 195, 201
Israel
  and "humanitarian assistance" in Palestine, 108
  occupation of the West Bank and Gaza Strip, 97

Jackson, Jesse, 61

Katrina, Hurricane, 140–41
Keane, Webb, 50–57
Kellogg Foundation, 59
Kennedy, Michael, 134
Klee, Pau: *Angelus Novus*, 176
knowledge, 17–18, 21–24, 29, 31–33, 235, 301–4, 307–9, 312
  and the limits of empiricism, 90
Knowledge Society of Soviet Union, 276–77
Koselleck, Reinhart: on messianic history, 189

Laclau, Ernesto, 45
Latour, Bruno, 237
Lederman, Rena, 15, 257, 259–60
Levi-Strauss, Claude, 310–11, 314
liberalism, 44, 53
  and constitutional norms, 240
  and governance, 243–47
  and rights, 191
  and the universal, 242, 246–47, 249
Linnekin, Joyce: "Tradition, Genuine or Spurious," 162–63, 166
literary studies, 54
Lupa, Victor, 209–14

Malinowski, Bronislaw
  diaries, 41
  1922, 38, 40
maps, 152–54, 302–3, 310
marketplace
  in sixteenth-century Venice, 68, 74–75
  in social science theory, 74–75, 78–79n26
Marx, Karl, 31, 308, 312, 316
Marxism-Leninism, 275, 314
masking, 43–45
mathematics, 82
Matthews, Frank, 61
Mbeki, Govan, 204–5
McDonald, Terrence, 59
mediation
  as analytic category, 74
memory, 81–89, 91
  nondiscursive, 217–18
  as a process, 90
  of violence, 92
method, Soviet concept of, 275–85
methodology, 15–16, 26, 88
  of anthropology and history, 83, 90
  See also method
Mignolo, Walter, 307
Mitchell, Silas Warner, 225
modernity, 114, 252–54, 315
  in Iran, 288
  of Oman, 185
multiculturalism, 62, 246
museums, 255

naming, politics of, 257–58, 261–72
narrative, 82–87, 92
National Historic Preservation Act, 148
nation-building, 95, 194–95, 200, 205
Neel, James, 122–32, 134, 137–38
neoliberalism, 44
New Orleans, 140–55
  disaster, history of, 153
  Holt Cemetery, 151
Nigeria, 240–41, 249

Obama, Barack, 156
objectivity, 85, 87
Oman, 181–90
open holism, 56, 64–65
oral history, 258–59
Ortner, Sherry, 59
Oslo Accords, 99
Otieno, Silvano Melea (S. M.), 191

Ottoman Empire, 69–70
Ouji, Mansur, 288–89, 292–93
Ouvroir de litérature potentielle (OuLiPo), 82

Paige, Jeff, 59
Palestine, 97–108
Park, Robert E., 74
participant-observation, 260, 263, 268, 283
Patrice, Lumumba, 173
Paz, Octavio, 314
pedagogy
 and Adorno, 282–83
Pemberton, John, *On the Subject of Java*, 110–12
Perec, Georges, *W or the Memory of Childhood*, 14, 81–89, 91, 93–94, 295
Peterson, John E., *Oman Insurgencies*, 184
Petit, Philippe, 178
phantom limbs, 14, 225, 236–38
Pierce, Stephen: "Discipline and the Other Body," 191–92, 243
"plural society," theory of, 74
political science, 227
positivism, 53
postcolonial studies, 53
postmodernism, 253
Power, Sarah G., 62
Pratt, Mary Louise, 67
Program in Comparative Study of Social Transformations (CSST), 58–59, 62, 65
 Eley Report, 60

racism, 54, 57, 61, 64
 in South Africa, 90, 94, 96n23
 of the state, 248
Ramos, Alcida, 133
Rand think tank, 167–68
Ranger, Terence: *The Invention of Tradition*, 158, 166
Rao, Anupama: "Discipline and the Other Body," 191–92, 243
Reagan, Ronald, 60–61
reflexivity, 17–18

regularity determinism, 55, 65
religion, in Soviet Union/Russia, 275–85
Romania, 208–15
Russia, 273–85

Sahlins, Marshall, 51, 56
Said, Edward: on reading canonical texts and archives, 75
scale, 19, 53–55, 93
Schneider, David, 51, 56
scholarship, 228, 236
sciences, 127, 229, 307
"science wars," 127, 132
Scott, James: *Seeing Like a State*, 149
Scott, Joan, "The Evidence of Experience," 141
Sebald, George, *Austerlitz*, 95n11
self, the, 89
sentiment. *See* emotion
Sewell, William, Jr., 52–59, 313
 Logics of History: Social Theory and Social Transformation, 53
Shaw, Rosalind: *Memories of the Slave Trade*, 217–18
Shepherd, Nick: "The World Below," 196, 197
Sider, Gerald: *In Between History and Histories*, 27, 217
silence, 89, 197
Simmel, Georg: "the Stranger," 78n22
slavery, 243
 in Sierra Leone, 217
 in sixteenth-century Venice, 67, 70–71, 75, 77n7
 in South Africa, 195, 200
Smith, Gavin: *In Between History and Histories*, 27, 217
social sciences, 73, 229, 237, 307
sociobiology, 126–27
sociology, 59–60, 82, 227
 and the "middle man" theory, 73
 and the "plural society" paradigm, 74
Sodikoff, Genese, 311
South Africa, 81, 90–96, 191–207
Sponsel, Les, 123
state, the, 43–44

352 INDEX

Steedman, Carolyn: *Landscape for a Good Woman*, 52, 312
Steinmetz, George, 52–53
   The Politics of Method in the Human Sciences: Positivism and Its Epistemological Others, 53
Stoler, Ann, 53–58
   Along the Archival Grain, 54
   and the Doctoral Program in Anthropology and History at UM, 58
structures of feeling, 26, 113
Stuhr, John, 232
subalternity, 148
   of children, 89, 93
subjectivity, 52, 241

Tanzania, 261–72
Taylor, Charles, 246
Tayob, Abdulkader, 199, 202
temporality, 28, 88–89, 111–14, 296
   of disciplinary frames, 142, 190
   and the future perfect, 111
   messianic vs. linear, 189
testimony, 68, 71, 90
Tetiz, Mexico, 39–40, 44–45
theory, 81
   of the Chicago school "middle man," 73
   of cultural mediation, 74
   of development, 182
   of the gift, 115
   Harold Garfinkel's critique of, 216
   Marxist, 79n26
   of memory, 89
   of "plural society," 74
   of Robert E. Park's "marginal man," 74, 76, 78n22
   in the Soviet Union, 275
Tierney, Patrick: *Darkness in El Dorado*, 20, 121–24, 129, 132, 134–36
Tilly, Charles, 19–20
time, 28, 88, 165, 177, 302, 305, 315
   conceptions of, 253–55
   See also temporality
tradition, 25, 240–44
   as an analytic category, 156–70
transdisciplinarity, 18, 108, 154–55, 238, 252, 255, 270
"Trans/Formations of the Disciplines" Conference, 5
transmodernity, 308
trauma, 81
Trouillot, Michel-Rolph: *Silencing the Past*, 27, 312–13
Truth and Reconciliation Commission of South Africa, 93, 96n17, 204
Turner, Terence, 123, 133–34
Tutu, Desmond, 193

uncertainty, 81–84, 88, 91–92, 181–86, 189, 211, 215, 221, 316
UNESCO World Heritage Site, 203
United Nations
   Emergency Force records on Gaza, 97
   in Gaza, 108
universalisms, 92, 95, 314
University of Chicago, 51–52
   sociologists, 73–74
University of Michigan, 50–52, 54–55, 65
   Black Action Movement (BAM), 61, 64
   Department of History, 57
   Duderstadt, James J. (president), 62–63
   Eisenberg Institute of Historical Studies, 52
   History Department, 57
   interdisciplinarity at, 57, 59
   Michigan Mandate, 62–64
   Power, Sarah G., 62
   Program in Comparative Study of Social Transformations (CSST), 58, 65
   racist clashes of the 1980s, 61, 64
   Student protests, 61, 64
   United Coalition against Racism (UCAR), 61
   WJJX, student-run radio station, 61
   and the Yanomami Controversy, 121–39

U.S. Department of Homeland Security, 143, 147

Venezuela, 121–39
Venice, sixteenth-century, 67–79
victimhood, 92, 95
violence, 22, 31, 41, 92, 96n19, 241–42, 245–46, 250
   colonial, 244
   in Israel and Palestine, 99–101, 104–5, 108
   in the name of tradition, 158
   on U.S. university campuses in the 1980s, 61
   and the Yanomami, 126–28, 130
Virgen del pueblo, la, 44

Walcott, Derek, 171, 312
Warren, Kay, 134
Weidman, Amanda J.: *Singing the Classical, Voicing the Modern*, 115–17
White, Hayden, 7
Williams, Raymond, 26, 314
Wolf, Eric, 315
   on culture, 74, 78n24

xenophobia, 94

Yanomami controversy, 20–21, 23–24, 121–39, 172, 174

Zapatistas, 309